MW00779828

CHRISTIAN ANARCHIST

Christian Anarchist

Ammon Hennacy, A Life on the Catholic Left

William Marling

NEW YORK UNIVERSITY PRESS

New York

NEW YORK UNIVERSITY PRESS
New York
www.nyupress.org

References to Internet websites (URLs) were accurate at the time of writing. Neither the author nor New York University Press is responsible for URLs that may have expired or changed since the manuscript was prepared.

Library of Congress Cataloging-in-Publication Data
Names: Marling, William, 1951–   author.
Title: Christian anarchist : Ammon Hennacy, a life on the Catholic left / William Marling.
Description: New York : New York University Press, [2022] | Includes bibliographical references and index.
Identifiers: LCCN 2021011566 | ISBN 9781479810079 (hardback) | ISBN 9781479810086 (ebook) | ISBN 9781479811250 (ebook other)
Subjects: LCSH: Hennacy, Ammon, 1893–1970. | Catholics—United States—Biography. | Anarchists—United States—Biography.
Classification: LCC BX4705.H469 M37 2021 | DDC 282.092 [B]—dc23
LC record available at https://lccn.loc.gov/2021011566

New York University Press books are printed on acid-free paper, and their binding materials are chosen for strength and durability. We strive to use environmentally responsible suppliers and materials to the greatest extent possible in publishing our books.

Manufactured in the United States of America

10 9 8 7 6 5 4 3 2 1

Also available as an ebook

In memory of Fern and Henry Marling

CONTENTS

ILLUSTRATIONS

Introduction

For protesting against World War I, twenty-five-year-old Ammon Hennacy spent two years in the Atlanta Penitentiary, nine months of it in solitary confinement. His credo of personal commitment later led to a sentence at Sandstone Prison in the 1950s for protesting against nuclear missiles. He also refused to pay "war taxes" to the federal government for over fifty years, for which the FBI hounded him continuously. No one on the pacifist Left—not Dorothy Day, his colleague Dave Dellinger, or his friend Claude McKay—sacrificed personal freedom as Hennacy did. To our era, when so much "protest" happens on social media, his actual sacrifices seem unworldly. This is the first scholarly biography of this iconic "Christian anarchist," as he called himself.

Putting his body on the line in protests, picketing, going to jail, and participating in hunger strikes were Hennacy's forte. He *embodied* his politics, but he was also a fine writer, who boosted the *Catholic Worker* to greater popularity in the 1940s and 1950s with his Thoreau-like prose. He was among the first to establish the US Southwest as a setting for ecological concerns, Native American protest, disputes over water rights, and conflicts over issues of individual conscience, long before such names as Rachel Carson, Wallace Stegner, or Edward Abbey became current (Abbey was a fan). Hennacy's *Book of Ammon* and *One-Man Revolution* are still in print and widely read.

Often embracing extreme poverty, Hennacy never lost his sense of humor or his high spirits; he ironically called himself a "one-man revolution." The core of his belief was the Sermon on the Mount and "voluntary poverty." His positive energy dominated, whether he was picketing the American Legion in Milwaukee, befriending prisoners of war in Albuquerque, advocating for the Hopis in Arizona, helping the homeless on the Bowery, or founding the Joe Hill House of Hospitality in Salt Lake City. Dorothy Day called him a "prophet and a peasant." The *San Francisco Chronicle* praised him as "the last of the great old-time non-conformists." Murray Kempton wrote in the *Village Voice* that "he was a real old time Wobbly, like those I'd read about in Dos Passos . . . the only truly homegrown American radicals. The most surprising part of all this was that Hennacy conveyed it with a sense of delight and humor."

Fifty years after his death, Hennacy's life reminds us that real political dissent is not a part-time activity. He worked nonstop with Alexander Berkman, Scott Nearing, Mother Bloor, Bayard Rustin, Claude McKay, Peter Maurin, Dellinger, Day, and other radicals, and he was possibly more committed. He synthesized pacifism, protest, vegetarianism, and ecological awareness into a daily practice—he *embodied* them—living his ideals every minute, but happily, as Kempton notes. He did not drive, he did not pay taxes, and he did not eat meat. Traveling all over the United States by foot and by thumb, he met and befriended thousands, leaving each person a bit of his "gospel of beauty." He was already publishing in "green" journals in the 1930s. Speaking at thousands of churches and colleges, on radio, and on television, and writing a stream of articles, he was an influence on countless people, and during the Vietnam War, he persuaded hundreds to become conscientious objectors.

While not today a household name, Hennacy deserves to be. He remains particularly important for the Catholic Left, and his example is recalled frequently by those involved with social justice movements. He has been rediscovered as an exemplar of vegetarianism, ecology, pacifism, tax resistance, voluntary poverty, and Christian anarchism. His practices may have set him beyond the pale in the 1930s and '40s when he developed them, but they have become central to American protest. His politics of voluntary poverty and ecological consciousness prefigure today's social-justice, green-energy, and gender-equality movements, and he remains a beacon for challenges that confront the world.

* * *

Chapter 1 introduces Hennacy's early life, his Quaker grandparents, his early vegetarianism, and his summer jobs selling cornflakes, during which he met his future wife, Selma Melms. At sixteen, working in a ceramics factory, he joined the International Workers of the World (IWW). In his precocious political education, he also met Mother Bloor, a famous feminist labor radical, and he hosted communist and socialist candidates for president while still in high school. Nor did he slow down at university, where he was a passionate Marxist in the tumultuous period leading up to his trial for draft resistance during World War I.

Chapter 2 covers Hennacy's trial in Columbus and his prison term at the Atlanta Penitentiary. Befriended by Alexander Berkman, he escaped sexual bullies but became the warden's nemesis. He led work stoppages and a food strike that landed him in solitary for seven and a half months. Rediscovering the Bible there, Hennacy made the Sermon on the Mount the core of his ideology. On release, he served another nine months in Columbus, Ohio, where he met Selma again and began to read Tolstoy.

Chapter 3 takes up Hennacy's travels after prison. He followed Selma to New York, where they attended the Rand School, immersed themselves in radical activity, and married. They held a number of middling jobs in New York during the Jazz Age, but, hungry to experience a bigger America, they planned a "Big Hike" around the United States inspired by Walt Whitman and Vachel Lindsay. They emerged from this two-year ramble, during which they visited almost every state and met thousands of people, with a profound sense of America's depth and diversity.

They returned to Selma's hometown of Milwaukee (chapter 4), inspired to "homestead" on Scott Nearing's model of self-sufficient farming. At "Bisanakee," as they called it, they were prospering, with two daughters, but lost their land during the Great Depression. To keep them solvent, Ammon worked at a dairy and then in the Milwaukee social services department. There he learned a great deal about structural poverty, met Roger Baldwin and Dorothy Day, tangled with the IRS and the American Legion, and got arrested again. He avoided prison, but his wife, Selma, joined a pro-war millennial religion called the I AM. Fearing that he would go to prison again, she fled with their children to Denver.

Chapter 5 explains how Ammon, convicted of World War II draft resistance but not sentenced to prison, traced Selma to Denver. He tried to heal the marriage, but was again arrested and jailed repeatedly for protesting. To escape his notoriety, Selma fled to the Santa Fe headquarters of the I AM. Hennacy could only find work south of Albuquerque near the Isleta Pueblo, but he discovered a new way of life, becoming an expert orchardman and writing about his "Life at Hard Labor." He became involved in the Latinx community and the Hopi Indians' native anarchism, which he integrated into his ideology.

Chapter 6 details Hennacy's move to Arizona to live closer to the Hopis. At age fifty-four, he supported himself as a migrant farmworker, an exhausting commitment to simplicity and poverty. He moved to Phoenix, where he became an *acequiero*, or expert irrigator, and jack of all trades for Lin Orme, an Old Pioneer who was against agribusiness and pesticides. Living in an adobe, Hennacy continued his "Life at Hard Labor" columns in addition to picketing or protesting weekly. After bringing Hopi culture to the counterculture through his writing and TV, radio, and college appearances, he was inspired by his long-simmering romance with Dorothy Day to join the *Catholic Worker* in New York.

Chapter 7 tracks Hennacy's arrival in New York in 1953, his formal adoption of Catholicism, and publication of *The Autobiography of a Catholic Anarchist*. Debating brokers on Wall Street and Jesuits at Fordham University, he became a famous face on New York streets, profiled by Elmer Bendiner and Dan Wakefield in books. Hennacy and Day were jailed repeatedly for antinuclear, anti–civil defense, and antitax protests. He picketed against nuclear submarines in Connecticut and Florida and against nuclear missiles in Omaha, where he again served prison time. His annual Hiroshima fasts lasted forty or more days and made him a favorite interview subject of Murray Kempton and Steve Allen. But the romance with Day cooled, especially during his second prison stint. He began to imagine a return to the West, where he aspired to start his own homeless shelter.

Arriving in Utah in 1960 (chapter 8), he opened the Joe Hill House, named for a famous member of the IWW killed in 1904 in Salt Lake City. The Mormons, with their self-help and antigovernment traditions, found him more to their liking than did the local Catholic hierarchy. He became a local icon, picketing the state capitol against executions, the IRS against war taxes, and the Dugway Proving Grounds against chemical weapons. Supported by Joan Thomas, whom he married in 1965, Hennacy spoke often and vociferously against the Vietnam War during the early 1960s, inspiring a new generation of conscientious objectors. He wrote *The One-Man Revolution in America*, a book about his favorite anarchists. Before that book could be printed, he suffered a heart attack and died on January 15, 1970.

The conclusion explains how Hennacy made his impact by *embodying* antistate, antiwar ideals, a practice associated with Gandhi and the tradition of "bold speech." This focus was at the core of his being, but his practice changed later in life. Those who put their bodies on the line, as he had, became his greatest heroes and heroines, and he had scathing words for the Cardinal Spellmans and Lyndon Johnsons, the "pipsqueaks," as he called them. The giants of his early life who had opposed such tyrants had declined in number, but Hennacy himself left a deep imprint on a new generation in the 1960s and 1970s.

In tracing his extraordinary life, this book argues that Hennacy created foundations for the social-justice movements of today. It also illuminates a broader history of political ideas now largely lost: the late-nineteenth-century utopian movements, the grassroots labor democracy of the IWW, the religious revivals of the 1900s, the socialist movements before World War I, the Catholic Worker movement, and the antinuclear protests of the 1960s. It attempts a nuanced look at what Andrew Cornell calls the "unruly equality" where religion and anarchist theory overlapped. Ammon Hennacy's life at the heart of radical libertarian and anarchist interventions in US politics not only galvanized the public then, but offers us a beacon today.

1

Early Life

September 22, 1918

He had been in solitary confinement for three months, every day receiving one slice of cornbread, one cup of water. To read there was only a Bible, and even though he called himself an atheist, he kept rereading the Sermon on the Mount. Legally he was a conscientious objector, in prison for advocating draft resistance during World War I, but the prisoner across the hall was a murderer, Dimiter Popoff, who had been groaning and begging for water all day. Ammon Hennacy, twenty-five, imagined the worst for himself.[1]

That morning the warden had said that, unless he confessed to a plot to blow up the prison, he would stay in solitary for the rest of his two-year sentence, as his hero Alexander Berkman once had. Hennacy did not know if he could take that. He had only talked to Berkman twice on the yard before being sent to the hole, but through a window he could see Berkman working in the prison shop. Conscientious objectors like the two of them were traitors, said the warden, adding that he thought they should be executed.

After the warden left, Ammon remembered a spoon that he used to write on the wall: "As soon as it was dark, I sharpened my spoon again and tried it gently on my wrist. The skin seemed to be quite tough, but then I could press harder. If I cut my wrist at midnight, I could be dead by morning."[2]

But that night he slipped into a reverie about his childhood on the family farm in Negley, Ohio. They had slaughtered the hogs every winter when the first snow fell. In his dream, sensing they were about to die, the pigs groaned like Popoff. Their deaths were messy, blood splattering and pooling on the floor until they quivered into silence. He had given up eating meat after that. In his dream he saw himself in a puddle of blood: that is how they would find him. What would Berkman think? What would his Quaker grandmother think? Back in Ohio he had believed in God and read the Bible a lot, especially the Sermon on the Mount, which said to turn the other cheek. In his sleep some spark inside of him, which he identified with his grandmother and called his "Celestial Bulldozer," now resisted suicide. He could turn the other cheek, and he would keep on turning it for fifty years.

* * *

Hennacy's values were rooted in that family, on that farm, where he had been born on July 24, 1893. Negley was a village in Ohio, in the western echoes of the Allegheny Mountains as they snuggle up to the Ohio/ Pennsylvania border. He was the first of seven children of Benjamin Franklin Hennacy and Lida Fitz Randolph. How they came to that place and the meaning of his childhood there assumed almost mythic status for Hennacy.

The hamlet of Achor, south of Negley, was the original settlement in the area, and that is where Hennacy was born. About two hundred people lived in the combined towns, mostly English and Irish. It was country opened by the Northwest Ordinance of 1787, and after the Revolutionary War, when its land grants were taken up, settlers poured in, displacing both white hunters and the remaining Native Americans.[3] When Columbiana County was incorporated in 1803, histories say it was still "dense forest or wilderness, with but a narrow road through it."

Everyone was a newcomer, but they got along reasonably well, and they elected government officials right down to a coroner. By 1830 the population was twenty-two thousand, and by 1840 it was thirty-five thousand. How should they organize themselves? The common answer was that they would do it by themselves, thank you. A country jail was built in 1819 and a poorhouse in 1829, both supported by local taxes. This faith in self-management, without outside interference, a sense of the common polity, would be passed down to Hennacy.[4]

By 1821 there were at least a hundred families in Negley, many of them Quaker.[5] Ammon would always claim descent from the "Friends" who had landed at Barnstable, Massachusetts, in 1720, having come from Cheshire County, England. Scholars say that this group was very egalitarian, having worked at husbandry, tanning, and weaving in Britain, professions that made it difficult to leave land or inheritances to their children. Thus they were against primogeniture, for women's rights, and concerned about providing for their daughters. Ammon would later not only use the Society of Friends as a synecdoche for strong women like his grandmother but also borrow from it ideas about how anarchism could work.

Hennacy's great-great-great-grandfather, Edward Fitz Randolph (1706–1750), was among those early Quakers in Pennsylvania, but it was his grandson Richard who came west and bought a tannery in 1810. According to one history, "He increased the capacity, adding fifteen vats to the four already there, and this tannery has since been carried on by the Randolph family." His industry made him a leading citizen, and he gave all seven of his sons the patronymic "Fitz" as a middle name, a style that Ammon would adopt.[6] The Ashfords and Vales, Hennacy's other maternal ancestors, arrived around 1812.[7] Ammon was named after one of them, Ammon Ashford, whom he recalled as "the only rebel in the family" and someone who "had been a '49er in California, a sheriff in Missouri who was shot in the leg by Jesse James," and "the local blacksmith when I knew him."[8]

Ammon's mother—Lida Fitz Randolph Hennacy—was born in Achor. Though very small, she bore nine children over an eighteen-year period (two died young). In her few photos she appears youthful but slight, and Ammon wrote that she weighed only eighty-seven pounds. When he was born on July 24, 1893, he weighed only three and a half pounds, he claimed, so small he was "put to bed in a cigar box." But he was a great self-mythologizer, who also said he remembered when his mother had "baked ginger cookies for Coxey's Army as they encamped on the meadow near us." It is unlikely that he would recall this march of the unemployed on Washington in 1894, since he was less than a year old, but it became part of his apocrypha, and he would join many similar marches. After Ammon, his mother bore Julia (1897), who was bookish and bright and later something of a radical.

When a third child, Frank, was born in 1898, a neighbor girl was brought in to watch them, indicating that the Hennacys were not poor. Lida was raised as a Quaker, but by the time of Ammon's birth, that faith had been eclipsed by the Third Great Awakening. So Lida went on Wednesday night and Sunday morning to the local Baptist meeting, and many of her relatives were buried in the Achor Baptist Church cemetery.[9] But Hennacy's invocation of her Quaker ancestry was invaluable to his imaginary, and he wrote weekly letters to her, as if she were the incarnation of his "Celestial Bulldozer."

Figure 1.1. Ammon and his sister Julia in 1897. Permission of Josephine Thomas.

Ammon sometimes disparaged his Irish side, writing that his paternal grandfather "came from Ireland in 1848 at the time of the potato famine" and that he "fought for the North when he was not fighting booze." He then "married a Pennsylvania Dutch girl by the name of Calvin and he was a tanner," an occupation he would have shared with Ammon's maternal ancestors. Ammon said that he only saw this Irish grandfather once, "when he came for a visit from California." Such itinerancy makes him difficult to trace, but there were Calvins living on the farm next to the Hennacys, and the death certificate for Ammon's father lists his mother as Sara Calvin, born in Beaver County, Pennsylvania.[10]

The Irish grandfather was not the kind one claims proudly, as he had given up all his children for adoption. It is not clear where the others went, but "Peter Brown, a wealthy farmer, adopted my father," wrote Ammon.[11] This Peter Brown was a direct descendant of the pioneer George Brown, and with the Baltzar Young family, these clans owned much of Section 14, which encompassed Achor. Young was the founder and Brown was a member of the Achor Baptist Church, so young Ammon's extended family were the local Baptist gentry.

Ammon's father, Benjamin Franklin Hennacy, worked on Peter Brown's imposing 325-acre Valley Farm (also called "Camp Bouquet Farm"), almost as much an indentured servant as an adopted son. Brown's grand brick house, built in 1835, had more than enough room for everyone, since Brown had neither wife nor children. The local gossips said that if he was not drinking, he was philandering, wrote Ammon. But his adopted son was a good worker and a natural politician, seeing to it that Ammon grew up respectable in Negley, crossing paths daily with his maternal relatives, the Fitz Randolphs.[12]

B.F. was "one of those fine looking, dark Irishmen," wrote Ammon, and a natural Democrat who made friends so easily that he was elected township clerk by the local Republicans. The paper of nearby Lisbon also praised him, setting the stage for his political career in that county seat. He oversaw the farm, its huge barn, and the extensive meadows on Beaver Creek, while also doing odd jobs for the government of Negley.[13]

Peter Brown grew some corn on his acreage, which Ammon remembered cultivating with an old white horse named Dexter. Later, in Arizona, he would use a mule to plant with the "Old Pioneer." It was a life close to animals, which Ammon liked, and he became an animal rights

Figure 1.2. A canning line at the Valley Farm, or "Camp Bouquet Farm," of Peter Brown, where the Hennacys lived and Ammon grew up. Public domain.

advocate early. That corn was fodder for Brown's purebred cattle, the first in the region, but a coal mine on the ridge behind his house was Brown's most valuable asset, though the road to it was frequently flooded. "One of the few things I remember from the farm is when they were hauling stone to fix mud holes in that road and I wanted to ride on the wagon, and they wouldn't let me, so I laid in the mud hole and kicked and got my clothes all dirty," he wrote. He mastered horse-carts too, which he used right up to 1935 during the Great Depression.[14] Ammon's sense of a bucolic boyhood, growing up close to nature on hundreds of acres of brush and berry bushes, is due to the extensive landholdings of his maternal relatives, and he could travel the whole county, staying with them overnight. The thing he did not like about the farm was the annual hog slaughter, which he avoided after his first exposure to it.

His most important childhood memory was of his grandmother Rebecca (Ashford) Randolph, who was his last genuine Quaker relation, sitting in her bonnet "in the east room by her Franklin stove and telling my three-year-old sister Julia and myself of how the peaceful Quakers loved the Indians and were not hurt by them." When he grew older, he was sent every summer to work in her garden. Thus, although as a child he never went to a meeting of the Society of Friends, his Quaker grandmother gave him its beliefs and culture, which became linked in his mind to gardening, self-sufficiency, pacifism, and Native Americans.[15]

This was also "Johnny Appleseed" country, and hobos passing through were told by townspeople to call on "Sister Randolph" for a free meal, and Ammon listened to their tales with interest, intrigued by their wanderlust. No wonder that she became symbolic of a golden past and, as he put it, "the first appearance of the 'Celestial Bulldozer' [divine spirit] which has prepared the way for my unorthodox life."[16] He would always feel close to Quakers.

As a child Ammon was somewhat sickly. "When I was a baby my mother says that I took slack [lime] from the coal bucket and plaster from the side of the door," he wrote. "I suppose I did not have enough lime in my system."[17] Bad teeth would be a lifelong problem. In prison in 1918, before contemplating suicide, his teeth hurt him so badly that he wrote to relatives asking for money to visit the prison dentist. On Brown's farm he played with the children of tenant farmers down the road. There were pranks with other boys, a crush on a girl, jokes about the housekeeper's cooking, and masturbation behind the barn. But there were no fights. He rode horseback many places and threw up when he ate too much watermelon. Excess was self-correcting like that, and he was happy in his own skin. "When I was a kid, I tried to get mumps so I would miss school, but got them months later in the summertime. I remember I had to sit out on a pile of lumber and shoot a gun into the air to scare crows off the corn; my only military experience."[18]

He attended the village school in Achor, a basic education that emphasized morality and will power: there was a saying on the schoolroom wall that "a man of words and not of deeds / is like a garden full of weeds," a notion of action from principle that would stay with him. He read the Bible from age seven onward, and he said that he followed in the newspapers the political controversies that he heard his elders discuss.[19] On the wall of Peter Brown's house was a portrait of abolitionist John Brown, whom Ammon thought for a long time was a religious figure; the area had been strongly abolitionist, and racial equality was one of Hennacy's articles of faith.

From the loft of Brown's barn, Ammon snacked on apples and rock salt, and looked over to a ridge used by the Adena and Hopewell people for rituals in pre-Columbian times. General Henry Bouquet had occupied this area during the French and Indian Wars, when he turned back the remnants of the Delaware tribe who refused to accept defeat after

Pontiac's Rebellion. The hollow beneath the ridge was known as Camp Bouquet. "Indians had camped there for centuries," wrote Ammon, but now "Methodists and Baptists had camp meetings there. . . . We could see the lights and hear the Hallelujahs as they shouted at nights in the later summer. Indians must have stood on this bluff and shot arrows at the game in our meadows years before, for we found arrowheads there." They also found big snakes that he later recalled when he saw Hopi snake dances. He connected these echoes of Native Americans lost to his grandmother; it would be decades before he learned that the Delaware had been slaughtered at nearby Gnadenhutten.[20]

Third Great Awakening

The original "Friends" of Columbiana County had been adherents to the main line of Quaker thought, but there were schisms by 1900. How active the tanner Richard Fitz Randolph was in the Meeting is unclear, but of the Vales more is known. Eli Vale was elected leader of the Hicksite Friends, an American group that followed the teaching of Elias Hicks, one of the first abolitionists. Hicks considered "obedience to the light within" to be the most important principle of worship. It was this Hicksite Quakerism of his maternal Vale ancestors that Ammon heard about and later saw as personifying the Sermon on the Mount.

When he was growing up, however, all of that was fading, as Columbiana County experienced the religious changes sweeping the nation. Many of the old Quaker families had moved farther west by 1850, and the Meetings had dwindled. Replacing them were an astonishing number of new theologies, including Christian Science, Jehovah's Witnesses, Disciples of Christ, and Mormonism, which would intrigue Ammon later. By 1900 eastern Ohio was a potpourri of religions. Locally the Baptists were ascendant, and while neither his mother nor his father was listed in the rolls of the Valley of Achor Baptist Church, their sponsors, the Youngs and Calvins, were key members.

Probably for its social capital as much as its theology, the Hennacys joined this church, which was up the road and across the creek from the farm. From the age of six, Ammon wrote, on Wednesday nights and Sunday mornings, "I sat through long Baptist theological sermons."

There was a six-week-long revival meeting during which he "cringed at the terrible threats of damnation from the pulpit." At age eleven, he "was baptized in the creek and gazed upon by a curious crowd." These baptisms occurred at a bridge a half-mile upstream from the farm, where there was a "swimming hole which I knew, but the preacher did not, so he stumbled on a rock and nearly choked me."

Ammon's conversion was heartfelt, and until the family moved to Lisbon he volunteered his time at the church: "During the winter and several summers I did all of the janitor work of the church: filling the huge hanging oil lamps and cleaning the chimneys, carrying coal and emptying ashes from the big round stoves—but then I got to ring the bell and that was something. I did this free of charge and gave $15 a year to the church which was much more in proportion than rich farmers gave. I felt that I should be a missionary." That he would be, but one who picketed the high temples of US militarism, standing in front of US marshals and asking to be arrested.[21]

Hennacy was always looking for odd jobs to save money for that future. At his grandmother Randolph's house one day, he sold a subscription for the *Commoner* to the preacher who had baptized him. This was the liberal paper of William Jennings Bryan, known for his "Cross of Gold" speech and advocacy of the "Common Man." The overlap of the Quaker grandmother, visited by the Baptist minister, who bought the liberal Democratic paper, appealed to Hennacy's sense of humor and testified to the catholicity of his influences. As part of Ammon's sale to the minister, he had to promise never to read another paper, the *Appeal to Reason*. Intrigued, he paid a local bricklayer fifty cents to subscribe for him. It turned out to be a socialist paper that published Upton Sinclair, Jack London, and Mother Jones. So instead of Bryan, these more radical voices took seats at young Hennacy's table.[22]

When Peter Brown died in 1906, the farm was sold, either to satisfy debts or for lack of biological heirs. Ammon wrote that "Brown left the farm to my father, but it was so heavily mortgaged that about all he got from it was the executor's fees." Thus B. F. Hennacy took his Democrat leanings, his wife, and his six children (Frank, Leah, and Loraine having joined the family) twenty miles northwest to the county seat of Lisbon. It was a bustling town, the birthplace of industrialist Mark Hanna (1837), and boasted one childhood home of President William McKinley. It had been a center of abolitionist sentiment and Civil War recruiting and was now the focus of regional publishing and government.[23]

B.F. opened the Hennacy Real Estate Agency in the post office building and was among the first local businessmen to have a telephone. He was remembered as a "colorful character" and civic promoter, someone counted on for donations: he advertised in the local newspaper and always bought a half-page ad in his children's high school yearbooks. Lisbon had better schools than Negley, with libraries and college-educated teachers, but right after the move, Ammon—to his later embarrassment—came down with rheumatic fever and lost a year in school. "In those days, doctors didn't know so much," he said later. "But for that whole year I was in bed most of the time. Too weak to walk." But he was lucky, for rheumatic fever was at the time the leading killer of young Americans.[24]

In Ammon's first year (1908) at the Market Street School, his teacher was Julia Briggs. He was not an "honor student," but she did commend him in the *Lisbon Buckeye State* as one of thirteen students never late or absent. Meanwhile B.F., carrying forward his political career, quickly won election as Lisbon's auditor. In the fall of 1909 he ran for mayor of Lisbon as a Democrat, losing by just twenty-six votes, having somehow been identified as the "wetter" of the two candidates, which was held against him in "dry Baptist" congregations. But he continued to be the standardbearer among Democrats and Progressives, well-known around town for his stylish bow tie and dark good looks.[25]

In Lisbon Ammon was able to connect his repulsion for the annual hog slaughter to a political stance. "The first radical I met was 'Curly,' a local vegetarian," he wrote. "I thought this was part of the rebellion, so the butcher joined the capitalist in the list of my enemies. . . . Then I read Upton Sinclair's *The Jungle* and had more reason both for being a vegetarian and being a Socialist." Ammon loved politics, talking about them with his classmates, his father, his cousin Jessie, and, most importantly, his second cousin Isaac McCready, who was a local atheist and radical. McCready instructed him to "get his Irish up" for his beliefs.[26]

Ammon found and attended a Presbyterian church, where he volunteered as an usher. His earlier conversion experience and moral feelings continued unabated into his teen years, so he was shocked to learn that two of the presbyters who gave communion were "disreputable and unchristian in their daily lives." This filled him with doubt and, in his daily Bible readings, he began to be disturbed by the bloodshed of the Old Testament. He went to the minister, who told him to pray, which he did. No answers forthcoming, he asked for guidance a second time, and was told to go to Youngstown, Ohio, to hear Billy Sunday.

Billy Sunday is paradigmatic of the later phase of the Third Great Awakening (1880–1920). A former pro baseball player, he was just beginning his extraordinary career as an evangelical Presbyterian. The meeting that Ammon attended was held in one of the quickly built "tabernacles" on which Sunday insisted, and it was his biggest show yet, producing 5,965 "conversions" and twelve thousand dollars in contributions. The meeting began right after Christmas 1909 and continued through February 1910. Unlike earlier revivalists, Sunday stressed "an emotionally-based 'experiential faith' that arose in reaction to immigration, industrialization, crime, poverty, and intemperance."

What sixteen-year-old Ammon saw at the Youngstown meeting shocked him. Although Sunday usually focused on the Prohibition amendment, the corruption of politicians, and the recovery of "old time religion," Ammon's repulsion suggests that he may have attended a "men only" meeting, at which Sunday described carnal sin in such detail that grown men fainted. These were "the ugliest, nastiest, most disgusting addresses ever listened to from a religious platform or a preacher of religion," wrote the Universalist minister Frederick William Betts. Sunday illustrated his definitions of sexuality and depravity with exaggerated gestures and language, a kind of religious porn. He also preached the inerrancy of the Bible, a literal hell, the second coming, and resurrection.[27] It was an early introduction to the power of rhetoric for Hennacy, as well as an illustration of how it could be used to vilify the body.

Ammon decided to leave the church. He told his father, who asked him to quit quietly and not roil his business and political aspirations, so he could run for mayor in 1911. Ammon took his rebellion out of town. On a Christmas trip to Negley he stood up in the Valley of Achor Baptist Church and announced that he was an atheist who did not believe in God or in the Bible. "I told [my father] that I had splashed in, and I was going to splash out," he wrote. He was scolded, but he felt that secretly his father was proud; in fact, he was never reproved for his political views, no matter how extreme, by his family.[28]

Now he was an atheist and a Socialist, as well as a vegetarian. He began to spend his Sunday mornings soliciting for the *Appeal*, just as thirty years later he would give the *Catholic Worker* to Pueblo Indians in Isleta, New Mexico, on Sundays. When the socialist editor of *Social Service* came to speak in Lisbon, young Ammon introduced him at a public meeting, and when the cofounder of the Socialist Party of Great Britain visited Lisbon, Ammon convinced his parents to board him. "My father talked radicalism intelligently with all of them," he wrote. His most daring act would be to put up a sign on the public square giving a definition of socialism. That awaited his father's election as mayor, but it indicates the extraordinary freedom permitted by his parents, and by the town.[29]

High School

At Lisbon High School he registered as Ammon *Ashford* Hennacy, claiming his Quaker heritage (his legal middle name was Leroy). But he already stood apart from the other thirty sophomores since he was slight—about five feet six, perhaps 120 pounds—and played no sports. Nor was Ammon in music or theater, and by his own account the future soapbox king of Wall Street was terrible at public speaking. Instead he became the "political kid." He took Latin and eventually German, which would allow him to speak to German POWs later. He was influenced in an important way by Elsie Roberts, an English teacher who became school principal. She taught him how to get the gist of a book by noting the best quotations and then combining them in a book report, a technique he would use the rest of his life in his voluminous reading. Equally important, his father had taken a typewriter as payment for some service, and Ammon began to type up his reports on it. He was one of a few students in the high school—and the only boy—who typed, and it proved an invaluable skill. His whole life he would type and type and type, using two fingers, very accurately though, sometimes a dozen pages a night.[30]

Lisbon High provided an education in civics that is startling in retrospect. It divided the entire student body into Greek debating societies, as did the local colleges. Ammon was in the Ionian Society, which chimed with the "scientific" track in his classes; there were also the Adelphian (public service) and Athenian (professional) societies. The societies held regular debates on topics such as suffrage, and they were all surprisingly well versed in rhetoric. Today this town is afflicted by strip mining and opioid addiction, but in 1910 its public high school was the educational equal of good schools in larger cities. Tongue-tied Ammon was not one of the debaters, however, and the Ionians lost every debate. "I [took] public speaking in high school," he wrote, "but I was the very worst in each class."[31] He was, however, studious. In an era when 70 was the average, his grades were good:

Algebra: 81
Physical Geography: 91
English: 84
Latin I: 74
English History: 87

All seven of his teachers were college degreed, one with an MA and one with a D.Phil. Five were women, continuing the strong female presence in his life. In styling himself as a radical, Ammon was not alone, for classmate Eletha M. Steeper was described in the yearbook as a "radical suffrage leader who was following in the footsteps of Mrs. Pankjurst" [sic] and there was also a young Black woman descended from fugitive slaves.[32] The political savvy and ferment at the high school were greater than we would expect.

In the fall of 1911, B. F. Hennacy ran again for mayor. The *Ohio Patriot* wrote that he "is a live wire, a progressive and a fighter. Whatever he goes after he means to bring home, if bringing is possible. His campaign of two years ago was warmly waged and as noted, was frightfully close to a victory in a town so much against him politically." And after the votes were counted, B. F. Hennacy was in fact "the first Democrat elected in Lisbon since the Civil War." But since he vowed to give Lisbon "a business administration," we can suspect there was a growing division between father and son politically.

His father's prominence got Ammon a winter vacation job at the local ceramics plant. There he discovered and joined the International Workers of the World (IWW), which had been founded in 1905 to encourage "revolutionary industrial unionism" and had strong links to socialist and anarchist labor movements, some from overseas.[33] He was just sixteen and a half, and this may have been the first he heard of anarchism. The Thomas China Company, a producer of insulators, had two large factories, but these IWW potters also were organized as Christians and attended Sunday services together. While not as radical as the western miners, whom Ammon later regarded highly, they illustrate the synthesis of politics and religion that he saw around him.[34]

This was the high point of Hennacy family life. Mayor Hennacy brought his personal charm to the mayor's court, delivering homilies to drunks that were reported in local newspapers, and Lida was the respected wife of the mayor. Ammon and Paul and Frank slept in one big bedroom, Julia and Leah and Lorraine in another. Ammon made new friends, and old acquaintances from Negley visited (he kept track of many in a notebook his entire life). In addition to a typewriter, he had a bike, and the run of the town where his dad was mayor. But in August 1912, his grandfather Jonathan Fitz Randolph broke his leg. He was eighty-four and living alone on his farm in Negley. Ammon volunteered to live with him temporarily, but the recovery stretched into the fall and winter. The high school for Negley was in East Palestine, and Ammon walked five miles there when he could not find a ride. Despite its remoteness, this was another excellent school, housed in a new building and ranked in the state's top third. The commute was difficult, because of snow and muddy roads, but he missed only three days. He averaged an 89 for "deportment" and received a 90 in English and a 93 in Political Economy, the subjects he was passionate about.[35]

East Palestine was also a pottery center and Ammon, with his experience at Thomas China and in the IWW, made friendships there. A Socialist named Ed Firth, who worked at the pottery and taught at the Sunday school, would recruit Ammon the next summer for a job selling cornflakes door to door. In spring he "ran the mile and the half in the county field meet" for East Palestine. "I was not so fast but I had a lot of endurance," he wrote: "I would run up the railroad tracks as far as McKinley's old home and back before breakfast."[36] But for most of 1912 his daily existence was physically daunting:

That winter I milked eight cows, morning and night, and worked all day Saturday. I sat behind a huge wood stove nights and studied, taking five subjects. Apples and cider from the barrel in the dark cellar form the pleasant memory of that winter. Sometimes when the snow was very deep I walked; at other times I went horseback or with horse and buggy. Mother Bloor came to East Palestine and I drove her, with horse and buggy, to organize the first Socialist local among the miners in my hometown of Negley. She was a wonderful person and an inspiration. . . . But this winter on the farm was enough for me.[37]

That job selling cornflakes across the Midwest the next summer was one of the best things that happened to Ammon. In door-to-door selling he had to develop a quick pitch, something that got his "foot in the door," a skill that he depended on the rest of his life.[38] And he believed in the "health product" that he was selling. But at first he was just as tongue-tied as he had been in his high school debating society. Gradually he acquired a pitch, his fluency improved, and he began to feel at ease cold-calling on strangers.[39]

As for the cornflakes, they were the health food of the day, brought to the United States by Rev. William Cowherd, a biblical literalist who noticed that Adam and Eve ate only fruit before the fall.[40] His followers set up in Pennsylvania and by the time that Ammon started selling them, there were at least forty-four companies making the product: Cero-Fruto, Mapl-Flakes, Flake-Ho, Korn Kure, Corn Crisp, Hello-Billo, and a dozen other corn cereals. Pennsylvania became the center of purity testing and lawsuits, so cornflakes produced in Pennsylvania were highly rated.

Since health foods were associated with vegetarianism, cornflakes also took another chair at Ammon's table. The "Jersey Cornflakes" that he sold came from Irwin, Pennsylvania, as did many crew members. They ranged as far west as Wisconsin in 1912, and the next summer Ammon would lead his own crew to Iowa, Minnesota, and east to Massachusetts.[41] When he came back, Hennacy was a nineteen-year-old senior. His sister Julia, having skipped a grade, was only a year behind him, but he had a sense of calling, loudly pronouncing himself a "Socialist." A friend "told me that I always got excited about things that were not important. He meant my radical ideas I guess." The local tobacconist said that "now I had disgraced him by becoming a Socialist."[42] The disapproval only stiffened Ammon's resolve and disposed him to find signs of decadence in the town. Protected by his father's position, he now put up his sign defining socialism on the town square. It was an act of oedipal rebellion, but tolerated by father and town in deference to political polity.

Socialism was also becoming mainstream in Ohio—this was the Progressive Era, and Tom Johnson was mayor of Cleveland. Ohio was still conservative compared to the East Coast, though, where scores of Eastern Europeans who had been recruited for the post–Civil War industrial boom had brought anarchist ideas with them. "Many immigrant shop hands came from countries in which working people had not yet gained the vote," explains scholar Andrew Cornell, and they gravitated toward the violent politics of Luigi Galleani, Alexander Berkman, or the militant side of the IWW.[43] But in Ohio and other midwestern states, the Progressives and Socialists could count on the liberal educated classes like the Hennacys, as well as on local unions and a more domesticated IWW. Mayor Hennacy liked to talk about these philosophies and their differences, and Ammon enjoyed having a sounding board for his own views.

At Lisbon High Ammon became well known in his senior year. Next to his picture in the 1913 *Olympian* yearbook the editors quipped, "His speeches have a noticeable weight." The traditional Class Prophecy began with a vision of Hennacy running as the socialist candidate for president in 1920 against Prohibitionist classmate Henry R. Brinker, who "was never known to unbend or revel once." The yearbook had much levity, and Ammon's literary society was identified as the source of several pranks, such as blockading the door to the seniors' rhetoric exams. In the humor section, a mock ad announced that "Political Advice of All Kinds" could be had from "A. Hennacy, Socialist." He was also featured in a fake ad for "Elephant Tooth Powder," but a second piece about "Esculapius Hennacy and Claudius Beaver" presiding over a circus was more prescient, as we will see.[44] Esculapius was the Roman god of medicine, possibly a reference to Ammon's vegetarianism and summer job, but also evidence that students were taught classical rhetoric, since Asclepius, the Greek version of Esculapius, was associated with *parrhesia*, the rhetorical practice of "fearless speech."

Hennacy's senior grades were very good: Algebra: 72, Geology: 92, Modern History: 97, Civics: 98, fourth-year English: 92, Latin II: 72, and German: 72. Now that he was living in town, he was absent only three days and tardy once, his conduct was "good," and these grades probably qualified him for the "First Honor Group."[45] Although politics interested him most, Hennacy also read the standards of English and American literature in high school: Shakespeare, the British Romantics, New England Renaissance poets like Longfellow, Lowell, Whittier, and, most importantly, Walt Whitman. Some assignments must have included imitations, because a few years later he would write in rhyme and meter to his fiancée.

Hiram College

Several of his teachers had graduated from Hiram College, one reason why Ammon applied there, but it was also affiliated with the local Disciples of Christ churches. In Lisbon, the dominant church was the New Lisbon Calvinist Baptist Church, the center of a network of Disciples churches. Not only was the religious base, with a focus on humanities, a better fit for Ammon, but bigger state schools leaned towards agriculture, engineering, law, and medical students. Local colleges were extremely popular in Ohio because students went home on weekends to do laundry and stock up on food. Room and board were the biggest expenses of attending college, costing $2.50 to $4.00 a week. Religion classes were not required at Hiram, but there were Bible study groups and "Disciples Clubs" and a high regard for foreign mission service, especially in Asia. President James A. Garfield was an alum and had been president of the college. Vachel Lindsay, the troubadour poet, had attended ten years earlier, and although his work was not taught, he was celebrated on the sly by students like Ammon. Hiram College was a step out of Lisbon for the first person in his family to attend college.[46] Before that, however, there was another summer of selling cornflakes to earn his tuition. Ammon put his brother Frank on his crew, and they went to Massachusetts, working Dedham, Worcester, Forest Hills, and Norwood. They wrote orders based on samples, then cases of cornflakes were shipped directly to buyers. They also traveled west, where Ammon would make great discoveries the next summer.

College started on September 5, 1913. Ammon, a twenty-year-old freshman, lodged with the Works family and stated that his "intention" was journalism. He signed up for seventeen credits and paid thirty-six dollars in tuition and fees. He was among the thirty-six fresh-men, dressed in coats and ties, who posed for freshmen photos.[47] Classes were the lesser part of his education the first semester; more important were friendships with Robert W. Peden, assistant editor of the *Advance* (the student paper) and William (Bill) Young, who was senior class pres-ident, captain of the basketball team, and big man on campus. Hennacy and Peden shared an interest in politics; the Mexican Revolution and the first Balkan War had started that year, and they probably read about the anarchists in the Mexican War, the Trotskyites, Emma Goldman, Mother Bloor, and the Ferrer Center. Senior class president Bill Young boarded at the same house as Hennacy, and by spring he had taken the freshman under his wing and involved him in high jinks. Ammon had much more social and political capital now than in high school.

A measure of his political focus is the *Advance*. It had devoted most of its space to sports, social events, and Bible study groups, but in Sep-tember 1913 it began a column on socialism, clearly by Hennacy. Then came an editorial on the topic, probably by Peden. On October 4, 1914, the paper announced a visit by the "millionaire socialist" James Graham Phelps Stokes, who was president of the Intercollegiate Socialist Society, a group organized by Upton Sinclair, Jack London, Clarence Darrow, and Charlotte Perkins Gilman.[48] Hennacy had invited him, and he was also setting up a Hiram chapter of the Socialist Society, the first college chapter established that fall.

As documents in the Tamiment Library at New York University make clear, Ammon had contacted the national headquarters of the Intercolle-giate Socialists in New York City. In 1913 he was already regarded as one of the bright young stars in the Socialist Party farm league.[49] Socialists who went on the lecture circuit were asked to question him, when they passed through, on attitudes in the Midwest and among the young. The Tamiment documents show that his responses were not only reported in the minutes but discussed at the national level.

Hennacy's socialist group read Richard T. Ely's *Socialism and Social Reform* (1894) and Karl Kautsky's *Class Struggle* (1892), which indi-cates an advance in his sophistication. Joining as founding members were four friends and Prof. Morton Adams, though the professor made it clear that he was an observer only. As for the James Phelps Stokes speech, Ammon wrote, "There was no hotel, and I said I would sleep somewhere else and he could have my bed. He said 'No,' that we could sleep together." In that era such "bundling" was common and not homoerotic. "He was tall and lanky and apologized when he knelt and said his Episcopalian prayers. I also had Fred Strickland and [Charles] Ruthenberg, the leaders of the Socialists in Cleveland, speak there," Hennacy added.[50] The *Advance* reported that Stokes "showed further that the socialistic movement is not a plan on foot to upset the present order by men dissatisfied for personal means," which was a popular accusation against the Socialists.

By accident Hennacy, a freshman, involved himself in a three-cornered faculty debate. His favorite professor was Elmer Ellsworth Snoddy in Philosophy, who was described in a yearbook couplet as "Never elated while one man's oppressed / Never dejected while another's blest." Snoddy's moral impulses were countered by hard-nosed Prof. Adams from Political Science, who showed up at meetings to pose tough questions. Taking a wider view was Prof. Howard Lewis of Political Science, who had just completed a survey of living/working conditions in the area. It is worth pausing for a minute on Lewis's description of the changing ethnic context from which Ammon emerged: "The old settlers are in fact becoming a pronounced minority, while the new-comers—Slavs, Bohemians, settlers from Georgia and West Virginia—are taking their places, buying their farms and, it must be granted, making more of an effort to improve them than did many of the older, more conservative element."[51] These professors used the Socialist Club meetings to score debating points of their own. The dean required that events like the Phelps lecture include a follow-up with an opposing viewpoint, so Prof. Lewis played the respondent on November 14. The college yearbook described him as having "bested" Phelps (who was not there to reply). In its humor section, the yearbook revealed that some tension existed between Lewis and Hennacy in class:

> PROF. LEWIS: The classic example of the unearned increment is that a man buys a bottle of wine and after leaving it in his cellar for ten years sells it for three times its purchase price. What do you think about that, Hennacy?
>
> HENNACY: Well, Professor, wouldn't you say that there was an element of sacrifice in that?

There is no doubt that Hennacy's Intercollegiate Socialists brought fresh views to campus. Mary Bosworth Treudley, in her history of Hiram College, cites them as "evidence of modernity" but notes that they were "balanced by the Disciples Club, also organized this year, which included John Pounds, pastor of the Hiram Church."[52]

Ammon had an article in the *Advance* almost every week, capping the semester with one on "War" on November 25 and a "Socialists Platform" on December 2. The first was printed in tandem with Peden's antiwar essay, which was retitled "An International Illusion." These show that Ammon had absorbed Kautsky's explanation of class consciousness and Ely's ideas on taxation. He was also honing a "plain style" of prose combining Thomas Paine, one of his heroes, and elements of the IWW philosophy: "Sixty per cent of our taxes are used to pay for former wars or to prepare for future ones," he wrote. "The workingman comprises eighty-five percent of the people. The Capitalists and their Parasites comprise fifteen percent of the people. Our motto is 'Workers of the world unite,' and as war divides the people, we are against it."[53] He and Dorothy Day would say the same thing to President Truman forty years later.

One of the appeals that Ammon used to interest students was the high cost of room and board. The *Advance* ran a series comparing the local prices of everything from butter to potatoes to those in nearby cities, finding Hiram prices almost twice as high. Tuition for a semester was thirty-four dollars, but room and board ran thirty-seven to sixty dollars. The paper published stories about the student co-ops springing up at Harvard and Ohio State, sending a reporter to perform an item-by-item comparison at the latter. Co-ops were the answer, said the paper, not only for students but for citizens in general, a view Ammon held his entire life.[54]

Ammon also had a rollicking social life, some of which can be reconstructed through Bill Young. "I liked him," Hennacy wrote of the class president, and they loved playing pranks together. "Away from home now I thought it was smart to smoke cigarettes, get drunk, play penny ante [poker] until daylight, steal canned fruit from the cellar of the Dean's house (for which I was sent home in disgrace for two weeks). This was all of my Baptist 'don'ts' coming out." No longer a strict vegetarian, Ammon smoked with Bill all the time.[55] In the slang of that era, Ammon and Bill were "rowdies." It was a problem commented on in the *Advance* and addressed by the dean. Mary Treudley notes that it "came up again and again through the whole period, as behavior inherited from the frontier came under the scrutiny of town boys and girls."[56] Hennacy embodied both the frontier and the town sides, as well as the ethnic displacements mentioned by Prof. Lewis. But he was not among the forty men expelled at the end of 1914 for organizing a fraternity that determined who played on the college sports teams: the Greek system was completely alien to him. Hennacy sometimes took his friends to Negley, where they camped in an outbuilding at his grandparents' farm and goofed off in the neighborhood.

Bill Young pulled the most elaborate prank on Ammon, one that showed Hennacy's good humor. Following a Hiram College custom, they took sacks and went into the woods to hunt nuts, which Young said were on the ground for the picking, but it got dark and Young got them lost on purpose:

> Bill said that we were near some small town and why not play a joke on the folks [at college] and ask to stay there, and we could get back in time for school the next day. "You go into that house there," he pointed and, "I'll wait outside." So I knocked at the door and a young girl came. I told her that my brother, Bill, and myself were orphans and we were hungry. She called her mother who asked me to come in. I told her all sorts of sad stories. She made me a sandwich and I ate it and asked for one for my brother, Bill, who was waiting outside. . . . I thanked her and went out to get Bill and I was met by a crowd who gave me the laugh, as I was next door to the eating house where we were three times a day and didn't know it. It was a good joke and I was kidded about it unmercifully.

This prank suggests some group planning, as if Ammon may have needed taking down a notch, and the *Spider Web* yearbook commented on it: "Hennacy and his brother Bill get lost in the wilds of the Nichols backyard." So everyone knew about it, but it also shows that, despite his politics, Hennacy was well integrated into campus life.[57]

Young and Peden were like big brothers, bringing Ammon out of his role as small-town iconoclast. Their approval showed him that he could attack icons without being marginalized socially: there were broader horizons within which he fit. Unlike in high school, these friends said, in effect, "You have interesting ideas, and we are listening." In spring semester, Hennacy ramped up his efforts, sponsoring a lecture on "Socialism vs. Social Reform" by C. E. Ruthenberg on January 15. This was a coup. The leading Socialist in Ohio, Ruthenberg had run for Cleveland mayor and for Ohio governor and senator. A genuine radical, he would soon be imprisoned for advocating draft resistance and would later cofound the American Communist Party. His speech was covered by the *Advance* of January 20, 1914, and his unwavering beliefs must have impressed Hennacy. A second article in that issue announced that the Socialist Club would begin selling "Striker Stamps" for miners in an IWW strike in Colorado, Hennacy's first fundraising effort, and also the first appearance of the West in his imaginary. Later he would be devoted to the memory of Joe Hill, an IWW organizer executed in Utah.[58]

Hennacy closed out spring semester with a blast of militant posts. On April 14 there was "Socialism: What It Is Not: Its Origin: What It Means: Its Applications." On May 12 he wrote a thousand words on "The Theory of Labor and Surplus Value." And on May 26 he published "The Class Struggle," ending with a call to action and signature line for readers to sign. These pieces contrasted dramatically with the rest of the paper, which was still devoted to sports, social events, "Town News," and Disciples Club meetings. How did he get away with it? The answer is that Peden, who was announced as the next editor-in-chief in May, was his backer. Celestial bulldozers are not made ex nihilo, and thus far Hennacy had generous sponsors.

But back home in Lisbon, Mayor B. F. Hennacy had a setback. A client from his real estate practice accused him of misusing sixty dollars from a trust. The opposition Lisbon newspaper promoted the story, and he decided not to run for reelection. By 1915 he would be living temporarily in Akron.[59] Avoiding the situation, Ammon opted for another summer on the road selling cornflakes, taking along his brother Frank again and two Hiram classmates. With his father's reputation under a cloud, he may simply have wanted to avoid the unpleasantness, but he would never live in Lisbon again.

He was now comfortable vagabonding around the country, and his crew banged on doors in several states, the most interesting of which was Wisconsin. They spent most of their time around Milwaukee, which had elected socialist mayors since 1910 and was a stronghold of the Progressive Party; even the Republicans were liberal there, represented by the famous LaFollette family. This was upper-crust politics compared to small-town Ohio, but life also opened up for Ammon socially: "In Lacrosse we roomed with people by the name of Martell upstairs over the Tribune building. There were three beautiful sisters. I took the younger one out, name of Bessie. Guess I kissed her several times," he wrote. "When I had my crew in Wisconsin I roomed in Portage at the home where a pale faced girl name of Helen liked me." Also in Portage he "sold a package of corn flakes to a young lady who seemed very nearly to glide down the banister to answer the door. She appeared holding a copy of Jack London's *Iron Heel* in her hand. I was reading the same book from the town library. This was the beautiful Zona Gale, author of *Lulu Bett*: she persuaded me that the University of Wisconsin was better . . . so I went to Madison in the fall."[60]

He had no trouble uprooting himself for a bigger political stage. He found a strong journalism program and forgot about his family, who were scrambling for a living in Akron. "I took journalism in the same class attended by Bob LaFollette Jr. There were a dozen Socialist legislators here, and I earned $17 space rates telling about them for the NEW YORK CALL and also credit in my course in journalism."[61] He tried a class on conventional economics, finding it "worthless." He worked a paper route for his room, he said, and "washed dishes at a frat house in exchange for meals." The contrast to Lisbon and Hiram was striking. Ever since he had embraced socialism, it had taken him to bigger worlds—he was being rewarded for his politics, for his rhetoric. So he spent his free time prospecting the leftist circuits of Madison. He took Miriam Gaylord, daughter of the socialist senator, to a film. When Randolph Bourne came to lecture, Hennacy and his roommate gave up their bed to him, and years later Ammon fondly quoted Bourne's maxim that "war is the health of the state." Emma Goldman came, lecturing on "free love" and "birth control," and Ammon introduced her: "I cannot remember what she said, except that she was adept at repartee when people tried to tangle her up in conversation."

That verbal dexterity impressed Hennacy, who had his "foot in the door" lines but little debating ability yet. Seeking practice, he went to a socialist meeting and got up to expound on the IWW, based on his experience in Lisbon. "An old time Socialist trade unionist who knew much more than I did criticized me until I was in tears. . . . I asked him how I could be a good speaker. He told me to be sure of my facts and not do as I had just done, talk about something that I didn't know anything about. Then, he said, to go to some town where I knew no one: get up on a soapbox and commence. After that first speech, if I was any good at all, I would be a speaker."[62]

While he was honing his ability as a socialist speaker, Hennacy was no pacifist yet. For example, he took the ROTC/military drill class at Wisconsin because, he later explained, "I wanted to know how to shoot, come the revolution." He also met Quaker Socialists and attended some meetings, but no synergy developed for him. Ammon was beginning to distinguish the religious sympathizers from bohemians and true believers. This lens was sharpened when, through the Socialists, he met a Mrs. Cooney, who caused him endless problems over the next years. She lived on his paper route and, with her aged husband's approval, she employed young men to squire her around town; Ammon became one of them, not understanding that the squiring was supposed to be sexual as well. When he did not deliver, Mrs. Cooney bad-mouthed him to his future wife, among others.

Ammon had been inhibited earlier by his family and his Baptist upbringing, but now he was free, and he soon found someone he thought perfect. Her name was Selma Melms, the daughter of the socialist sheriff of Milwaukee. She moved in that polite socialist circle of Wisconsin that Ammon had sought to crack. He was the only outsider at a lawn party when he saw her, and it took him four days of follow-up to get a date, which she accepted only because he said he had to leave in ten days: the University of Wisconsin raised its out-of-state tuition from $24 a semester to $148, and there was no way he could earn that much. He was already writing romantic poetry to her before he left town:

> To Selma from Ammon.
> Sweetheart, each time you touch this pillow soft
> May it recall love's caresses and waft
> Them back to me; till with an added one
> Our love has yet a happy course to run.

Many years later, after they were separated, he wrote that "Selma was the broad-faced peasant type that always appealed to me. Love is blind, and how much the fact that I was a happy Irishman, much more radical than the staid Germans of Milwaukee, and that Selma was the first radical girl I had ever met . . . had to do with our engagement is difficult to determine." Despite this later condescension, his letters show that he was as deeply in love as when he would be courting Dorothy Day twenty years later.

The Melmses were living, as a perk of the sheriff's job, over the county jail. It was there, he wrote, that "I kissed her, she fainted, and I was scared. Her mother wouldn't speak to her for 6 weeks because she had bobbed her hair. I think she really fell in love with me as it was a chance to get away from home, although her father was a fine man. I went back to Ohio very happy." They were both smitten and saw one another each of those ten nights. Back home Ammon composed a twelve-item document titled "My Wife," spelling out what he sought: "I want a New Woman, who in common with her more unenlightened sisters, finds joy in being possessed by me; who delights in receiving burning kisses from my lips." Second, "I do not want her to have a spaniel-like devotion; I want a faith that is firm and patient, not blind. We both do honor to the divinity of our beings by each trusting the other with the power of going alone if necessary." Third, "If perchance poverty requires tedious duties, they shall be looked at as incidents and as services of love rather than as an aim in life or duties." Fourth was "a love of the open country, of hikes and tramps." His other points amplified the same sense of patriarchy: his idea of a New Woman was basically a New Follower.[63]

Ammon did not go straight back to Ohio State. In fact, he did not leave Milwaukee for another month, doing some door-to-door selling and then returning to his family, which may have appealed for his economic help.[64] First he found work in an Akron machine shop, joining the union on a Friday, only to find himself fired on Saturday for endorsing the IWW. When he got home that day, there was a notice of eviction for nonpayment of rent on the front door. Then came a letter from Selma breaking up with him (Mrs. Cooney had gotten to her). Was he depressed? Hardly: "I got work on the Busy Bee bread wagon, with a horse and wagon route," he wrote, and that worked out. "My smallest sister had been born when I was away at school, so when I arrived home with cookies—part of the 10% breakage which I was allowed—Lorraine promptly called me 'Ammon-cookie.'" After work, he wrote political love poems, such as "To My Sweetheart, Selma," trying to win her back.

> I dare to live for a great idea
> My aims from a greedy world apart
> To place naught above the common weal
> This and more because of you, Sweetheart.
> . . . .
> To be strong to love and agitate;
> Not before the rich to fawn and kneel;
> Strongly to doubt and investigate.
> My Lover and I our love thus seal.

He asked Selma to come to visit and, surprisingly, she agreed, but they did not visit his hard-pressed family. Arriving by train, she met him at Akron, and they continued instead to Lisbon and then to Negley, as if he wanted to show her his roots rather than his current reality.[65]

Ammon's comment above about his sister Lorraine is among the few regarding his siblings in this period. We know that he took his brother Frank on his summer trips, and that his sister Julia worked at a Kresge's drug store in Akron, but not much about the others. Lola would become radical, but in 1915 she, Lida, and Lorraine were still in school, a big responsibility for their mother in the family's reduced circumstances. B. F. Hennacy himself was adrift, his career in politics over and his real estate profession unrecoverable. According to Ammon, he was drinking too much. As the eldest son, Ammon helped out, but in a limited way: he was stricken by political fevers and by love, the kind of idealist whose family ties are tenuous at best when there seems support for his agenda elsewhere.

Just as Ammon was about to start at Ohio State, however, his father found a sales position in Columbus with Fuller Brush, so the whole family moved there. The next "term at Ohio State was one of the best years of my life as a student," he wrote. He brought his political know-how from Hiram and Wisconsin: "I was the head of the Intercollegiate Socialist Club and secretary of the Socialist local downtown. In my classes in philosophy and sociology was much room for my radical agitation. I had never been sad about my radicalism, and with this love of Selma in my heart I felt that I could conquer the world."

Things began to move faster. Ohio State was huge and more diverse than his previous colleges, he was involved in even more socialist activities, and he had moral and romantic commitments. The most important connection he made in this period was to Scott Nearing, the radical economist who had just been fired by the Wharton School for, among other things, denouncing Billy Sunday. He and his wife would later write *Living the Good Life* (1954), a classic for the back-to-the-earth movement of the 1960s, but in his classes he was already stressing the agricultural variants of socialism. Nearing brought Ammon's farm upbringing into his political outlook—he too was a vegetarian— and became a lifelong friend.[66] Hennacy also took philosophy with a Professor Leighton, whom he liked except for the fact that he headed the local Preparedness League, an effort to train college students and older men for a war. Hennacy was dead set against all wars, especially a European war. Some Socialists were pro-war, but that conflicted with fundamental religious beliefs that Hennacy still held. In Columbus he went briefly to the Congregational church of Rev. Washington Gladden, who had refused money from the Rockefellers, saying it was tainted, but he also went to a local spiritualist church, where he asked a question and "heard" the eerie response that "Peter is happy in heaven." He thought that meant Peter Brown, who had raised his father. These religious flashes indicate that he was not entirely an atheist in his preprison period.[67]

Preparations for war became a litmus test for Hennacy and for the Left generally, even dividing anarchists and Socialists among themselves. As Cornell has detailed, many Socialists thought that taking the side of England and France against Germany was more important than pacifism. But radical anarchists—the Galleani followers, Carlo Tresca, and Mexican anarchists—urged young men to dodge the draft or leave the country.[68] Hennacy was still a Socialist, so he was spooked by the number of liberals preparing for war. One of his professors, Louis Arner, had written a socialist book, but now he "had turned for the war." Another of Hennacy's heroes, the Rev. Edward Ellis Carr, had been the socialist candidate for president in 1912 and advocated draft resistance at huge rallies in Cleveland and Columbus, but then he too recanted.

Hennacy was seeking some ideological rock on which to stand when he got a clue in his sociology class, where he was assigned to speak against socialism, while a rich girl spoke for it. He turned the assignment on its head: "My argument was that Socialism was not radical enough, that anarchism was the real ideal. I didn't believe it then but that was the only argument I could think of." But he found that this class exercise, his first public avowal of anarchism, was rhetorically persuasive. He had to stand absolutely alone and not back down or equivocate. His new self-confidence showed up even at home, where his mother found him "saucy."[69]

Thereafter Hennacy insisted on resistance, whatever the cost. He had a lingering investment in the Socialist Party, which still considered him one of its promising young stars. He tried to balance these interests: "Despite the fact that our presidential candidate, the Revolutionary Rev. Carr, and many other leaders were to turn pro-war," he wrote, "we youngsters knew that we had Debs, Ruthenberg, Wagenknecht and many others holding with us." But then Debs, front runner for the Socialist Party nomination, decided to run for senator of Indiana rather than for president. That left the nomination to the less radical Allan Benson, who finished with 3 percent of the total vote and blamed the party's poor showing on "anarchists, falsely regarded as Socialists, aided and abetted by certain foreigners whose naturalization papers should be cancelled while they themselves are deported to the countries from which they came." Though Ammon would later forgive Debs, he found deeply insulting the charges of Benson and the complete collapse of socialist principles in war time: it was a key moment in his intellectual development.[70]

He devoted all of his free time to politics in 1916. The *Ohio State Daily Lantern* reported on his speeches throughout the spring, revealing the fusion that he was working on: "Utopian socialism is based upon a mystic ideal which has greatly influenced men and nations, creating an ideal out of the mind and seeking to shape society to that ideal, according to Ammon A. Hennacy, junior arts, who spoke at the Intercollegiate Socialist Society Friday night in Page Hall." No longer organizing discussion groups or selling Striker Stamps, Hennacy was the main speaker, and he was learning to tailor his talks to his audiences: "That $2655, the amount required for the firing of a 13-inch gun, is equal to the amount required for a college education was [a fact] given in a talk on the waste of militarism and the capitalist system given before the Intercollegiate Socialist Club by Ammon A. Hennacy junior in Arts Friday night. The Socialists could easily run this country on what is now wasted by the inefficiency of the capitalistic system due to imperfect methods of agriculture, manufacturing and distributing, according to Hennacy."[71] Forty years later he would be imprisoned for opposing even bigger guns, nuclear missiles near Omaha, but during the summer of 1916, there were no missile sites to picket.

He had been writing to Selma almost daily, even as his fame grew locally, and during the summer she came to visit. As before, they avoided his family, but they visited Chicago, courtesy of his socialist friend Ed Smith from Hiram. Smith had a private fortune and "rented an apartment for us for a week in Chicago when we hiked and [he] kept buying tickets for concerts, etc., to keep us there. His wife was away, and Selma cooked for him." The "hikes" were more to Ammon's taste than to Selma's—she was a city girl and suffragette whose greatest aspiration was to be an actress. The summer was a pause, but soon Ammon was back on stage.[72]

In the fall of 1916 the *Lantern* reported that Hennacy was teaching a course on socialism, with twelve lessons "mapped out by the Rand School of Social Science of New York City. One of the instructors in this course is Professor Beard of Columbia University." Those interested were told to report to the socialist headquarters at 121 1/2 Town Street on Sunday night for Hennacy's initial two-hour lecture. With his experience on three campuses over three years, Ammon was now a proficient public speaker and political organizer. Trial evidence would suggest that he had a hand in other protests, such as the anti-rent movement. He had no doubts about his ideals, but he seems not to have gauged how emotional the war debate was off-campus, or how severe the crack-down could be.[73]

In the spring of 1917, with other members of a small group that still supported Rev. Carr (who had not yet turned), Ammon wrote a leaflet and a placard for distribution. It would be held in trial that the "small group" legally constituted a conspiracy and that they also printed rent-strike flyers. The leaflet was the milder of the two antiwar documents:

YOUNG MEN
DON'T REGISTER FOR THE WAR!
It's better to go to jail than
To rot on a foreign battlefield.

The poster was more combative and class conscious:

YOUNG MEN
are you going to
REFUSE TO REGISTER
for military service in a foreign country
While the rich men
who have brought on this war
Stay at home
and get richer by gambling in food stuffs?
WE WOULD RATHER DIE OR BE IMPRISONED FOR THE
   SAKE OF JUSTICE, THAN KILL OUR FELLOW MEN IN
   THIS UNJUST WAR.
Signed .... Young Men's Anti-Militarist League[74]

Unlike some antiwar Socialists, Hennacy infused his appeal with religious undertones. Yet it was not to Rev. Carr but to Debs and Ruthenberg that he now felt closest. Had he simply written the materials above, or posted them and then disappeared, he might have escaped the subsequent dragnet. Instead, he put himself in the front lines of antidraft advocacy, which was construed nationally as treason.

These flyers appeared just as James Cannon, a New York Socialist, was scheduled to speak at the corner of Broad and High Streets, next to the state capitol, the most important corner of downtown Columbus. Hennacy was probably the organizer of the event. He wrote that

by 8:30 there were thousands of people at the meeting, and I could not see over their heads. A Jewish comrade came along with his junk wagon and I stepped on top and addressed the crowd. Cannon had not yet arrived; he never did come. The police told me there were too many people around and I would have to come down. I expect there were 10,000 by that time. I argued that I had a permit, but they reached for me. I ran across the street to the State House steps and continued for half an hour. Here they had no authority over me.[75]

After he talked for thirty minutes there, Ohio state troopers arrived and arrested Hennacy and another Socialist Labor Party member. They were held overnight for disturbing the peace and released in the morning, with their trial scheduled for May 30, 1917. At this point Ammon was only charged with a misdemeanor, but in his view it was a huge opportunity to disrupt on a larger scale. He filled a suitcase with his antiwar leaflets and hit the road for the next seven weeks. He no longer saw himself among the equivocating Socialists but instead aligned himself with "true" radicals like Emma Goldman and Alexander Berkman.

There were informers everywhere, so he traveled cautiously. "My method was to go to a town and look up a comrade whose name I was given or whom I knew from my previous soap-boxing," he wrote, but "often the comrade had already turned pro-war and I had to leave in a hurry before he turned me in." His first stop was Cleveland, where he was introduced for a talk by Ruthenberg, who had just coauthored the antimilitary "St. Louis Statement" of the Socialist Party. They came from different class backgrounds, but Ammon respected Ruthenberg, who would soon be in prison too. The Cleveland Socialists gave Hennacy enough money to get him to his next destination, and he left his leaflets to be distributed after his departure, a tactic designed to make their authorship difficult to trace. It is clear that everyone understood the leaflets to be unlawful, even if morally justified. Leaflets typically carried a printer's mark: by the time the original printer identified Hennacy, he would be in another state, in this case Pennsylvania. Or so it was hoped: his movements would be traced at trial, demonstrating his intent.

He probably spent a couple of weeks in the Ohio border counties that he knew so well. From there he crossed into West Virginia to visit Ed Firth, his friend from East Palestine, who was living in Huntington. Then he went to Cabin Creek, a mining town owned by Consolidated Coal and the scene of bitter strikes, but his contact had moved away, and the United Mine Workers were pro-war. The situation felt too dangerous, so he walked out of town on the railroad tracks at night, carrying two suitcases of leaflets. When sufficiently far away, he knocked on the door of the only cabin with a light on. He was welcomed by farmers, probably in the historically Black enclave of Levi (now Rand). This was his first experience, albeit brief, living with African Americans. They were more than accommodating, he said, but were puzzled by his refusal to eat sowbelly for breakfast.[76]

He got a train at Charleston the next day, heading back to Columbus for his trial. On board he was wearing a huge button marked "PEACE," he wrote, "yet the dumb troopers, who entered the train . . . and said they were looking for seditious literature, opened my grips and seeing the books on top of the literature, muttered something about my being a student returning from college." He arrived home only the night before his trial, but he audaciously sent his radical sisters and friends to leaflet the university neighborhood, which was lightly policed, while he distributed in the more heavily patrolled downtown areas. "There were no squad cars and radios in those days, so a person did not have to be very smart to outwit a cop," he wrote later. "I put stickers on nearly all the downtown store fronts." Did he not understand the danger? He was not only advertising his "treason" but also repeating again the offense for which he was about to be tried, making proof of intent easy. Details of these activities would come out in trial; they could not be dismissed as one-time or innocent. "Finally at 2.30 a.m. I was caught and put in solitary."[77]

It is doubtful that he understood that this would be his last day of freedom. He was twenty-four years old and very much a romantic and a self-righteous idealist. He did not expressly believe in God, but he believed that human beings were good, and that truth would win out. He would be in the Atlanta Federal Penitentiary for two and a half years. He would need every bit of strength and belief from his Ohio days that he could muster in solitary confinement.

2

Prison

Trial

When Ammon asked for a lawyer, a detective named Wilson said that, unless he registered for the draft, he was to be shot "on orders from Washington." Wilson showed him a paper with the headline "Extreme Penalty for Traitors," adding that the other protesters had given in and registered.[1] Then he was put in solitary, to prevent patriotic inmates from attacking him, said Wilson. Nor could he visit the barber to spruce up for his hearing because, Wilson added, the barber might cut his throat. No lawyer ever appeared, though the group was later represented by a public defender.

Ammon had never been in jail before, and these tactics were new to him. For weeks he had been on the move, talking with like-minded friends, with no idea how unpopular his ideals had become. The temper of the time appears in *Buckeye State*, the Lisbon newspaper, which emphasized the importance of flying the flag, printed the name of every man eligible to be drafted, and endorsed a halt to naturalizations of Germans. By the time Ammon walked into court, almost seventy-five hundred Columbiana County men aged twenty-one to thirty had signed up. Not only Lisbon but all Ohio was watching his case, which did not occur in an empty courtroom, as he later claimed. The regional newspapers sent reporters to Columbus, and their readers apparently felt that Ammon was getting what he deserved.[2] Noted the *Buckeye State*, "Hennacy's mother and father and most of their family have been in attendance at the trial from the start. The father said that it was his opinion that his son, Ammon, would be convicted and that he would receive a salty sentence. Young Hennacy maintains the same air of playing the martyr in a great cause for the good of humanity. Only a few of the extreme socialists support him, most of them declaring that they believe the government should be heartily supported against the German military tyrants."[3] Ammon later claimed that a newspaper asked his mother if she was afraid that he would be shot: "Her reply was that the only thing she was afraid of was they might scare me to give in."[4] If this incident happened, the newspaper has yet to be found, but it became Ammon's favorite gloss on the trial. Taken together, the reports confirm that Hennacy was indeed "saucy," as his mother had remarked earlier, and was now staking everything on his pacifist/antiwar position.

There were others on trial in addition to Hennacy: Harry E. Townsley (the printer), Cecil Bailey and John Lewis Hammond of Marietta, and Robert E. Pfeiffer of Coal Run. Nor was the trial quite so one-sided. Judge Sater forbade the prosecutor from asking about the political views of prospective jurors, and at trial the accused were defended by an eighty-three-year-old Quaker ex-judge named Moses B. Earnhardt, who worked for free and filed many motions on their behalf. Earnhardt's main argument was that the leaflets had been printed before the draft law was enacted and only distributed afterwards, so technically they were legal. However, Townsley, the printer, had kept a letter from Hennacy after passage of the law asking for more copies, which clinched the case against both. Charges against Pfeiffer were dismissed for lack of evidence, since he testified that he had only "found" the leaflets Hammond left on his porch. US Assistant Attorney General James M. Stengst then subpoenaed Pfeiffer and eight others in a barrage against Hennacy, Townsley, Hammond, and Bailey.[5]

The evidence has been preserved. A good deal of it involved connecting the dots to link all the accused, since they had scattered over eastern and southern Ohio. One particularly damning bit was a postal money order that Ammon bought in East Palestine to pay Townsley for the posters, indicating that he wished to cover his tracks (Townsley's shop was only a mile from Ammon's house in Columbus). There was another letter from Hennacy to Townsley, postmarked from Huntington, West Virginia, showing that they were planning the printing. There was even testimony from suppliers making it clear that Townsley knew what the paper and ink were to be used for.

The evidence found in Justice Department Archives in Atlanta and Chicago shows a well-developed case. Ammon commissioned not only

Figure 2.1. Hennacy's antidraft and rent-strike flyers from his trial. Permission of US Bureau of Prisons.

the large posters and window stickers but also several thousand "dodgers," which were four-by-six-inch flyers to be passed out in crowds anonymously. Also in the evidence were posters Ammon ordered for the Anti–Rent Payers League: *"Down with Rent, Interest, and Profit: Mr. Rent Payer, STOP PAYING RENT."*[6] These were seized from the Hennacy house at 133 Hunter Street in Columbus. The anti-rent materials, which he never discussed later, were an outgrowth of his advocacy of co-ops and rent protests. Ammon admitted to being the author of all of these in a later motion to exclude them from evidence. While the anti-rent materials had no bearing on the charges at trial, they made draft resistance appear to be part of a larger left-wing plot. Hennacy was no violent Galleanist anarchist, but he was deeply involved in the most radical action available. And he was going it alone, like his heroes.

Ammon wrote that his trial was attended only by his family, but many newspaper reporters commented on the sizeable and odd audience, which included a socialist washerwoman and a Native American ("Karakas Redwood, who was some kind of Yogi"), whom Ammon referred to several times in his letters. The record shows that at least four newspapers reported on the trial, all of them recording District Attorney Stuart Bolin's thundering summation on July 3:

One hundred and forty-one years ago tomorrow the immortal words were written which were to fire our forefathers until they were free from the English tyrant. Today a greater tyrant threatens us. George the III did not cut off the hands of little children and bayonet the enemy alive to barn doors as the Beast of Berlin has done. In 1776 such men as Hennacy would be defending King George and in 1861 it was men like him who would have allowed the slaves to remain slaves. Judge Earnhardt would have you believe that this despicable coward, Hennacy, is a hero. He calls him by the resounding name of "conscientious objector." I tell you this man does not have a conscience. The money of our state has been spent to educate him in our university.[7]

Judge Sater's charge to the jury was that "no matter how fragrant [sic] Hennacy's part was in his plot, if it were proved that Townsley did not print the circulars after May 18, both should be acquitted."[8] It took the jury, some of whom Ammon claimed were sleeping, about thirty minutes to decide that both were guilty. The verdict was reported as far away as Cincinnati and Cleveland. Hennacy was to serve two years at the Atlanta Federal Penitentiary, followed by nine months in the nearby Delaware County jail.

He did not go to Atlanta immediately, because the verdict was appealed, and although he and Townsley were eligible for bail on posting nine thousand dollars, neither could do so. Earnhardt's appeal to quash the evidence was based on the lack of a warrant for the seizure of specific materials from Townsley's shop and Hennacy's house. But DA Bolin had heard that before, rattling off four federal case decisions that justified the broad seizure of evidence. When the judge overturned the motion to quash, the old Quaker lawyer had no other cards to play.

On the train trip to Atlanta, Hennacy and Townsley were chained to their berths. "I had never occupied a Pullman berth," he wrote ironically. They arrived on Friday, July 13, 1917, and were promptly separated. Ammon, then twenty-four, was assigned number 7438 and sent to a cell to begin what he later called a "greater baptism," learning the world of prison etiquette. His first cellmate was an old forger whom he calls Peter Brockman in his autobiography.[9] Brockman sized up Hennacy as his next punk.

We undressed and Peter came over and sat on the edge of my bunk. I edged away but could not get far. "Don't be afraid. I'm your friend," Peter said, "I've been here four years, kid, and I sure get lonesome. Several skirts write to me off and on, but the one I planted my jack with has forgotten me long ago. The hell with women anyway! You can't trust 'em and a fellow is a fool to marry one."

"I'm tired, Peter, I want to go to sleep," I said jerkily as he commenced to caress me.

"No one goes to sleep so early in this hot jail; the bedbugs are worst this time of year. This is a man's joint and you'll have to learn what that means, kid."[10]

Hennacy wrote that he resisted Brockman with the aid of Alexander Berkman, who was also a prisoner at Atlanta. He had heard of Hennacy's arrival, and Ammon would be inspired by his example throughout his Atlanta time, especially Berkman's earlier ability to endure two and a half years of solitary. Through a prison runner named Blackie, Berkman sent Ammon a note explaining that "your cell mate has paid $5 worth of tobacco to the screw in your cell block to get the first young prisoner coming in to be his cell mate. . . . Watch him, for he is one of the worst perverts in the prison. There is no use in making a fuss, for you may 'accidentally' fall down four tiers. Get $5 worth of tobacco from the store and give it to Blackie and he will give it to the guard and pull strings." Berkman also told him to attend Mass, so they could meet and talk.[11] This was Hennacy's introduction to a new social reality that permanently altered his sense of "protest."

Berkman was a living legend who had attempted to assassinate coal mine manager Henry Clay Frick after the Homestead Strike, seventy miles east of Lisbon, about the time when Ammon was born. He had spent fourteen years in prison, written *Prison Memoirs of an Anarchist*, and was far more radical than Ammon. He and Emma Goldman, his partner, believed in violent means and were willing to put their lives on the line for revolution. Ammon had read Berkman's *Memoirs* (1916) and written him a letter, "and now I was to meet him personally." Led by Blackie, Hennacy was taken to Berkman in the prison yard on a sunny day: "His kindly smile made me feel that I had a friend." Berkman explained how to get letters out, how to speak without moving your lips,

Figure 2.2. Ammon Hennacy's intake card from the Atlanta
Penitentiary. Marquette Archives.

and that on rainy days they could meet in the Catholic chapel, for the
chaplain was a sympathetic ex-boxer. He also left Ammon with a code
of five important rules:

1. Don't tell lies.
2. Don't snitch on other prisoners.
3. Decide what you will and won't do and don't budge.
4. Don't curse or ever strike a guard, because then they could attack.
5. Don't be seen talking to Berkman; send a note through Blackie.

The intransigence of this prison stoicism appealed to Ammon, who
incorporated it into his ethos. He was able to fend off Brockman
with "good natured passive resistance" for several weeks, until he got

transferred to a new block with a four-bed cell.[12] Berkman became not only Hennacy's guide to prison survival but also a mentor who understood the rules of the game inside and outside prison. Socialists like Carr and Ruthenberg did not compare; they had not been through anything this rough (though Ruthenberg would soon serve serious time). Berkman inspired Hennacy's full embrace of anarchism, and his use of violence did not alarm Ammon, who was not yet a pacifist.

Two of Ammon's new cellmates were counterfeiters. The third was Johnny Spanish, a legendary labor racketeer, robber, and Mafia hit man from the Five Points gang in New York City. Spanish, who had spent ten years in Sing Sing, impressed Ammon by speaking well of that prison's reform-minded warden, Thomas Mott Osborne. Initially Hennacy suspected all wardens, but Osborne and rehabilitation became a lifelong interest. Another of the counterfeiters, John, was boss of the painting gang and, taking a liking to Hennacy, had him transferred to his gang. "And when he left in about 6 months, I was made the boss of his crew," wrote Ammon. "I had a pass to go anywhere I wanted inside the walls."[13]

Before that would happen, he had to learn to avoid other prisoners' dramas. Contraband was a constant, and early on a fellow prisoner tried to plant a shiv on him. Letters came in and went out by secret channels; Ammon learned to use those quietly, with appropriate bribes. Radical newspapers with conservative names, such as the *Conservator* and *Irish World*, were available through John T. Dunn, who became Hennacy's closest radical friend inside. He was a Catholic conscientious objector from Providence who was boss of the plumbing gang. There were a dozen other conscientious objectors, and they all knew each other, but the warden had dispersed them through the cellblocks, thinking they might conspire if grouped in one place. These COs were either European anarchists, old-time IWW members, nonanarchist foreigners who did not speak much English, or members of small religious sects. Some of these new acquaintances, like Dunn, Ammon would visit after prison, others on his Big Hike. But in prison they did not do anything together—the warden was more correct than Ammon could admit. It is clear, however, that he was closer to the Catholic Dunn than to any of the other religious pacifists.[14]

He still admired Berkman's absolutism, though, and looked for opportunities to be as radical, thinking he could forge himself in Atlanta as

Berkman had at Allegheny Prison. His first opportunity came when the editor of the prison paper, *Good Words*, asked him to write something. Knowing that his real opinions would never pass the censor, Hennacy decided to use those of Henry D. Thoreau, writing, "A prison is the only house in a slave state where a free man can abide with honor." When this appeared on April 1, 1918, he was pleased with his subversion.[15]

During his first prison job, on the construction gang, Ammon slowed down the delivery of wheelbarrows of cement to the job site by constantly stopping to tie his shoelaces, by pretending his "buggy" was defective, etc. He wrote proudly of this to his parents—he was still allowed correspondence. But when the guards killed two prisoners, one of them Black, he found out that subversion was not a game. He heard about the incident and imagined it later in an unpublished play. As he scripted it, Sam, a Black northerner, was smoking covertly in the toilet, when he was given up to the guards by a "rat" named Lorenzo. "You lousy bastard of a screw, can't a nigger smoke if white folks smoke?" Sam asks the guard. "No nigger can curse me," says the guard, who shoots him.[16] There is no doubt that everyone in the prison then knew what happened, and it is Hennacy's first-known literary effort, aside from his poems to Selma.[17]

Present or not, he was incensed about the murder, but his cellmates knew the rule. They may have agreed that prison was racist, but they probably pointed out that he did not bunk with the Blacks. They said he "should worry about the living, for the dead were the dead. . . . That if I wanted anything to do, I should raise a fuss about the poor fish served on Fridays."[18] Ammon did not eat from the table where fish was served because there was a vegetarian table, but, annoyed by his cellmates' lack of sympathy for the Blacks, he decided to organize a protest, and the fish would serve as a pretext.

> I got cardboard from John Dunn and painted signs which I put up in all the toilets around the place telling the prisoners to work on Fridays but stay in their cells and refuse to go to dinner or to eat the rotten fish. The guards and stool pigeons tore the signs down, but I made others and put them up. The first Friday 20 of us stayed in our cells. The guards came around and asked us if we were sick. We said we were sick of that damn fish. The next Friday 200 stayed in their cells, and the next Friday 600.[19]

But someone informed, and on the third Monday Ammon was summoned to the warden's office and told he had been overheard plotting to blow up the prison. A guard named DeMoss framed him, he wrote later. On June 21, 1918, Ammon was sent directly to a lightless, triangular room known as the Dark Hole.[20]

The Dark Hole was not only punishment but also sensory deprivation. He was stripped to his underwear, the only light came from under the door, and there was nothing to read. In place of a bed there was a pallet on the floor, and he received just the slice of cornbread and cup of water mentioned earlier. The only events were auditory, the prisoners marching to work every morning, the trusty approaching with his meal, the door opening and closing. After eight days it was difficult to remember how long he had been there.

On the tenth day he was taken to the Light Hole, which had one twenty-watt bulb and a small dirty window facing east. He could not see the sun, though, because a tall building faced his window, but if he got down on his knees, he thought he could see Berkman's head as he worked in the tailor's shop in that building. Even if he was just imagining it, that was another reason to persevere. "White bread, which I got then, tasted like cake," he wrote. There was "a bunk attached to the wall on the right; a plain chair and a small table, with a spoon, plate, and cup on it. There was a toilet; and a wash basin attached to the wall."[21] These were on the wall next to the door, the one place in the cell where a convict could write without being seen. It was here, in a crack in the wall behind the toilet, that Ammon found a stub of pencil on his second day. It was here that he would come every day after reading his Bible passages to write notes on toilet paper.

When he entered prison, Ammon was agnostic. Six months earlier he had been sampling churches in Columbus. Now he received a Bible through the Protestant chaplain. It was the only book permitted and, though he had read it in his Baptist youth, he thought he might reread it. He was so bored, he said later, that he would have read a telephone book. On the toilet paper he noted the good quotations, just as Elsie Roberts had taught him back in Lisbon.

I commenced with Genesis and read at least twenty chapters a day. I also walked what I figured was four and a half miles a day. Berkman sent me a copy of Edwin Markham's "The Man with the Hoe" and I learned it by heart and recited it aloud several times a day. For the first few weeks the time did not go so slowly, as I was busy planning a routine. I found that on one day, perhaps a Thursday or Friday, I would suddenly be called by the guard to go across the hall and get a bath.[22]

In this passage, Ammon names three of his four main activities in solitary. First, he read the Bible closely, then reread, as there was little else to do: "I made up games with pages and chapters and names of characters. . . . I had memorized certain chapters that I liked. As I read of Isaiah, Ezekiel, Micah and other of the prophets and of Jesus, I could see that they had opposed tyranny." His appreciation of the Bible centered on the Sermon on the Mount and those voices he thought supported it. Second, he had a variety of exercise routines. He used his chair as a dumbbell, he shadow-boxed, he did isometrics and arm circles, he even tried handstands. Like a rat in a box, he prowled, eight-and-a-half paces from one end of his cell to the other. He did this for hours. As he paced, he recited or thought about his day's reading, boiling it down to common themes. Third was the unusual event: the shower, the shave, and the haircut—his head was shaved bald—or a visit from Deputy Warden Girardeau.[23] Eating was the fourth routine, with the Black trusty bringing him his meals: oatmeal every morning at 7:00, beans and bread and coffee for lunch at 11:30, and grits with meat and collards for dinner around 5:30. The beans were a problem, because they often contained pebbles that could break his teeth. He gave his meat to the trusty in exchange for notes from outside. Berkman sent him a piece of candy by this route, but he never saw any fruit.

He also slept a lot, taking both morning and afternoon naps. He was often tired, because bedbugs attacked as soon as they found his warm body when the lights went off, just as they would at the Catholic Worker House in the 1950s. He tried to be asleep by 10:00 p.m. when the guard flashed a light on him. The only three sounds that happened every day were distant train whistles: one in the morning, one in the midafternoon, and one at night. He clung to his routines and these markers of time, but the days and nights blurred. He told himself that if Berkman could do two and a half years of solitary in Allegheny, then he could do two if necessary. He was fortified by his love for Selma, though she had not written, and by his Celestial Bulldozer feelings, reinforced by the Bible. He explained himself in a letter to his family after he was moved to the Light Hole:

> Since June 7 I have been in "solitary." I am in a large closed cell by myself: only being allowed out in the hall for a shave on Thurs and across the hall for a bath on Fri. I have no privileges—no paper, letter, or anything to read except the Bible and since Sept. "Good Words." As there is a conflict between the authorities here and myself about what is just the right thing for me to do, I suppose I will lose my "good time," will not be home until July 13th [1919]. On Nov 8th they moved me upstairs in the Isolation Bldg. I get the fresh air here and can see outdoors and hear the new arrivals making music during the music hour. I get plenty to eat and am treated OK. I have not been sick any. Tell Leah I'll soon be as fat as she is. I take exercises two hours a day and get plenty of sleep. I have read the Bible thru 5 times and find some new things in it.[24]

The "new things" that he liked were in the books of Matthew, Mark, John, and James. He added that "much of the Old Testament, and Peter, Paul, and Jude I did not like."[25]

On September 12, 1918, Chief Warden Fred Zerbst came to visit. Ammon did not know that Zerbst, a student of penology, had written to his parents, assuring them that Ammon was okay. He wanted Hennacy to sign up for the second general draft, which started August 24, so that he could put Hennacy back in the general population. "I told him I had not changed my mind about the war," Ammon wrote. "He said that I wouldn't get anything around here acting that way." Ammon said he was not asking for anything; he was just doing time. "He said I would get another year back in the hole for this second refusal to register, I told him that was o.k."[26]

In the letter to his family that Ammon was finally allowed to write, he told Julia that he was "trying to think of a name" from their Negley farm days "and suddenly it would come to me. I worried more about you folks and Selma not hearing from me than anything else." Gifts from outside may have been sent, he said, but he had not received them. He asked his brother Frank to write about his work, and he told Lorraine that there were "lots of little birds by [my] window." He wondered if Paul still slept in the attic and whether Frank and Julia had followed Lola to the middle floor of the Columbus house. He requested that roses be bought for Selma, who seemed to be estranged by his actions.[27]

Ammon believed that the guards would try to break him the way they were breaking Popoff across the hall. During one of his barber visits he saw Popoff with bandages on his head: it seemed that Popoff was going insane, an indication of what might lie in store. Ammon wrote notes about Popoff's treatment for his sister Lola to send to newspapers, smuggling them out through the Black trusty. This time in solitary was sapping him.[28] On September 21 Warden Zerbst came back, saying that Ammon had reached the normal maximum for solitary and would be let out the next day if he promised not to plot to blow up any more prisons. Ammon was unable to resist the temptation to talk back.

> "You know I didn't do that," I said.
>
> "I know you didn't," Zerbst replied, "but what do you suppose I am warden for? If I had told the prisoners that you were put in solitary for leading that food sit-down, all of them would be your friends. When you are accused of planning to blow up the prison, they are all afraid to know you." Zerbst marched out, but he came back in five minutes.
>
> "Have you been sneaking any letters out?" he asked.
>
> "Sure," I replied, smiling.
>
> "Who is doing it for you?" he demanded.
>
> "A friend of mine," I answered.
>
> "What is his name?"
>
> "That is for you and your guards and stool pigeons to find out."

Zerbst stormed around the cell, irritated that nothing seemed to work on Hennacy. "You'll stay in here all your good time and get another year, you stubborn fool," he said as he left.[29] Ammon wanted to live up to the example of Berkman, but also to feel supported by his family, by Selma, his cousin Georgia, and socialist well-wishers who sent him socks or chocolate. He was trying to live by principle, but he now faced the cost: the prospect that Zerbst would withhold his "good time" until the end of his entire sentence. He could be in solitary until he cracked.

Ammon wrote that he paced back and forth for hours after this visit. Eight and a half steps to the wall, then back. He tore the buttons off his clothes so that he would have to sew them back on. He lost faith. "I had not had a note from anyone in months," he wrote: "Here I had been singing defiance at the whole capitalistic world . . . now I wondered if anyone really cared. Perhaps by this time Selma might be married to someone else with a real future ahead of him instead of being lost in a jail. That last letter I had received from her was rather formal. . . . How could one end it all?"[30]

He fell asleep worrying about Selma and listening for the evening freight's whistle. The next morning the deputy came by and, remarking that Ammon "looked rather pale," said that number 7440, who had come in with Ammon, had just died of flu. The great flu pandemic of 1917, which killed several million outside, was sweeping the nation and had now reached inside the prison, where thirty had died in the previous fortnight.[31] The deputy said that if Ammon did not get outside and breathe fresh air, he would probably die too. "Talk about the weather," said Ammon, for "I was not interested in achieving the reputation of a rat." The deputy asked, "Who sends out your letters?" Ammon approached until they were almost touching: "It was a prisoner or a guard." He thought about the flu: if he could die, that would simplify things.

That afternoon at bath time, the guard left Ammon's door open, making the sounds from Popoff's cell louder still. He was in some sort of shackles. "As the guard came down the hall, he opened Popoff's door, dipping his tin cup in the toilet and he threw the dirty water in Popoff's face." If he were next, how long he would last?[32] This was the night that he sharpened his spoon, thinking about suicide. "I thought I ought to write a note to Selma and to my mother." What would he write? "Tell Julia that I remember the good times we used to have on the farm. . . . Don't forget to send American Red Beauty roses to Selma for her birthday Dec. 9."

Then he fell asleep, dreaming of the hogs they had slaughtered in Negley, which somehow mixed with Victor Hugo's stories of men hiding in the sewers of Paris and IWW songs and Popoff's groans. His subconscious told him that he "should not give them the satisfaction" of committing suicide. That would make them the victors, when he was the righteous one. He would not only survive; he would turn the other cheek, and keep on turning it. As Joan Thomas later wrote, what he discovered that night was Christ: like Christ, he embraced all of the contradictions in his life, all of his bodily suffering, and affirmed himself.[33] He would become the pacifist he thought the world needed.

When he woke up, the sun was shining. He got down on the floor, looking for Berkman's shining bald head. How would the world ever know about Popoff if he gave up now? He started to sing an IWW song. "I was through with despair," he said. "I wanted to live to make the world better." He spent the next days in "reviewing all of the historical knowledge that I could remember and in trying to think through a philosophy of life. I had passed through the idea of killing myself. That was an escape, not any solution."[34] "I remembered what Berkman had said about being firm, but quiet. He had tried violence but did not believe in it as a wholesale method." Ammon examined his childhood conversion to the Baptist faith—"frightened into hell by proclaiming a change of life"— and he decided to take a slower path this time. "Gradually I came to gain a glimpse of what Jesus meant when he said, 'The Kingdom of God is Within You.'"

The next day, during his daily pacing, he accidentally hit his head on a wall and had an insight: "Here I am locked up in a cell. The warden was never locked up in a cell and he never had a chance to know what Jesus meant. Neither did I until yesterday. So I must not blame him. I must love him." Loving the warden would be hard. "He and the deputy, in the chaplain's words, did not know any better; they had put on the false face of sternness and tyranny because this was the only method they knew. It was my job to teach them another method: that of good will overcoming their evil intentions." He read and reread the Sermon on the Mount. "The opposite of The Sermon on the Mount was what the whole world had been practicing, in prison and out of prison; and hate piled on hate had brought hate and revenge. It was plain that this system did not work."[35]

This is, of course, a conversion narrated after the fact to make sense of experience under extreme pressure, but that is not to gainsay it. Ammon Hennacy forged himself on a very hard anvil, under enormous pressure: he could either crack or crystallize a new self. Two months after his suicide temptation, he heard the prison whistles blowing and church bells ringing and understood that the war was over. He got a note from Berkman telling him not to be so happy, that this day, November 11, 1918, was the anniversary of the hanging of the Chicago anarchists accused of the

Haymarket Riot of 1887. For Hennacy it became as important a date as his birthday; he would not only honor it every year but also ask that his ashes be mingled with theirs.

"I had ceased by this time my nervous running back and forth like a squirrel in my cell and was now taking steady walks," he wrote. "I had conquered the urge toward masturbation, which is a constant nightmare for the first few months when one is by himself. I was now going to build myself up and not get sick and die. I would show my persecutors that I would be a credit to my ideals."[36] The physical self-mastery is important, but he continued miserably for several months. In early February of 1919 the federal superintendent of prisons, Francis H. Duehay, came from Washington to inspect the Atlanta facility. Duehay had taken an earlier interest in Eugene Debs, and now he tracked Berkman. Curious about why Hennacy was being held in solitary so long, Duehay went with Zerbst to visit him. As they entered the cell, they saw on the wall the poem that Ammon remembered from *The Appeal to Reason* and carved with his spoon:

SURPLUS VALUE
The Merchant calls it Profit and winks the other eye
The Banker calls it Interest and heaves a cheerful sigh
The Landlord calls it Rent as he tucks it in his bag;
But the honest old burglar he simply calls it swag.

Duehay began to stalk about the cell, calling Hennacy all manner of names, but Zerbst frowned, not liking to hear his inmates berated. Hennacy stayed silent, acting the part that he later called "God's Coward." It is a phrase from John Wycliffe (1320–1384) and means that the wise man removes himself from the scene of temptation. Although Hennacy learned this bit of theology later, that day he practiced it instinctively. He refused to fight with Duehay, and suddenly the superintendent turned and said to Warden Zerbst, "Let's make out parole papers on this stubborn fellow. Half of the time I can't trust my own men. This Hennacy is honest and can't be bribed."[37]

Zerbst, who went on to become an important figure in several legal cases, was nearly as tough and idealistic in his own way as Hennacy. He too professed a system, and Ammon finally understood that he was arguing with a theory of human nature rather than with a man. Those beliefs were wrong, he thought, a conviction that would grow deeper as he traveled the United States over the next decade. He would counter Zerbst with the ideas of Thomas Mott Osborne, the reforming warden of Sing Sing, whom he would endorse in his own prose for thirty years.

The morning after the superintendent's visit, a "runner" came down to measure Hennacy for an "outgoing suit." He told Ammon that Duehay and Zerbst regarded him as a nuisance, unlikely to inform on anyone. They wanted to pass him on to the next jail, in Franklin County, Ohio, where he still owed nine months. His remaining days went quickly, until the deputy warden showed that he had one more trick. Arriving for a valedictory, he announced, "We give, we take. You tell us who is getting out your contraband mail or you'll stay here another five and a half months and lose your good time and then another year for refusing to register."

Hennacy had been whipsawed by this technique many times, so it was not a total surprise, but he had really believed that he was close to the end. He choked up, beginning to cry, but held back until the deputy left. Deep inside he felt strong enough, and the next morning he began to tick off his good time on the wall. As he was adding a day, Johnson, the trusty, came in and said, "Getting out of this jail, Hennacy." Though he was sent across the hall for a shave, he still did not believe it. Another guard gave him his ten-dollar out-going money and a bunch of withheld letters. Next, they told him to put on his out-going clothes, but he still sensed something was wrong, because the warden had not come down to shake his hand.[38]

Nonetheless he walked out the front gate of the Atlanta Penitentiary, free for about a minute, until met by a plainclothes official who said he was under arrest for refusing to register for the second draft in August 1918. The first draft of 1917 had only covered men between twenty-one and thirty, but many unfit and older men had volunteered. The second draft covered *all* men from eighteen to forty in addition to volunteers. By the end of war, two million had volunteered, 2.8 million were drafted, and 350,000 had "dodged."[39] Ammon and the officer took the streetcar two miles downtown to the Fulton County Tower, where Ammon was lodged with Joe Webb, a nineteen-year-old murderer. He was permitted to write and receive letters now and got back in touch with Selma. "She had received some of my contraband letters from my sister. She was cordial and not married to anyone else, so there was still hope."[40]

The most important thing that happened here was that his "red-haired cousin Georgia" again appeared, this time bearing a copy of Tolstoy's *Kingdom of God Is within You*. This was the second most influential book Hennacy would ever read:

> I felt that it must have been written especially for me, for here was the answer already written out to all the questions that I had tried to figure out for myself in solitary. To change the world by bullets or ballots was a useless procedure. . . . Therefore the only revolution worthwhile was the one-man revolution within the heart. Each one could make this by himself and not need to wait on a majority. I had already started this revolution in solitary by becoming a Christian. Now I had completed it by becoming an anarchist.

Tolstoy oriented Hennacy toward an individualistic, anti-authoritarian, Christian pacifism. "There is one thing, and only one thing," wrote Tolstoy, "in which it is granted to you to be free in life, all else being beyond your power: that is to recognize and profess the truth." Indeed, it seemed he had written to Ammon: "Universal military service may be compared to the efforts of a man to prop up his falling house who so surrounds it and fills it with props and buttresses and planks and scaffolding that he manages to keep the house standing only by making it impossible to live in it."[41] Tolstoy's prohibition of violence, even in self-defense, and his giving up of revenge, became basic to Hennacy's faith.

Ammon was not completely done with socialism and communism, but he became increasingly suspicious of them. Tolstoy's agrarian vision of Christian anarchism accorded well with his rural upbringing, his faith in the soil, and his interest in Scott Nearing's theories. Tolstoy believed that nonviolence was the absolute core of the Gospels, and that simple folk practicing vegetarianism and resisting all "government" had the best prospect of achieving self-realization. Ammon would adapt and try out similar philosophies, but he embraced Tolstoy's vision right to the end of his life. Also coming to visit was Mary Millis, a Cleveland Socialist and Christian Scientist who lived in Georgia, who brought a copy of *Science and Health*. At the time it did not appeal to Ammon, but it was the beginning of a long flirtation with Christian Science, from which he would draw some of his ideas about health.

Ammon's cellmate, Webb, was a swaggering, flamboyant nineteen-year-old, scheduled for execution. Ammon, now somewhat conversant with the rules of evidence and appeals, thought that Webb was being railroaded.[42] He seemed to need an advisor or older brother. Through his Socialist Party connections, Ammon put Webb in touch with an "influential friend," E. M. Eubanks, who got Webb a stay of execution and a new trial, with an eventual commutation to life in prison. Webb was anything but repentant. He later escaped from the chain gang and, when recaptured, posed for the press smoking a cigar and grinning. Living with murderers taught Ammon about the dark side of human nature—he was not naïve—but it did not diminish his positive view of human possibility, the necessity of prison reform, or the "one-man revolution."

As a Socialist who had served time, Hennacy could now call on party connections. Instead of an old Quaker ex-judge, he was represented by Samuel Castleton, the Atlanta lawyer who would later represent Eugene Debs, who had been arrested for an antiwar speech in Canton. Sharing this lawyer indicates Hennacy's national stature in socialist circles. Castleton thought he could get Ammon's second sentence reduced to six months if he "was not too radical."[43] It took seven weeks for the case to come up, and when it did, it was assigned to a judge who grouped all his conscientious objector cases on one day. Appearing just before Ammon was a "Holiness preacher" who had refused to register for the draft but reconsidered the night before trial, when God came to him in a dream and told him to obey the powers that be. He received twenty-four hours in jail. The judge asked Ammon if he too had changed his mind. Ammon answered that he had: he had entered jail as an atheist and a Socialist, but now he was a Christian and an anarchist.

"What's an anarchist?" asked the judge pointedly.

"An anarchist is someone who doesn't need a cop to make him behave," replied Ammon. This would become one of his set phrases, and he continued with another: "Anarchism is voluntary cooperation with the right of secession. The individual or the family or the small group as a unit instead of the state. As Jefferson said, 'that government is best which governs least, as with the Indians.'"[44] It is doubtful that he said all of this, but the previous weeks had crystallized his views. He would engage in these exchanges so often that they became games, in which Tolstoy and Jefferson were speaking through him. As a Socialist who served two years, he was one of a hundred, but as a "Christian anarchist" he was unique. As a Christian anarchist who was, in this clash with a well-disposed judge, willing to serve time again for his beliefs, he distinguished himself at a new level.

The judge conferred with District Attorney Hooper Alexander in whispers, as Ammon told the story, before declaring the case dismissed. The DA motioned Hennacy and Castleton to chambers, where the judge explained that he liked a good fighter and, though not a pacifist himself, he recognized that something was wrong with the world. He asked Ammon if he had money enough to pay his own way up to Columbus to serve the additional nine months, and Ammon replied that he had been saving the two dollars a month the Socialists sent him as candy money.

The Delaware County jail in Columbus was like being at home. Relatives came to see him, and he patched things up with Selma. They had traded romantic poems before he went to prison and they revived the habit. He wrote her a poem on June 10, 1919, that he titled "Bobby Bolshevik" and signed "with greatest love to Selma from Ammon." ("Bobby" here refers to bobbed hair, a fad in the 1920s.)[45]

> I don't care for golden stresses
>   Or dark-hued raven locks,
> Worn by girls whose every action's
>   Just to be orthodox.
> For the mind that dwells on fashions
>   Is so useless and so meek—
> Behind these bars, I thank my stars
>   For Bobby Bolshevik.
> For when we're traveling in a hurry;
>   See the time it saves;
> For my wife needs not to bother
>   With curls and marcel waves
> And when she snuggles in my arms
>   So "helpless" and so weak;
> There are no pins for fear of "sins"
>   With Bobby Bolshevik.

> At early morn her wooly head
> > Rests snugly on my breast;
> He love-lit eyes look into mine;
> > Her lips on mine are pressed.
> For on this morn in early May
> > I have sure reached the peak
> Of happiness; I must confess;
> > With Bobby Bolshevik.

The voice of male privilege speaks here, not one that reveals any trace of Tolstoy or the Sermon on the Mount, but it does model Ammon's thoughts about marriage and the future. Bobby is an anticonsumer woman, without the need of cosmetics, still a lover of the Left, who will depend on him as they hit the road. The "Bolshevik" part was mostly alliterative ornament. Only a few of Selma's poetic responses are preserved, but they all deflect the "heroic resister" role into which Ammon's patriarchy cast her in favor of something milder:

> I sit today and wonder
> If it really can be true
> That we workers are so stolid
> That our fighters are so few
>
> . . . .
>
> They have gone to prison for us
> Have suffered every wrong,
> Yet they perish in their suffering,
> And we look blindly on.[46]

Rereading this exchange, Ammon's second wife, Joan Thomas, commented that Ammon's prison time confirmed him in his role as the "Man of Honor," for whom "women, for all that they are deeply loved, are at best a most secondary game."[47] This is an astute observation, as are two more that Thomas made. The basic relation of men is to war, she wrote: "In contemplating War we fail to reckon how War makes Life so much more interesting." Secondly, a man who has lived through a major world upheaval like World War I *must* have a relation to it. If he rejects war, then "it is much more interesting to a man to *fight* for Peace than to live peacefully with his woman."[48] Although his later relationship with Dorothy Day would be almost worshipful, the style of the fight that Hennacy believed in would come between them too.

Ammon's other letters from the Franklin County jail overflow with requests for small favors: to write to distant contacts, to send small amounts of money to people, and to remember him to Lola, Lida, and Leah. He reported on his reading, his jail routine, and his weight (he emerged from Atlanta weighing 131 pounds, only a tad below his usual 135). There are more references to Debs, Wagenknecht, and socialist publications, and he wanted everyone who came to visit him to bring the daily paper. "Two profs from the University were over here to see me," he wrote, adding, "Send or bring some Pepsodent." His teeth had decayed more: "I have been downtown to the dentist's several times by myself to get my teeth fixed. I got a white tooth put in where that broken one was. I have three fillings more yet."[49]

Apparently he was trusted to come and go on some tasks, and he was loaned out to "neighbor ladies" to mow their grass or shovel their coal for pay. But this only happened when the warden was on-site; when he was not, Ammon was confined to his cell and read. In letters he asked for Twain's *Huckleberry Finn* and Jack London's *Moon Face* and *Martin Eden*. There he probably read Vachel Lindsay's *Handy Guide for Beggars* (1916) and *Adventures While Preaching the Gospel of Beauty* (1914), which must have whetted his appetite for the Big Hike.

B. F. Hennacy had found a new job at Fuller Brush in Toledo, introducing the whole family to what would become their fall-back trade. The role of this company in Ammon's life would be great, and Selma also thought about selling Fuller Brushes, since the company hired women during the war.[50] Lola was already living in Toledo, and the entire family would shortly relocate. Ammon, however, thought that he would not be with them, certain that he would be married: "A girlfriend of Selma's is to be married on May First next year and we have decided to be married at that time, too," he wrote to his mother, explaining that "in Wisconsin if you register your names at the courthouse, it is the same as a marriage. No ceremony need be performed. Selma and I are thinking of being married that way."[51]

But Selma's perception of Ammon was different. For her he appeared to be extremely nervous, quick to judge, and unable to sit still—he looked like damaged goods. She did not visit until September 24, 1919, almost six months after his release from Atlanta. She stayed in Columbus two weeks, living with his mother, who stayed behind, and bringing fresh clothes to the jail. The tenor of that time for Ammon is clear in his note to his mother:

> We have had a dandy visit: Selma has been over about ten hours each day: we eat supper here in the jail together. . . . Selma and I have agreed that this visiting together and loving only teases us and that it is better for us to get registered sometime between the time I leave jail and the first of the year in Milwaukee. She will explain to you. We would live at her house probably until about May first when we would come to visit you and Lola for a while . . . and take hikes around the country. Then we would start out west.[52]

There are no letters from Selma confirming this, but his pent-up wanderlust would soon overflow in an odyssey that added to his idealism.

Among the last letters that Ammon wrote from the Columbus jail was his resignation from the Socialist Party. "I cannot belong," he explained, "because they want Socialism by voting, when striking and the idea of One Big Union to enforce labor's demands will do more good." The IWW was, in his opinion, closer to Christian anarchism. He also rejected the Italian anarchists "and their way of bringing about 'letter conditions'" (violence) "but I will stick up for Berkman or Emma Goldman any time." Instead, he said, he would join the Communists.[53] This was an important divide: Hennacy rejected paying taxes and voting, but he also rejected the violence of the anarchists who followed Luigi Galleani, soon to be important in the Sacco-Vanzetti case. He had decided that the individual pacifist was the locus of action.

Religious Syncretism

Most political philosophies begin with an estimate about human nature and, as April Carter has noted, Thomas Hobbes is the ogre in the cave of those estimates. Hobbes, like Hennacy, had a great interest in the human body, which he too understood to be in a cybernetic loop with the mind. Extrapolating from that, he reached the conclusion that if everyone pleased themselves, humankind would reach the state of "warre of every one against every one." All those "wants" must come into conflict at some point, and Hobbes concluded that a strong state was necessary to protect us from the despots. Strong self-controls were not part of his estimate.

Hennacy also based much of his thought on the body, but in prison he learned that body-and-mind feedback permitted self-discipline and a sense of the "good" to arise. It was a choice and always available. Where there were "wants," there were also "self-denials." The Sermon on the Mount was not some abstract religious ideal: do unto others and love thy neighbor were the foundations. "Anarchism, having faith in the innate goodness within everyone," Patrick Coy writes, "seeks to establish the Golden Rule by working from within the consciousness of the individual while all other systems of society, working from without, depend upon human-made laws and the violence of the state to compel people to act justly."

If thy neighbor turns out to be an ogre, said Ammon, you must still turn the other cheek, or better yet, just move away. Removing oneself from scenes of conflict is the commendable solution of "God's Coward," as Wycliffe had termed it in 1831. Hennacy liked that phrase. But both options were better than sheltering under a state that could kill you or your neighbor or whole nations at will. Hennacy's choice was a profound and positivistic embrace of free will. After emerging from prison and reading widely, he found buttressing insights and practices all around. Chief among them was Tolstoy, who famously declared, "Everybody wants to change the world, but no one thinks of changing himself." Thoreau, Gandhi, and Dostoevsky soon joined Hennacy's pantheon as he read deeper.

But what kind of Christian anarchy had Hennacy arrived at? It was *syncretistic* in the best American fashion. Like his heroes Whitman and Thoreau, Ammon took tenets of Romanticism, especially a respect for nature, and combined them with a transcendent personal Christianity. As David Kuebrich has shown, Whitman himself believed he was writing for a future religious democracy, a citizenry of spiritual athletes who, as he put it in "Song of the Broad-Axe," would "think lightly of the laws."[54] As for Thoreau, he believed strongly that *only* religious experience counted, argues Allan D. Hodder, and that "nature was the perfect expression, even embodiment, of spiritual reality."[55] Similar readings of these two writers were Hennacy's building blocks.

His more traditional religious elements, beyond the Sermon on the Mount, came initially from the Society of Friends, specifically the "unprogrammed" branch's practice of "expectant waiting upon God" that his grandmother had talked about. But this should not be construed as anything like "quietism"; his grandparents had followed the Hicksite group of Quakers, who embraced the active abolitionism of John Brown. Hennacy looked rather for parallels and commonalities in other belief systems as his own evolved. These were not necessarily permanent liaisons; he would move away from Christian Science later when it did not recognize conscientious objectors, though his beliefs about health remained in accord with theirs. As this suggests, his religious syncretism had such a strong orientation to contemporary politics that a shift in current events might make him drop one "influence" and pick up another, as Ruthenberg had been replaced by Berkman. Other examples were that his youthful enthusiasm for utopian communities lagged when he later discovered how bureaucratic they were; and his interest in the libertarian, decentralized practices of Henry Nunn's shoe company and Fuller Brush ended when they fired employees ruthlessly during the Depression. He built up a very strong suspicion of structure that was only overcome, and that temporarily, when he embraced Catholic personalism.

Hennacy often recognized "fellow believers" by their common hero/ines. He and Selma loved Walt Whitman, Thoreau, and Vachel Lindsay. Later on, he and Dorothy Day "recognized" each other partially by their mutual admiration of not only Tolstoy and Dostoevsky but also Joan of Arc (who, as Dorothy often remarked, was canonized for her faith, not for her rush to battle). Ammon would require exposure to a compatible groundswell in American Catholicism, which, as Mark Pfeifer has shown, was still regionalized, before he incorporated it into his worldview.[56]

But these influences, like political contexts, could change in their valences for Hennacy. In midlife, when he was more set in his personal beliefs, he became a stickler for unwavering constancy. When he read deeply in Gandhi, who said, "My life is my message," he admired that "embodiment," which he sought for himself almost as much as pacifism, and his fasting came to epitomize an acting out of ideals with his body. In his later years, when he had seen heroes and heroines fall away from their purity of practice, the core of his syncretism was nearly reduced to one's willingness to die for one's beliefs. He felt that he was as willing to die for the personalism embodied in the Sermon on the Mount as Berkman had been for a more violent brand of anarchism—that was the test. His evolution from an initially broad Protestant syncretism to his must-be-lived-in-the-flesh variant was a dialectic between the restraint symbolized by Wyckliffe's remarks ("God's Coward") and the rhetorical insistence that the Greeks called *parrhesia*, or "bold speech," examined in the conclusion of this book. In 1919, belief without action was already insufficient for Hennacy.

3

New York City and the Big Hike

Ammon was still in the Columbus, Ohio, jail when Selma, through her father's Socialist Party contacts, won a scholarship to the Rand School in New York City. She seems not to have told him until it was fait accompli, and she left without him, but he half-heartedly decided to follow her. The school was formed in 1906 by followers of the Socialist Party to give a broad education to workers, politicizing them but also functioning as a research and publishing arm. It even operated a summer camp for socialist and trade union activists.

"I went to the Rand School more because Selma would be there than for the Rand School," he wrote. New York City also fit well with her artistic aspirations, and after her arrival she applied for Ammon, and he also won a scholarship. Perhaps he thought that in New York his prison story would be recognized; he was thinking about writing a play based on it. The city in 1919 was the center of what Andrew Cornell terms "bohemian anarchism," a romance between the most extreme political factions and the arts that stretched from Greenwich Village to Harlem. It was also the dawn of the Roaring Twenties, and the city embraced free love, booze, and financial speculation. Stars like F. Scott Fitzgerald and Duke Ellington were emerging, but many *artistes manques* sat on the curb.[1]

Hennacy went directly from Columbus, not visiting his family, stopping only in Warren, Ohio, to pick up a loan of $150 from old friend Ed Smith. He was twenty-six years old when he arrived at Penn Station, where Selma, her father, and a male friend named Mazur met him. Mazur was visibly surprised to see Ammon kiss Selma. Feeling liberated, Selma had been seeing other men while Ammon was writing letters from jail. Now he understood her silences.

She was living in a rooming house, sharing with two other women, and Ammon got a room on the same floor. The large milling crowds were unnervingly like the penitentiary, so he followed Selma around. At the Rand School he chafed at seeing another man put his arm over

Figure 3.1. Selma Melms, 1920. Permission of Josephine Thomas.

the back of her chair. "I was quite 'mushy' and this seemed to get on her nerves," he wrote. "I had always thought I could dance, but after coming out of the jail it seems that others did not think I could. I asked Selma to dance up at the Gym one night, and she did not do so, but danced with a couple other fellows and . . . this made me quite sore." Ammon did not "get" the bohemian atmosphere; it did not seem idealistic to him. He was writing an article for the IWW paper, and at a talk Mother Bloor had recognized him from the stage, which restored him a bit.[2] Selma started complaining, he wrote, "that she could not get any work done with me in the same house." They had hardly kissed and certainly not had sex, but he wanted to "caress her when others were around, and this made her sore." He followed her around so much that she called off their plans for marriage. Angry, he went to see Mother Bloor's daughter Helen, implying that he too could see other people, hoping to level the playing field. That did not work.

But when he threatened to move to Massachusetts to take up union organizing, Selma gave in and they moved into two rooms on East Nineteenth Street off Third Avenue. On December 24, 1919, they called their friend Louis Arner to go with them to register their marriage before a city clerk. The next day, Christmas, they visited Mother Bloor's daughter Helen, probably at Selma's insistence: Helen was surprised to learn that Ammon was now married. But later there was a spontaneous party, speeches were made, and someone gave them a book of Swinburne's poems.[3] After they had moved in together, Ammon wrote to his mother that "Selma goes under her own name," enclosing a clipping about their new status from the *Milwaukee Leader* and a picture taken of the couple three years earlier. In the photo, both are tight-lipped and earnest. Selma has bobbed hair and looks slightly taller than Ammon.[4]

"The second night I slept on the couch and the first night I was so bashful that when I was all undressed I jumped into bed and, while Selma was undressing, looked out of the window, I was so bashful. The many fears that I had about sex proved to be laughable."[5] But even as part of a couple, he added, "I was still very nervous and in no position to hold down a job. When visiting anyone I could not sit still for five minutes but would commence to pace the length of my 'cell' with my hands in my hip pockets. [Selma] would whistle, and I would sit down ashamed of myself, but soon would be walking around again. A husband like that must have been a trial to live with."[6]

In letters home, Ammon assured his mother that they were okay financially. "Mr. and Mrs. Melms have been extra nice to us. Yesterday we received a large box of bread, candy, cake, sugar, cheese, eggs, etc. Mr. Melms sent each of us a check for five dollars. We do not need any extra money. We put $50 in the bank so as not to risk losing it." He put the best face on this new life, writing that New York City was more like Lisbon than his parents could imagine:

Each morning at 8:30 we are awakened by a garbage peddler going by with a cow bell. Down in the East Side you find everything in the street and as much dirt and disorder as in a country village. . . . Selma and I generally study until after midnight and then get up about 9 a.m. Classes [at Rand] do not begin until 3 p.m. I like the work in Public Speaking extra well. We are going down to the library to get some books this morning. New Year's night we were down in the real Chinatown and had some chow mein and chop suey. There is a big oyster and sea food restaurant near us where we often go to eat. Enclosed find a letter for Lola. With love to all of the kids.[7]

In fact, New York was so much bigger than anything either of them had experienced that it was overwhelming. In the US census of January 11, 1920, Ammon and Selma are found living at 203 East Eighth Street on the Lower East Side. He was twenty-six, she was twenty-four. They lived in a building of Yiddish-, German-, Russian-, and Polish-speaking immigrants. They were the sole native-born inhabitants, and the only other English speakers were from Ireland.[8] Ammon, and his ideals, must have been completely unmoored. They had a revolving cast of friends, jobs, and schools, mostly from their old socialist networks. When Ammon later composed his *Autobiography*, he began the New York chapter with that radical meeting at the Rand School where Mother Bloor "was speaking about my case."[9]

But in fact the couple's first reaction to the city's bustle had been to get a cottage at the anarchist Ferrer Center and Stelton Colony in Stelton, New Jersey, about an hour away from New York, from which they commuted to the city. Ferrer was dedicated to the martyred anarchist pedagogue Francisco Ferrer and stressed unstructured classes dedicated to free thought, religion, sex, and hygiene. As Cornell notes, the center "served as a meeting ground in which the city's many anarchist groups interacted with one another and the broader Left. On Friday nights, multi-ethnic crowds of manual laborers and intellectuals packed in to hear talks delivered by famous figures such as the lawyer Clarence Darrow and the muckraking journalist Lincoln Steffens."[10] The center had foci in children's education and art; it embraced Greenwich Village and such painters as Robert Henri, George Bellows, and Man Ray. Ammon and Selma were influenced by the pedagogy more than by the artists.

But there was a waiting list for a cottage, and after a few weeks in the dorm, they decided that neither it nor the alternative—a tent on the grounds—was for them. By May Day 1920, they were back in the city, where Selma danced at the Rand School commencement while Ammon sold amnesty-for-CO buttons in the crowd.

They moved to a room at 267 West 127th Street, close to Columbia University, presumably because of Selma's interest in the drama program. Harlem was not yet Black, but it was an area in which rent strikes were popular, and Ammon had championed these in Columbus. At first he liked the area, explaining in a letter to his father that "it is two blocks beyond Central Park where we rode on that bus when you were here, and right by the 6th Ave elevated. . . . The room is really nice. . . . Two windows, a leather couch, a two-burner gas plate, with a pretty screen to hide it, hot and cold water in the room. Two nice tables and four chairs. . . . It is on the first floor, and the rent is $9.50 a week. We feel that we are lucky to get the room." They would soon discover that it was infested with bedbugs, but it was here in April that they had their "little illness," as Ammon called it, an unplanned pregnancy terminated with help from a nearby Margaret Sanger facility.[11]

Hennacy's focus in the tumult of his New York period was on finding his political feet. Religion receded in importance temporarily—there is no mention in his correspondence of attending any religious services— but in this regard he was not unusual. Dorothy Day was then writing journalism about taxi dancers in New Orleans and following her lover, Lionel Moise, to Chicago. When she published *The Eleventh Virgin*, a roman á clef about these escapades, the *New York Times* called it a "tiresomely 'adolescent' novel."[12]

At first Ammon worked as a carpenter's assistant for five dollars a day "with the possibility of $7 later on." He hoped that his socialist boss, Mr. Greenwald, would start a builder's co-op and turn the organizing aspects over to him. Selma worked "for two hours at dinner time at a cooperative cafeteria. . . . She gets a dollar and a meal each day."[13] By July Ammon was working as a mason, chipping off the façade of a building and mixing cement. "I am getting lots of muscle, and have a good appetite and sleep well," he wrote. "Selma and I are going out to Coney Island Sunday and the next Sunday up the Hudson to an I.W.W. conference."

Despite his rejection of the Socialists, he was attending their convention to write about it for the paper of the IWW, which was his focus. But he and Selma were also meeting with pacifists every other week, calling themselves the "World War Objectors." He met Alfred Wagenknecht again and Benjamin Glassberg and Roger Baldwin of the ACLU. They all agreed that, after the Russian revolutions of 1917, socialism was passé. Goldman and Berkman had been deported to Russia but had not yet returned with their shocking revelations, so there was a pause in the evaluation of communism.[14]

Like many young radicals, Hennacy probably had a sense of living *en attendant la revolution*, but he was still a long way from purging his life of capitalist details. He and Selma saw plays they liked, and it is clear that they were reading a lot together. Their favorite was the metaphysical novel *Carmen Ariza* (1916) by Charles Francis Stocking, a pacifist and Christian Scientist. This book would be a tremendous influence. South America was in vogue in the American imagination, so much so that Ernest Hemingway would satirize the craze in *The Sun Also Rises* (1929). Stocking painted South America in pastel colors as a place of adventure, but also romance and spirituality. It would inspire Ammon and Selma to travel for four years. That was the dream that they lived for, not the "Jazz Age."

Their idea of *Carmen Ariza* blended with Henry David Thoreau and Walt Whitman's *Leaves of Grass* (which they read to each other), while looming large in the background was Vachel Lindsey's *Adventures While Preaching the Gospel of Beauty*. They were deeply moved by Lindsay's vision of the "everyday beatific."

> People do not open their eyes enough, neither their spiritual nor their physical eyes. They are not sensitive enough to loveliness either visible or by the pathway of visions. I wish every church in the world could see the Christ-child on the altar, every Methodist and Baptist as well as every Catholic congregation. . . . I say we do not see enough visions. I wish that, going out of the church door at noon, every worshipper in America could spiritually discern the good St. Francis come down to our earth and sing of the Sun. I wish that saint would return. I wish he would preach voluntary poverty to all the middle-class and wealthy folk of this land, with the power that once shook Europe.[15]

Figure 3.2. Ammon Hennacy's passport photo, 1923. Permission of Josephine Thomas.

That "voluntary poverty" and the St. Francis link fit with the Sermon on the Mount, but at this point in time Ammon and Selma were most interested in the vagabond aspect. They were planning their Big Hike, in December buying heavier clothes for Ammon and "a great big [trunk] that Selma can put most of her things in for safety here as well as to be used in traveling." Ammon was now working at a restaurant where he could eat all that he wanted. The dream of Columbia University had not worked for Selma, so she was taking private acting lessons. Ammon reports on their weights (they always weighed themselves around Christmas): she was 155 and he was 135. Just before Christmas, Ammon's parents visited, bringing along his younger brother Frank and his wife, Minnie. Ammon and Selma "tried to tell Minnie something about Birth Control . . . but she has little guts."[16]

By January 1921 they had moved again, because of bedbugs, to Hell's Kitchen (554 West Fiftieth Street). Only a block from the Hudson River, their new (1920) building was next to the Franciscan Catholic Church of Saints Cyril and Methodius.[17] Their building had a dozen small apartments, but unlike the rest of this generally Irish area, it was in a Croatian corner. The neighborhood faced New Jersey, and since Prohibition had begun in January 1920, the number of abandoned warehouses made it a popular storage area for bootleggers.

Their social world may have been IWW and Rand/Ferrer, but the most durable influence of this period would continue to be Scott Nearing. Ammon had met him in Ohio in 1914, but now, through their Rand School connections, he and Selma were invited to dinner at the Nearings. They came away impressed: "As soon as supper was over, he got up and put on an apron and commenced to do the dishes. He said his wife got the supper and that was enough for her to do," wrote Ammon. His notion of white male privilege foregone was undercut, however, when he added that he would soon hear Nearing debate a Columbia professor while "Selma will stay at home and keep the small son of the Nearings . . . otherwise he would have to come as they have no one to attend to him."[18] His ideal of Betty Bolshevik did not include domestic equality.

Nearing and his wife would not publish their groundbreaking book for thirty years, but their homestead project had started, and Ammon kept in touch through the 1930s. Nearing had finally joined the Communists too, reinforcing Ammon's sense that the Socialists were a lost cause. Nearing would visit the Soviet Union in 1925 and China in 1927 and wrote for the *Daily Worker* for several years, but he was mustered out of the Communist Party for his pacifist views, which were very close to Ammon's. Meanwhile, the building "cooperative" did not materialize; Ammon later regarded it as a hoax invented to placate him.[19] He and Selma graduated from the Rand School. They went out for chop suey with the Nearings, they saw A. J. Muste, and they attended *The Blue Flame*, a play about reincarnation starring Theda Bara that may have stuck in Ammon's imaginary.[20] By March their planning for the Big Hike was taking priority over other aspects of life. Selma's job at the tearoom was ending, so "she brought home quite a bit of sabotage . . . fixed nine-course suppers for me."[21] Until they left she was going "to work around the Birth Control office free in order to learn things there" that they could disseminate on the road. Margaret Sanger, a Socialist who would found Planned Parenthood, was an influence on both of them. Ammon now worked at the League for Mutual Aid and two part-time jobs: one was soda clerking in Penn Station, the other dishwashing, which he planned to continue "until about April 16th when we will start to roam this part of the country."[22] Despite his nervousness, New York was broadening him: he met a male coworker who wore earrings—he had "36 pair of them, wearing a different pair every day"—and Ammon found this possible sign of gender fluidity interesting rather than off-putting.[23]

The Big Hike

The Big Hike was to start in the mid-Atlantic states, with the couple hitchhiking, camping out, working along the way, and spreading their views in Vachel Lindsay fashion. It was anarchist individualism mixed with romantic vagabondage. Leftist friends and influences would be visited (such as Walden Pond), as well as prisons that housed conscientious objectors and Socialists. They would walk, waiting until someone offered a ride. They would sleep in parks or, asking permission, in farmers' fields and barns (but they were often invited inside). They met over five thousand people, and Ammon kept track of many in a notebook.

"We have a camera and will send you pictures," Ammon wrote to his mother. He probably carried a Kodak vest-pocket Model B (which cost $2.75) from which 3 x 3 prints could be made.[24] Some of the 3 x 3–inch snapshots survive in university archives and show them surprisingly well dressed. "Each of us has a knapsack. . . . We have a small pup tent and two rubber garments called Ponchos that fit around your neck and cover you all over like a sheet to the ground." They wore leggings, army shoes, and hats, and carried a change of clothes, medical supplies, and small tools and books. Selma would later wear knickers that, with her bobbed hair, gave her a masculine appearance.

They warmed up with a visit to Sing Sing, where they visited Ruthenberg. "I had not met [him] since 1917 when he introduced me at an anti-conscription meeting in Cleveland. He was the same quiet, thoughtful and pleasant comrade . . . typical of the old time Russian revolutionists who could do countless years in prison without forgetting his ideals."[25] Next they gave away their furniture and bought a "small balloon silk tent which had the bottom sewn in, weighing seven pounds, and we could both sleep in it." With their hundred-dollar food fund, they set off on June 21, 1921 (the third anniversary of Ammon's entry into solitary). This would be another significant date for them. Ammon carried a forty-five-pound pack, Selma one of thirty pounds. Ammon also carried a pedometer, on which he recorded his steps for years.

Their general goal was South America, but on this first day they stopped at the Inter-Collegiate Socialist offices, then at Margaret Sanger's, and finally at the Rand School, where Norman Thomas hefted their packs. They had a vegetarian dinner with friends and at 10:00 p.m. finally took the subway from Fourteenth Street to the Battery, though the packs made it hard to get through the metro turnstile and people stared at them. They took the Staten Island Ferry and a streetcar to the end of the line, then walked from 11:30 p.m. until 1:00 a.m., camping in a field. They woke in poison ivy, under a scarecrow, which frightened Selma.

After breakfast they set off for the Carteret Ferry to New Jersey, and on the ferry, as would happen so often, they were befriended by a couple who gave them a ride, invited them for tea, and let them sleep in their grassy meadow. The second morning they woke surrounded by roses. The next day, the same: two more rides were offered, the first couple buying them ice cream and the second dropping them by a chicken farm owned by an old-time anarchist interested in Ammon's acquaintance with Berkman. So it went, until they entered the Toms River region of New Jersey, where they did their first real camping. They walked forty-eight miles one day (measured on Ammon's pedometer) and stayed in Atlantic City with a former prisoner from Atlanta.

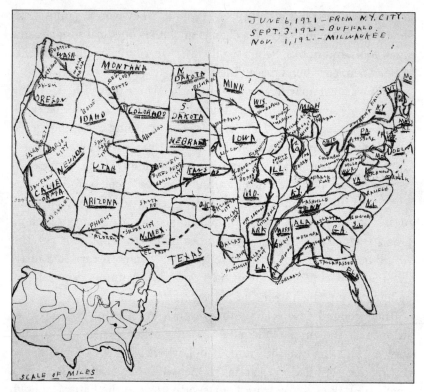

Figure 3.3. Ammon's map of the Big Hike. Permission of Josephine Thomas.

Then they headed toward Camden to pay tribute to Walt Whitman.[26] Appropriately enough, the family living in his house invited them in for dinner. Overall, though, it was Lindsay who was their inspiration; like St. Francis, he had walked thousands of miles, writing about it in a rhythmic iambic pentameter. He cast himself as the apostle of sunshine, but warned that "one should not be a gypsy forever. He should return home. Having returned, he should plant the seeds of Art and Beauty. He should tend them till they grow."[27]

The Big Hike was really four trips, separated by stops to work, sometimes in places they considered living permanently. The first trip lasted from June 1921 through September 1921. We can see from Ammon's hand-drawn map that it departed from New York City and went through New Jersey into Virginia, then up the Potomac River to Harper's Ferry before turning south into the rest of the state and ending at

Norfolk. In the middle of this hike, they caught their strangest ride, on a boat pulling barges up the East Coast to Maine, from which they worked their way down through Vermont and Massachusetts (visiting Walden). They crossed upper New York State, seeing Niagara Falls and reaching Buffalo on September 3, 1921. Traversing Pennsylvania to Ohio, they visited his relatives in Akron and stopped in Negley, then went on to Michigan and Wisconsin before resting in Milwaukee with Selma's family. They would return there repeatedly. In Milwaukee the first thing they did was send postcards to people who helped them; by the end of one trip, they had sent out 350 of them.

On the first trip alone they covered 3,606 miles, walking 651 of them. On the second trip (February 22, 1922, to June 20, 1923), they walked 341 miles and rode 1,582 miles.[28] Then they spent over a year in Atlanta. Their return to Milwaukee (June 20–July 28, 1923) was via Springfield, Illinois, where they stopped to see Vachel Lindsay, who was not home but camping in the Rockies. They ended up again in Milwaukee, walking 341 miles and riding 1,582. Ammon counted this out-and-back trip as one.

They stayed only nineteen days in Milwaukee before taking a third trip to the utopian commune of Fairhope, Alabama, where they stayed and worked for almost a year (August 1923 to June 1924). This was an important stop, as they tried to put their Ferrer School training and ideas on progressive education into practice. Again Ammon counted this as one trip. The fourth trip (June 21, 1924, to July 30, 1925) took them from Fairhope out west and back to Milwaukee. On it they walked 681 miles and rode 4,033, and Ammon met his first actual Native Americans. This last and longest trip went all over the West, including Utah, before pausing in Berkeley, where Ammon worked with both the Communist Party and the Fuller Brush Company. They also visited Los Angeles and the Grand Canyon, before returning to Milwaukee.[29]

Over the four years, Ammon and Selma visited or stayed with about a thousand people, whom Ammon often seemed to know in advance. He kept a meticulous address book: his political contacts, old friends from Negley and Lisbon, contacts at Hiram, Wisconsin, and Ohio State, all the conscientious objectors he had heard of, and all his relatives—they were all in the book. Sometimes the addresses were not specific, and there were few phone numbers, but he did not mind knocking on doors and asking. Each person got one line in the book.

Ammon worked along the way, sometimes for a week or more if a farmer needed help bringing in a crop or milking cows, which was his most common way of earning their bed and board. Other work he did was weeding, chopping wood, orchard work (especially pruning), berry picking, mule driving, barge driving, teaching, and digging and sacking potatoes. During the long stays in Atlanta and Oakland, he worked as a Fuller Brush salesman, as a busboy, and as a waiter. Once he worked for a Christian Scientist trying to develop new entrances to Mammoth Caves, while Selma learned to make and sell pine needle baskets. She frequently cooked for bachelors and elderly couples.

They walked a lot, but they also rode on the back of a motorcycle, on a barge, in countless cars and trucks, on a few trains, on a coal sled, on a wagonload of logs, on buses, with moonshiners, with a US marshal looking for moonshiners, with Black Morehouse College students, with Ku Klux Klan members (by accident), with a Jewish dentist, with a Black chauffeur, with drivers who liked to race cars at night, on a load of cotton, with a gravedigger and an undertaker, on a cog railroad, and, standing on the running board for thirty miles, with a Mexican family.

They slept in many strange places: at a reformatory (part of a prison visit), at Waldheim Cemetery in Chicago near the graves of the Haymarket martyrs, in their friend Ed's private apartment for three weeks, in a few hotels, in barns in winter, with the last living Shakers, on countless dining room floors, in hay lofts, in the entrance to Mammoth Cave, in a tobacco drying barn, with Mrs. Millis (who had visited Ammon in Atlanta), in a doctor's house, in public parks, with a Greek conscientious objector, on the lawn of a town square, in the Woodman's Hall, in vacant buildings, in a camp of Greek goatherds, in a peach orchard, in San Francisco's Presidio Park, in Jack London's Valley of the Moon (Sonoma County), and for two days in the Carson City, Nevada, home of a telephone operator who, having directed them there, did not appear due to her work schedule. But she had left out a Catholic magazine about the wisdom of peasants that made an impression on Ammon.[30] Everywhere they seemed to elicit trust.

They ate ravenously to fuel themselves, usually what was at hand and always vegetarian: chicory and grits, quarts of blackberries, pies of all varieties because Ammon loved pie, sorghum and biscuits and jam for breakfast, cornbread, lemon pie, corn liquor, a bushel of peaches, and doughnuts. They breakfasted on watermelon, made a dinner of cucumbers, and thought they had found the best ice cream in the country.

Some of their encounters stand out. As they approached Sawnee Mountain, Georgia, on their second trip, people warned them about ambushes. A grocer told them that "there's a woman on horseback halfway down the side of the 'mounting' who makes a sign to a man in the bushes, and then they rob you and throw you down into the Bottomless Pit."[31] Reassured by fellow travelers, Ammon and Selma joked about this and set off the next morning in sunshine, picking flowers as they climbed. Suddenly as they rounded a curve, there *was* a beautiful woman with rouged cheeks on a horse, blocking the road. She *was* signaling to someone over the ridge. "I thought you was two fellas," she said, turning to them: "Y'all from the North I suppose? None of we folks would be packing them packs." As she moved her horse to allow them to pass, Ammon and Selma noticed "what appeared to be a spring but . . . was a large hole in the ground." Catching their glance, the woman said, "Nobody knows how deep it is." The young couple continued down the far side of the mountain to its base, where at dusk Ammon asked a farm wife if he could buy milk. "You come over the mounting?" she exclaimed. "Din't none of the robbers git you?"

The next morning in town they learned that the horseback woman, about thirty-eight years old, and her sixteen-year-old daughter alternated as lookouts for several groups of moonshiners, giving a variety of signals when revenue agents approached. Ammon and Selma found it funny that everyone believed their side of the mountain was safe, but the other side dangerous. It became their parable about human nature.[32]

Camping in the public square of Bradford, Arkansas, Ammon woke up before Selma and decided to go buy milk for their breakfast of cornflakes. "When I came back, I heard the town loafers laughing as they gazed toward our tent," he wrote. The razorback hogs that roamed about freely had decided to investigate the new arrivals. Selma was seated in the tent's entry, waving a shoe at the snorting, dancing cohort. "One of them had a cornflake box wedged around his snout, another had eaten our stock of lemons, and still another was nudging the tent to see what could be found."[33]

In Colorado Springs they decided to walk to the top of Pike's Peak rather than take the tourist cog-railway. It was hot and the Fourth of July, but they knew it would be cold at the top and dressed appropriately. Ammon carried one pack for both. The first two miles were okay, but they had never hiked at altitude. By dusk they had only reached the Halfway House but decided that the remainder could not be as bad, when it was in fact a lung-bursting 28-percent grade. They walked twenty steps and rested, walked and rested. Then "we walked a hundred steps and laid down on our blanket. I became tired and sleepy before Selma did and she carried the pack. . . . Then she began to give out and I took the pack. . . . Finally, we slept about five minutes each time we stopped to rest. We agreed to sleep in the snow if we did not see the light of the hotel by the time we rounded the next corner." But they did see light and "slept on the floor of the kitchen with several other hikers until we were awakened at 3:30 a.m. by tourists arriving by the auto road to see the sunrise." They joined them and took pictures. But what really lingered in memory was a breakfast of the "finest coffee, doughnuts and pie that we had ever tasted." Ammon's journal entries on the hike, notes Joan Thomas, "emanate that closeness, a camaraderie that obviously is genuine." They would make a parallel hike fifteen years later with their daughters when their marriage was crumbling.[34]

In Atlanta, Ammon bumped into Deputy Warden Girardeau from the penitentiary on the street: "He did not remember my name at first, but recognized me as a former inmate. He began to invite me to his church, and then remembering his treatment of me, made some excuse and hurried away. I had theoretically forgiven him before I was released from solitary, for I knew that he was a slave to evil thinking and did not have any conception of any other method of treating prisoners. I was glad to prove to myself that upon suddenly meeting him, I did not have a feeling of hatred toward him."[35]

Atlanta was, curiously, the first place they stayed, for almost a year. They considered its long-term possibilities, and Ammon got a Fuller Brush job immediately: "I led the office [in sales] here for the first 2 1/2 months," he wrote to his father, who was selling brushes in Toledo. But he complained that his closest rival "has two fellows working for him. They go to school part time. The three of them make long hours and extra good sales and the rest of us are supposed to keep up with the three. . . . Is this allowed by the company?"[36] For all its faults, Fuller Brush met some of Ammon's work criteria. It was very rational but decentralized, with detailed procedures and a clear structure. It had goals and quotas, but all were left to do their own work. It emphasized the quality of its products, as well as habits of daily cleanliness. Given that it epitomized the capitalism Hennacy detested, how did it fit with his ideals?

Fuller Brush made Ammon test some of his ideas. His cornflakes experience inclined him to the door-to-door work, but Fuller also allowed workers to control their hours and sales techniques, and it was somewhat democratic. Innovation could flow from workers up to the leaders and even alter production. Fuller himself believed in producing the best product possible, in positive thinking, and in Christian modesty. He was fond of quoting from the Gospel of John: "If I honor myself, my honor is nothing."[37] Like Ammon, he drew inspiration from his mother—"I could never look my mother in the eye again if I was guilty of a dishonorable act"—and he was a convert to Christian Science.[38] These facts and the ethos of his organization appealed to Ammon. Fuller had worked alone for a long time, but when he finally hired salesmen, experience taught him "that no potential dealer should ever be rejected on the basis of physical handicap. Many star sales producers for the Fuller Brush Company in later years were missing an arm, a leg, an eye, or were too old or too young or too unintelligent. We even had a successful dealer who, having lost both legs in an accident, made his rounds in a wheelchair."[39] Fuller was also the first to hire women as door-to-door salespersons, paving the way for Avon Cosmetics, so he looked like a progressive, libertarian capitalist.

But Fuller also believed in lots of meetings at which salespeople shared techniques and information, and there were several every week.[40] He treated his salesmen as "dealers," which meant they were not subject to withholding taxes; this was important to Hennacy later, because he could avoid paying taxes for wars or the military. One of Fuller's innovations was a series of regional distribution centers, and when Ammon worked in Oakland, this system created several new products—Californians needed brushes to clean cars, not chimneys—and also organizational changes that were passed up to headquarters. Ammon, as we will see, was in the thick of this. While in Oakland, he also absorbed the lessons of branch manager Rex Rechow, who "urged his dealers never to spend more than ten minutes in any house. Rechow's sales per call were low by the company standards, but his total volume was consistently higher than that of anyone else."[41] Ammon later used a similar technique in his sidewalk politicking.

Ammon and Selma's interest in Christian Science (CS) deepened on the trip. While Ammon was working as a temporary Fuller dealer in north Georgia, Selma lived in another town, where she attended CS meetings and became interested in the Bible. Reunited, they began to study CS together. The problem for Ammon was that CS did not permit conscientious objectors. He tried at the Wednesday night meetings to show that Mrs. Eddy, the founder, had articulated the principles of conscientious resistance, "but it was useless, for most of the members were married to the worship of wealth and the status quo, except in medicine." CS was not aligned enough with his other beliefs, and Mrs. Eddy would soon be debunked. They were already avoiding medicine, but Ammon did feel that CS helped Selma understand his religious pacifism better.[42]

Their goal of travel in South America was still alive in Atlanta. "Selma had been looking at maps and decided . . . to study Spanish and prepare for hiking in South America," Ammon wrote. "Meanwhile I read several histories of South America . . . had our passport pictures taken, and upon swearing that I had not been convicted of a felony (which was true), our passport was granted." But they postponed the trip "until summer and, thinking it over, decided that we ought to hike up North again and say hello to our folks, for if we went to South America, we might stay a long time." They had saved over nine hundred dollars while working and thought about buying a car but decided against it, possibly because Ammon did not drive.[43]

They headed to south Florida, where they expected to ship out to South America, wanting to reconnoiter the area, but they found the people there unpredictable and the atmosphere rough. They learned that couples were not permitted to travel steerage from Tampa to South America; they could only sail passenger class for "moral" reasons. The tipping point came when they were sleeping near the beach and woke to the braying of forty-two mules that had escaped their pen. The mules ran around and around their tent as the owners chased them until 4:00 a.m. Then at 5:00 a.m. a neighbor "got God" and began to scream to

Him for an hour about the mules. That decided them to return to Milwaukee, then go to Fairhope, Alabama, where they could teach in the school. From Fairhope they could check out other boats to Brazil the next year.[44]

They had learned a lot about the South, not least about the deep entrenchment of racism, but also about the ways that southern liberals excused it, although they were white and enjoyed the attendant privileges. Ammon read deeply in Fairhope history, which prepared the way for their return trip. They left Atlanta on June 20, 1923, and arrived in Milwaukee on July 28. Of the 1,923 miles on this portion of the Big Hike, they had walked 341. They got several rides from Ku Klux Klan sympathizers and defenders of slavery, during which they tried not to talk much. They were asked daily what church they belonged to, and they always answered, "The same one that Jesus did." If questioned further, Ammon would say, "Jesus did not belong to church, he got kicked out of church."[45]

But these homeward rides took them off course and they ended up in Mississippi, where they crossed over into Arkansas, meeting up with a conscientious objector from Leavenworth whom Ammon knew.[46] After this visit they walked eighteen, twenty-three, and twenty-six miles with packs on successive days in the July heat. Selma wanted to get home by July 29 for the socialist convention—her father would be a main speaker—so they took a train to St. Louis and then to Springfield, Illinois, where they again tried to meet Vachel Lindsay, but he was again off hiking. They arrived at Selma's house a day ahead of schedule, weighed themselves, and ate ravenously. In the next two weeks Ammon gained fifteen pounds and Selma ten.[47]

The Fairhope Colony

The Fairhope Colony had offered Ammon and Selma temporary jobs, so in the fall they headed to Alabama. It looked like a place to practice the Rand theory of organic teaching while earning some money. The colony had been founded in 1894 as a radical "Single-Tax" town by twenty-eight followers of economist Henry George.[48] By purchasing four thousand acres on the eastern shore of Mobile Bay and subdividing it into individual leaseholds, the followers hoped to simulate a single-tax colony in which all taxes were paid from the rents of the lessees. The goal was to "eliminate disincentives for productive use of land and thereby retain the value of land for the community." The colony's school was started in 1907 by Minnesota progressive Marietta Johnson and was praised in John Dewey's *Schools of Tomorrow* (1915). Celebrities such as Sherwood Anderson and Upton Sinclair had wintered there, and the school was at its height of fame in the 1920s. It had no tests or grades, and no homework until high school. Active involvement in handcrafts and folk dancing was required. Ammon was hired to fill in as a history teacher but, as he told the story, the school was undisciplined and biased. On his first day he told the class that their books "of a dominant religion or exploiting class" were wrong. Most history was guesswork, he said, "as we did not know for sure about yesterday."[49] He decreed that on Fridays there would be an hour of absolute free discussion, and he ordered in the *Christian Science Monitor, Single Tax Courier, Milwaukee Leader,* and *Wall Street Journal.*

Then a local minister of the Church of Disciples heard about Ammon. He was also head of the KKK, which must have shocked Ammon, given his familiarity with that church in Ohio. The minister denounced Hennacy as a "jailbird," unmarried cohabiter, and agnostic—in short, someone who ought to be run out of town. In keeping with his philosophy of turning the other cheek, Ammon invited the man to speak to the class, but he did not show up. Eventually this history class met not at its scheduled time but on Wednesday nights from 8:00 to 11:00, without credit. It "was the Organic method with a vengeance," Ammon wrote skeptically.[50]

Meanwhile Selma organized an outdoor production of *The Winter's Tale* and played the part of Autolycus. On weekends Ammon shoveled manure for a Quaker farmer and packed tangerines at a local fruit shed. Through these contacts they found the local Quaker meetings, which they attended together for the first time. "They were of the same Hicksite sect as my grandparents," Ammon wrote happily.[51] Here was a religious group he could work with, but their patience with the school's lax discipline wore out in spring. In May they made a last attempt to follow their romantic *Carmen Ariza* vision to South America, but their ship tickets fell through. They had lingered in Alabama from February 28, 1922, to June 30, 1923.[52]

They went back to Milwaukee, but returned to Fairhope the next spring, thinking to use it as their base for a trip out west. This adventure would start in New Orleans and proceed to Houston, Amarillo, Santa Fe, and Taos, then go up to Colorado Springs and Denver, over the Rockies to Salt Lake, up to the Northwest, and finally down to San Francisco. It would be the longest of all, and they would end up walking 397 miles and riding 4,404 in a trip ending May 30, 1924—but the highlight was California.[53]

Dropped off by a traveling salesman in San Francisco, they crossed the Bay Bridge to Berkeley a few days before Thanksgiving 1923. They had chop suey to celebrate. The next day they rented a room for sixteen dollars a month on the third floor of a nice old Victorian house at 1930 North Delaware Street near Ohlone Park.[54] Their excitement about Berkeley was apparently visible, because two reporters for Oakland's Hearst newspaper interviewed them for a feature on new arrivals: they said that they had "been to every state in the union and liked California so well, but had not settled down here for good."[55]

Ammon went to the Fuller Brush office the next day, because they needed funds for his typewriter (thirty-five dollars) and Selma's tuition (thirty-five dollars) at the California Arts and Crafts School. At night Ammon studied agriculture through the UC Extension, an introduction to the science of soils that later accelerated his alarm at the ecological crisis in the Southwest. But his tuition of $115 was more than they could afford, so he attended lectures and studied on his own. Fuller Brush had given him a territory that started the next week. By the end of the next month, he had sold four hundred dollars' worth of brushes, an indication that he now excelled at getting his foot in the door.[56]

Investigating the local socialist/communist/anarchist scene, they found the West Coast very different. Ammon was still interested in the Communist Party. "I had never really attended any local meetings of the Communist Party while I had been traveling," he wrote. "The local in Berkeley was composed largely of Finns [who] asked me to teach American history in their Sunday School. [The students] were eager and likeable young folks, but they were not allowed to think for themselves, being on the jump to salute with the clenched fist and answer 'Always Ready' at the suggestion of the older comrades. Ready for what? They did not know."[57]

At Fuller Brush he agitated to organize the office more rationally, based on single-tax ideas and what he had learned in his jobs back east. He thought the Berkeley bunch too laid-back and possibly corrupt, writing to his mother,

> I guess you read that outline that I had the salesmen in Berkeley adopt. Frank showed it to Dad [Fuller]. Some of the money grabbers out here did not like it, but as long as I remain one of the leaders in the office, they cannot say much. Some of them think I am a spy sent from Hartford by Dad Fuller to catch them in their crooked work and want to get rid of me, but my assistant manager stands up for me. . . . Some of the brushes out here cost an awful lot more than they do in the east. Enclosed find an order blank. You can see the difference. . . . I want to get a country territory in Wisconsin when I get back in a couple of years.[58]

He was already thinking of a Scott Nearing "back to the earth" venture, though what Selma thought about giving up her aspirations is not known. A top salesman, Ammon received a turkey for his efforts at Thanksgiving. It seems that their vegetarianism admitted occasional lapses, for they invited Mother Bloor to dinner. She had just returned from the Soviet Union, where she participated in several conventions, and she was hitchhiking across the United States writing stories for the *Daily Worker*.[59] This was the first turkey that Selma had roasted, but Ammon wrote his mother that "no complaint was made by anyone at the table." Ammon and Mother Bloor relived their 1912 horse and buggy ride in East Liverpool, but she seems to have been too doctrinaire for him, as he wrote that she still "had the enthusiasm of youth" but not "the inquiring mind which had caused her to leave conservative surroundings."[60]

"By the time the winter was over," Ammon wrote, "I was so disgusted with the dogmatism of the communists who desired Russia and the revolution to be mentioned in season and out of season, and although I still admired Ruthenberg, I resigned from the party."[61] He shared his grievances with Scott Nearing, who was on a speaking tour of the Bay Area, but Nearing had just joined the party, dropping his pacifism temporarily, though not his vegetarianism. Ammon argued that Tolstoy's model of personal revolution was better, both in ideals and practically, but Nearing supported Mother Bloor and the Finns. Ammon was increasingly suspicious of any organization, in part because of "deceitful stunts the [Fuller] salesmen are advised to pull." In his view, one should "1) know your article well, 2) don't oversell the customer but be sincere, 3) Have perseverance with *yourself* and not just with one customer, because old man average will take care of your income." He applied this critique of Fuller Brush to the tactics of the Socialists and Communists, because none reflected any inner conviction. They were all large organizations. This philosophy developed through the winter of 1924–1925 and apparently leaked into his conversation. When the young couple was invited to dinner with the new president of Fuller Brush, "much to the disgust of the division manager" whom Ammon had grown to detest, he talked about the study of soils, agriculture, and beekeeping. After that he was no longer a hotshot in the Berkeley office. As for Selma, she continued her weaving and art classes, but was not acting. For leftists, they remained curiously unaffected by Berkeley: "The West had not engulfed their souls," Joan Thomas observed.

One night in May 1925, Ammon suggested to Selma "that we give up our South America trip, finish those portions of the United States which we had yet to visit, and settle down in the country near some small town in Wisconsin and raise a couple of children." They had already been talking about names: Carmen, from *Carmen Ariza*, and Sharon.[62] There was no sense of urgency, though, and their trip home was just as meandering as their previous journeys. From Berkeley they traveled north to Carson City and Yosemite, before turning south and going down the Central Valley to Los Angeles. They also planned to see the Grand Canyon, Denver, Omaha, Sioux City, Fargo, and Madison. They would ride 3,845 miles and walk another 368 miles before arriving in Milwaukee. As usual they attracted interesting, generous people to them.

Although they did not suspect it, the most significant of these was a vegetarian and Rosicrucian near Lake Tahoe. He told them that "Ascended Masters" were preparing a new race of people near there in the mountains "to lead the world out of chaos." They listened quietly, not unsympathetic to his ideas on reincarnation and abstinence from alcohol, meat, and tobacco. Privately Ammon felt he "had heard enough of California boasting," but Selma was more receptive, and listened attentively to the tenets of the I AM movement, which had a center at Mount

Shasta. She would eventually become a follower, and the couple would split up because of her involvement in the sect.[63]

On the way to Los Angeles, they stayed with old friends from the Rand School, "Sophie and D," who lived on the far northeast outskirts of Los Angeles. Sophie worked as secretary for a script writer, while D ran a sign shop. These friends showed them the usual Hollywood sights, telling Ammon that socialist and communist authors were writing screenplays for profit. Even Upton Sinclair, one of his childhood heroes who had moved to Monrovia, California, in 1920, was exploring this option. Known for his sexual abstinence and anti-alcohol and vegetarian beliefs, Sinclair had written a novel titled *They Call Me Carpenter* (1922) about Jesus in Hollywood. When they visited him in 1925, he asked for an account of Ammon's time in solitary, which he wanted to add to his play *Singing Jailbirds*. Ammon told him that *The Jungle* had made him a vegetarian in 1910, but Sinclair was now a meat eater, and they finally found little to agree on except the value of optimism.[64]

One night Sophie and D announced that they wanted to come along on Ammon and Selma's road trip. They had a car but also obligations, and they proposed to split expenses if Ammon and Selma could wait a month. With nothing pressing, Ammon found a job on a "bee-ranch" owned by a young Quaker woman near Whittier, where he and Selma slept in an out-building. Ammon, just done auditing the bee-keeping course in Berkeley, worked with the owner. She "would work all day with a low-neck dress, bare arms and fairly short shirts, sometimes with a veil and sometimes without one," he noted, but she "was rarely stung." Her other helper, however, used a smoker to stun the insects and tied his shoelaces around his ankles to prevent the bees from invading his pants, and he was stung often. "The quiet Quaker woman did not excite the bees . . . and they seldom harmed her."[65]

A month later the foursome hit the road, Sophie and D sleeping in the car while Ammon and Selma camped beside it. It took them four days to drive to the Grand Canyon, where they descended to the Colorado River and visited the isolated Havasupai tribe, who must have piqued their imaginations, because they stayed a week in the canyons, emerging on the south side to visit the Zuni pueblo. The landscape was dazzling, and Ammon made a note to read more about the tribes. They traveled on to Santa Fe, where the car broke down and the couples parted, with Ammon and Selma scrambling for a plan, since they were low on funds. Frugally, they worked their way back to Wisconsin by foot, rides, and bus.

Christian Science

In addition to blisters, sunburn, back strain, and sore limbs, the young couple experienced two serious medical situations on this trip that increased their interest in Christian Science. Selma developed neuralgia that afflicted her face, sometimes causing partial paralysis, but it disappeared at her parents' home in Milwaukee as they were reading about the Christian Science theory of mind-body connection. The miracle was repeated when Ammon, experiencing episodes of "lumbago" (lower back pain) for several hours every morning, decided to fast. After four days during which he drank lots of water and took hot baths and enemas but ate no food, the lumbago disappeared. Later on he found that "if I read the Christian Science book for an hour . . . in the morning I was cured. I have done the same thing several times with colds this winter. As long as people continue to believe that certain diseases are contagious and are afraid of certain diseases, just so long will that fear produce the disease under adverse circumstances."[66] It was not that he denied the existence of disease—the 1917 flu pandemic had been real for him—but that he glimpsed "holistic healing" before that phrase was fashionable.

In March of 1923 he wrote to his mother that "Christian Science says that all other methods change one disease for another, and in the cases of medicine an antitoxin or vaccine will show after-effects worse than the disease . . . [They] say in proportion as you discard fear, hatred, envy, vengeance and selfishness and bring yourself in harmony with what they call Divine Mind or God, you will be able to have power over sin, sickness, poverty, misfortune."[67] These aspects of CS aligned with his religious ideas—the *Christian Science Sentinel* quoted Walt Whitman approvingly—and he recycled them thirty years later in his Catholic Worker soapboxing on the Bowery.[68] Reading the Christian Science literature spurred him to fast, to reintegrate himself physically, but other parts of the CS creed he disagreed with, such as the teaching on war, socialism, and marriage.

Ammon and Selma probably felt a sense of relief that this nomadic chapter of their lives was over. As Joan Thomas wrote, one "has to suspect that they are getting sick of it; also aware of age; after all, Ammon will be thirty-three the coming July, Selma thirty the coming December. If they spend another five years tramping around, even in so great a place as South America, they'll be pretty old to start a family, especially by the standards back then."[69] The bureaucracy of the Socialist Party, of the Communist Party, of the Fairhope Colony, and of the Fuller Brush Company had returned Ammon inward towards his Tolstoyan ideal of self-sufficient, small-scale farming and a one-man revolution. But they felt they knew the world now: they had met literally thousands of good people, been given rides and fed and housed by so many strangers that Ammon was confirmed in his belief in the fundamental goodness of people.

4

Bisanakee and Milwaukee

The Agrarian Dream

When they arrived at her parents' house in Milwaukee in July 1925, Ammon and Selma had only one hundred dollars left. It was soon his thirty-third birthday (she was thirty) and they were full of energy, returning to one of the most liberal, cultured cities of the Progressive Era. Within days they found an apartment, they gained back the weight they had lost, and Ammon went to work in a restaurant. Still wearing his pedometer, he counted how many steps he was taking (it worked out to 336 miles a month). But now everything was prequel to the self-sufficient farming project. For three days Ammon worked in the restaurant's vegetable room, then out in the dining room. He was appalled at the customers' waste of butter, suggesting to his boss that it be reused on toast. He was full of ideas: the restaurant "had very little system. Floor-men could have done the work which six were doing if each had been given certain tables. As it was, they were not allowed to rest or stand still but had to walk around whether there was anything to do or not."[1]

Scott Nearing's homesteading model, integrating pacifism and individual anarchism with self-sufficiency, was their overwhelming influence. Impatient to put it into practice, they went on weekend jaunts looking for farm property, knocking on farmers' doors, and finally finding "Old Man Zicher." He was willing to sell them ten acres for one hundred dollars down in New Berlin Township, Waukesha County, west of Milwaukee. It was the swampy northwest corner of the township, but it would be theirs.[2] After the down payment, they paid only the interest on the mortgage, which Zicher held. But they paid promptly, and he gave them apples in return, which Selma baked into pies, and when things got tougher Zicher accepted these in place of interest. A character from the pages of *Poor Richard's Almanac*, Zicher dressed poorly but

Figure 4.1. Ammon and Selma in Milwaukee just after the Big Hike. Permission of Marquette Archives.

held mortgages on many farms. He "never said much, but he knew how to farm. . . . The others talked big and failed," Ammon wrote: "At a party one night all were gathered and Zicher looked like the hired man." But Zicher never transferred titles on properties until they were completely paid off, for he had seen a lot of failure.[3]

Helped by Selma's younger brother Edmund, Ammon hand-dug a cellar and began to build a house. Neither had done this before, but their grandparents had, so they figured it was in their blood. Ammon, conditioned by life on the road, carried rocks up from the swamp to build a fireplace, while Edmund took charge of the rough framing. The house went up so quickly that on September 1925, Ammon could write to his mother that "this week we will paint the inside and next week will put linoleum down." When the house was finished, they started on a twelve-by-twenty-four-foot chicken shed and cow barn, which was completed in March 1926, and then on a separate ten-by-twelve-foot shack for Edmund. He slept at the house so often that the new dog (an expensive pure-bred German shepherd) obeyed him rather than Ammon. Heat was provided by fifty old railroad ties that Ammon and Edmund hauled up to the house for fuel. Then the young couple insured everything for eight hundred dollars.[4]

Despite the rural location and aim of self-sufficiency, their ready cash came initially from a Fuller Brush route. Due to his experience, Ammon got a good territory covering New Berlin, Vernon, and Museko Townships, which were two miles east of Waukesha but crossed by the Interurban rail line. Because of the swamp, Ammon had no direct road access to his territories, but he used an Interurban stop as his business address, even in his newspaper ads: there he met clients and delivered brushes. He also delivered brushes at the Oak Knoll Tavern on Route 59. He walked almost everywhere, fifteen to twenty miles daily. He wrote to his mother that he was making eighteen dollars a day: "I have been doing quite well selling brushes and expect to do better as I get acquainted."

Eventually the *Waukesha Daily Freeman* heard about the idealistic newcomers. In December 1925, Ammon gave the paper a summary of their four-year trip, saying that "sentiments of Walt Whitman caused us to put packs on our backs [and] camp out among the natives of the community." In the article Selma became a graduate of Columbia, Prof. John Dewey had introduced them to Fairhope, they camped among the Native Americans at Taos, and they once traveled seven hundred miles on fifty-four cents. "After a year in California we decided that a snow-storm and a change of climate were much better than the fog of Berkeley, the Booster spirit of Los Angeles, and the artificiality of Florida." No mention was made of politics, Ammon's time in prison, or their utopian experiment.[5]

The initial plan was for a truck garden, but it was fall before they moved into the house. Putting food on the table fell to Ammon, since Selma paid the mortgage interest with her pies, worked on baskets, and was carrying their first child. On his Fuller Brush route Hennacy had at first walked, but after two months of winter he decided to buy a bicycle. "I have ordered a 'Pope-Arch-Bar Superb,' the strongest bicycle I could get," he wrote to his mother: "The bicycles at Sears are somewhat cheaper, but I would have no place to get them fixed, and it would be poor business to ride over my territory in a Sears brand, for people might as well get their brushes there too."[6] This was the last time he ever wrote with excitement about buying something new.

They had shipped ahead a sewing machine, a *Webster's* dictionary, and an atlas, but otherwise the furnishings were minimal. During winter evenings they planned their spring garden using his texts from Berkeley. Otherwise, he had only a small library, mostly Tolstoy. They made some of their clothes, and they gave their land a name—Bisanakee—that compounded the local Native American words for "quiet" and "place." It became their address (Route 5, Box 21, Bisanakee). Poring over seed catalogues, they ordered from three suppliers, to see which strains grew best. And after planting the next June, they bought pullets and a milk cow that they christened "June." During bad weather, Hennacy was rereading Tolstoy.[7]

Every day he rose early to milk the cow. On weekdays he ate "three slices of toast bread with hot milk over them as breakfast" and carried an egg sandwich to eat at noon. The farmers he called on usually gave him a cup of coffee. Selma did not get out much, but she gave some dramatic readings at a nearby school. Her mother was against the whole project and, when Selma announced her pregnancy, was outraged because there was no running water. But the Hennacys believed that a self-sufficient family was key to agrarian anarchism.

Nature surprised the young couple with an early frost on September 25. Ammon hurried home to salvage what he could, shocking the corn, sunflowers, and buckwheat, and Old Man Zicher came over with his team of mules to plough under Ammon's rye for the spring.[8] Selma canned the ground cherries, but this harsh weather put them on notice

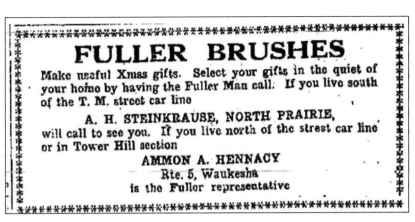

Figure 4.2. Ammon's ad for his Fuller Brush route, November 11, 1925. Public domain.

that the agrarian life would not be easy. With the house done, Ammon and Edmund had dug a cistern that fall and strung wires through the forest, intending to install a telephone. There were now four rooms and a Navajo rug on the floor.

Selma had been raised an atheist, but Ammon was trying to lead her to Christianity. He clung to the idea that CS would be that path, so he corresponded with the *Christian Science Watchman* through the winter of 1926–1927. They even arranged a CS midwife for the birth, but Selma's mother was not having any self-sufficiency nonsense and insisted that they at least consult a doctor, which was fortunate, as Selma's water broke early. Ammon had to rush home on the Interurban to be on hand for the birth of Carmen Hennacy on June 17, 1927.[9] Mrs. Melms then refused to visit Bisanakee (as she did again after Sharon was born), isolating Selma from all her family except Edmund, who liked Ammon. The midwife stayed a week, cooking and cleaning, with Ammon washing the break-fast dishes. His parents did not visit either, but they sent baby clothes, and by his thirty-fifth birthday, Ammon was a proud father, holder of a steady job, and living in a house he had built: he seemed to have put his beliefs into practice. But Selma, alone all day with the baby and the dog, was growing unhappy.

Removed from the political fray for several years, Hennacy was only dimly aware of the uproar over the scheduled 1927 execution of Sacco and Vanzetti. One day in August he went into Waukesha and saw the headlines. "They killed two good men," he recalled exclaiming. He went home and cried. But he saw no chance to do anything locally and believed, from reading Tolstoy, that any involvement in politics was futile. He was rejecting all politics, believing that "what we *do* is more important than what we believe or what we think others think of us." And at Bisanakee he was synthesizing an early version of his eco-personalism.

In a letter to his sister Lida, who was becoming radicalized, he recommended that she too read Tolstoy, the Bible, Whitman, Ibsen, and Shaw. No Kautsky, no overtly political texts. His credo in 1927 did not require radical political engagement. Rather, he was adding a second floor to his house, with three more rooms, cementing the walls of his cistern, and hiring a mason to build a real fireplace. As he was dry walling the first floor, he wondered if even "time spent reading the daily paper with its scandals is worse than wasted."[10] He was still trying to interest Selma in religion, so he explored the local churches. Close by were Lutheran, Jehovah's Witness, and Catholic churches, but he and Selma continued to attend the CS meetings on Sunday and Wednesday, and they "read the lesson every day."

Figure 4.3. Ammon and Selma's homestead at Bisanakee in winter 1928. Marquette Archives.

He racked up brush sales of $3,250 in 1927 and wrote home boastfully that "with all of my building and not working on Saturdays, I am still seventh out of thirty-five for the year in sales."[11] But selling brushes began to weary him. There were mandatory Friday-night sales meetings in Milwaukee, one annoyance, but he also chafed at the sales quotas and bureaucracy. Salesmen had to pay for their brushes in advance, and "the boss always wanted you to order out more than you sold in order to make his sales look big."

At home he was the doting father. Carmen, he wrote, "has learned to watch for me and says 'Daddy.' She likes to jump up and down in her swinging chairs. Has six teeth now, but not very much hair. We have not allowed her on the floor [which was still dirt]. I will take one of our beds made of 2 x 4's and fix it into a large pen for her to play in. Then when the weather is better she can have her swing outdoors."

The Great Depression

When the stock market cratered in 1929, Ammon and Selma were relatively insulated. They did not experience the initial wave of disillusion that swept over progressive politics, though more urban observers despaired. Europe had never truly recovered from World War I, with the punitive reparations imposed on Germany leading to hyperinflation there, and relations with other countries were just as polarized as they had been before World War I. But now Old Man Zicher was suggesting real repayment. Ammon took out a two-thousand-dollar loan, thinking they could afford the twenty-two-dollar monthly installments, but his economic life began to collapse. Brushes were nobody's necessity and Ammon, focused on his dispute with CS about its policy on pacifists, spent more and more of his free time home at Bisanakee giving "the matter of becoming [Christian Science] serious consideration."

A second child, Sharon, was born on October 23, 1929, the day before Black Thursday. Fuller Brush sales were already falling, and on the back of the birth announcement he sent his parents, Ammon complained that the company had changed the commission structure: "I would have to sell $40 more in 2 periods in order to make $27 less." But right through November, he did not recognize the scale of the collapse. He collected signatures for an International Peace Letter in the local churches. He was fascinated by Sharon, who was big, and he thought that she "had guts, like Selma," whose blue eyes she had inherited.

Customers began to cancel the Fuller brushes they had ordered. "If collecting is as bad in Cleveland as it is around here, you will have a hard time getting money," Ammon wrote to his father, but he kept his hand in with Fuller, thinking that the commission structure would change back. A neighbor, he noted, was supporting himself by cutting down dead trees and selling the wood. Ammon let him chop down one of his trees and went halves with him. If there was involuntary poverty, he would deal with it, but he quit selling brushes.

In March 1930 he hired on as a milk wagon driver at Fox Dairy. He had worked a milk route in Akron in 1916, and this route was eerily similar: it served 230 customers over a two-mile stretch, using a horse-cart. The pay was one hundred dollars a month and two quarts of milk a day. "I went on my bicycle after midnight and stacked my wagon full of milk, etc. and went out in the cold. Fox had very good cottage cheese, but their milk was the same as others. I got a lot of new customers by bragging about the cheese." With his daughters bouncing about the house, however, he had trouble sleeping during the day.

Then he heard about a social work job in Milwaukee and thought about applying for it, but hesitated because he was an ex-convict. He took the exam anyway, making the short list of twelve. He was forthright about his prison time; the question was whether the city could legally hire him, and only the courts could decide that. Meanwhile he tried to sell more cottage cheese. To make ends meet the Hennacys took in a boarder, but she left in June. Then they got rid of the cow, which had developed tuberculosis. There were new expenses, as Selma wanted a piano for the girls. They threw a birthday party for Carmen, and she was invited to other parties, which required presents.

The dairy job had problems. "If I sold something extra to a new customer then I was 'short' and when I turned the money in later, then I was 'over.' Fox would charge you with being short, but never credit you with the money turned in which should have been over."[12] Ammon saw an opportunity for the kind of "direct action" that he had once liked. "The men asked me to head them and . . . I did so, but by the time I got to the office they all laughed. I told Fox about it and he laughed. He said he would give me the money due, but I was fired. I asked him what about the other men. He said, 'You don't work here anymore, what do you care?'"

While Ammon would later refer to this incident as a strike, it is clear from his letters that it was only a partly successful "job action." The times were too tough for anyone to go on strike. The Hennacys were looking at a fall without income when the decision came from the Attorney General's Office: since Hennacy had not been guilty of a felony, he was eligible for the social-service job. So the Hennacys moved back to Milwaukee.[13]

Giving up Bisanakee was hard. Two daughters were born there, and their homestead might have succeeded but for the Depression; now they had to sell the German shepherd and walk away from a dream on which they still paid twenty-two dollars a month. Two years later Zicher would buy back their ten acres for two thousand dollars and pay off the remaining seven-hundred-dollar bank loan. Ammon was not bitter: "We got $1,300 for our six years' work, and we were allowed to live there in the summer for a few years, so that the girls had the benefit of country life in their first years."[14]

Milwaukee

The move to Milwaukee was cathartic, but diminished the physical component of Ammon's life, leaving a restlessness that he filled with writing and proselytizing. As he refocused on politics, he gradually discovered a local Catholicism conducive to his views, one that led to Dorothy Day and the Catholic Worker movement. Unlike most other religious movements, Day and Peter Maurin's Catholic Worker movement had responded to the Depression, and their pacifist and agrarian ideas paralleled Ammon's. Never as enthusiastic about the agrarian project, Selma was probably relieved by the return to town, where she could focus on the girls and the charismatic side of CS. But rather than joining in Ammon's interests, she would secretly join the I AM movement that they had heard about in California.

Their first residence was the second floor of a frame house owned by her grandparents in Walker Square, a working-class neighborhood. Selma persuaded her grandmother to try CS methods to try to cure her grandfather, to no avail.[15] Meanwhile, at the Department of Outdoor

Relief, Ammon determined the eligibility of families applying for aid.[16] "Of course an anarchist had no business working for a government," he wrote, "even a county government. I admitted this to all and sundry and compensated in my mind for this dereliction by speaking in hundreds of Protestant churches on Christian anarchism."

Some of his applicants were meek, and Ammon felt he was not helping them enough for his $2.50 daily pay. Others were bellicose: these Ammon came to regard as his specialty, practicing a "moral jujitsu" that he said he was learning from reading Gandhi, who added fasting to Ammon's interests. Not only did Gandhi's ideas parallel Ammon's other influences, but his focus on the body as site of political expression, which has recently received scholarly attention, was something that Ammon liked.[17] It helped that someone in his office believed in Ammon and his eclectic interests: his new boss, Benjamin Glassberg, had been one of his teachers at the Rand School.

The clients he met often tested Ammon's pacifism. One man demanded five mattresses, said he had a gun and would use it; this was the way he had gotten his wishes from previous social workers. "Let's go upstairs and see what size mattresses you need," suggested Ammon. After more back and forth, Ammon saw that only one mattress was needed. When he said so, the man laughed agreeably. Trying to stay warm in winter, clients ran up larger gas and electric bills than the department allowed. When the department did not pay, their utilities were turned off. It cost five dollars to turn them on again, so Hennacy simply marked them for payment, taking up the fight with Glassberg, who eventually relented.

Another recipient wanted shoes. "What did you do with the pair I got you last month—sell them for booze?" Ammon asked. When the man claimed that he wore them out looking for work "up north," Hennacy said, "And you came home in your bare feet?" The man laughed and the incident was over: humor often worked. Some ethnic recipients of aid ate different foods than the department's Wisconsin suppliers provided. When Italians asked for spaghetti and wine, Hennacy wrote a letter to the board pointing out that the "statistical menu" for the "average family" was not working.[18]

The incident that most affected Hennacy involved a giant Polish tanner suspected of earning unreported income. Marion Myszewski had threatened to knock out the previous caseworker. Ammon visited to tell him that as a result his food aid was being cut off. "He locked the door, drew down the blind, and took up a butcher knife and made at me. I was sitting at a table and did not get up." He stopped short and said he was giving Ammon fifteen minutes to approve a grocery order. "He said he would carve me up if I did not mark down the groceries. . . . He did not care if he went to the House of Corrections 'as I have been there before.'"[19] Hennacy said he had been in prison too—in solitary confinement. The giant cursed and swung at his head. Hennacy sat still. The man went behind him, shouting that he always got what he wanted. Ammon felt the knife on the back of his neck. "This went on for nearly an hour. He called me all the vile names he could think of. Finally, he came after me more energetically than before and said I had to do something. I reached out my hand in a friendly manner and said, 'I am not afraid of that false face that you have on. I see the good man inside. If you want to knife me or knock me cold, go ahead.'" The man relented, impressed by Hennacy's pacifism. "What is your strongest weapon," Hennacy asked, "your big fist with a big knife? What is my strongest weapon? It is the fact that I do not get excited—some call it spiritual power. What is your weakest weapon? It is your getting excited and boiling over. . . . So I use my strongest weapon against your weakest weapon."[20]

At least that is how Hennacy would tell the story for decades. He felt the incident was so powerful that the next day he wrote it up in a letter to the local Christian Scientists, with whom he was still arguing. But in fact, he had previewed case notes on the Myszewskis, who received rent, food, and clothing assistance. The problem was that a local alderman had insinuated to them that the Department of Outdoor Relief was crooked and he had "fixed" their requests for them. Like his predecessor, Hennacy also wrote case notes: in his write-up, there was a threat of violence, but no knife. He found their complaints justified: he wrote down the grocery list and approved $5.70 for children's shoes, $4 for a doctor bill, and $15 for clothes. He reinstated the milk that had been cut off. Convinced that the wife was working but did not share her income with her husband, not even allowing him tobacco, Hennacy gave Myszewski more than he expected.[21]

The "hand-or-knife story," in which Hennacy contrasted the hand he extended toward the tanner with the knife the latter wielded, fits nicely into what activist Barbara Deming has called the tradition of the "two hands of non-violence," or parables about the power of pacifism.[22] This story became one of Ammon's favorite soapbox illustrations, a tool that he honed to a point. He had met many types of people on the Big Hike and now he was making a good-faith attempt to solve their problems in a financially strained, highly bureaucratic system. He had run up against the limits of what institutions could do, but he found a bit of room to act individually, to tailor solutions to specific cases, which permitted him to act out a bit of Tolstoyan personalism. The hand-or-knife tale marks a step beyond his encounter with Warden Zerbst; he had decided not only to love his neighbor but to turn the other cheek even if there was a chance of dying. No more would he work at being "God's Coward."

In late 1933 the Hennacys moved to the Shorewood neighborhood, just blocks from a good public school. Theirs was a six-apartment brick building, with a public pool nearby where the girls would learn to swim. During the summer Mr. Zicher allowed them to visit Bisanakee, but it was an hour's ride each way on the Interurban. As Ammon wrote to his parents, "It looks like this depression is here to stay so I suppose I will have a job here for some time, and it will be difficult to get another one."[23] The Hennacys at home were preoccupied by schooling. The Fairhope pedagogy had impressed them and, warming to CS, Selma was resisting vaccines, vitamins, and any teaching about germs. When a kindergarten teacher asked Sharon if she was sick, she said, "I'm Science. I don't get sick." Encountering anti–Christian Science attitudes in the public schools, Ammon and Selma increased the amount of schooling they did at home. "At present my wife, by means of blocks and kindergarten facilities which we have at home, is teaching the girls as much of the facts of reading, spelling and figures as they ask for," he reported.

Christian Science was under attack at that moment, dimmed by revelations in *McClure's* magazine that Mrs. Eddy had lied about her life. Her "science," said *McClure's*, was simply hypnotism. Then John V. Dittmore and E. Sutherland Bates published *Mary Baker Eddy: The Truth and the Tradition* (1932), a debunking so severe that it caused Mrs. Millis, who had introduced Ammon to CS, to quit. "I should think that the disclosures of the real facts of Mrs. Eddy's life and methods would have sufficed to turn you away from membership in the organization," she wrote to Ammon and Selma.[24]

Selma tasked herself with her daughters' education but inclined against having more children. But then, although they used condoms, she got pregnant again. She chose to abort, and Ammon respected her wishes. "I figured that she was the boss in such things," he wrote. Through a friend named Walter Parks, who worked for the health service, they located a provider, who charged twenty-five dollars.[25] Afterwards, working on a degree in teaching drama at Marquette University, Selma decided the best education should be "similar to that of Isadora Duncan, where the idea and not the form is important."[26] She took the girls to music lessons, sublimating her own artistic aspirations, and Ammon proudly attended evening recitals. They soon consulted Carleton Washburne, an advocate of John Dewey's education theories, who had developed the "Winnetka Plan" of progressive education. He won over Selma, who rented an apartment near his school in Winnetka, Illinois, which Ammon would supposedly visit on weekends while continuing to support them from Milwaukee.

After six months, however, they both found Winnetka "too gold coast," or affluent. Ammon said he would move wherever they could get a progressive education. Privately, Selma seems to have been fed up with Ammon's renewed political enthusiasm. He had so much physical energy that, unmoored from the labor of the farm and Fuller Brush route, he seemed likely to do something that would put him in prison again. Then she would have two girls and no income. He was itching for political action, and the newspapers bruited the inevitability of war. He spent less and less time at home.[27] On Saturdays he stood in front of the library selling *Conscientious Objector* and *Social Work Today*. Some in his conscientious objector group were Catholic, and they showed him a new paper, the *Catholic Worker*, the first issue of which had been published by Dorothy Day and Peter Maurin on May 1, 1933.

As scholars Robert Putnam and David Campbell have shown, there were many ethnic/local Catholic constituencies concerned about inequality, economic issues, and government inaction; they were less concerned about orthodoxy and the pope.[28] In Wisconsin, as Michael Pfeifer shows, there were new Marianist groups, some allied with antiwar views, and other groups with Old Church sentiments not unrelated to Tolstoy's.[29] These were increasingly popular, making the area good prospecting for Dorothy Day. She had become a Catholic only in 1927, with "a very definite point of view about poverty, unemployment, and my own vocation to try to do something."[30] A Tolstoyan and ex-Communist, she met Peter Maurin in 1932 when he appeared in her doorway. "He fancied himself a troubadour of God, going about the public squares and street corners indoctrinating his listeners from a singsong repetition," Day wrote: "Being a born teacher, he did not hesitate to repeat his ideas over and over. . . . Peter would sing out, 'To give and not to take,' and the chorus would respond, 'That is what makes man human.'" Maurin's *Easy Essays* had ignited Day's journalistic and organizing talent at the *Catholic Worker*, but the real blaze required the Depression. In these propitious conditions, Ammon and Selma arrived in Milwaukee.

While Selma was in Winnetka, Ammon hung out with his radical friends, seeking the kind of path the *Catholic Worker* would soon offer. He even met Goldie Berg, one of Selma's Yipsel friends from New York City, to plan several political events. Once he rode down to Chicago in her car without telling Selma, who was furious when she found out "and stayed that way for months."[31] When Ammon's father died in June, Selma refused to attend the funeral, so he hitchhiked alone to Ohio. When he returned, she announced that she was taking the girls to New York to further their musical education. Their *entente* publicly was that this was an idealistic, self-sacrificing venture undertaken for the girls' sake.

But then Ammon discovered another reason for the move. One Saturday he went to sell *Social Work Today* at a union office, but it had closed and in its place was a sect called "I AM," the cult started by Guy and Edna Ballard of Chicago. He spoke with the local leader, Brother Bill, who confidently called Ammon a "Communist." Wondering how a man he had never met would know his past, he wrote to Selma mentioning the incident, and she wrote back that he had stumbled onto her I AM chapter. Thinking that perhaps he was getting it wrong, Ammon wrote to old friend Mrs. Millis, asking if the I AM was somehow better than CS on war and conscientious objectors. She wrote back that I AM seemed no better; he did not check further.

In 1933 Ammon had unsatisfying work, no family, and no sense of mission. He felt office bound: "There are more people applying for relief now than any time during the Depression. I am not visiting anyone now but am busy helping take care of new people that come in the office."[32] He needed to fortify himself with a meaningful context, so he wrote letters to famous thinkers such as Reinhold Niebuhr and Mahatma Gandhi, and they returned polite, neutral replies. He wrote to Vanguard Press proposing a book on American anarchists and their resistance to the military; then he wrote a long account of his prison time. He reconnected with Roger Baldwin, now leader of the American Civil Liberties Union, but most importantly, he met Bill Ryan, a communist organizer who had fought in Spain until he was disillusioned by the Stalinists, and his Hungarian wife, Alba, whose friendship sustained him for the next ten years.[33]

Living at 1331 West Greenfield Avenue, he wrote nostalgically to several old Hiram College friends in 1934. The extraordinary outpouring of letters indicates another reevaluation of where he had ended up.[34] In an essay on Emerson that he was reading, Ammon came upon a line from Robert Frost: "I bid you to the one-man revolution / the only revolution that is coming." It aligned with his reading of Tolstoy and Gandhi: so many influences seemed to point in the same direction. It was useless to think that anyone else was going to change unless awakened by example—his example.

First off, he led the social workers in starting a union, though he feared putting his friend Glassberg on the spot. They won a pay raise from $140 to $175 a month. He began speaking widely and meeting people with whom he would correspond for decades, many of them World War I conscientious objectors. He wrote to them about a new round of resistance. Despite his unsettled situation, he was energized by World War II.[35] In the elections of 1936, Hennacy reluctantly supported the Socialist Norman Thomas, but seems not to have voted. After the election Hennacy wrote his first letter to the *Catholic Worker*: "Enclosed find 25 cents in stamps for a sub to your Catholic Worker. I am not a Catholic, but I like your paper. Father Kennedy of your church here spoke of your interest in war objection. . . . My anarchist comrades generally think they have to be atheists in order to be radicals, and my church friends are generally afraid to take the absolutist stand against war and to turn the other cheek in daily life—it's lots of fun."[36]

The Catholic Worker Movement

The paper that Hennacy began to pass out had reached a circulation of one hundred thousand per issue by 1935. Peter Maurin was the source of its "personalism," though the term had been used by Walt Whitman in 1868.[37] Trained by the Christian Brothers in Europe, Maurin had attached himself to Le Sillon, a French fringe movement, until discouraged by its bureaucracy and its retreat from the Sermon on the Mount. He emigrated to Canada, where he pioneered an agrarianism modeled on that of St. Francis. "Very little about modern life appealed to Peter," write Day's biographers. Having read some of her articles in *Commonweal*, Maurin appeared in Day's kitchen in New York in December 1932. She "was uncertain at first how much she wanted to do with a Prince Myshkin [Tolstoy's anarchist hero] in the flesh."[38] It took him four months to convince her to start a newspaper to advance his ideas, which he thought should be called "Catholic Radical." But the paper that appeared on May 1, 1933, reflected Day's long-standing interest in labor issues. Though the *Catholic Worker* made Maurin's "Easy Essays" famous, he often felt its politics were not radical enough, believing the paper should argue for life in small agricultural communities. "There is no unemployment on the land," he said over and over.[39] But he was not good at organizing the communities, and the urban-oriented Day did not really take to farming.

The length of the *Worker* varied from eight to thirty pages, but the front page was usually dominated by a striking wood-cut graphic by Fritz Eichenberg or Ade Bethune. Long position pieces by Day, Maurin, Thomas Merton, and, later, Hennacy started to the left or right of the graphic and jumped inside, where there were shorter articles, letters to the editor, announcements, and some ads. Daniel Berrigan, Robert Coles, Jacques Maritain, and Michael Harrington were other notable voices that eventually appeared, but anyone could publish an opinion. There was no attempt at balance or fairness, and the pages were sometimes visually crowded or sported white gaps. The *Catholic Worker* looked rough-hewn; that was its charm and persona, familiar to anyone who has read a protest newspaper.

It was a lifeline for Hennacy. When Day came to Milwaukee to speak early in 1937, he had been selling the *Catholic Worker* outside several churches. In 1935 he began writing long letters to it in response to William Callahan, the managing editor, who argued against the traditional Catholic position on "just wars." Callahan argued that the premise of *just wars* made it necessary for the *CW* to be *against all wars*. This was the affirmation he had not found in CS, and it reopened him to larger organizations.

In 1936 Callahan and other pacifists of the Mott Street House in New York announced "the formation of a Catholic organization of conscientious objectors."[40] Four months later the group was named "PAX" and Callahan became director. Dorothy Day backed it, arguing that resistance should not be passive but should involve total noncooperation. When summoned to the New York Chancery, Day would not back down. "We had to follow our own consciences, which later took us to jail; but our work in getting out the paper was an attempt to arouse the consciences of others, not to advise action for which they were not prepared," she wrote.[41] Callahan came to Milwaukee to speak at Marquette University in 1937, but Hennacy somehow missed that event. He wrote Callahan a long letter, frustrated when he did not reply immediately.

One cause of Hennacy's slow approach to the *Catholic Worker* was that he was attempting to woo Selma back. In personal letters to others, he was boasting of his daughters' ballet and piano skills. He wanted to believe that they (only eight and six years old), as well as Selma, shared his pacifist/anarchist credo. When asked in school how many of their fathers had served in World War I, Carmen wrote,

I am proud of my father, but I don't like the way he *boasts* about it all the time. And says how great he is. I think he could of done it without all the boasting. I *do not* belong to "Brownies" and I am not going to join "Girl Scouts." When they ask me why I don't join, I answer them with this: "I am too busy and do not have time for it." Which is very true (because I take tap dancing, toe dancing, poems, and plays. I also take piano). But when they ask me for another reason, I tell them, "Well, my Daddy did not go to war and does not believe in it." Which is the most important reason. I think that is all I have to say about it. I am nine years old and am in the "A" grade in school.
Carmen Hennacy.
P.S. My father's name is Ammon Hennacy.[42]

Ammon was ecstatic, copying Carmen's statement into several letters. So when Selma returned to Milwaukee in April 1937, either out of money or to give the marriage a final try, he did not join the Catholic Worker movement immediately. He found a new, very large house for them at 2638 North Frederick. By May he was characterizing Selma's return as permanent. They tried to rent out two of the rooms, to no avail.[43]

Hennacy talked so much about Dorothy Day and the *Catholic Worker* that Selma felt that he had "fallen" for her. "Dorothy Day destroyed my marriage," she later told Joan Thomas.[44] She did not want any part of Ammon's next prison term, which she was sure was coming, and during which she would have to raise two children alone. He had promised to give her his small pension from his Social Service job (which she apparently thought would get her started in the tight-knit world of the I AM), but in mid-October they were still in the big, unaffordable house on North Frederick.

During the winter of 1937–1938, Hennacy wrote for the first time to the Doukhobors, a group of Russian agrarian pacifists who followed Tolstoy and seemed to embody most of his beliefs. He also wrote to Tom Mooney in San Quentin, promising to send money raised from a rally he was organizing for the Haymarket martyrs. Through this rally he met Henry L. Nunn, who was president of the Nunn-Bush Shoe Company, a model of corporate socialism and a sponsor of the Haymarket event. Was this fusion of seeming opposites possible? Open to the possibility, Hennacy went to Nunn's office, discovering that he was at least notionally vegetarian as well as Tolstoyan. "I would have been proud to go to jail, but in 1917 I did not know any better," Nunn told him.[45] Ammon's sense of possibility in such friends and in his new affiliation with the Catholic Worker movement overflowed in his letters.

Then Selma took the girls to Fairhope, with Ammon's approval. In letters he described the trip as part of their educational quest. But in Fairhope there was no I AM group, which had become central for Selma, and the colony had become middle-class. In the winter of 1937–1938, she abruptly moved out of their North Frederick house, probably without telling Ammon in advance. He tried to put a good face on it in a letter to Abe Kaufman.

Here is something that I want you to keep entirely to yourself and family, as least for the present. We are planning to take an auto trip to New York City in the early part of August. It is likely that Selma and Carmen and Sharon will stay in or around New York City indefinitely. They do not know just where they can fit in the work in music, drama, and dancing and also with schoolwork. Selma feels that it is best to be located where the children can advance. . . . As one might say, my anti-war activities are in our budget, and it is foolish to think that my pay checks will continue for the next fifteen months without stopping. If my activities land me before a firing squad or in prison, Selma can take care of herself better in New York than she can here. She never did like Milwaukee. I have a civil service job which pays $170 a month. . . . I plan to stay here and send Selma all I can. If later it is possible to get some kind of job in New York, although it pays less, it would be better for me to be there too. Selma will have her Ford, and the children their new bicycles. All other furniture will be sold here. Some books, pictures, clothes will be taken along. What does it cost to attend the Ethical Culture School?[46]

In a second letter six weeks later, he revealed that Selma had left him, though he was trying to help her set up in New York.[47] No letters reveal Selma's thoughts at this point, but to judge from his letters, Ammon's were indeed centered on Dorothy Day, to whom he did not mention his domestic woes. He returned to Milwaukee, where he received a letter from Day advising him to cut the length of *God's Coward*, the manuscript he was working on. But in his enthusiasm, he added several thousand words. In letters he trumpeted how Day was introducing him to priests and *Catholic Worker* officials. With Abe Kaufman, he continued to discuss the misguided idea that he could afford the Ethical Culture School ("over $300 per child per year," Kaufman wrote). For the next twenty years he would send Selma and the girls most of the money he made, sublimating his guilt for following his conscience.

By September Hennacy was living at 804 Cass Avenue, where he rented a room for three dollars a week. He boasted to his Cleveland relatives of his parsimony: "I get raisin-bran bread at the bakery a day old, for 7 cents a loaf. I buy up enough canned goods after pay day for a week. I buy 5 cents worth of grapes for dinner. I bought a 5 lb. pail of honey for 55 cents. A sailor lives across the hall. He is on W.P.A. at $60 a month and worries how to get along on that while I spend $26." This was the unglamorous beginning of his "voluntary poverty," in which he did with as little as possible. For the most part he liked it. It confirmed him on Gandhi's path. It was easy enough to wear old clothes and live in reduced circumstances. Missing Selma, he decided to write about their four-year hike around the United States, a travelogue that he titled *High Roads and Hot Roads.* He believed that it was just a matter of time before one of these manuscripts sold: "Harper's are reading my book now. I also spoke to Farrar and Rinehart. . . . And I spoke to Vanguard who will also read it, if necessary."

Money was clearly on his mind when the plan for their daughters' high-end education fell through. "I suppose the girls will go to the public school in their vicinity, [but] I do not know Selma's phone number," he explained to Abe Kaufman. Hennacy explained that the arrangement was just "for the winter," but in mid-October Selma moved to the Stratton Arms Residence Club at 330 West Eighty-Fifth Street. Ammon was sending them everything he could, but the costs added up: the piano teacher wanted seventy dollars a month. Ammon soon learned that she was in the I AM movement. Then Carmen was put back a grade for a deficiency in math, a shock. Since Selma did not work, Ammon paid for everything, sending Selma over $140 of his $170 monthly pay.[48]

Due to his spare diet and reading in Gandhi, vegetarianism was a daily practice, so when Carmen wrote that she and Sharon were becoming vegetarians, he was thrilled and remembered an earlier conversation: "She said: Daddy, why don't you eat meat? I answered that as I did not like to kill pigs and lambs and chickens, it was not right to ask others to do this for me. There was a wiener on the plate and she said 'Maybe that pig just died, maybe nobody killed it.' Then again a few years later she told me that animals had to die to make shoes for us."[49] Unstated in Carmen's letter was that her conversion came via the I AM piano teacher. The daughters were too young to join the movement formally, but it was clear that the piano teacher was proselytizing. Then he heard from Abe Kaufman that he had visited Selma:

> I must confess that we were very much depressed at the thought of such intelligent and delightful people giving way to the I AM Movement. We

felt that, in a sense, we share some of the responsibility for this having happened to Selma, for if we had been able to meet earlier, it might have been possible for us to get them interested in something more socially useful. I am telling you this even though I do not know whether you are fully aware of the meaning of the I AM Movement. It seems to us to be extremely fanatical, unnecessary, "anti-Red," and of no social usefulness. On the other hand, it hurts to see such lovely and healthy girls like Carmen and Sharon educated in the teachings of this sect. Selma seems to conscientiously believe in the absurd teachings which she described to us.

When Hennacy wrote back, he attempted to find his own overlaps with his wife's faith:

I do not know as much about it as Selma and the girls. . . . The basis of their belief is that the great souls who have lived in ages past have not died just like dogs, but have been reborn in bodies every once in a while, and have carried on the work for progress. . . . I have always believed in this idea of re-embodiment. I have studied Theosophy and Rosicrucianism with Scott Nearing years ago. . . . Part of the Theosophist idea, which I had too before I was interested in Theosophy, is to be a vegetarian, and not to use liquor or tobacco or gamble. I have held that idea for years. Also that those who think right and do not let anger and hatred and jealousy control their feelings will not be sick. . . . All of them are basic principles to the I AM idea. The new thing that the I AM seems to bring is to make the whole idea ACTIVE NOW. They say that if we call earnestly for the help of the great souls—Ascended Masters they call them—then they will help not only the individual person but keep injustice, war, poverty, etc. from ruling the world. . . . What is wrong in "decreeing," as they call it, earnestly for justice and peace? . . . Now about this man Ballard, or any of his accredited Messengers, I will wait until I meet him to say what I think.

He was soon to get his fill of decreeing, but at this point he tried to be fair: "So far in my contact with the local I AM's, I find them about as intelligent on pacifism as the average worker or professor. . . . It has at least made them vegetarians."[50]

Suddenly Guy Ballard, the founder of I AM, died in Los Angeles on December 29, 1939. Almost a million followers waited to learn if he had become one of the Ascended Masters. His body was quickly cremated while his wife and son formulated a work-around, one that stated that "ascension" involved reincarnation in a finer physical form.[51] Using Jesus as their model, the heirs claimed that Guy had recorded a "dispensation" before his death, providing for Ascension directly to heaven without a body. Guy Ballard, having already been George Washington and Richard the Lionheart, would henceforth be known as Ascended Master Godfre.[52] About the same time, US Postal Service inspectors interested themselves in claims made in the books of I AM's Saint Germain Press. Were they "true," and did the Ballards believe them? The IRS launched an investigation, and both cases went to trial. Son Donald and widow Edna told members to shun all contact with nonmembers. While Hennacy was planning to visit New York to check on his submissions and family, Selma was thinking of following the leaders to Los Angeles, but again she did not tell Ammon.

By August 1939, she and the girls were living in the Los Feliz neighborhood of Los Angeles, where they had rented a cottage for thirty-one dollars a month. Since Ammon was planning to be arrested for draft resistance, perhaps he would be content that they were settled. On Christmas Day 1939, as was his habit, he wrote many letters: "The day war was declared in Europe my wife wrote saying that she heartily agreed that if and when we got into war, I should quit my job and go to Leavenworth and that God would take care of her . . . [but] Sandstone [prison] will take care of those getting two years or less." He would end up in Sandstone eventually, but not for resisting World War II.

Hennacy was trying to get a lot done before going to prison. Antiwar speeches on the air were foremost, and his first was a fifteen-minute radio address in Cincinnati in mid-January 1940.[53] As for his writing, he received a rejection for his prison book, but he sent it to another publisher and finished up a third manuscript, *Christian Anarchism*, the research for which put him in touch with Agnes Inglis at the University of Michigan Library, where he would deposit manuscripts later. He was trimming his already spartan diet, eating only breakfast and lunch, getting ready for prison, but experiencing bursts of energy. Though he had begun to write for the *Catholic Worker*, he still scattered his efforts, placing a piece in *MAN* in February, and sending *God's Coward* out to a Boston publisher.[54]

World War II

In May 1940, President Roosevelt asked Congress for $900 million to build forty thousand airplanes: US entry into the war was at hand. Prison was appealing, but Hennacy was conflicted, as he recounts in a letter: "I am 47, have about seven good teeth, two children and a wife dependent upon me, so why not register and claim exemption, they say."[55] Selma would have his pension payout, about three hundred dollars, "until she can get something to do," and the girls had already received a lot of musical training with which to make a living for themselves. But a few days after Roosevelt's request, the El Centro earthquake rocked southern California, causing nine deaths and twenty injuries, and the I AM hierarchy started to think about Santa Fe as a headquarters.

By the end of May, the Corsair fighter was already making test flights, indicating that Roosevelt had deceived the public and Congress all along: the plane he had just requested funds for had already been built. His denunciation of Italy proved to everyone on the Left that he was determined to launch a war. Hennacy, Bill Ryan, and Abe Kaufman debated how to respond. Kaufman, over forty-five, signed up in July, knowing he would not be drafted. It was a more serious case for Ryan, who was under forty-five. The draft law allowed for conscientious objectors: there were five different types of 1-A-O deferment (Available but an Objector), and Ammon would have been 1-H ("deferred due to age"). This did not sit well with him, and the general skepticism of the Left about Roosevelt seemed justified, as he now lobbied Congress to extend the draft twice in 1941, registering all men from eighteen to sixty-five. Militarism was everywhere. In Milwaukee the county airport was being renamed General Mitchell Field and turned over to the National Guard.[56]

In August of 1940 Ammon took a vacation, ostensibly to visit his family in Los Angeles, but also to check out the Doukhobors in Washington State and British Columbia. His correspondent, Helen Demoskoff, had painted a tableau of Tolstoyan principles in the face of government oppression. Due to the Depression, their numbers were healthier than usual, almost seventeen thousand, as they absorbed draft resisters.[57]

But when Hennacy arrived, he found many cultural barriers: not only did the Doukhobors speak a dialect of Russian, but they interpreted the Bible literally, and their cultural isolationism, necessary in Russia, included a refusal of all politics, Luddite attacks on machinery, and women pulling plows. Attractive as he had found them on paper, theirs was not his idea of resistance. Like many of his heroes, he wanted to offer resistance *in the world*. As he rode the bus down to Los Angeles, Hennacy wrote of the Doukhobors' vegetarian diet admiringly, but their villages were strikingly primitive, he admitted, without electricity or phones, like hamlets in the trans-Caucasus of 1880.

When he got to Los Angeles, Hennacy spent most of his time with Carmen and Sharon, swimming in the Pacific and hiking in the San Gabriel Mountains. Carmen had won a summer swim meet and he was proud, but he was not tempted to move to LA. "Jobs are scarce there," he wrote to Roger Baldwin, "so I will remain here [Milwaukee] as an 'involuntary virgin' as one of my friends designates the situation." He was reassigned to fieldwork, so after three years in the office he could stretch his legs. Being on the street, he could freely distribute his pamphlet *Christian Anarchism*, as well as other literature. As described in this treatise, his anarchism was still based on Tolstoy, with ideas gleaned from Fairhope, Thoreau, Gandhi, and the Doukhobors: it was light on Christianity aside from the Sermon on the Mount.

Then he heard Peter Maurin speak at the Holy Family House, admiring the way he corrected a heckler who charged him with misquoting Marx. Maurin said that Marx had stolen this idea from "the anarchist Proudhon." The heckler asked Maurin if he too was an anarchist and he responded, "Sure I'm an anarchist. All thinking people are anarchists, but I prefer the name Personalist." Hennacy wrote that "Peter was a wonderful man. The second man of stature I had known: Berkman being the first."[58] This was very high praise. Despite his new field assignment, Ammon delivered the *Catholic Worker* to employees at their desks, which caused problems. This proselytizing got the American Legion to prod the county to prosecute Hennacy. Before the judge, Ammon claimed that he never distributed *his own* opinions to workers or clients, and that he only held up the *Catholic Worker* silently outside the building, on his own time. His seeming discretion impressed the judge, who then asked Hennacy questions about Tolstoy.[59] An account of the trial in the *Milwaukee Journal* gives a sense of Hennacy's reawakened militancy. "Some county employees, members of the American Legion, had complained to [Judge Oliver L.] O'Boyle about the activities of Hennacy and urged that charges be preferred against him before the civil service commission. Hennacy, who is now above draft age and calls himself a 'Christian Anarchist,' has told O'Boyle that he does not believe in the draft or war. He was sentenced as a draft dodger during the World War. He assured O'Boyle that he would not voice his views on county time or when making relief investigation calls."[60] This dust-up fortified Hennacy, but he knew that his chance of serving time was growing faint, and it irked him to be regarded as an old gadfly. He and A. J. Muste began organizing support services to send money, chocolate, and letters to the younger men who would go to jail. For a while that absorbed his energy; then Abe Kaufman recruited Ammon to do homework for a new War Resisters League pamphlet: "Mail us as soon as possible three or four of what you consider the best statements by Tolstoy, Gandhi, or Thoreau, stating the case of those of us who are absolutist. . . . We consider you the best informed of our Tolstoyan members and are anxious to have the quotations which you think are more significant."

Ammon threw himself into it, returning nine pages in forty-eight hours. These he compiled in the room he rented from Selma's brother Edmund. This would be his last Milwaukee address. Outside of his writing, he was buoyed only by Bill Ryan, who told stories about celebrity leftists in Spain such as Hemingway. "Bill was now an anarchist and also an atheist," Ammon wrote, "though he felt that the ethics of the Sermon on the Mount were a true moral guide. We visited each other nearly every day."[61]

In his Christmas 1940 letter to his mother, Hennacy claimed that he had reduced his monthly expenses from twenty dollars to eighteen. Renting from Edmund and Ethel helped, and he paid only five dollars for food and volunteered to babysit their children some nights. "Ethel does my washing, and I do not have to buy a paper, so it is better all around." He noted happily that the I AM movement was struggling financially.[62] Then in January 1941, Hennacy was called on the carpet at work and forbidden to hand out the *Catholic Worker* or *Conscientious Objector*. Ironically, the conflict came to a head because the revved-up war economy meant the Outdoor Relief Office had fewer clients. The board proposed to lay off twenty-five of the four hundred staff members. Hennacy was thirty-fourth in seniority, but the board had an annual "performance grade," on which he ranked lower due to his proselytizing. He went to Glassberg and a new list was drawn up, on which Hennacy was again thirty-fourth. "So I am safe until the war hysteria gets going strong," he wrote. But he felt that working for a government at war was repulsive.[63]

Eager to do something, he was still corresponding with the Doukhobors. But he wanted Selma and his daughters to go with him. They flatly refused. Selma was committed to the I AM, which was closing its big court case over its legal status. Another possibility was to move to Los Angeles to be near them. Sharon sent him a poem, "Come Back, My Child."

> I know you have been away so long,
> Away for many years,
> But when you return, you'll be welcomed with joy,
> My blessing you will hear.
> Then with my love and blessing,
> You shall be locked away in my heart,
> You shall stay with me forever,
> In my home never to part.

That pulled him, but the path to the girls ran through Selma, with whom he was now angry for "deserting" him. In letters to others, he wrote that "very few women have the nerve to stick by their husbands when they stand for an ideal." He repeated this view all spring, imagining that life with the Doukhobors would be better.

A problem appeared now that haunted Hennacy the rest of his life. To pay for the war, President Roosevelt proposed dramatically higher taxes on corporations and individuals, and a 5 percent "Victory Tax" on all individual incomes over $624. The Victory Tax would supposedly be credited back to individuals after the war, but it was a stunning expansion of state financial control of the individual. "I will not voluntarily pay one cent of war tax or sign a voucher to have any amount taken from my pay check," Hennacy wrote: "If, however, it is taken without my consent from my employer, then I will set aside a like amount for the support of families of those doing time." His refusal put him in bed with strange company, such as Charles Lindbergh, whom Roosevelt had just labeled a "dupe of Hitler." On the other hand, Ammon's compensatory plan enacted a kind of personal penance on behalf of the nation, rather creatively Gandhian. It showed that he was not unrealistic, and others could follow suit. Taxes for the military never disappeared, however, leading Hennacy to three decades of work-arounds.

He decided in June that he would go check out the Doukhobors again. He planned an August train trip that departed from St. Paul and arrived several days later in British Columbia, and from there he would go to Los Angeles to visit his family. On the eve of his departure, he wrote a letter to Dorothy Day. He was not yet going to Catholic services, because they sang the "Star-Spangled Banner" at the end of Mass, and it was a rather perfunctory letter, filled with his boilerplate biography. But it ended "Yours in Christ" and was the beginning of an epistolary relationship that would last twenty years, and Day would write often about his trial in a few months.

When Hennacy reached British Columbia, he realized that the Doukhobors already had a patriarch (which was close to his imagined role), whom his friend Helen respected greatly. There was not even a position open for *eminence gris*. "I hope to be able to live with them when my children are grown up," he wrote. "They want me to live with them and write their official story. I would like to do this after I am 60 and the girls are through school." Thus the Doukhobors were assigned to a kind of "retirement" possibility in his life.

In Los Angeles he was surprised to learn that Selma and the girls had moved without telling him or even her relatives. They did not have a phone, so Hennacy had to suss out their new place. When he found them, Selma claimed that the constant piano practice had annoyed the neighbors, who complained to the landlord. So they moved to "Hollywood Junction" at Santa Monica and Sunset Boulevards, only a half-block off Sunset and decidedly less genteel than their old neighborhood.[64]

It was a tense reunion. Ammon had to sleep on the living room floor because the "aura" of a nonfollower was thought by I AM members to contaminate believers.[65] Selma had been in a car accident, which she blamed on Ammon: she had been angry at him and swerved on a wet train track, hitting an uninsured car. She lost some teeth, hurt her leg, and had to sell the car for forty dollars. She told him that if he went to prison again she would consider him dead. He spent most of the day out of the apartment with his daughters, at the beach or hiking. One day downtown he bought the girls a small sewing machine for $7.50, which Selma angrily said ought to have gone for her dentistry. She had not worked since moving out four years earlier and now, when she needed to, she couldn't.[66]

Back in Milwaukee in September, Ammon went downtown during an American Legion convention to pass out *Conscientious Objector* and the *Catholic Worker* on the steps of the library, a deliberately provocative move. When the library closed at 6:00 p.m., he followed the Legionnaires to their convention, where he sold twenty papers without any problems. He was looking for trouble, eager to go to jail. His friend Bill Ryan had declared his intent to refuse to register, and now a trial date was set. He and his wife moved in September to a cabin in Maine for some time together. As Ammon envisioned the future, "They will pass a draft up to 65. There will be no opposition. I will refuse to register and take whatever I get. I have $450 in a pension fund which my wife can use. . . . I have not heard from her, but suppose she is for the war as all of that crazy I AM religion is."[67] He wrote a two-page letter to the US district attorney on December 19, 1941, almost begging to be arrested: "I predict that we will not conquer Fascism, although we may defeat Hitler; we will have a Fascist dictatorship under the name of Democracy upon us. . . . I enclose also the statements written to you in September 1939, and September 1940 on the same subject." The government simply ignored him

It was a brutal January, with temperatures falling to between -15°F and -25°F every night. Even in this weather, Ammon made the long walk home from his political meetings, a five-mile, ninety-minute trek, sometimes late at night.[68] "I walked home past a hundred trembling people in doorways waiting for a streetcar, and saw ten cars in a row coming the other way," he wrote. He tried to keep his spirits up by writing long letters to Dorothy Day and others at *CW*. He was anticipating the return of the Ryans from Maine for trial in February. They were hitchhiking, despite the frigid weather, and Ammon told them to stay with his mother in Cleveland.[69]

On February 4, the I AM lost their California case and decided to leave. The logic was that their prayers ("decrees") had protected that state from Japanese invasion, and now they were withdrawing their protection and dire things would happen. They moved to Santa Fe, New Mexico, with Selma and the children following. Ammon sent them money, but Selma wanted more. Rent was expensive, she said: she had an apartment, then a small house, and the girls needed a piano and lessons. Then he did not hear from her for a while, finally learning from Roger Godwin that she had moved to Denver, which was cheaper and where the I AM also had a chapter.

The Trial

In solidarity with Bill Ryan, Hennacy pressed for his own case to be heard simultaneously. Greater numbers meant more publicity, and he wanted to have something to lose. He worked hard on a statement to read in court. On March 23, 1942, he told Glassberg that he expected to be imprisoned, so he was resigning.[70] He was spending more time at Catholic churches, but where he used to sell a dozen *Workers* every Sunday, now he sold only a few. Then on successive Sundays he sold none, writing ruefully that "I saw 200 plates of corn in the [church] basements all laid out for the worship of St. Bingo."[71] Milwaukee, once a socialist bastion, had become pro-war. He lacked support, any kind of base at all. Anarchism had "evolved in fundamental ways during the 1940s," Cornell writes, and "newer and more native formations were arising on both coasts," but there was little foment in the heartland. Hennacy sensed that he was behind the wave and perhaps thought that prison would reconnect him.[72]

He wrote to Bill that "the FOR [Fellowship of Reconciliation] group will have a special meeting for you in the First Methodist church." But there was no cohort for the meeting.[73] Ammon printed up five hundred copies of his "refusal to register" statement. He left a copy at the *Milwaukee Journal*, but he had many, many copies left. He even wrote to Day, "If you know anyone whom you would like me to mail a copy to send me their address and I will mail it."[74]

The *Milwaukee Journal* was tired of Hennacy. It put his picture on the front page, with two paragraphs of his statement, and branded him a "draft dodger." At the trial the *Journal* decided that Ryan was the story, Hennacy an imposter. On May 12 both men read their statements, and the DA accused Ryan of a felony and Hennacy of a misdemeanor. Ryan had to post bail or be jailed, but Hennacy was released on recognizance after fingerprinting. The *Journal* made out that Ammon was insulted. Under the headline "Loses Chance to Be Martyr," it wrote, "The worst happened Tuesday to the 'Christian Anarchist' Ammon A. Hennacy. He tried to be a martyr and the federal authorities wouldn't let him. The long haired 48-year-old Hennacy came to court with a suitcase full of clippings . . . and his pajamas in a suitcase, ready to go to jail 'because the world is horrid. . . .' Hennacy eventually signed his bond with great dismay and trudged off home, carrying his briefcase and looking like a man whose meat has just been snatched from his plate."[75] It was public humiliation. He wrote to Day that he had brought a briefcase with copies of his statement, but "I had no pajamas. . . . Anyone who knows anything about jails knows that you don't take your pajamas there and that you don't go there until you have had a trial."

The DA and Marshal then made a clever end run around him. After the fingerprinting, they presented him with a draft card and asked him to sign it. When he refused, they mailed it in a registered letter to his address, where his sister-in-law signed for it, thinking she was doing him a favor. That receipt was all that was required: Hennacy was registered for the draft.

Due to his refusal to sign at the draft office, the FBI began to track his movements.[76] By the end of May 1942, Ammon realized there was nothing left for him in Milwaukee. His agrarian dream had failed, his family had left, and his job as a social worker had proven that organizations were useless. Bill was going to prison. The *Catholic Worker* and the Doukhobors looked promising, but he wanted to be in touch with new, younger anarchists, like Dave Dellinger and Bayard Rustin, who seemed to be making things happen, especially in the conscientious objector camps.[77] With nothing to lose, he took the bus to Denver. Selma and the girls were there: maybe that meant she had left the I AM.[78]

5

Life at Hard Labor

Denver

One month after Pearl Harbor, Ammon Hennacy was on the road, trying to find his wife and children, but he had continual access to the
CW and was reading deeper into its vision of personalism, which he felt
he had been practicing for decades. Peter Maurin may have "brought
from France an intact and meaningful Catholic tradition capable of
orienting the person toward transcendence," as Marc Ellis has written,
but Ammon felt he had been practicing the tradition of Whitman, Thoreau, and Lindsay, not to mention that of Borden Parker Bowne, who
had published *Personalism* in 1908.[1] Personalism did not seem like an
import.

From Denver Selma wrote that, since she was moving so often,
Ammon should just mail money care of General Delivery. This way she
avoided giving out her address, which he had proven adept at finding
in LA. When Ammon sent his six-hundred-dollar pension payout and
word of the day of his arrival, she wrote back that he should have waited
to be fired, in order to collect unemployment too. In fact, she did have a
permanent address: she was renting at 1472 Josephine Street, near City
Park and South High School, which Carmen was attending.

Hennacy stopped in Chicago to meet other war resisters, including
Claude McKay, the Harlem Renaissance poet and IWW member. Arriving in Denver on a Sunday, he knew exactly where to find Selma: at
the I AM meeting. There, in a store front, several other people were also
waiting. When Ammon said he wanted to worship with his family, a
burly I AM official blocked the staircase. He had to wait downstairs, the
official said; he could see them when they left. He sat on a bench with an
engineer from Spokane, also trying to see his wife, and a man who had
fooled his wife into thinking he was I AM, so he was allowed into the

house. "Are you allowed into your house?" he asked Ammon. "I don't even know where it is," Ammon replied.[2]

Minutes after the service was over, Sharon came in the outside door, having snuck away from Selma, who was trying to get home without seeing him. Walking back to the bus stop with Sharon, Ammon pried out their address, and they passed a dairy, where he would find a job. At the bus stop he pointed out to Selma that he was supporting them, and she agreed that he could sleep on the floor, but only for three nights.

Many dairy co-ops had opened to meet the growing city's needs, and City Park Dairy consolidated several in 1906. It was a union shop, which Ammon liked, so he put forward both his union and his dairy credentials.[3] The company had free, on-site dorms for workers, which solved one problem.[4] New workers were needed constantly to replace those who were drafted, but the union was the AFL Teamsters, a very authoritarian, pro-war organization. Its business agent, Mr. Coffee, came around to collect Ammon's fifteen-dollar initiation fee, explaining that he was lucky to join before the fee rose to twenty-five dollars. A few weeks later, when Hennacy went to his first meeting, he saw over five hundred men in the room.

His dorm room was the size of a cell, with a bed and cupboard but "without the bodily conveniences," he wrote. About fifty other men lived on-site, in a noisy area between the offices and the cow barn, so they heard the cows all night. There were common baths and a mess hall with surprisingly good food; the pay was ninety dollars a week, but twenty dollars were deducted for room and board. He wrote to friends that he was giving Selma sixty-five of the seventy dollars that remained.[5] The cows were milked twice a day, with Ammon's shifts being from 1:00 p.m. to 5:30 p.m. and from 1:00 a.m. to 5:30 a.m. He warmed to the work, recalling his cow at Bisanakee. He befriended old and skittish cows, cajoling them into the stalls, making sure that his hands were warm before milking. His coworkers kicked the slow cows and cursed them if their milk came slowly. Ammon got into a spat over this, which was resolved when he volunteered to milk one older cow and to carry the coworker's pails. This got him assigned twenty of the most machine-shy animals. Other milkers began to resent him, the new guy and cow lover, baiting him when he passed by, but he carried their buckets to the cooler.

The dairy was in many ways a place Hennacy liked, a cross between prison and farm, but with the freedom to leave to proselytize and to go hiking on weekends. In the evening, between shifts, he could take the streetcar into Denver for meetings of the Fellowship of Reconciliation (FOR). On weekends he walked downtown and passed out the *Catholic Worker*, feeling freer than in Milwaukee. He was reading deeply in Gandhi, who taught that nonviolence begins with what we eat, that a nation could be judged by how it treated animals. He began wearing a Gandhi cap, which was commonly mistaken for a yarmulke. Walking by a Jewish sanitarium, he heard two old men comment, "Oy, what a young rabbi!" On the occasions when he was able to see Selma and their daughters, they went hiking, even up Lookout Mountain, where they visited Buffalo Bill's grave.[6]

At the first union meeting, a motion was made to invest a thousand dollars in Liberty bonds; he tried to speak against it but was ruled out of order. The priority was to end the meeting quickly so everyone could go drinking. At the next meeting, when a union official moved to forbid conscientious objectors from joining and Ammon objected, the agent told him that while the rule did not apply to him, it came from the national boss, Dan Tobin.

"Soon after that," he wrote, "I was selling CW's and CO's in front of the public library downtown one Saturday afternoon. A cop came up and asked what I was selling. I handed him copies and said, 'The best papers in the world.'" The policeman said that Ammon needed a permit and arrested him, an event familiar from Milwaukee, but here it was worse for his domestic situation. The I AM was pro-war, and Selma was deeply involved, spending several hours a day "decreeing" against assorted politicians. Even Carmen and Sharon had to decree for an hour a day. The Denver I AM community was paranoid and prurient. Ammon had hoped for some time together, but Selma would not let him close. Carmen and Sharon were picked up for meetings by two California teen I AM members, who drove them both ways. "The I AM wants to make them feel that if their father as much as touches their elbows, it is something carnal," he wrote: "My wife tried to be nice at times, and at other times was very argumentative. She made it clear that I could not live there permanently unless I belonged to the I AM."[7] Personalism and the *CW* offered no guidance in dealing with such a group.

In response to World War II, the I AM had published "The Octave of Light," a millennial tract by which Selma justified her views. "This [millennium] is supposed to happen by Xmas," Ammon wrote to a friend. "The Jehovahs have the [same] thing happening another way, with themselves as leaders. The Lemurians have it happening with an island rising up from the Pacific, and themselves to establish a new civilization."[8]

Ammon celebrated his fifty-ninth birthday by writing to Bill Ryan, who was serving time at Sandstone. He sent Bill one dollar a week, trying to evade the prohibitions on nonfamily mail by using some of Selma's I AM stationery, since religious mail was allowed. But he was caught, angering Ryan's wife because this endangered Bill's mail privileges. In a letter to Bill he described his family's situation: Selma had a good flat for forty dollars a month with heat, and a fridge, stove, and hot water to boot. The girls could ride their bikes, and there were cherries free for the picking, but Selma's knee was still stiff from her LA accident. Despite the problems, Denver seemed an improvement over Milwaukee for all of them.

Then he got arrested again. This time he was held four days because the local FBI thought he was a Communist. He asked them to contact Harry Connor, the FBI head in Milwaukee, to vouch for him. Meanwhile, he had to appear in daily line-ups, at which police coached witnesses to identify those they were after, raising the chance of false charges, which made a deep impression on him. Finally the FBI returned word that, despite refusing to carry a draft card, Hennacy was free to move about the country.[9] The local FBI told him to visit the chief of police, which he did, and the chief said he could sell papers wherever he wanted. But the next week he was arrested again, and this time he contacted Roger Baldwin of the ACLU in New York, who threatened to take the case to the Supreme Court.

His arrest made the Denver newspapers, which Selma and her coreligionists read closely for "signs." After his release he stopped by her house but found no one home. He thought they had gone to the mountains, but when she finally returned, Selma confessed that she had been to Santa Fe. She said she could not live in the same city with a husband who was always embarrassing her and her religion, as well as the girls. Ammon decided to think of Selma's move as "temporary," like her earlier moves to Winnetka and New York City, and he even helped her to pack. "Looking at the thing fairly," he wrote to Bill, "if a person believes in such a theory, then they ought to be as near the source of inspiration as possible. Chances are I'll make it down there about every two months to see them. Round trip is $13. . . . Selma will get a job in Santa Fe, although it will be harder." He resigned himself to life at Park Dairy, settling into his monk-like cell.

Thanksgiving passed and Christmas approached; Ammon began his end-of-year epistolary routine. Letter writing kept him going when the days grew gray. He wrote to Dorothy Day that he was working on a way of not paying taxes to support the war: "At the FOR meeting . . . I got up and said that as an absolutist I should not pay any war tax next year. . . . However, if I paid it, to ease my conscience I would notify the gov't that I would pay twice as much to . . . FOR and the *Catholic Worker*." This compensatory self-taxing was an idea he came up with in Milwaukee, but now he put it into action. He also wrote warmly to female pacifists and the wives of pacifists, some of whom he knew only as names in the *Catholic Worker*. "Write and tell me about yourself and your pacifism," he wrote to one. As Joan Thomas remarked, "His letters, so myriad, stem at this time in his life from an intrinsic loneliness."[10]

Then Hennacy asked the business secretary of the City Park Dairy union if he had any contacts in Santa Fe, since he planned to visit. On December 15 he wrote a polite letter to Roy Lemons, a union official in Albuquerque, and two days later he wrote to Bill, "I am going down to Santa Fe next Wed. to see my family. I have official notice from my wife that I am not welcome and will not get to see them, but I am taking the chance."[11]

When he arrived in Santa Fe, Selma had already moved from her first house to a cottage near the old plaza. She could not keep the address secret because Ammon was paying her utilities, the records for which were public. He was charmed by the cottage: it had two fireplaces, two-foot-thick adobe walls, and beamed ceilings, and backed up to the Santa Fe River.[12] She had two pianos, one for each girl, but she did not want him around. She forbade his overnight presence (in the house he was paying to rent), saying that the Christmas meditations of the I AM were a sacred period. She asked for even more support, and he took perverse pride in turning the other cheek. "I would not coerce her by withholding money, going to court, or in any other unchristian action," he wrote to Ryan. "In time the girls will be able to see the truth. I am willing to wait."

While he liked the city and the Native American influences, there was no dairy in Santa Fe, which got its milk from Albuquerque. It was there that he finally found work just by "walking out the north end of town asking farmers about a job. . . . Finally I came to Blumenshein's dairy."[13] The owners were old Catholics with two married sons and a hired man named Bertie. They ran 150 head of Jersey cows and did all the work themselves, living rough and ribald in ways that shocked Hennacy. They played lewd tricks on each other, cursed all day and night, and tormented the feeble-minded Bertie. Room and board were included here too, but when they found out that Hennacy was a vegetarian, they served him a plate of afterbirth. "That ain't meat—eat it!" they yelled. He went outside and threw up. After six months Blumenshein decided that Bertie could do all the work and Ammon was happy to leave, never mentioning his crude employers again until late in life.

Old Man Simms

He found another job immediately at Simms's Dairy, also north of town.[14] Like Nunn, Albert G. Simms would be an influence on Ammon. He was a successful businessman, slightly older than Hennacy (now sixty), with roots in the golden age of self-made men. Born in Arkansas, Simms had learned accounting and settled in Mexico in 1906, then moved to New Mexico, where he learned the law and held a dozen elected positions. He met and married the widowed Ruth Hanna McCormick when they were both members of Congress. She, from Illinois, was heir to the McCormick reaper and Hanna shipping fortunes and owned the 250,000-acre Trinchera ranch in Colorado. Using her money, they had bought eight hundred acres just north of Albuquerque for their home, dairy, farm, nursery, and cultural center.[15] Here they built "Los Poblanos" in 1934, curating every aspect of its ballroom, chandeliers, and carved wood ceilings. Almost incidentally they established a dairy with herds of purebred Guernsey and Holstein cattle.[16]

Figure 5.1. Ammon Hennacy at hard labor in Albuquerque. Permission of Josephine Thomas.

At first Hennacy was blind to Simms's role in the "water wars" sweeping the upper Rio Grande Basin, but this would be his initial education in western ecology and politics. Large and small property owners sued each other over the river's meager flow. Downstream obligations to Mexico, Native American tribes, and other towns were seldom met, as landowners from Albuquerque and the north diverted millions of gallons a year for irrigation. Still more water sank in the swampy oxbows and sandy flats of the river, replenishing the aquifer. "Prosperous investors such as Albert and Ruth Hanna McCormick Simms saw a great opportunity, and they quickly moved in to buy the formerly nearly worthless swampy field," write scholars Fred M. Phillips and colleagues: "But everyone could not share their enthusiasm. For most of the indigenous Hispanic farmers, the MRGDC [Middle Rio Grande Development Council] was an octopus that slowly squeezed them out of their livelihood."[17]

Simms, and Hennacy's later boss Charles C. Shirk, were constantly in the newspapers as plaintiffs or defendants in these lawsuits. Simms gambled that by driving out the small guys he could make the swampy oxbows into productive land. Hennacy worked first under one of his managers, a wily straw boss who taught him the lore about Simms and the Rio Grande. Naïve at first, impressed by the strangeness, Ammon described his new routine in a letter:

> If I do the work well, [Simms] will raise my pay to $70, which is what I was getting in Denver. Here I get up at 3:30 a.m., go out to the corral and get the cows and lock them in their places, wash and dry their bags, milk or strip a few if I have time and then turn out one "string" as they call it, and get in the next string. Six strings altogether. Then breakfast around 8:30 and clean the barn until around 10:30. Rest until 1 p.m. for dinner and then rest until after 3 p.m. when the business starts over. Through about 8 p.m. and have supper. A man and his two sons, another Mexican who lives nearby, and two young boys comprise the help—except two other Mexicans who help the son haul alfalfa each day. . . . We are a mile from the Sandia mountains. . . . It is here the McCormick boy and a friend fell off a cliff while climbing a few years ago. Ruth Hanna McCormick married Mr. Simms who owns this place. . . . No Social Security card is needed here, so I pay no Victory Tax.[18]

It was healthy, outdoor work that he liked, and it gave him time to read and write during breaks and evenings. He even borrowed books from the Simmses' library.[19] He liked Ruth, whose first husband had also died in a climbing accident, in part because she was "born in my hometown of Lisbon." But Albert Simms was crusty, having introduced himself to Ammon by saying, "The men who work for me here call me the old son of a bitch." But later that year, when Ammon published his "Tolstoy booklet," he asked Simms if he could use the ranch as a mailing address, and "he said to use it."

For this booklet he "read all of the 22 volumes of the Scribner [Tolstoy] edition and took hundreds of pages of notes, listing them on the subjects of Thou Shalt Not Kill, Christian Anarchism, The Simple Life, and Religion."[20] This had been prompted by the FOR "refusal to register" pamphlet, but was now expanded significantly.[21] Hennacy's precis of Tolstoy was basic Christianity and, while not responding to Hobbes's objection that humanity will always revert to a state for protection, he does anticipate a later debate between John Rawls in *Theory of Justice* and Robert Nozick's minimal state, or "minarchy," response. Rawls said that though some people may be bad, "rights" cannot be bartered. But they can be provided for, he said, without any need for formal government, by a kind of personalist distributism. Ammon agreed.

As he was writing these ideas down, Hennacy learned from the straw boss that before meeting Ruth, Simms had broken his first wife's will to collect an already forgiven fifty-thousand-dollar debt. He had also cheated an Italian family out of their land. The straw boss, recounting these things while they worked in the greenhouses, told Ammon to go ahead and pick some tomatoes for himself. Ammon cautiously picked a small one, but the straw boss said, "If you take a small one, you'll always be taking small ones; take a large one and you'll always have the best." Later, when Simms asked why there were only small tomatoes left, the straw boss answered that it was the breed. The ethos of the water lords, Ammon saw, spread downwards through their employees and came back to bite them.[22]

Ammon liked the dry, high (fifty-three-hundred feet) climate of Albuquerque, declaring that no one who had seen it would return to the "extreme heat and cold and wet weather" of the Midwest.[23] The town had a Spanish colonial past dating to the 1600s, growing larger in the 1880s when the Atchison, Topeka, and Santa Fe Railroad arrived. In the 1900s it was discovered to have an "ideal climate" for tuberculosis patients, and its location on Route 66 brought more people in the 1920s. It was a place with promise, and the population quadrupled between 1925 and 1941, when the US Army took over the airport, renaming it Kirtland Field.

The Sandia Labs on Kirtland soon began research on nuclear weapons, and though Ammon was at first focused on the Hispanic and Native American populations, he would soon write about the weapons. He had his books shipped from Denver, a sign that he was staying. He figured out how to make the sixty-five-mile trip to Santa Fe for $2.50 by striking a deal with a bus driver. Ever thrifty, he was still writing letters on old stationery from Milwaukee and Denver, but he considered New Mexico home.

His working life became a mosaic of small jobs. In slow times at Simms, he worked for an apiary, bottling honey, as he had in California, and "trap-nesting some prize chickens."[24] For a while he lived in a trailer, only bathing once a week, but he planted peas and revived his gardening interests. When sister Julia sent money from Ohio, he spent two dollars on one hundred pounds of wheat, which he cleaned, roasted, and had ground into flour for his family, hoping to remind them of Bisanakee. Selma did not say thanks, and she returned all the *Catholic Workers* and *Conscientious Objectors* with his articles that he had sent to his daughters. While honoring his role as pater familias, he began to wonder if he was not effectively divorced. He flirted with a girl named Pat in Simms's office and had casual sex with a Mexican woman.[25] What seems to have kept him formally married was his intense affection for his daughters.

Next he discovered that the land barons "loaned" out their workers as if they were chattel, for he himself was "sent" to a millionaire named Gardner west of the river. Like Simms, Gardner was gleeful about cheating others but furious when cheated. He was expanding his hen houses, so Ammon candled eggs for him and operated an egg sorter. He was paid the same and, while working for Gardner, lived in Simms's adobe with no plumbing. He hauled water from a well for cooking, and he used a nearby copse for relief. Here he started another small garden: "Planted beds of onion, spinach, lettuce, peas, string beans, carrots, and have irrigated them twice," he reported. "Have ground-cherries planted in a box in the house. Red-winged blackbirds by the hundreds coming and going. Work without any shirt or undershirt in the p.m. but put on two at night."[26] He wrote a lot, and Dorothy Day had become his muse; he wrote to her several times a week. But he was also writing letters to the *Albuquerque Tribune* and working on a novel about a Taos Native American girl, modeled on Sharon, titled *Unto the Least of These*.[27]

In Santa Fe Carmen and Sharon were performing at concerts and playing with the symphony, so he went to see their important performances, brimming with pride. But Selma kept him at arm's length. "My wife is getting more hard-boiled than ever," he wrote. "I bought a bus ticket and was supposed to go see them tomorrow. . . . Carmen's 16th birthday, but my wife writes forbidding me to enter the house, saying that if I come, she will get the court to keep me away. . . . She says I may meet the girls one day in the park in July."[28]

At night he wrote to conscientious objectors and old friends such as Roger Baldwin, who was starting Vanguard Press. He sought out local Quakers and spoke against the war and the draft. On Sundays he walked into Albuquerque, though it was a pro-war town, to hand out papers. His formal employment with Simms lasted until the spring of 1944, when he published his refusal to pay income taxes. Simms had tolerated the Tolstoy pamphlet, but now said, "You will be arrested tomorrow. . . . I will be disgraced for having harbored you in my employ."[29] So Simms sent Hennacy, like a serf, back to Gardner, who sent him to Charles C. Shirk on the south side of town.[30] Here is the core of the statement, re-published January 13, 1945, in the *Catholic Worker*:

I again refuse to pay any taxes to help prosecute a war which is a blas-phemy against God and a crime again the poor boys who are slaughtered at the command of scheming, senile and hypocritical politicians. To pay taxes toward the support of peacetime conscription, whereby the war sys-tem is saddled on us forever under the name of "democratic training" is being an accessory before the fact of legal murder, and I refuse to take part in it. In my statement of refusal to register for this war in Milwaukee, Wisconsin, as printed in the *Catholic Worker* for May 1942, and in my re-fusal to pay taxes in March 1944, I have given sufficient reasons to support the logic of my action, predicting the following events which are now history. Power politics are supreme; Communist Russia grabs Baltic and Balkan countries, while England creates her bloc in Western Europe and the Mediterranean, denies freedom to India, and swears to "hold what we have got." Meanwhile our boys are doing the fighting and dying, sup-posedly for the repudiated Atlantic Charter. The common soldier and the common citizen are aware of the situation and whisper about it but lack the courage to be different from the crowd.

"The tax office did nothing about it," Ammon wrote.

Shirk Dairy and Upland Orchard

His new employer, Shirk, was buying up the apple orchards. His land occupied a verdant bend on the east side of the Rio Grande. He had started Shirk Dairy around 1910 and grown with the city. Before pasteurization was widespread, even a city like Albuquerque had north- and south-side dairies. Cows were milked by hand and large tracts of arable land were devoted to raising silage, for which Shirk was famous: a picture in the *Albuquerque Journal* showed his son with twenty-two-foot-tall corn plants. Ammon lived an almost bucolic life at Shirk's for several years. Shirk paid him one hundred dollars a month and two quarts of milk a day, "plus living quarters, stove, bed and fuel." He was officially an orchardman: "Today I started my new job on this ranch in the garden. Wage the same, but as a Tolstoian and vegetarian I like the work better." He also worked in the dairy and started learning the art and craft of irrigation. The farm would soon employ German prisoners of war, housed at the nearby airfield, with Ammon as their nominal boss.[31]

From Shirk's it was a two-hour walk or a thirty-minute bus ride to downtown Albuquerque, where he could talk at churches against the draft and war. But he was increasingly drawn south to the Isleta Pueblo and sometimes went to the Catholic church there. He began to write articles for the *Catholic Worker* about this life, which Dorothy Day liked, especially an early one about the cows he milked.[32]

> I thought that I had been used to handling cranky people on relief, and I ought to handle cranky cows too. So I asked the boss to give me the job of stripping her. He was surprised, but I have been doing it since. I am not afraid, but I have to watch myself, for she kicks at me nearly every time.
>
> This small farm lies in the shadow of the Sandia mountains (watermelon in Spanish). They are 10,000 ft. high. . . . Days are bright, nights cool; no snow; no rain this time of year; beautiful sunrise and sunset every day. Extinct volcanoes to the west. I am privileged to see sunrise each morning, as I am then cleaning out the barn. At night I finish at sunset, so I lose none of the beauty of this country in my work.[33]

This piece was one of the first in his new persona, the literary face of Christian anarchism and voluntary poverty. He had the same family and ethical dilemmas as before, but his new locale seemed to make his prose more descriptive. These columns in the *Catholic Worker* came to be known as his "Life at Hard Labor." He made his life into a demonstration that "voluntary poverty," advocated by Catholics from St. Francis to Peter Maurin and by Americans like John Woolman and Henry David Thoreau, was entirely possible in 1944. Not all of his new writing is translucent, but the short pieces, often edited by Dorothy Day, reveal a modern, threadbare Thoreau in the making. The tax statement above reminds us of how Thoreau the writer stepped out of his bean fields, but for Hennacy the contemplative background was increasingly the West and Native Americans, especially the Hopis, about whom he wrote two pages for the *Catholic Worker* in April 1945. This was the start of another transformation.[34]

Though earning a pittance, one of Hennacy's projects was to buy Carmen an expensive watch for her graduation from Santa Fe High. She had been promised a scholarship to the University of New Mexico, where Ammon believed that she would go, but Selma intervened: it had to be Northwestern University. But she did not tell him and, as in New York, she had no idea of what private schools cost. At graduation in June 1945, Ammon stayed overnight in a hotel, thinking he would give Carmen her present in the morning. But he could not locate them, not then or in the next week. It was Shirk, on his way to Colorado to sell a load of apples, who delivered the bad news. He had stopped at Selma's in Santa Fe to leave a bushel of apples, at Ammon's request, but no one was home and the landlady said they had moved to Denver. Ammon was shocked: "I knew nothing about it. Don't see how she has the money to move around."[35]

Letters indicate that Selma finally wrote to him, and that he sent her money (for which she said thanks). She confessed that she had sold the pianos and furniture that he had paid for to finance her trip. She would not reveal her address, so he wrote back care of General Delivery. Not until Christmas would Hennacy see his daughters, on what would be his last cross-country hitchhiking trip. In letters he did try to sweet-talk Selma back into civility, addressing her as "bunny rabbit" and bringing up the Big Hike, but she was in no mood for reconciliation. First, she sent back Carmen's graduation watch (to General Delivery), saying that it didn't work. Then she fired off a five-page letter accusing him of defaming the I AM. A few lines deliver the tone of the whole.[36]

I gather from your remarks that you are part of the Stalin-sting and *smear* campaign. Get the attention of someone, make a seeming complimentary remark about another person, then *just before you* close, send out a few stinging *smear* statements.

Do you know that several *past friends*, whom I *did not* contact, while visiting Milwaukee, are *wholly disgusted* with your attitude?

In Los Angeles I told you there were a million communists in *key* positions. Your answer: "That is an exaggeration." *Look* and see what is being *uncovered* these days! So shall you see *other* things revealed—that you have *scoffed* at. This experience closes my *physical door* to you. . . . *You have* nothing to offer but *words*. I have proved some things; I have *much more* to prove.[37] (emphases in original)

Five days later Ammon made a patient reply. "You knew that I was opposed to war when we were married," he wrote: "You claim that I have always left you in the lurch when you needed me. . . . But I have sent you 4/5 or more of what I made."[38] He would get to visit his daughters briefly in 1945, but after that he did not see them until 1948 in San Francisco, when they were young women at arm's length from the I AM.

Hennacy did not mind working for Shirk; it was opening new vistas. "Yesterday I went with my employer after some young cattle he had left for the summer in the Jemez mountains, 80 miles n.w. of here. Very beautiful scenery. Went through 4 pueblos; different colored corn was drying on the ground, red peppers hanging against the adobe walls; small irrigated field, Jemez River on one side and the beautiful colored walls of the canyon on the other. Further up were huge pine trees; 10,000 ft. elevation. I like this desert country. . . . Why would anyone live in a city after seeing this?—that is what I thought."

He was feeling like part of a community too. In the two-room adobe behind him lived the seven Sandovals, whose daughter Lipa befriended Ammon. Mrs. Sandoval frequently invited him to dinner, where Lipa laughed at his handling of tacos. Shirk may not have been a good farmer, but he allowed the Sandovals and locals to glean the orchards after harvest and Ammon liked that, recalling the hobos who tramped through the orchards in Negley.

But then suddenly Shirk sold the orchards to Chester B. Gibson, who also mismanaged them and eventually sold them back to Shirk. They moved pieces of land like checkers in the water wars. Hennacy stayed on, technically in the employ of his original boss. Now that he could see their inefficiencies—something of Old Mr. Zicher lingered with him—he judged both men to be slack farmers. "I have picked about 800 bu. [of apples] and only 150 have been sold. . . . Shirk loaned my services to Mr. Gibson for the orchard work. Plenty of apples left to pick yet; if we had buyers for many of them . . . it would all be done in a hurry. As it is, we will pick until a freeze comes."[39]

By fall Ammon was mentioning the prisoners of war who were beginning to appear. "A young German prisoner is helping me these days. He and others go around without a guard." Probably at Ammon's urging, Shirk tried to find more workers: "My boss put an ad in the C.O. paper . . . would like to have more C.O.s here."[40] The CO conservation camps back east were very successful. The COs made excellent workers, but there is no evidence that Shirk found any; instead, he used more prisoners of war. As more POW camps were established, Wheeler Field became a destination for German prisoners. It was a hastily built basic bombing school, adjacent to the city airport, with most of the Germans housed farther south at Roswell and Lordsburg. Those who came to Kirtland were judged no flight risk, put in "hutments" beside the main road, and hired out to farmers like Shirk. They were a sideline to the training of bombardiers on the range that stretched from Los Lunas to Rio Puerco, covering 2,450 square miles by 1942. There were day and night bombing runs beginning in January, which Ammon could hear every night.

The POWs were a daily reminder of the war. When Gibson hired his first POW, Hennacy dusted off his high school German. He liked the German's work ethic and silence, his familiarity with pruning and with bread and cider making. "For the last month a German prisoner picks apples with me in the orchard," he wrote. "No guard is around. He is 23. He was brought up a Nazi and still is one. I know a little German and he a little English, so we get along." On Sundays "when I go into town with the C.W.s I walk on the highway past the prisoner's [sic] barracks and they wave at me and during the week kid me about 'going to the Kirke [sic].'" Ammon got in the habit of going early, to "say my own prayers my own way. I also say them in the orchard, which is just as good, I think. I fraternize with [them], which is against the Army rules, but I am not in the Army."[41]

Nature Writing

Like Thoreau, Hennacy began to meditate in his letters on the rhythms of work: "When chopping wood, I have thought of the deep breaths taken, and the satisfaction of the slowly growing pile of wood. While if a buzz saw were used, there would be much more danger of losing a finger—and instead of the sweet smell of the wood there is a dusty, musty smell."[42] He was exploring the nearby Mexican settlement: "Half a dozen Mexican families live in shacks between the shack I live in and the orchard. I keep them supplied with fruit. The children are such sturdy and interesting youngsters. They invite me in for beans and chili often and I can eat without a spoon—using a tortilla. They get a lot of fun out of my attempts to speak Spanish."[43]

Despite the loss of his family, he was rediscovering a love of agrarian life, and his writing was more "in the moment," despite some forced notes. In many of his pieces in the *Catholic Worker* he anticipates the nature writing, twenty years later, of Josephine Johnson, Annie Dillard, and Edward Abbey.

The first stop my boss, our Mexican housekeeper, and myself made was at the twig encircled stump where the mourning dove had her very poorly constructed nest, the worst built of any bird. She was gone. At our approach, Little Brother attacked the air wildly with his bill and when we came nearer, he flapped his wings at us, standing up bravely. Little Sister—for they are always born in pairs—never blinked an eye, resting peacefully as if aware of her maternal function which later was to tell her not to leave the eggs entrusted to her care.

Thousands of bees buzzed contentedly among the blossoms of our thousands of apple trees. The seeming far-away sound of the mourning dove, the chirp of the robin, and the shrill note of the meadow lark drowned out in our consciousness the noise of the product of the Merchants of Death in training over our heads. My boss says that the meadowlark calls out "John Greenleaf Whittier." I had not thought of the call of this bird as being a Quaker name before.

As my boss and our housekeeper were planting young trees, they came near where I was irrigating, for the water from our well runs day and night from April to November; and as he glanced up at the airplane overhead he said, "We have done more good for humanity this morning planting fruit bearing trees than the munitions makers of all time."

Here in the orchard all impatience, ill temper, wrath at the perverse sinfulness of mankind, disappear. A calmness, a peace reigns, the oneness with Mother Nature: grower and producer, hemmed in for activity in our Rio Grande Valley by the rolling mountains to be seen at every hand, and presided over by the same Father Sun whose rays had given light and warmth to his worshippers in the neighboring pueblos.

As we left the orchard for dinner, my boss, veteran of the Villa campaign, World War I, and myself, veteran pacifist, closed our morning worship in God's Outdoors: a church with no membership list, no Mammon worship, and free to all who release themselves from the bondage of the city; whose only admittance is calloused hands and whose only sacrament is kindness toward all of God's creatures, including man. Spontaneously we sang the doxology and "My Country 'Tis of Thee."[44]

Just before Ammon was about to leave on his Christmas visit to the East and see his daughters, Scott Nearing showed up. Together they "had a supper of vegetarian salad with cider and cottage cheese at a friend's house and then visited at the home of principal of the Indian School there . . . [who] invited me over to meet some young Hopis. [If] I have a vacation next year, I may go and visit the Hopis."[45] When he did, that tribe would give him an invaluable perspective on voluntary social organization.

The best of Hennacy's *Catholic Worker* columns came as the war raged, from these orchards, possibly because of his need to use the resources at hand as the canvas for an abstract message to be read by a distant audience. The simplicity of his life had something to say. Both as theme and as technique, "simplicity" became, like a Shaker chair, the art of revealing how much can be done without:

At this dairy I live in an old adobe house. Father Sun, as the Indians speak of the ball of fire, rising over the Sandia (Spanish for watermelon) mountains to the east filters through the mulberry and cottonwood trees to my open door. I turn in bed and relax. A prayer for those near and dear and for those loved ones far away; in and out of prison and CO camp, and in and out of man's holocaust: war. The night before I had cooked unpolished rice sprinkled with raisins. With milk, and the whole wheat bread I have baked, my breakfast is soon finished. It is now 8 o'clock. I go to the dairy to see if any change has been made in plans for work for the day. If my student friend in the milk truck appears, he will take my letters to the mailbox; otherwise I will take them myself.

Readers warmed to these domestic snippets and wanted to know what he did the rest of the time, especially in his evenings, an interplay that suggested more topics for columns: below is Ammon's follow-up.

The mailman comes in the afternoon. Perhaps today I receive several letters from boys in C.O. camps, discussing Tolstoy and bringing up questions which puzzle them. It is now 6 p.m. and I go to the dairy for my quart of milk, perhaps carry a can of water also, and chop wood for half an hour. Evenings are cool and even in the summer a cover is required. The apple, cherry and peach wood burns brightly in the fireplace. Even twigs burn well in the range.

It is now early April and asparagus, which has come up for years throughout the orchard, presents a fine supper for the vegetarian. Many times with a half pint of milk, a little pepper and shortening added, it makes a filling and delicious meal. At other times slowly fried and mixed with rice it gives a flavor resembling oysters. (Some meat-eater may correct me, for I have not tasted oysters for thirty years.)

A picture of Jesus at the carpenter's bench finally wore out after I had put it up and taken it down when moving around. My half-pacifist young Lutheran minister friend, Leeland Soker, gave me Sallman's "Head of Christ." My unorthodox array of "Saints" on the wall are Tolstoy, Debs, Thoreau, Jefferson, Abdul Baha, St. Francis, Vanzetti and Gandhi.

Tradition tells of treasure hid here in this house at the time of Indian raids. For the house was once an old fort in the times when the whites were encroaching upon the Indian country. The treasure that I have found here was buried, all right—buried deep within my personality, and it took the peace and quiet, the productive labor among kindly, common and everyday sort of people to discover it.

Unlike Thoreau, for whom the purpose of writing fine detail or observing nature closely was ultimately a connection to a transcendental Oversoul, Hennacy kept his details in the here and now. The point was the work, a Franciscan focus on doing good in nature's order, not on transcending it. It is through work that harmony emerges: work relates to food, food to taxes, and taxes to vegetarianism. The more one reads of Hennacy, the more logical his worldview seems:

> Old timers here and there along this Rio Grande have watermills where corn is ground between two stones. They go with exceedingly slow motion but there is no cost, and these stones have been grinding for centuries. If it is possible to get my blue corn and wheat ground at such a mill I will do so; if not, the hammer mill of my employer can grind it. The primitive way of cutting wheat, binding it by hand (for few people raise wheat and use a binder here) and threshing it out by hand on canvas seems queer. By itself it may seem foolish, but taken as part of a pattern of life it has meaning. Orthodox economists tell us that the farmer who uses a horse and a plow and very little machinery cannot afford to compete in the market with the farmer who uses up-to-date machinery.
>
> It happens that I do not care to own property and have it taken away by the government for non-payment of taxes, for most of the taxes in my lifetime will go to pay for World War II and to prepare for World War III. One who eats meat can raise a few hogs and chickens in the country and here turkeys do well. For a vegetarian who simplifies his needs, the cash that is needed for certain purposes can be earned as a farm laborer; and most of the food to be consumed can be raised on an acre or two. To raise food for animals and then eat the animals is expensive. Why not raise the grain and eat it yourself?

Even as Hennacy parts in ultimate aim from Thoreau (who was not a vegetarian or a pacifist), he finds the voluntary poverty of the Concord sage useful and imitates Thoreau's publication of his budget. So we peer with curiosity into Ammon's private economy:

My Budget
I keep ten dollars for expenses and send the remainder to my wife and girls. During the month of May 1945 my expenses were as follows:

Whole wheat flour, 25 lbs .... $1.25 (could grow own wheat)
Vegetable shortening, 3 lbs...................... .68
Cornmeal, 5 lbs.. .46 (could grow own corn)
Oleomargarine, 2 lbs............................... .38
Rice, 4 lbs... .58 (price is too high)
Raisins, 2 lbs .... .23
Syrup, 5 lbs .... .47
Yeast, salt, sugar, etc................................ .50
—Total 4.55

Electric light bill 1.00
Bundle of CO and CWs 2.40
Postage stamps, haircut, etc. 2.05
—Total $10.00

I bought a quantity of pinto beans (seconds) last year and still have some left. Have a few jars of apple butter which I put up last fall. Get a quart of milk free from the farm daily, and asparagus, wild lettuce, and later fruit and vegetables. Irish potatoes do not grow well here. The ones that you buy at the store now are not worth the money, so I buy rice instead. Another year I should get a few hives of bees. Reading of the bread-making at Mott St. and of Cobbett's old-fashioned way of bread making, and of Catherine de Heuck's rye bread encouraged me to persevere until I can now say that I make as good bread as I have ever tasted. Here is my method. . . .

And what he proceeds to describe is his method of making *tortillas*. The deadpan humor, this new prose style, the unexpected understatement would not have been possible for Ammon if he had not removed himself from the tensions of Milwaukee and Denver, been forced to look hard at a new reality, and taken up his new local resources. There were new styles of anarchist thought developing in Berkeley and Seattle, where young anarchists like the poet Kenneth Rexroth were breaking away from the insurrectionist Italians and doctrinaire Marxists, but for Ammon in Albuquerque they did not seem very different from the bohemian anarchists he had seen in Manhattan in the 1920s. In New Mexico he saw something new and different: a decentralized communitarian agrarianism undergirded by centuries of Indo-Hispanic and Catholic practice. He wove these elements together gracefully, for example, in describing his growing mastery of irrigation.

> It is Sunday morning. I get up at 5.45, eat a hurried breakfast, take my good clothing in a grip along with about 50 *Catholic Workers* and go to the orchard to look over the situation of the water, which has been running all night. Here the water has gone into another row and missed half a dozen acres; there it is dammed up with weeds and a furrow. I channel the water in the proper places and look over the next row for potential breaks and turn the water into this new row. I oil the pump, and then a dash of cold water livens me up. Change my clothes and walk a mile down the road to the seminary chapel, where I give a CW to each person as they enter for 7:30 mass. Then I walk the ten miles toward town. Many times a workman picks me up.

Suffice it to say that Hennacy's mastery of the tortilla would have seemed exotic at his mother's house in Cleveland, not to mention his easy intercultural relations. True, he was appropriating cultures he did not understand, but in 1945 he was doing the great service of introducing lay Catholics, union members, and eastern intellectuals to a world most of them had barely heard about. But he was not writing travel literature: the point was that right there, among each and every one of them, was the antidote for what ailed them, an "indigenous" model of a simpler, more satisfying, equalitarian life. He illustrated this solution without stridency, without even seeming rhetorical. But he had an even more effective campaign in mind, a narrative from the point of view of the natives to whom he distributed *CW*s. He did not pretend to "know them," but he worked to integrate them into his columns. Below

at length is a passage in which he presses his own case without conde-
scending, more difficult than it might appear, especially for Ammon:

> One Sunday morning in June I arose early, picked a cup of mulberries
> from the bush at my door, which with sugar and cream and some bread
> made a delicious breakfast. I had borrowed a bicycle from Lipa's brother
> Joe, and after attending to the irrigation of the orchard I started down
> the road to the Indian reservation in which is located the Pueblo of Is-
> leta, seven miles to the south. The road was uphill and down and quite
> sandy, so that progress was slow. Here it wound along the edge of the bluff
> overlooking the two ribbons of the Rio Grande with a wide expanse of
> sandbars between. Horses grazed on the lush grass along the river in the
> lowlands near the Santa Fe bridge. Coming into Isleta a rather large adobe
> house with buildings of the same material occupied the corner between
> the road and the bridge. An Indian with an exceedingly large brimmed
> hat was feeding some animals. An auto, partly dismantled, stood in the
> yard. Just south of the bridge is the dam which throws the water through
> the spillways for the reservation. . . .
>
> The houses were on narrow semi-streets winding here and there, as in
> Santa Fe, and each yard held farm machinery, wood, and the familiar
> wagon in which I had often seen the Indians from the orchard on their
> way to town. Nearly every woman who came to the door spoke to me in
> English and thanked me for the paper. Several extremely wrinkled old
> men came to the door, and although they may not have understood just
> what it was they received, thanked me for the paper.

Ironically, as Hennacy was creating this setting and persona, there was
hardly anyone in the vicinity who knew that he was writing. His audience was elsewhere and largely urban, reading itself into his imaginary.
There was no one to correct, to argue with, or to contradict him.

> On the bicycle as I was going through the Pueblo toward home, several
> children and older folks recognized my white attire and waved to me. A
> jeep full of guards from the German prison camp passed me, and one of
> them who knew me wondered what I was doing down there. They had
> often met me as I had passed their camp on the way to church on Sunday
> mornings. Nearing home, I stopped for a drink of water at the home of

cousins of Lipa whom I had met before. As soon as I got home, a look at the well in the orchard proved that the water was running properly. I was very hungry and prepared a good bowl of rice and raisins with a dash of cinnamon and nutmeg, then went to the orchard to turn the water into another row for the night.

Aside from Dorothy Day, who no doubt edited these pieces, there was no other voice on the Catholic Left so rural and folksy or so western in 1945. There were few other agrarian, ecological pacifists at all. Even Scott Nearing was for the war.

One More Big Hike

To get enough money to visit his daughters in Evanston, Hennacy worked seven days a week without overtime to earn a month off at the end of 1945. With the gift of a woolen sleeping bag from Shirk, he set out at sunrise on December 15, headed "eastward over the pass toward Amarillo." It was like the Big Hike, except that he was fifty-two years old and spending a very cold month on the road was not something he had done since high school in East Palestine. Walking and accepting rides, never thumbing, he reached Tucumcari just as the temperature fell below ten degrees. "I came about an hour after dark to a farmhouse and asked if I could sleep in a shed or barn. It was bitter cold, and the man asked me in the house to get warm. Later he insisted that I occupy a spare bed in an enclosed porch, saying that I could sleep in my sleeping bag any time. His forecast was correct, for of the twenty-two nights that I did not stay with relatives, this New Mexican was the only farmer who allowed me on his place."

The days of the easy road were over. The next day "hundreds of cars passed without noticing me," until finally a young couple stopped and "crowded themselves to allow me to sit with them in the front seat. We struck a snowstorm as we arrived in Oklahoma City." The roads were full of soldiers hitchhiking home for Christmas or, if they had money, riding in packed buses. Tourist camps and even Salvation Army dorms were filled. At one point Ammon slept in the drunk tank of a jail, and it was cold there too. The days were very short; he got disoriented by the early darkness and lack of signage in Sterling, Illinois, going into an all-night diner for coffee and to regain his bearings. The owner let him sleep on potato sacks in the basement, where at 5:00 a.m. a waiter woke him: "A trucker would take me as far as Joliet."

That was the worst day of the trip. "Sleet on the highway and windshield. . . . The truck broke down and after much walking and a few rides, I met my wife and girls. The activities of their sect did not allow my radical aura to befog the atmosphere, so I went to Milwaukee for Christmas."[46] He did learn that "both girls earn their tuition, which is very high, clothes, etc. They aim to become composers. They still follow that I AM religion along with my wife, but they are sweet, unspoiled girls."[47]

In Milwaukee he expected to see Bill Ryan, who was now free, but his wife, Alba, held a grudge due to the mail kerfuffle, and was keeping Bill away from his old crowd (though later she would help Hennacy in Salt Lake City). So Ammon went to Cleveland to visit his mother and sisters, who offered to buy him a bus ticket back, but he rigidly objected to any purchase that might result in a tax paid to the government. Instead, he walked west out of Cleveland, getting a ride from a fearless woman who said she always picked up strangers. She dropped him at a coffee shop, whose owner was having a nervous breakdown, so Ammon stayed and worked for the family for two days. He felt called, he wrote: "All things work together for good to those who love the good—God."

This trip had begun with a simple desire to see his daughters, but it was becoming eerily spiritual. When he stepped out of the coffee shop on the third day, a taxi stopped apropos of nothing and took him all the way to a Toledo convent that Dorothy Day had visited a few weeks earlier. "Knocking on the convent door, I asked for Sister Columbiere. I was ushered into the parlor and soon the sister arrived, wondering how I knew her name. I showed her a copy of the December CW in which her name was mentioned, which she had not seen." After dinner he attended benediction in the chapel, "hearing with pleasure the clear voice of Sister Columbiere singing." He slept in a loft over the garage, leaving in the morning with enough snacks to feed him all the way to Chicago.

Among the old radical friends he met again in Chicago was Claude McKay, the Harlem Renaissance poet. McKay was a friend of Dorothy Day and a recent Catholic convert, disenchanted with communism. He had traveled to the USSR and seen Stalinism, and then gone to Spain,

Figure 5.2. Ammon Hennacy with his daughters, Sharon and Carmen. Permission of Josephine Thomas and Marquette University.

where he had met Bill Ryan and "felt for the first time the full significance of Catholicism as a way of life and bedrock for an entire civilization." McKay was in failing health after a 1942 heart attack, moving between temporary jobs and friends' apartments, and looking for a stable place to write. He had just suffered a disabling stroke while working for the Port of Newark, and he was in Chicago staying with Catholic friends, whose network would soon send him west to Hennacy.

Passing back through Chicago, Ammon managed to see Sharon outside her practice studio near Northwestern and to walk with Carmen for a few blocks, but his daughters, the motive for his travel, had minimal time for him. Leaving town, he was picked up by a man who asked where he was going. Somewhat disconsolate, he said, "To the monastery." In his autobiography he claimed to have seen the mirage of one, but he had been playing with the notion of visiting the New Melleray Trappist monastery near Dubuque, Iowa, because Dorothy Day had recommended it. After his ride dropped him off, he walked toward it in a blowing snowstorm. "Cars had slipped off the road, but the pilgrim on foot made it all right. Nine miles farther on I heard the bells of the monastery tolling on the right."

Founded by monks from Waterford, Ireland, in 1849, this monastery supported itself by making caskets. The theme of mortality, combined with the weather, made for a somber visit, but Hennacy was taken in hand by Brother Joachim, with whom he discussed vegetarianism over dinner. The monks ate no animals, Hennacy learned, "not out of any special regard for animals or health" but out of penance. That was news to him and somewhat Gandhian, a potential addition to his developing ideas of embodiment. Everyone went to bed early, Ammon included, because they got up at 2:00 a.m. and prayed until breakfast at 8:00 a.m. Ammon was intrigued that fifty-seven monks slept in one room "somewhat like voting booths with canvas partitions. They sleep with their robes on." It reminded him of his Denver dairy cubicle and of SRO hotels on the Bowery in New York, and he stored away this model, using it later when he opened the Joe Hill House. He stayed until 2:00 p.m. the next day, when Brother Joachim led him out into the bitter cold.

It took several rides to get across the "long, dreary stretches of Nebraska." He believed that he passed "the exact spot where Crazy Horse had put blankets on the hoofs of horses and escaped the U.S. military patrol a half a century before."[48] Then he walked and rode to Denver, where he visited old friend Helen Ford. He left after a day, hitchhiking as far as Walsenburg, Colorado, where he spent a very cold night under a bridge. "When I awoke, two inches of snow covered me," he wrote: "I had not been cold during the night, but my fingers were nearly frozen by the time I had tied up my pack."[49]

By the time he reached Albuquerque, he had walked 490 miles of this 3,000-mile trip (he still had the pedometer). But he had misunderstood the terms of his leave and "Shirk only paid me for half a month when I came back, but will pay me for all the Sundays I work, so I will make $150 more in a year and will send it to the girls. It is not likely that I will take a vacation this year, if Selma is not working."[50]

There was a note of relief in Hennacy's letters as he settled back in. "As soon as I got to New Mexico," he wrote to his mother, "I did not cough anymore." "Mr. Shirk is giving me a flat top desk with drawers and a filing cabinet that he got from the airbase. Tell Julia that I am reading *The Perennial Philosophy* by Aldous Huxley." He was now sharing his small, unheated adobe in the orchards with an ex-soldier "who rooms next to me and needs all of the blankets in this cold weather, so I sleep in my sleeping bag."[51]

By the spring of 1946, Hennacy was becoming the advocate of his Latinx neighbors. "White people do not pay Mexicans . . . enough for their work. Shirk paid Lipa's brother, Joe, $60 a month for the first year and now pays him $65. While he pays good-for-nothing drunken whites $100 a month. Joe is the best worker he has. But white people say 'He's a Mexican. I would not pay him as much as a white man.' Same to the Indians—and with Negros in the South." He was now a regular guest in Lipa's kitchen, and he delighted in her children, who greeted him in Spanish. "Spanish people stick with their families very much and generally visit a lot and help each other when in trouble," he wrote. "A common expression among . . . Mexicans and Indians is 'He has no manners. He's a white. What do you expect?' The dirtiest Mexican or Indian child has more manners than more grown up young white people. Shirk's 11-year-old boy has no manners at all."[52]

In May he received a telegram from Claude McKay, who had dropsy now, a consequence of his heart disease and high blood pressure. He was looking for someplace high and dry in which to recover; in fact, he was arriving in two weeks. Ammon and Sister Agnes de Sales met him at the Rio Grande station and took him to St. Joseph's Hospital, where they had found him a room. There was such Jim Crow racism in town that they had to enlist Monsignor Garcia to make even that possible, and the bed they got him was on a porch.[53] "He was nearly dead with diabetes, heart trouble and dropsy when he arrived and had to be put under an oxygen tent," wrote Ammon, who visited several times a week. "Claude told me that his mother and grandmother died of this same condition. He does not seem to realize how bad he is. His legs are not swollen anymore, as they were when he came, but water is in the main part of his body. It is a wonder that he stood the shock of moving. I will go in again this Thursday night."[54]

Ammon, now entering an intensively Catholic phase, prayed daily for McKay. "Claude passed the crisis and in about six weeks was well enough to be released," he wrote. But McKay was hardly ready to travel.[55] Ammon had thought he could use a cottage at Shirk's, but now Shirk said that it would not be free for several months. Finding a place for McKay to recuperate should be easy, Ammon thought, but he was rejected at six places where he inquired. He was surprised by the systemic racism: "I would be glad to have him live with me," Ammon wrote to his mother, adding that his place was too small: "I never realized how prejudiced most people are."[56] Finally, Hennacy and Monsignor Garcia found a room in the Mexican section of town, where McKay wrote most of *My Green Hills*, but not until September 1946 was he fit to travel.[57]

Ever since childhood Ammon had cultivated an interest in Native Americans. He and Selma had spent a week at Taos pueblo during their 1925 travels.[58] After moving to Albuquerque, he met Hopis through his contacts at Isleta, which he wrote about in "Ammon among the Indians" (*Catholic Worker*, July/August 1945). According to scholar Brian Haley, he probably learned about Hopi draft resisters earlier that spring from the conscientious-objector weekly *Pacifica News* (March 30, 1945).[59] He also reviewed Laura Thompson and Alice Joseph's *Hopi Way* (Chicago, 1944), a copy of which he sent to Thompson. She responded warmly with added insight on the Hopi draft resisters: "The refusal of the men to register was apparently a part of a pattern [at Hotevilla] which extends as far as objecting to signing their names on any document whatsoever. In the case of the draft, this behavior fit in with their pacifist attitude toward life."

After reading up, Hennacy decided that the Hopis were the "most anarchist" tribe, and he began to take their side in all conflicts, even against the neighboring Navajos. He would visit, make friends with, and write about them for almost twenty years, leading Haley to write that Hennacy was "key" to the ascent of the Hopi as "the Counter-Culture's Favorite Indian."[60] As early as August 1945, he was musing about living among them and wrote to Chester Mote. In September he wrote to Don Talayesva, whose autobiography *Sun Chief* he had been reading, part of his research on the Hopis at the University of New Mexico library.

The Isleta pueblo south of his orchard home had been his initial window into the Native American world, but its complex past precluded the kind of ideological and cultural clarity that Hennacy sought. During the Pueblo Revolt of 1680, for example, many Isleta people had fled to Hopi settlements in present-day Arizona, "returning with Hopi spouses." But he also found a key there. In the 1800s "friction with members of the Laguna Pueblo and Acoma Pueblo . . . led to the founding of the satellite community of Oraibi."[61] For Ammon this indicated a system of peaceful conflict resolution that had its deeper roots in the ancient Hopi communities to the north. "I had been visiting the Indians at Isleta pueblo all along. When the Atom Bomb was exploded at nearby Alamogordo in the previous July none of us knew at the time what it was." For Hennacy it was the time to go north and west.

Isleta had taught him much, but it was the Hopi conscientious objectors he truly admired.[62] In his letters home, he was full of praise:

> Very few of them are converts to Christianity. Five of them went to jail against the war. In their language there are no swear words. . . . They do not drink; have no jails, police, courts, and no one has ever committed murder or suicide there in 1000 years. . . . I am writing to some of them and will visit them in time. In dealing with one another and outsiders, the worst sin is to have revenge or try to "get even" with anyone who does them wrong. There is nothing in the Christian religion as practiced by the churches which is any improvement on the Hopi religion.[63]

This was a very idealized view, full of exaggerations, but their supposed purity aligned the Hopis with the Gandhian "embodiment" that glued his syncretistic religious views together. Pacifism had to be lived in daily work and bodily practices, which it appeared that the Hopis were doing.

Ironically, it was Shirk, who liked to take long road trips to sell apples or to research property, who piqued Hennacy's interest in moving on. That trip to the Jemez pueblo had been the start.[64] Then Ammon met Chester Mote, one of the Hopi COs, in Winslow, Arizona. Mote, who ran four hundred sheep in Keams Canyon, had been jailed by the government when he refused to reduce their number. In theory Ammon sympathized, though he was not unaware of overgrazing as a problem.[65] Then some small slight by Shirk left Ammon disgruntled. He suddenly gave notice and moved with his few possessions to Flagstaff, in northern Arizona, where he could be closer to the Hopis. It is fair to say that in New Mexico Ammon learned, like Claude McKay in Spain, "the full significance of Catholicism as a way of life and bedrock for an entire civilization."

6

Becoming "Ammon Hennacy"

Phoenix

Ammon lived rough in Arizona, working the fields with migrant laborers.

> I slept at the home of a friend in Phoenix and got up early before daylight, went down to the "slave market" at Second and Jefferson, and jumped on the first truck going out of town. I did not know if I was going east, west, north, or south. I worked in a field for a big produce company and at night asked whether I could have a cabin to stay in. Shacks were only for Mexicans and not for white men, they said. I walked down the road and met a Molokan who said he had a shack up the road which I could live in, free of charge.[1] I was soon sleeping on an old spring mattress. I got an old stove and fixed the place up.[2]

By his fifty-fourth birthday, he had also found a typewriter and was pecking out letters and articles. Soon he had a piece on prison reform published in the *Arizona Republic*.[3] Through an extremely hot summer, Hennacy worked the fields for sixty cents an hour, harvesting beet seed, cleaning ditches, and cutting wood (which paid seventy-five cents an hour). While picking lettuce he met a right-wing employer who was illiterate: "When we signed our names to our checks, this farmer made an X mark." When he saw another fellow mark his check with an X, Ammon understood the farmer, distrustful of giving his name to the government, to be asking *sotto voce* if he had a Social Security card. So he said no, adding that he did not want to pay tax to the government. The illiterate farmer approved of that, but Ammon was probably struck by how the political Right and Left met on that issue in this place.[4]

In other fields, Hennacy picked cotton. Only he and the Native Americans did not own sacks, renting them from the boss for twenty-five cents a day. The cotton was tall, harder to pick than the short variety, while the field was a mile long and a quarter-mile wide. "I had never picked tall cotton before," he wrote: it "was difficult to extract and hurt your fingers." The Navajo next to him said it was supposed to be "clean picking," no parts of the boll allowed, and as they worked down the rows, the Navajo spoke of his childhood in reservation schools, of government projects that supposedly "rehabilitated" the tribe.[5] The cotton pickers were the real dispossessed, Ammon learned, and his own shack looked good by comparison. Using the style he developed in New Mexico, he extended that approach to his writing about this life, which was unchanged since 1920.

> I went early in the morning to Phoenix, where the bonfires were burning at Second and Madison. Here Mexicans, Indians and Anglos, most of the latter being "winos," were waiting to select the truck in which they would go to work. Just now there were only cotton trucks, there being a lull in citrus picking. Cotton pickers carry their own bags behind them like giant worms. There were eight trucks and several pickups. Most of them were shaped like the traditional covered wagon with canvas. There were benches on either side and in the middle. I walked around searching for someone I might know, but my friends of the lettuce fields were wary of cotton picking, considering this the hardest job to be had and one to be taken only as a last resort.
>
> "Last call! Take you there and bring you back. Three dollars a hundred. All aboard gentlemen!" shouted a good-natured Negro in a bright mackinaw. The truck to which he pointed was box-shaped, of wood veneer, with a short ladder leaning inside from the rear. I entered and found a seat between a colored woman and a colored man. After a few more calls the doors were shut and we could see each other only as one would light a cigarette. Later the truck stopped, and we were joined by a large group of laughing Negros of all ages. There were three whites besides myself and one Indian. Our destination was nine miles beyond Buckeye, which is thirty miles west of Phoenix.[6]

Although fifty-four years old, Ammon persevered, but he could pick only thirty pounds. Even the alcoholic Navajo picked forty-two pounds, and some experienced Black pickers had sixty pounds by lunchtime. "Good pickers can make from $8–12 a day," he wrote, "but I was not in that class." He brought and distributed the *Catholic Worker*, and often he picked with the Navajo. He loved the camaraderie, the songs, and the Black women who served up coffee, chili, wieners, and pie at modest prices for lunch. He met "gandy-dancers" who were between jobs mending the railroad, all of the down and out. "I come out here so I can keep sober," one picker told him: "As I have eight kids, I have to keep working."

Then one of the farmers discovered that Hennacy had irrigated in New Mexico and offered him $7.50 a night to work his fields. That was not much, but it was more than he earned picking, so he accepted.[7] He had stopped wearing his Gandhi cap (India was free now) and began to cultivate a rich mane of hair. He was tanned from fieldwork, healthy from his diet and clean air, but not yet ready to settle down, so he kicked around all summer, living northwest of Phoenix, then working in a dairy, irrigating at night, cutting wood and brush. He still wrote faithfully to his mother, saying he might follow the fieldwork from Prescott to San Diego and back. By October 1947, however, he was hooked on Arizona and had decided to stay, and an important part of the decision was Lin Orme.

The Old Pioneer

Known locally as "the Old Pioneer," Lin Orme Jr. was born in 1872 in Missouri. His father had been a prominent Phoenix lawyer, a farmer, and sheriff of Maricopa County at the time when the sheriff executed court orders in land cases.[8] Lin Orme Jr. stepped into his shoes, serving on the prison board and becoming its chair. Sticking more to ranching than his father, Lin Jr. began importing Belgian draft horses and other purebred livestock that Ammon was familiar with. He also became known as president of the Salt River Valley Water Users Association, a group synonymous with irrigation canals and dam building in the Goldwater era of Arizona politics.[9]

Ammon initially wrote to his mother that he did not think much of Orme.[10] But they had common interests and over time they grew close. Both were self-sufficient, respected the land and those who worked it,

Figure 6.1. Lin Orme, "The Old Pioneer." Permission of Arizona Memory
Project, State of Arizona.

and held free speech to be sacred. Orme had liked Hennacy's article on prison reform in the *Arizona Republic*, and he was health conscious and interested in vegetarianism. "He always says for me to get a grapefruit from the tree every day and gives me a bowl of beans every Saturday," Ammon wrote to his mother.[11] Like Nunn in Milwaukee and Shirk in Albuquerque, Orme was an enterprising and economically independent businessman. Hennacy would have similar relationships with Platt Cline, a Flagstaff publisher, and Frank Brophy, a Phoenix banker. All had grown up in the culture of public debate and polity that Hennacy learned in Lisbon High, none of them believing that government could do much for the individual. They were not pacifists, but they were passionate about free speech. In 1916 when the IWW was driven out of Bisbee, Orme was outraged, saying, "If they can drive the I.W.W.s out of Bisbee, they can drive the Ormes out of Phoenix."[12]

Working for Orme, Hennacy got an education in "rural ecology" before that phrase was coined, for Orme disapproved of industrial farming. At first Ammon occupied a small adobe a hundred yards from the main house. But after "I had worked for him on and off," Ammon wrote, "he invited me to live in a three-room cottage to the left of his house. It was back from the road and quiet. Only an oil lamp, but there was running water. I got the rent free in order that I would give him first chance on my employment, such as mowing his lawn, chopping wood, cutting weeds, etc." Toward the end of Orme's life, Hennacy cooked for him and lived in his spare bedroom. As for religion, Ammon noted that Orme was "a nominal Episcopalian who did not go to church. . . . [He] appreciated the ideas of Jefferson and his life on the land. His [other] 160-acre farm was rented out to the big company I had first worked for. He knew of my radical ideas and read the CW."[13] During Hennacy's residence, that other ranch was gobbled up, as huge land companies moved in, and the crops they raised and agricultural methods changed completely. They used DDT, as Ammon would note in 1952.

Hennacy was "definitely happy in Arizona," Joan Thomas wrote, in part because it was the place where he would finish creating his public persona. His letters were filled with a new sense of generosity. "Before noon the date man (who is a blind vegetarian) brought in a full plate of dates and figs. . . . We decided that was a better dinner than anything we could cook, so we ate them. I filled a suitcase with 8 cabbage heads and gave them to my [Native American] friend from the day before. . . . Been sending the girls $30 a week for 5 weeks. Got them a Hopi doll; also one for my honey Louise [Lupa's daughter in Isleta], who now lives with her mother in Los Angeles."[14]

In Arizona he was also distant from these domestic groupings, reducing the drama in his life. "No longer the family man," Thomas explained, "he was turning himself into the legend he had been—on an unconscious level—constructing for years."[15] There are four areas that particularly contributed to his self-fashioning in Arizona: (1) the Hopis, (2) fasting while picketing, (3) work in and writing about the fields, and (4) Dorothy Day.

The Hopis

When he met Chester Mote on his initial trip to Arizona, Hennacy began his education in "Hopi traditionalism." This was not in Tolstoy or the Bible or any books he had read. Mote and his friend Thomas Banyacya were conscientious objectors who had been at Tucson Federal Prison Camp from 1942 to 1945. Mote and Banyacya had clarified their pacifist views in long discussions, but their antiwar position was only one point in a broad battle against the road building and federal policies on grazing and schools that had fractured the tribe. The resulting split was so divisive that when there was a drought, the tribe's factions staged competing rain dances. "It generally does happen to rain right after the Hopi make their prayers," Ammon wrote ironically. "This year there was a cloudburst within a few minutes after their ceremonies, and cars couldn't get through for 2 days."[16]

The intra-Hopi dispute went back to 1882, when a "friendly" faction had sought US intervention against Navajo grazing incursions. This pro–US government faction believed in a centralized structure and in cooperation on schools. Opposing them were the "hostiles," who settled disputes by simply moving away, shunning schools and new roads. When the dispute had boiled over in Oraibi in 1906, the hostiles left and founded Hotevilla—which Hennacy thought an ideal anarchist answer, even if the long history of the hostilities undercut his notion of an indigenous pacifism. But the new village itself did not follow the ancient prophecies completely either, which created more factions, and accusations of witchcraft even bubbled up. The important thing for Ammon, however, was that there had been no violence: the dissident faction simply moved out to an open area and started its own town. No courts, no state, no police.

According to scholar Brian Haley, Hennacy first met Banyacya in person in March 1949, when the hostiles—twenty-six traditionalists from Shongopavi, Mishongnovi, and Hotevilla—met and wrote a letter to President Truman. For Hennacy the issues and protesters reflected his deepest political concerns.[17] He in turn was their perfect conduit to the outside world, someone who would publicize their fight in leftist, antiwar, Catholic, and Quaker circles. The Hopis did not have so much as a typewriter, but Hennacy could count on Rik Anderson, a Quaker in Phoenix who owned a Varitype on which they produced hundreds of copies of the letter to Truman. The traditionalists would read one at the National Congress of American Indians in April 1949. Hennacy was their "first and most significant non-Hopi audience," writes Haley, and became their best publicist.[18]

In August 1949 Hennacy and Anderson were invited by Banyacya and Mote to the Mishongnovi snake dance, where Hennacy met and interviewed the traditionalist leader Kuchongva. "I asked questions to the radical Hopi chief all one afternoon and later wrote it up and had my Hopi CO friend Thomas Banyacya correct it," he wrote.[19] The article appeared in the *Catholic Worker* in February 1950, presenting the Hopi worldview to a broad popular American audience for the first time.

In the spring he organized a Hopi protest trip to Washington, to coincide with a larger pacifist demonstration. Lin Orme allowed him time off for this, another advantage of working for him, and Ammon's new friend Joe Craigmyle, a former CO, did most of the driving in his new Willy's pickup truck, with Banyacya pitching in (Ammon still did not drive). They outfitted the truck as a camper. Chief Dan Kuchongva would be the feature attraction, with Banyacya interpreting. They also stopped in Texas to see Dr. Shelton, who published a vegetarian/health magazine, and then in Cleveland, to visit Ammon's mother. The visit to Shelton, as explained below, was due to Ammon's intensifying practice of fasting while he picketed. When they finally reached Washington, all of Hennacy's conscientious-objector, Catholic, Quaker, and radical contacts quickly became the Hopis' new friends. He also met Dave Dellinger,

Figure 6.2. Hennacy, Craigmyle, and Hopi leaders in Hotevilla at a children's initiation ceremony. Permission of Josephine Thomas.

with whom he had been corresponding, who became a lifelong friend and printer of *The Book of Ammon*. Since Ammon had printed a few pieces in Flagstaff's *Arizona Daily Sun*, on his way back from Washington he stopped to meet Platt Cline, the publisher. The libertarian Cline had been reading the *Catholic Worker* and was sympathetic to the traditional Hopis: he had sent a reporter to cover Kuchongva's May 1949 meetings at Hotevilla and then provided Banyacya with notes.

That fall Ammon also traveled to radio stations KPFA in Berkeley and KPFK in Los Angeles to advocate for the Hopis. Then Orme sent him to the Maricopa County fair for eleven days later in 1951 to watch over his prize livestock. Hennacy enjoyed this kind of thing, sleeping on a cot by the stalls, but, like the visiting tribes, he noticed that the organizers themed the fair with a giant Kachina doll holding a bow and arrow. This was their idea of honoring Native Americans, though Kachinas did not have anything to do with weapons. "Fifteen of the Hopi including Dan and Thomas were down protesting to the Gov. about his wanting to have the Hopi be like white men," wrote Ammon. "I was the only white man besides the reporters present during the 3½ hour meeting."[20] The bow and arrow were removed. Ammon's annual public letter to the tax authorities, which was published in the *Catholic Worker*, contained numerous mentions of the Hopis, showing how he relished the role of Hopi advocate.

But he overstepped himself in the spring of 1953, when Platt Cline showed the traditionalists a draft of "Loma," an article that Ammon planned to publish in the *Catholic Worker*. The introduction to the article was a tender description of the naming ceremony for Thomas and Fermina Banyacya's new boy; then the piece proceeded to three political issues: (1) a lawsuit launched by the tribal council's lawyer to reclaim Hopi lands lost to Navajo and Anglo encroachment, (2) Arizona's attempts to legalize the sale of liquor to the Native Americans, and (3) Secretary of the Interior McKay's desire to assimilate all Native Americans. Also included was a letter from the traditionalists to Senator Goldwater charging him with hypocritically supporting proposals that would harm Hopis.[21] The first and last issues were too volatile: Cline said that Hennacy had failed to consider how describing the naming ceremony might offend the Banyacya family, who were Mennonites and Tribal Council supporters. As for attacking Goldwater ad hominem, that was a nonstarter for Cline.

According to Platt Cline, there had been some previous dissatisfaction when Ammon used real names in his articles, but, if it had been conveyed to Hennacy, it never registered.[22] He believed in authenticity, in names and facts, but Cline fancied himself as one who moved behind the scenes, exercising his political influence. He feared that "branding the REAL Hopis as 'Christian anarchists' at this time, in a newspaper considered very 'radical' would give characters like Lewis, Pyle and Goldwater just the sort of ammunition they could so well use to do very great harm to the Hopi." As he wrote to Ammon, "This is not your problem, but the Hopi problem . . . and they approve the use of these channels, because they have asked me to do these things I have done."[23]

Ammon disagreed, clinging to his idea of the Hopi traditionalists as pacifist anarchists, and writing to Cline in June 1953, "The Hopi surely are not Democrats or Republicans, Socialists or Communists, and the way they live is true anarchism whether they say that or not. Cultures are not extinguished by being true to their ideals and being radical; they are done for by compromise and watering down and become [*sic*] prosperous. I am not worrying about the Hopi though." He continued to publicize their cause and to work on their behalf.

In June 1954, Ammon appeared again on Pacifica's KPFA radio in Berkeley to speak on the Hopi, and the station used quotations from the traditionalists' 1950 letter to Commissioner Nichols on the cover of the program guide.[24] Ammon then turned his attention to his annual August protest against the atomic bomb. He now planned to stay in Arizona—"to be where I can see you [the traditionalists] and be inspired by your fine lives"—for the long term. The dust-up was finally regarded as minor by all parties, and on his way east, Ammon stopped for visits with the Clines and some of the Hopis.[25]

In Ammon's November 1954 article summarizing the trip, he noted these visits, but the article marked the end of Ammon's most intense advocacy for the Hopi traditionalists. He never abandoned his belief, however, that they were prime models of pacifist anarchism. "Hennacy visited [the] Hopi five times between 1958 and 1968," writes Haley. "In a 1960 kiva meeting, the four Traditionalist leaders, Katchonvga, Banyacya, David Monongye, and John Lansa, told Hennacy 'You are a hero' and presented him with a turquoise bolo tie."[26] He wore that turquoise with pride the rest of his life. Although *Book of the Hopi* (1963) by Frank Waters and Oswald White Bear Fredericks had a wide impact on the sixties hippies, it was Hennacy who broke this ground. In fact, his departure from Arizona created a publicity vacuum that the traditionalists needed to fill by prodding Waters to write a book. Hennacy is a "starting point for tracing the pathways of cultural transmission and culture making that gave rise to the hippies' love of the Hopi Traditionalists," writes Haley.[27] They were an important part of his public persona.

Fasting

Hennacy had fasted in the Atlanta Penitentiary, but in 1950 in Arizona he began *long* fasts, with three new differences. First, his early fasting had been part of a health regime. Following a tenet of CS, he thought that illnesses were caused by food and personal habits. During the Big Hike he thought that he had cured his "lumbago" (backache) by fasting. His way to health was to "reset" the body balance by a period of fasting.[28] His early fasts lasted only a day or two, and most of them were in

Figure 6.3. Hennacy picketing in Phoenix. Permission of Josephine Thomas.

Milwaukee and Albuquerque, while he was selling the *Catholic Worker*. He was young, he took breaks, and those were cooler climates.[29] As late as 1945 in Albuquerque he still considered fasting an adjunct to vegetarianism, advising a correspondent to stop "eating a little lamb when your wife cooks it."[30] Fasting was not yet a political act for him.

A key influence was Dr. Herbert Shelton, mentioned earlier, a naturopath in San Antonio, who like Hennacy had been imprisoned for draft resistance during World War 1.[31] In 1939 Shelton began publishing *Hygienic Review*, to which Hennacy subscribed, impressed by Shelton's claim that Gandhi followed his principles. From 1949 on, he corresponded with Shelton; he routed that trip to Washington with the Hopis through San Antonio in order to meet Shelton. Shelton "says that too much starch, sweets, etc. is worse than meat for some diseases," Ammon wrote Day, who had been discovered to have a tumor.[32] He recommended Shelton's thirty-day fast to her, but Day said she had neither the time nor the energy for that.[33] After Hennacy's death in 1970, Shelton contrarily wrote that "working like a Trojan while going on a long fast at least helped to weaken his heart. No doubt the coffee and other such drinks helped too."[34]

Contrary to Shelton, research concludes that undertaking a twenty-one-day "Daniel Fast" "can significantly improve several markers of overall health, particularly those related to cardiovascular and metabolic disease." Religious fasting is ancient, and, as researchers show, there are many Christian fasts lasting longer than those Hennacy undertook, particularly in Greece.[35] There is no definitive evidence on the net effect of fasting, but recent studies suggest there might be a difference between short-term, intermittent fasts and long-term, continuous fasts.[36] According to T. M. Sundfør and colleagues, the former work with circadian rhythms, the gut microbiome, and sleep patterns to control weight, but they produce more intense feelings of hunger. Continuous fasters are more apt to report feelings of wellness and that their diets were easy to follow. Ruth Patterson and Dorothy Sears note that many Mormons and Seventh Day Adventists fast, with positive outcomes, for short periods. One thing that most fasters agree on, however, is that fasting opens a lot of time in one's day. Without meals to plan for, food to buy, meals to prepare, or their social settings, the faster has at least two extra hours a day. This added time is sometimes spent reading or in self-reflection, and sometimes in public, with people who are eating or in normal life. In any case, fasting promotes a departure from the ordinary. Ammon's routine, as he wrote to Day, was to "rest half an hour morning and afternoon when I picket and then have all day Sat. and Sun when I won't picket, as the tax office won't be open. So I'll make it. . . . Knowing I will see you will be better than food and a good reward for my fast."[37]

The second difference between his earlier fasts and his new, longer fasts was that, as the letter above indicates, Hennacy's fasts became part of his greater ideological project. His Quaker friends Rik and Ginny Anderson gave him advice on how to make fasting a political statement, where to stand for visibility, how to word his signs effectively, how to synchronize fasting with biblical themes, and when and how often to take rest or water breaks. Fasting was not just a "vegetarian response"; rather, it was planned, required a training period, and was publicized beforehand. Passersby now saw Ammon "doing penance," a practice he had progressively built up, an act that synthesized religion and political protest. Due to his fitness, there seemed to be no consequences, but he was fifty-seven years old when he began this practice intensively, and living in a hot climate. His innate performativity led him to record his start and end weights, his fluid uptake, and his recuperation times, but he did not record subtler states. Every fast was a "success," with Ammon reporting no loss of energy and his weight returning to normal. They became heroic political testimony, proof of right living, and penance for the Bomb.

Third, he began to associate fasting with Catholicism. He had been highly alert to the religious dimensions of fasting, first in Gandhi, then in the Native Americans. When he saw his first Hopi snake dance, he noted that "they were in the middle of their 16 days of fasting and prayers in the kiva in preparation of their snake dance next week," and no "sales of soda pop" or any other bad food were allowed.[38] His was purely an onlooker's appreciation, but these were confirmations of the private meaning of Hennacy's Christian fasts, which came to include an idealization of Dorothy Day, his model of Catholic discipline. As early as 1950, he wrote to her from Oraibi,

> To make sure that you are not missing the main thing of my fast I will repeat that on the third morning of my fast while at mass I felt a deep meaning to the spectacle of Jesus on the cross and made up my mind right there that I wanted to join the church whenever I felt the same way about the sacrament of communion. It can't come through the intellect— only through a deep feeling. It was then that I felt that spirit of compassion or love for the poor people of the congregation who knew no better than to follow materialism. I have let the wickedness of the church keep me from God. . . . Whenever the times come that I can feel as I should about communion then I will tell you and join the church.[39]

Fasting was both a kind of inverse transubstantiation and part of proving himself worthy of Catholicism and of Day. It was also an effective public relations component of his antitax pacifism, but he wanted Day to understand that it was more, that it was genuinely spiritual. And there is no reason to doubt that.

The effects of long fasts are different. An increase in heart rate may occur in the first week, due to ketosis. Heart palpitations can occur from lack of water and salt, and while Hennacy drank plenty of the former, he consumed little of the latter. Some fasters report a kind of high on extended fasts, a clarity of purpose. Low carbohydrate levels cause blood sugar levels to drop, and the body begins breaking down fat to use as energy, which for most people results in light-headedness and passivity. After his first extended fast (August 1951), Hennacy wrote to Day that he was extremely tired. He rested up at Rik and Ginny's, but it took him several days to recover. After his death, Joan Thomas wrote that he was found to have "paper thin heart walls," but there's no proof that fasting caused his death.

Writing from the Fields

Hennacy continued to write evocatively in Arizona, but now he integrated writing into his political resistance and growing Catholicism. Often inspired by Dorothy Day, this writing has an intimate quality, a personalism that shines through its minimalism, contrasting with the fullness of his "life at hard labor" aesthetic in New Mexico. As early as 1951, Hennacy wrote about the dangers of pesticides and herbicides in farming, before the more scientific account of Rachel Carson (*Silent Spring*, 1962). He created a nonfiction desert setting before Joseph Wood Krutch wrote *The Twelve Seasons* (1949) or Wallace Stegner wrote *Beyond the Hundredth Meridian* (1954). Edward Abbey, who would write *The Brave Cowboy* in 1956, read Hennacy's writing and was a fan. In 1962 Hennacy wrote about what he called "the anarchistic implications of the Green Revolution."[40] Unlike the professional writers, Hennacy worked as a farm laborer and was often exhausted when he wrote.

In the fields, Ammon had become what the Spanish called an "*ace-quiero*," or expert irrigator. This was not only a job but a philosophy: the *acequia* system, exported from Spain to the Americas, has been shown by modern studies to "promote soil conservation and soil formation, provide terrestrial wildlife habitat and movement corridors, protect water quality and fish habitat."[41] Equally important to Ammon, the *acequia* system was truly communal. It was an ethical system, incorporating not just the "first in use, first in right" creed he had seen at Shirk's farm but also a real "water pluralism" in which "principles of equity and fairness" proceeded from the belief that "water is a community resource that irrigators have a shared right to use, manage, and protect."

Hired as an entry-level "ditch rider," Hennacy soon recognized that "when land is used for irrigation [farming], regular rain is not enough."[42] He observed and questioned landowners and Mexican laborers until he had mastered the system of gravity-fed irrigation they had inherited from the Spanish (who had inherited it from the Romans, who inherited it from the Arabs). Often he was up all night, opening channels for water and removing blockages in pitch darkness: "Had to let the water run four hours this morning in the garden subbing up and getting the ground wet without that on top getting wet," he wrote to Dorothy Day: subbing was the upward osmosis of water to the proper level, which he often had to discern in darkness. "Will write this p.m. as I am irrigating tonight for James and otherwise won't get any writing done."[43] This work was very erratic, depending on the type of crop and the natural rainfall, so Hennacy was always on call.

> Last night was a lot of wading in mud up to my boot tops, getting the water to run right. Did rest in my sleeping bag once for three hours, but not really sleeping. Did I tell you that the other night around midnight there was a great BAA-ing of sheep around midnight and the boss got up? He looked all over and in a far corner found two lambs. He happened to guess right and took them to the mother and all was quiet again. . . . I never could eat veal or mutton even when I lived on the farm and was not a vegetarian FOR THE LIVES OF THESE ANIMALS HAVE TO BE CUT OFF BEFORE THEY GET A START JUST FOR OUR GLUTTONY!

Unlike Thoreau, who was in many ways his model, Hennacy was immersed in other working people's problems: "The chicken man quit!—and with 4,500 baby chicks I get up—or rather stay up—until midnight and feed and water them. A new man is coming next week, and I will have more time on Sundays."[44] Always there was *the land*, and reading Hennacy's letters, one feels its requirements and rewards:

> I irrigated last night and did not work today but will irrigate tonight and work tomorrow. . . . Been pleasant all day, forking piles of wheat, and will bind them in sheaves tomorrow. Went down the road a mile where the farmer has the mules and drove them up with the mowing machine. On the way back stopped along the road and got figs from a tree and boxed some up and will mail them to you [Day] and to my girls tomorrow. Hope they are still good. They taste better if put in an icebox a few hours before eating them after the trip. The wife of this farmer thought that *Catholic Worker* meant that we were all good *workers* on the farm. Alas, she should know. . . . Nights are still nice and cool, while the days are not much over 100 and not too hot yet. I need more sleep though in hot weather and eight hours is enough to work. The Mexicans are turning the vines back out of the rows so the cantaloupes will not get wet when we irrigate. Won't be long now until we have some. I have about 100 watermelon vines; ought to have plenty of those.[45]

One might ask where the "anarchism" is in such a passage? Where did Hennacy stand relative to the East and West Coast schools? His answer would be that "voluntary poverty," an ascetic pacifism, requires a laboring life, not theoretical speculation. Yet, as visceral and local as his written observations are, Ammon could still see the big picture because he read so much and so widely. References to census reports, vegetarian magazines, pesticides, classic fiction, the *Los Angeles Times*, and *Life* magazine pepper his letters, often integrated with details from the dirt under his feet. The ultimate glue uniting Hennacy's local and global, as Patrick Coy notes, is "personal responsibility." Governments are not going to solve problems, individuals are: "The census report shows that there were 18,400 farms in Ariz in 1940 and 10,300 in 1950. Every state has *fewer* farms except California and the Carolinas. Draining swamps and bulldozing cut-over land brought more land under cultivation. . . . [I] planted okra and late watermelon tonight. Eating peas this last 8 days and will do so every day while there are any. Never buy any in a can. Had one carrot, 4 radishes, a chard leaf with salt and peanut oil for salad, along with plenty of peas for supper." This is not a non sequitur:

this is the observation of a national malaise and a personal response. In Arizona his prose acquired this "implied metaphor" factuality, in which things comment on conditions in a way self-evident to him: "The big company ranchers had a meeting a few days ago grouching against the state ruling for sanitary conditions for migratory worker camps. Say it will break them—but they sure like the 45-cent subsidy on cotton. Cotton growing all around here now."[46] The ubiquity of cotton is more than a comment; it is the source of the preceding phenomena.

The antigovernment part of "living anarchism" caused Ammon more problems as his fame grew. Even though the Old Pioneer sheltered him, IRS and Treasury agents followed him wherever he went. He had refused to pay income taxes for fifteen years, but he was still walking free, an affront to the IRS. No wonder that he felt he was an example, a one-man revolution. Neither did he pay state or local taxes, or home telephone or gas taxes if he could avoid them. When he could, he bought goods from tax-exempt Indian traders. No doubt he paid those small taxes built into the prices of bus tickets and utilities, but he was the least taxed man in the United States, and for reasons that he talked about constantly: people should understand that they could do it too. When they did, according to Ammon, then the military industrial state would wither and fall.

On his trips into town to picket, Ammon let the Feds and IRS know where he lived.

> There was a T-MAN, with direct orders from Washington to keep after me until he gets the nearly $400 I owe here in Arizona. . . . The army captain for whom I was working told me about it at noon, although he was not supposed to say anything. He said he would pay it out of his own pocket, but I told him not to. He will pay me in advance each day I work in the future. The T-man wanted him to call them each day I worked so they could come out and garnishee my wage. I told him not to get in too much trouble. He didn't mind it unless they keep bothering him daily until he can't get his work done. . . . He told me of a neighbor who owed $4.70, and the tax man took scores of hours of his time looking over all his records, etc., and finally found *they owed him* instead.

Hennacy had a way of turning skeptics, like this army captain, into sympathizers. They liked his antistate attitude, but they had not thought through the implications of their other political views, and Ammon enjoyed trying to convert them.

The Old Pioneer and Ammon bonded over hard work, self-discipline, absolute free speech, a taste for personal and political freedom, and skepticism about progress, especially of the mechanical sort. They both hated pesticides and herbicides, as Ammon wrote in 1950: "This . . . DDT kills off weak flies and makes stronger ones . . . like sprays that kill weak weeds and make stronger ones." Two years later he wrote, "I went into town with the old man [Orme] this morning. Coming back, we saw cotton pickers *actually crawling* on the ground picking up the loose cotton from the mechanical picker. The stems or the stalks had been cut off. In the old days before picking machines, people could stoop or reach, but now they have to crawl for a living."[47] They took a great satisfaction in the gardens they planned together, something of a ritual, with Ammon doing most of the work. Orme would borrow a mule from a neighbor, then direct Ammon in the preparation of the garden layout. Later Ammon would add other vegetables that he wanted.

> The Old Pioneer brought twine and we measured out straight rows. We hitched the blind mule to the plow and the Old Pioneer led as I made— not the straightest row in Missouri or Arizona—but one good enough for the purpose. We came back over the furrow to make the ground even on both sides of it. By 1 p.m. I had returned the mules and had started to plant. The rows are 81 feet long. I have never worked elsewhere in such fine mellow ground: not a hard lump of dirt to be found. . . . The furrows were about a foot and a half in depth. I leveled off the ground between them with a rake, then took a hoe and chopped halfway down the edge of the furrow to make sure that the ground was fine and crumbly as a bed for seeds. Then I made an inch furrow along this edge where I judged the line of irrigation water would about reach.[48]

This was not gentleman farming but gardening for their kitchen table. Ammon applied his accumulated knowledge to each new crop he put in, because he was eating this food. He did not go to the store much; the home garden was an important part of his vegetarianism and voluntary poverty.

The Old Pioneer was becoming ill, however, and considering his son "undependable," he entrusted many ranch details to Hennacy. Being so stationary made Ammon easier for the FBI and Treasury agents to find. When Orme moved Hennacy into the main house in the last month of his life, Ammon wrote,

> The Old Pioneer is a gem. The T-man went to the hospital to serve him the garnishee papers on me and he refused to have them served. Told him that he couldn't scare me or get anything out of me. Young Orme is afraid of his shadow—a nice fellow but a milquetoast. Of course the Old Pioneer will write out no more checks to me, but I will still live here. He told the T-man that hundreds of farm workers never paid a cent of taxes, and the T-man replied "Yes, but they do not flout the authority of the government as this Hennacy does."[49]

They liked roaming the fields in their last days together. "Mr. Orme looked over his fields today and said, 'I'll never sell this place. What is money worth? Why 100 families could work and produce what they needed on my land.'" Orme would have been surprised to learn that he shared a vision with Tolstoy and Peter Maurin. Toward the end of his life, he turned for solace to Hennacy: "The old man got onion sets, radish and carrot seeds. . . . We sure like to work in the dirt. Nice sleeping out in that east porch; we hear the birds first thing before daylight."[50] Ammon judged that all this would end. "Young Orme was served papers yesterday to pay everything I earned to the tax man. The Old Pioneer is coming home tomorrow from the hospital [his second visit]. I do not want to worry him with the coercion of the tax man, so will offer to leave here rather than embarrass him."

The Old Pioneer was still quotable, and Ammon wrote down his best lines. "Jefferson's plan of not having great wealth inherited was the right idea," said Orme. Whittaker Chambers reminded him of the drunkard who fell asleep in a manure pile: "The scream of a woman awakened him, and he staggered into the dance hall proclaiming, 'I have come to defend the honor of woman.'" One day he told Hennacy that he "shoveled like a Mexican," which he said was a compliment, because Mexicans shoveled with economy of effort and physical efficiency.

Then Orme had a stomach operation on March 14, 1953.[51] A week before he died, Ammon wrote to Dorothy Day, "The old man is pretty weak. I woke up at midnight feeling there was something wrong and said extra prayers for him." He cooked and cared for Orme until he actually died on March 25, 1953. "The Episcopalians conduct the funeral," he wrote to Day. "It is okay to say in the *CW* that Fr. Dunne baptized him [and] he received extreme unction. . . . As if in celebration and pleasure the chickens laid 13 dozen and 7 eggs today. The most by five eggs that we ever got."[52] As if in celebration: a kind of transubstantiation.

Dorothy Day

Dorothy Day, whom Ammon met in Milwaukee in 1937, was the person around whom the new Arizona Ammon coalesced. Their relationship developed only as the possibility of cohabitation with Selma faded. Ammon had long felt that Selma lacked courage, and he suspected the I AM of being her response to his political/religious convictions. Although he sent her money for ten years after she left, she denied him parental rights in a fashion that would be illegal today; however, she raised the girls of whom he was so proud in spite of great obstacles. But although sympathetic, he ran out of patience. He was lonely.

Dorothy Day was his ideal: a working mother, a Christian pacifist who had spent time in jail, a powerful leader, and an evocative writer whose large audience seemed to come to her naturally. She embraced voluntary poverty. She was four years younger than he, and she had lived as rough as he had. But as the charismatic face of the Catholic Worker movement, the fifty-three-year-old Day led a public and bureaucratic life that was more demanding than Ammon imagined: she had to think about many people, the hierarchy of the Catholic Church, and the consequences of her every action.

Hennacy did not fully grasp another part of their differing life experiences. A native New Yorker, Day had taken lovers in her Greenwich Village years and lived in Europe with the *bon vivant* Berkeley Tobey, who married eight times. Meanwhile Hennacy, like his hero Gandhi, was chaste for a long time. Day had had an abortion, attempted suicide, been jailed with prostitutes in the Tombs (an infamous New York City prison), and lived common-law with several men, including the anarchist Forster Batterham.[53] Hennacy doted on his daughters and stayed married. By the time Hennacy met her, Day had not only started the *Catholic Worker* but also the Hospitality House and the Easton farm commune. She was more worldly and knew about the vagaries of idealistic men. She used her charisma to foster cooperation, whereas Hennacy was a prickly iconoclast, an ideologue in all things, and missing half his teeth. He had been living a celibate life, but farm work and diet kept him in robust health. With his mouth closed, he was handsome but still naïve.

The relationship began when Day spoke at the Social Action Congress in Milwaukee in 1937, while Ammon was working in Roger Baldwin's office downstairs. The *Catholic Worker* was spreading like wildfire when Day arrived to speak upstairs in the *Liberator* office. Hennacy only got in a few words with her afterwards, and the next day when "she spoke at Marquette to a room full of nuns, priests and students . . . I was only able to come late to the meeting and had to sit in the very front row. In answering questions from patriotic questioners, she mentioned something of my pacifist record, saying that I was not a Catholic but that when the next war came, she would be with me in opposition to it."[54] We can imagine that he glowed, and there followed an exchange of letters in which Ammon stated his bona fides as usual: prison time, IWW and union membership, tax resistance, and picketing. It was no different from the introductory letters he wrote to dozens of people.

> If I could believe in the Catholic religion, I *would certainly be heart and soul in your movement.* As it is, I do what I can to break down the misunderstanding and animosity of Protestants toward Catholics in general by bragging about our folks and handing out Catholic Workers in all the Protestant churches where I speak.
>
> Ellen Glasgow spoke of a time when she was tempted to become a Catholic. She went on a pilgrimage to the top of the hill at Assisi, as she was drawn to St. Francis. On the way she saw a poor broken down horse . . . hauling several well-fed monks up the hill and she thought "St. Francis was alone, but the Franciscan friars are a multitude." That I think is all the more reason why people like you and Peter need to keep going, to undo all of the patriotic junk that the majority of Catholics put forth. You see how [Jacques] Maritain tries to justify a Just but not a Holy war.[55]

He did not insist on his vegetarianism as a point of difference between them, but it is implicit in his style of creating meaning by juxtapositions (in this letter, it is the horse, the fat monks' indifference). They exchanged a letter a month through the late 1930s. Ammon mentioned his estrangement from Selma after she moved alone to New York City in 1938, though he would not call it that. When she published an excerpt of "God's Coward" in the *CW* in November 1941, he was ecstatic. That was when he boasted that Day was introducing him to priests and CW officials.[56] When Selma moved to Los Angeles, his letters became more personal and he felt he could crack jokes about Catholicism—calling the liturgy the "lethargy"—but her publication of his life story in the December 1941 *CW* was deeply gratifying. "I feel very much honored," he wrote.[57]

The fiasco in Milwaukee was a low point, but she was there for him. Publicly lampooned in the papers, he wrote the long letter to Day quoted earlier. He had expected to start a new chapter in his life, probably in prison. Instead he was directionless. Faith appeared often in his letters, as when he wrote to Day that "I have been in solitary, where I did not believe in a God or anything (at first), so I can take it now when I do believe that God is everywhere and that nothing apart from Him is present in my experience or has any power over me unless I give it power, which I refuse to do."[58]

That was explicit enough for Day, though at first she found him insufficiently "Catholic." By 1943 the pressures of her work mounted to the point that she thought about giving it up. Her pacifism had brought her into conflict with the church hierarchy. She was living in the chaos of the Mott Street Catholic Worker House and also dealing with the problems of the communal farm at Easton. She took a six-month leave of absence to move near her daughter, Tamar, who was a major concern.

For Day, Ammon was at first just a correspondent, one of hundreds to whom she wrote. But this man wrote back immediately, sometimes twice a day. He did not have a Bible in Arizona, so she sent him one. He wrote back that "because I love you and you sent it, I will read it daily. I told you before, but will repeat it here, that my prayer for my girls, my wife, you and Bob [Steed] and the rest and myself is: 'Great God of Truth and Love bring peace, protection, enlightenment, and encouragement.' Many times a day at the end of a row of field work I open my billfold with your picture in it and say this prayer. You may say you are weak, and you may really feel weak at times, but to me you are strong." He compared her to Joan of Arc, which became a humorous leitmotif between them.[59]

Hennacy's value to Day, as her recent biographers make clear, was "to put a human face on the conscientious objector debate." However, "giving Hennacy space in the paper cemented the image of *The Catholic Worker* in the minds of many as an un-American publication."[60] That she continued to do so argues that she began to take him seriously. In the fall of 1944 Hennacy broached the topic of becoming Catholic, but Day suspected an infatuation: "It makes me so queasy when you say you are going to become a Catholic for love of me. When you say you feel spiritually the Church is your home, I feel better. But your eyes should be on Christ, not me." He was planning a trip back east, and they discussed a meeting in Chicago at the Peter Maurin House.[61]

Living in Albuquerque in 1945, Hennacy had seen what Catholic community meant to his Hispanic/Native American neighbors. He walked ten miles into town to give out *CW*s, and that road was also a meditation path, with Day often in his thoughts. He was selling more papers, up to twenty-five per service, sometimes fifty at one church. It seemed like a sign, and it is fair to say that by January 1945 he was ready to reach out to Day. He wrote to her that he was "working in the orchard since the first at $75 a month, a quart of milk, fuel and rooms.......*Phone 8933.*" The latter was boldfaced and underlined, his way of saying, "It is now possible for you to call me."

In April he wrote, "As you know, when I was in solitary I swore and cried, sang Wobbly songs, until after a long time I really *felt* what Jesus had gone through in the Garden and on the Cross—before this I thought I was *alone*. Guess that gave me a self-starter, so I don't have to be cranked up again. . . . Making good bread now. Will plant some wheat this week, thrash it a la Tolstoy by flail and grind it for bread next winter. Going half naked in the orchard."[62] Learning to read Hennacy by his analogues (from jail to the orchard) and the puns (self-starter to bread) must have taken Day some time.

But there was something darker nearby, over Sandia Peak, that now caught his attention. "Have you heard about this atomic bomb? A big light in the sky at 5:30 a.m. on July 16 was a tryout for the bomb s.e. of us here, at Alamogordo. The steel tower from which it was thrown vanished like vapor. The contrast between the peaceful Indians around here and the crazy white people who acquiesce in this bombing is marked."[63] When the actual atomic bomb was dropped, Day rushed to state the *Catholic Worker*'s position: "Truman is a true man of his time in that he was jubilant. He was not a son of God, brother of Christ, brother of the Japanese, jubilating as he did. He went from table to table on the cruiser which was bringing him home from the Big Three conference, telling the great news; 'jubilant' the newspapers said. Jubilate Deo. We have killed 318,000 Japanese."[64] Their letters crossed in the mail.

Shortly afterward, Ammon had a mystical experience, probably the point of his personal Catholic epiphany. After attending a Quaker meeting one night, he awoke to see "a blue flame burning in the middle of the room. I went to it wondering, for I knew that there had not been a fire in the stove for 12 hours, and this was not near the stove. The fire burned, and yet I couldn't see that there was any wood or coal or anything to provide fuel. I put my hands in the flame and while it was warm, it did not seem to burn or scorch me. Perhaps this took three minutes, and when I opened my eyes, the flame was gone." He wrote a poem about the experience that appeared in the *Conscientious Objector*, part of which reads,

> Appearing naked before this Divinity
> Today I go about my work:
> I write letters to friends and receive letters in return
> I have a tolerable peace of mind
> Yet now after having knelt before the Flame
> I know that wars and famines can come and go
> And I shall not be moved.[65]

The confluence of events must have seemed portentous. There was the definitive break with Selma, the new spiritual direction he took from the Hopis, and his fasting/picketing. He grew convinced that Dorothy was the one, so his letters from Phoenix grew warmer. His closing changed from "Yours in Christ" to "I love you always Dorothy" or "To you who are my inspiration always, my love and thoughts."[66] For her part, Day held Hennacy at an affectionate distance. She was surrounded by men—the *CW* was "a movement of men because Peter Maurin set his seal upon the work." In the office were Bob Steed and Stanley Visnewski. Maurin himself needed care now that he was old and had taken to wandering. Hennacy was not formally Catholic, but there was no denying the energy of his personality in those letters, now twice a week, and Dorothy began to reply by air mail. As Patrick Coy notes, Day said that Hennacy was one of the three men who permanently affected her life.[67]

On December 19, 1949, Dorothy Day came to Arizona to meet Ammon. They stayed in Phoenix two days, then traveled around the state. They made close emotional contact, they held hands, and perhaps they kissed. The visit can only be established in retrospect, since they were together, not writing to each other daily. Day biographer William D. Miller confirms the importance of the visit: "She left on Sunday night, January 1, and, just as Ammon had been at the bus station to greet her, he was there to see her off. . . . When she left, he felt that a fresh inspiration had come into his life. No doubt Dorothy encouraged him in his writing and no doubt too, she encouraged him to think about coming to Mott St. to amplify his 'One Man Revolution.'" Ammon wrote immediately after her departure, "Your touch helped me realize and do more than usual." The next day his letter mined their histories on a common ground.[68]

> We were probably at many of the same meetings in NYC from Dec 10, 1919 to June 21, 1921 when I lived in New York. I was pale-faced and dizzy, just out of prison and it took several years before I could cease pacing the length of my cell. . . . But I do go to mass on Sunday because I love you. . . . We have grown up and proven ourselves these thousands of miles apart across the years and it is right that we should pray for each other, help each other and in the right spirit love each other.[69]

He wrote to his mother that

> Dorothy Day was here for 2 days around New Year's and we had a fine visit. Went around to see the radical priests and some anarchists. . . . She was affectionate toward me. I do not know of any woman I have any more love and respect for. . . . I went to mass twice with Dorothy but did not kneel—read the missal. After she left and I had time to get my breath, I

realized that after the girls get through school, I will devote the rest of my life to Dorothy and the Catholic Worker movement. The kind of love I have for her is impersonal although I do like her as a person too.[70]

He thought he and Day would support each other, writing to her that

I have a long way to go before I can come up to you in the true spirit of love, but your respect and love make me aim higher and live truer, if there is such a word. . . . If one has never had sex experience, they may look forward to it (or away from it) as something especial. Well, sometimes it is, but twenty times you do the same thing and there is not the right spiritual and mental attachment and you are lucky if twice there is a real union that one can remember after a year. . . . We have no illusions about sex so we can put our minds to work. I'm not getting theatrical either, for right now I would like to embrace you and kiss you.[71]

Such sentiments often appeared at the end of his letters, but sometimes the next paragraph would concern a local protest march or gossip. In the letter above, which shocked Day a bit, Ammon continued in the next paragraph about the perfidy of a rancher who was "taking up desert land, drilling deep wells and watering his big cotton fields and now a whole community has to haul water and can't get money from the FHA to drill their own wells. This big well takes it all." But his closing salutation was, "Try to get here this August if you can. I love you always and you can count on me inside or outside as the case may be."

It was a month after Day's 1949 visit that Hennacy evolved a plan to take the Hopis to the big Washington, DC, protest. But the end point was to visit New York, see the Catholic Worker House first-hand, and be with Dorothy. When he arrived, their paths crossed only for a few days. Overworked and under pressure, distraught by Tamar's troubles, Day had gone to Lake Park, Florida, on a retreat. There she responded to an early draft he sent of what would become *Autobiography of a Catholic Anarchist*:

Your whole writing about me seems sentimental, too rapturous, and I did not like it at all. The rest of the chapter is wonderful, but I am going to censor what you write about me. . . . My life is public enough without all this emotional writing. . . . Mary Thornton wrote to me in shocked accents that you were in love with me. Young people who are used to looking upon me as a mother are repelled, just as children are repelled in the lack of understanding of the life of their parents. For one thing you are nearly sixty and I 55. A mature age, when calm affection and friendship, deep and sincere, can be respected, but romantic love cannot. There is something quite sane about this. Such love is associated with youth and the time of mating, and the idea of procreation . . . so also to the natural mind, the idea of sexual love is out of place at our age. It is next to impossible to write about such love of people in their sixties without seeming ridiculous or revolting. I am utterly frank in writing to you this way because I want to prepare you for the fact that I am going to ruthlessly cut out of the book any reference to me along these lines. At our age we should be turning to God, not to each other.[72]

When Ammon protested his sincerity, she wrote back: "Dear Ammon,—it is so hard for me to answer your letters because they move me so, and besides I want to be alone to answer them. . . . Your letters make me love you very much, you are so sincere, and one can see the growth in simplicity and humility too. I don't feel in the least worthy of the affection you give me."

Biographers Loughery and Randolph describe a "long, affectionate correspondence," but Miller feels the relationship was "sophomoric."[73] One thing clear is that Dorothy was deeply moved. On retreat in August 1952, she wrote a prayer-meditation in which she asked God to "give him light to come with humility to the baptism font, to be confirmed a perfect Christian." She had "a great longing that Ammon become a Catholic, and I ask this now." Whatever happened, she would "continue to love Ammon and have faith in him, and look up to him, and count on him whether or not he ever becomes a Catholic. And I won't say anything to him about it because I want you to do all the work."[74]

To Ammon she simply wrote that he should be glad that "I am gone and you can settle down to work, physical and mental. We did not have too much time together, really just a couple of days. . . . You talk about being shy with me. That is because you are only in love with your idea of me, not really me. How can you be when you have seen so little of me, a few days?"[75] Yet she closed this letter, "Remember always, I love you and pray for you, and I count on your prayers."[76]

If there was anything sophomoric about them, it was that they passed notes to each other. In one that survives, Day wrote, "You know I loved the feel of your hands, when you held mine to say goodbye. It is so strong. A man's hand should feel capable of working. A woman's hand too should look as though she used it. God bless you Ammon, you are sweet and good. And give my love to Mr. Orme. Next time I come out I'll stay there."[77]

Hennacy had returned to Orme's ranch recharged, thinking of Day as he worked the fields. "My idea of God in May 1950: God is a power line, and a person can pray and do anything he wishes, but unless he connects with this power line, he is not connected up. . . . Churches should be these transformers to do the connecting."[78] The image of the power line reminds us how Ammon was connected to his landscape and simple, material life, which Dorothy did not share. For him simple facts shine with faith, his analogs and parallels express love; his physical work *embodies* his faith: "6 p.m. Been a peasant all day, forking piles of wheat and will bind them in sheaves tomorrow. Went down the road a mile where the farmer has the mules and drove them up with the mowing machine. . . . Both grapes and figs grow well here, so we will have to have our own 'vine and fig tree' sometime as we go along, Dorothy."[79] Sometimes he would be light-hearted in a post-script: "The mockingbird woke me this morning with a new sound like a far-away bell. Hope you had a good trip. I love you really—although not in a ROMANTIC or RHEUMATIC way."[80] That was quintessential Hennacy.

Since his 1950 trip to Washington with the Hopis, Ammon had become a highly visible figure: he picketed the White House carrying a sign that said "75% of income tax goes to war." That got in the papers. According to Joan Thomas, he not only embraced fasting completely on this trip but admitted that there was something "vainglorious" about it.[81] In August he wrote to his mother about plans for a five-day fast on his annual picketing, and he sent out letters to ninety-four Phoenix clergy asking them to publicize it. Part of him hoped to be arrested, because he thought Dorothy's activities would lead to her arrest back east.[82]

Fame

For his next tax protest in Phoenix in August, Ammon wrote to authorities in advance, providing them with his writings, his interviews, and his arrest sheet. He requested permits, which he had never done, adding that he would protest without them. He went to Mass every morning "out of love and respect for Dorothy." This was his new modus operandi, the crystallization of "Ammon Hennacy" the public figure.

When he began his picketing, it was an unusually cool period in Arizona. The IRS took away his signs, but Rik Anderson made new ones that read "Personal property of Joe Craigmyle."[83] Ammon was only carrying them for Joe, they said. That was also what might be called "full Hennacy," a credo summed up by Coy as requiring "above all else, the reduction of the state. . . . He saw national government as the largest example of the organized return of evil for evil. He stood squarely in a long line of anarchists and libertarians who held that the one and only modus operandi of government is coercion and force. After reading Thoreau, Garrison, and Tolstoy, he understood all governments, even the best, to be founded upon the police officer's club—the very opposite of the teachings of Christ."[84] It was a measure of his new stature that the *Los Angeles Times* covered the protest, at the end of which Hennacy's weight had fallen from 143 to 129. He said he felt fine and regained ten pounds immediately, then headed north for the Hopi snake dance. He was thinking about starting a Catholic Worker House in Phoenix, he said, like the one he had visited in New York, but he decided to put that plan on hold. For one thing, he was not formally a Catholic and many other things were happening: Bill Ryan, whom he still called his best friend, was editor of the month at the IWW magazine and asking for material.

In January 1952 Dorothy Day published an autobiography, *The Long Loneliness*, which had a page and a half about Hennacy. She contrasted his rugged, outdoorsy, "personalist approach of Berkman" with the "doctrinaire and dogmatic" Bob Ludlow, who wrote most *CW* position papers. The text made it clear that Ammon was the man of action and an important part of her life. Ammon was tremendously pleased: "I think she exaggerates a little, but I do the same about her. . . . Dorothy is the most holy person there is now living, and it is well that people can read about her if they get tired of their material way of living."[85]

As Ammon became well known, a wake of publicity trailed him. Not only the *Los Angeles Times* but national news magazines picked up the tax-protest story: "Dorothy Esser of *Time* magazine talked with me for 20 minutes yesterday," he wrote. At these interviews Ammon gave away copies of Dorothy's book, purchased from his own meager funds. He also reviewed it wherever he could.[86] Dorothy had planned to visit Phoenix again in March 1952, but she was diverted by a crisis at the *Catholic Worker*. Hennacy was also busy, debating banker Frank Brophy on Phoenix radio and being interviewed by Platt Cline on Flagstaff radio. He was sparring with Senator Robert Taft, and he received a letter from Manalil Gandhi, who would reprint some of Hennacy's articles. "Got a lot of fan mail," he wrote to Cline ebulliently. "It is as though he experiences himself too fully," Joan Thomas wrote.[87]

Planning to see Day again in the fall of 1952, Ammon elected to picket and fast in August, then travel by bus—stopping to see friends and relatives—to New York City. The picketing/fasting went well, and he wrote to Day that he "lost 17 pounds in all. Feel fine, except that I can't eat much at once. Had two light fried eggs, orange juice, and two slices of toast for breakfast. Didn't want anything sweet. Couldn't eat another bite. . . . See you Sunday."[88]

In November, after making sure that he understood it, he planned to join the Catholic Church. "Likely it will take 3 months," he wrote.[89] He had glimpsed a new life, which would be New York City, the *Catholic Worker*, and Dorothy Day. She wanted him to go on religious retreat with her in August at the Maryfarm, thinking his baptism might occur there. But this conflicted with his annual picketing/fasting, and Ammon was still a day laborer. It is easy for religious people to forget: he put in forty- to sixty-hour weeks. To go on a retreat he would have to double down on his work schedule: "I get up at 4:30 and put in my 8 hrs. before it gets too hot, binding up sheaves of wheat for the old man's chickens. . . . Irrigating tonight and likely 3- or 4-nights next week. Not easy to sleep in the daytime, but the irrigating is easy work and pays well. I made $213.90 in May working at 75 cents an hour." That is four seventy-hour weeks of hard farm labor by a fifty-nine-year-old man, and he worked a hundred hours the next week so that he could afford the trip.[90]

He began picketing on August 3, 1952, writing in advance to the IRS and noting that it would be the seventh anniversary of the atomic bomb.

"And we are still making them, but *not with my taxes.*"[91] This publicity hit the Phoenix papers with unexpected results. A group of barrio kids knocked on Lin Orme's front door one evening just after his picketing, when Ammon happened to be inside. They asked for "Yancy."

"Never heard of him," said Ammon, "but my name is Hennacy."

"You are the guy!" they said. "Come outside here on the concrete and we'll rub your head on the cement."

"Who sent you?"

"None of your business. We go all over after communists. You are a communist and *The Catholic Worker* is communist."

"Beat me up right now," Ammon said. "I won't hit you back."

They did not attack him, though he thought he saw them three times in the next week, but he was never sure and would not have called the police anyway. He was cautious because of his experience in the Denver jail when the police encouraged witnesses of crime to mistakenly identify him. "They were not especially vicious, but had been told lies," he wrote. "They were not to blame for their actions."[92]

Few converts have struggled over their decisions more than Ammon. He worked out his own relation to original sin, the pope, the liturgy, church hierarchy, indulgences, heresy, the saints, sex, etc. Mostly he defaulted to the bedrock of "individual conscience," a habit since his Quaker-influenced youth. Still, he was agreeing to a disciplinary religious structure for the first time since then. He was worried that he did not understand enough to be baptized.

Since there were too many loose ends in Phoenix, the event occurred in Hutchinson, Minnesota, on November 17, 1952, on a trip that was a stand-in for his eventual move to New York. Father Casey, the house priest of the *Catholic Worker*, conducted the service and reassured him. "We agreed that if a Catholic in conscience felt that it was a sin to register for the draft, pay taxes for war, and otherwise be in denial of The Sermon on the Mount, then that person was bound to disobey man."[93] Dorothy Day was his sponsor, and he was baptized Ammon St. John the Baptist Hennacy. That night he made his first confession. After taking his first communion, he was back on the road, to speak in Wisconsin, then Minnesota, and finally to return to Phoenix.

He immediately wrote to Day to apologize for not coming to New York:

A week or so there would not have been enough for me. I have begun to see here and at the two farms just what you are up against and how much love you really have. I have never before had such a length of time when I have been in a truly spiritual atmosphere and I begin to see what I have been missing. While love for you has brought me to see all this— something had to do it and why not you? I seem to always feel strong, both physically and mentally and in courage, and if this is my built-up heritage (much of it done in solitary) then I want it to make you feel stronger when you need it—for we are very close to each other as you know—and we don't need to touch each other physically to have this happen—although a sweet touch of hand or lips does help. . . . I am keeping those rose petals as something, as an emblem of your affection.

If the intimacy of their relationship is striking, so is Dorothy's spiritual mentorship. As Ammon wrote,

Thinking back to the other day, there were three definite steps in making me see the necessity of That Other which you whispered to me: your kneeling when they sang; the peace we all had when working with the wool—the sense that Mike, his very fine boy, and all of us were brothers; and the short story of Tolstoy about a man who saw the futility of any other life except that of giving up all for God and embracing voluntary poverty—all of this has given me the feeling that I spoke to you about coming over from Staten Island, that in my heart I have decided that the Church is the Home which I need.

Day made another trip to Phoenix after Christmas 1952. They spent the period from New Year's Day until January 7, 1953, together. She gave an inspired and inspiring talk at St. Francis Xavier Church on January 6. Afterwards he wanted to take her to see the Hopi and Platt Cline, but she wanted to rest. She did meet Lin Orme briefly.[94]

The postcards that passed between them in the following weeks are embarrassingly tender. "Dear Heart: . . . I am so happy from the afterglow of your visit. I'll be walking on air for weeks. It's all too good to be true, yet as you say, to sin against hope is awful, so I'll keep on hoping for the very best. I felt as close to you that night in the back of St. Mary's when you were praying out of sight in the front, so I suppose I am getting the proper D E T A C H M E N T—so also I'll feel close to you when I'm here and you are there in the East. Love always."[95]

A few days later he wrote, "Dear Heart, Hope you got some rest away from the One Man Revolution." And the next day, "Dear Heart, You are all the world to me, Dorothy. You make me strong. I think we make each other strong, through God—for you are the one whose strength made me find him." These letters reveal Ammon living in a unity of the spiritual, emotional, and physical that was extraordinary: "Dearest Dorothy: Want to talk to you some more. Cleaning the ditch so the water can get to the orange tree and drilled 3 holes so water can seep in and get to the roots better. Was sweating and no shirt on at 10 a.m. About 11 a.m. I took a grapefruit off the tree and ate it; that's when I like it best—except when I drink some fresh juice out of a glass with the one I love the best, like that communion glass we had at Ginny's that last morning."[96]

After his return, Hennacy discovered that other local teenagers had broken into his adobe. Only a few articles of value were missing, but the Old Pioneer was furious. "Those kids should be whupped," he said. Ammon demurred; he had picketing to do in town. When he returned from it, Orme was in the hospital for a long-avoided operation on his ulcer. Ammon went to visit, learning that Orme needed a follow-up operation. "Just got up now at 3 p.m. from sleeping," Hennacy wrote to Day. "I don't know how much is true about dreams . . . but while I was sleeping I was dreaming about hiking near Pittsburg and I was in someone's attic looking for something when all at once I saw the Old Man sitting there, very tired, with a smile. He said, 'I wouldn't "whup" them. I wouldn't "whup them now."' Then I awoke." Lin Orme had died that night.[97]

Ammon stayed on in Arizona a while. He was writing his autobiography, and it was going well. Dorothy had already put his name in the masthead of the Catholic Worker, where he was listed as associate editor. She was also sending him letters to the editor to answer, from the sort of well-meaning but querulous reader who wanted to know how the paper could claim to be Catholic. He was already giving practiced replies: "First, we appreciate your frankness, and your interest in our efforts. The CW picks up the worst of the human debris at the bottom of the cliff resulting from the dog-eat-dog system of capitalism. We get the ones that professional social workers despair of."[98]

He wanted to leave, but his care for Lin Orme had created obligations. "They want me to stay here until I go East in August [after another round of picketing]. I sleep in my own place but cook on the electric stove, as I have so much to do with his yard, the chickens, etc. I spend about two hours a day on it. Get about 86 dozen eggs a week, wash the dirty ones and grade them and put them in boxes." But the project he had shared with Orme seemed pointless now. "With the Old Man's death possibly Ammon felt no need to stay in Phoenix," Joan Thomas wrote: "He was so very much on fire with Dorothy Day, *The Catholic Worker* and, yes, I venture at this time the Catholic Church."[99]

When Rik and Ginny Anderson, Hennacy's pacifist friends in Arizona, discovered that he was joining the church, they hazed him for weeks. Ginny quoted James Joyce and suggested that the church was illogical. Even T. S. Eliot had only gone so far as Anglicanism, she noted.[100] In protest they had not distributed any of the *Catholic Workers* that arrived in his absence. "Rik, and to some extent Ginny, are the only ones who were not glad that I joined the Church," he wrote to Day.[101] Most of his correspondence in his final Phoenix days was with Dave Dellinger, his printer. Ammon was spending all his money on the book, over $850 by midsummer, and he deferred to all of Dorothy's edits, which were good. *The Autobiography of a Catholic Anarchist* was going to be something. In August 1953 he did his last fast and picketing in Arizona, then headed north to Flagstaff, where he and Platt resolved their differences. He took the bus to New York City as a fully fledged public figure, very different from the fieldworker who had arrived six years earlier.

7

The New York Years

Hennacy stopped at two *Catholic Worker* farms on his way to New York to get an idea of their agrarian practices. He knew a bit about farming and does not seem to have been impressed by the first farm he saw. The second was the Peter Maurin Farm on Staten Island, where he also worked on his *Autography*, sometimes sleeping at Dave Dellinger's in New Jersey. There he proofread and collated the pages of his book, the folios proceeding to Dellinger's print shop in New Jersey to be bound. A sympathizer loaned five hundred dollars to buy paper, and Fritz Eichenberg of the *CW* produced a sketch of Ammon for the cover.

It was a low point for the Catholic Worker, which had moved from Mott Street to Chrystie Street. "After the war, there were very few houses," said Tom Cornell, "and only one third of the newspaper circulation. [Dorothy] was no longer sought after. *America* didn't print her name for fifteen years. Friends of mine found that their vocations [in the priesthood] were questioned and even denied if their association with the Catholic Worker was any too enthusiastic."[1]

The new location was a dirty brick building with a fire escape hanging down the front and a store window filled with slogans. "I had visited Mott Street for a few minutes in 1938 and 1939," wrote Ammon, and "spent the day after Easter of 1950 there." The people he saw on Chrystie Street could have been a resume of his past: migrants and their children, indigents and alcoholics, and idealistic youngsters, all somehow living together in the shabby order that radiated from a core of Catholic beliefs. It was a form of anarchism that he had not yet experienced. "I was not yet sold on the advisability of majoring in 'feeding the bums,'" he said. "I was for more and more propaganda."[2] It is not that he was against charity, but he saw his brand of Catholicism as streetcorner advocacy—as much the Sermon on the Plain as the Sermon on the Mount.[3]

Ammon had followed the *CW*'s office politics but from afar, with scant notion of the internecine battles. There was a raucous dispute between followers of Peter Maurin's personalism and a newer, European import known as distributism. Personalism focused on change through individual action, charity, and the self-sufficiency of Maurin's agrarian communes. Distributists thought all that was naïve: more structure and egalitarianism were required, and did not most people live in cities? They called personalism "reactionary" due to its roots in French social Catholicism. Ammon represented a blended view, which scholar Mary Segars sees as a link between Maurin's philosophy and "such American thinkers as Thoreau and Emerson."[4]

Maurin had suffered a long cognitive decline and died at the Staten Island farm on May 15, 1949, leaving Dorothy Day without an ideological interlocutor. Ammon's arrival in August 1953 marked not a Maurin replacement but a different type of male energy in the *Catholic Worker* offices. In practical terms, he would soon replace Robert Ludlow, a social democrat who formulated the *CW*'s positions.[5] He also replaced, at first, Tom Sullivan, the managing editor, who departed for different reasons. Though Ammon was the new managing editor, he aspired to be the new fire-breather. He disagreed with the distributists not only on economics but also on their allowance for "just wars." Unlike Maurin, however, Ammon wanted to live in the middle of things: he had lived the agrarian life and found it a narrow platform for effecting change. They lived in the city, not the country, and he found his new colleagues' conception of farming rather romantic; they had not been up in the middle of the night "subbing" the irrigation canals. Ludlow had been an "office anarchist," Ammon said, whereas he himself planned to be in the street, expanding his Phoenix picketing practices to one-on-one engagement. He had been in training for this.

Dorothy Day, meanwhile, every day had to arbitrate dozens of disputes, and was not as romantically available as Ammon had imagined. She was firmly in the personalist camp, but she acknowledged useful points in the distributist agenda. Sullivan, as managing editor, had arbitrated among the editorial factions, but Hennacy did not know enough Catholic theology or personalism to do this, and frankly he did not care. He did recognize unpalatable elements in distributism, however, which counted Hillaire Belloc and G. K. Chesterton among its exponents.

Figure 7.1. *Catholic Worker* caricature of Hennacy pounding a
sword into a ploughshare. Public domain.

Both had supported World War I, and Ammon, as usual, distinguished
friends and enemies by their icons and associations.

Religiously, Ammon was still apprenticed to Father Marion Casey, the
draft-resisting priest who had baptized him. But he was satisfied that his
Catholicism was deep enough to support his pacifism, that "voluntary
poverty" was better than codified equality, and that this was the "big
tent" of Christian pacifism that he had always sought. All people needed
to do was to live the Sermon on the Mount, as he did. Soon a young
ex-seminarian named Robert Steed, who had left Gethsemani Abbey,
would appear and become managing editor, freeing Hennacy to speak

on the street, which Steed saw as his talent. "He would say the most insulting things to people in a cheerful voice, with a smile on his face," said Steed: "He was so convinced he was right." Hennacy in turn became a kind of father figure to Steed.

In the *Catholic Worker* office, Hennacy had a desk and a new, practical attitude. "As radicals we live in the camp of the enemy," he wrote,

> and we can't make the rules that they have to govern us. We have to do the best we can and by that I mean *we have to do the best we can*. And not alibi and do little because we can't do it all. We can't be free of some entanglements like paying a small sales tax or tax on transportation, but these are exceptions. We can make the whole tenor of our lives anti-capitalist. We don't have to pay taxes on tobacco, liquor, shows, medicine, even if for a time we have a tax taken out of our pay.

This was quite a concession, but not as big as the one needed to live in the CW House.

Life in the Chrystie Street House

At first Hennacy, who had been living in unheated adobes for years, had the only single room for men, at the very top of the house, where he slept on a cot. This floor was a miasma of smells rising from the overheated lower floors, so bugs and vermin loved it. Steed, who soon joined him in this room, said there were so many bedbugs that they put the legs of their beds in cans of kerosene to prevent them from climbing up. "But they fell off the ceiling on us anyway," he said, "though Ammon claimed that, as a vegetarian, they would never bite him."[6]

They bathed only two or three times a week, for there was seldom enough hot water and little reason to smell nice. They got clothes that fit well enough from the donations room. It was true voluntary poverty, but Ammon had lived just as primitively in Arizona at first, and he saw propaganda value in it: "The fact that the CW folks do have bugs and lice and filth and deal with people who lie, steal, drink and fornicate, makes any change that might come over these derelicts come through knowing the sincerity and unselfishness of the CW."[7]

"The only hierarchy at the Catholic Worker House," said Steed, was determined by who had keys to the house and who did not.

> It was sort of "You've been here long enough. Why don't you start pulling your weight and take responsibility?" There'd be somebody sort of in charge of the house during the day and at night. We'd sign up on a roster at the beginning of the week and [take] assignments, so there'd be somebody to answer the phone, answer the door. During each of those times, there were certain kinds of responsibilities. At night you had to wash the floor, turn out the lights, wait for the bread to arrive for the next morning. In the morning . . . there'd be somebody in charge of the soup line, and somebody would take over after that.[8]

It was, in fact, the model of a self-organizing anarchist collective.

For a while Ammon's roommate was Michael Harrington. "I still had these very middle-class habits," said Harrington. "It was sort of ridiculous in the dining room . . . where we had rats and roaches, but I would hold Dorothy's chair for her. Dorothy was very feminine."[9] Hennacy "would needle Harrington, now committed to the Socialist Party, with stories he knew of socialists." "When I'd first wake up," Harrington recalled, "I wouldn't open my eyes. I'd first listen to see if he was around, because I knew he'd be waiting, just waiting. He would say, 'I knew a socialist in Ohio in 1911 who became a white slaver. I knew a socialist who used to beat blacks.' I mean, he knew every horror story about socialists."[10] In schooling new recruits, as several have mentioned, Hennacy took on Maurin's role, and he probably found Harrington a bit too Ivy League.

There were "some fellows in the kitchen" who cooked all the food, though with "too much starch in the diet," wrote Ammon. It was in that kitchen, Judith Gregory has written, "that the daily routine began."[11] They lit the stove well in advance of cooking, so that the roaches would leave. "I took a liking to roaches," Gregory said. "They seemed to breed in the desk drawers. Cockroaches waving their feelers gave me an impression of alertness and a certain shy sociability that I found charming."[12] In this kitchen Ammon met and was charmed by Dorothy's daughter, Tamar, "one of the matter-of-fact, practical women of whom there are very few in this upset world. I played with her children and off-and-on had a little conversation with Dave Hennessy [her husband]."[13]

"Ammon was a thin, active man of medium height," Gregory said, "always simply and neatly dressed, with wavy grey hair, cut short except for a stiff, curly flourish in front. He walked briskly with a springiness like his alert gazes and his witty responses in conversation. He worked hard and kept a strict schedule: answering letters on a typewriter in the office, selling papers, fulfilling speaking engagements and fasting every year, starting Aug. 6, one day for each year since the United States bombed Hiroshima and Nagasaki in 1945."[14]

On his first official day at work (August 30, 1953), Dorothy gave Ammon a huge pile of correspondence to answer. He plowed through it until September 3, to most letters responding with the boilerplate that he had already mastered, augmented by his new affiliation. These letters were peppered with "we feel" and "our way of living" and "In Christ, Ammon Hennacy, for the staff." He worked at "representing the CW."[15] As Joan Thomas has written, "Dorothy, for a time at least, does take Ammon over. And most willingly on his part. With something of an old-fashioned Southern courtesy, he refers to Dorothy as 'Miss Day.'"[16]

Dorothy had said to establish weekly routines "now that I was a soldier of Christ," Hennacy wrote.[17] So he created a weekly rotation, taking the soldier part rather literally. On Monday evening he sold CWs in front of Cooper Union College, where up to two thousand people attended free lectures. On Tuesday afternoons he held forth at Pine and Nassau in the financial district. Afterwards, "I continued my soapboxing on Wall Street" at the corner of Broad, adjacent to the New York Stock Exchange. Tuesday evenings he moved to the New School, where he met non-Catholic liberals. On Wednesdays he took the subway to the Bronx and stood at Fordham University gate, "about the noisiest place in New York City," to meet a Catholic crowd, many of whom recognized him later and elsewhere.[18] On Thursdays he picketed Woolworth's from noon to 2:00 p.m. and sold CWs nearby at Fourteenth and Broadway from 6:00 to 8:00 p.m. "Competition there is great," he noted, "for two or three street merchants will be shouting their wares." On Fridays he sold CWs at Forty-Third and Lexington, not far, Judith Gregory noted, "from a Catholic church whose politically reactionary pastor he loved to bait." On Sunday after Mass, he sold CWs in front of St. Patrick's

Cathedral. "He talked with anyone willing to talk with him, or likely to listen to him," Gregory said. "He was energy unbounded, propaganda in person, embodying his belief."[19]

On Monday, Wednesday, Thursday, and Saturday mornings Ammon worked at Chrystie Street, answering mail, writing for the *CW*, or working in the shelter, which was packed. "Ordinarily we have enough people to do the office work and the giving out of clothing [but] right now there is not one extra bed," he wrote. "When I came from Arizona . . . it happened that one fellow who worked in the file room left; otherwise I would have slept on the floor in the library, where about 16 sleep each night."[20] Though he came from the tranquility of Arizona, Hennacy warmed to the chaos of Chrystie Street. If this was pacifist anarchism, he was amenable.

A variety of men and women used the shelter. "People drift in who are maladjusted mentally and physically," he wrote. "Some of them stay a day or two and some have been here for 18 years. More come and go. We do not ask them to do any certain thing, but some cook, others clean, others sew, and nearly all help mail the paper out. Many sit around and do nothing. We have no staff meetings or discipline."[21] But there were minor insurrections. At one point, Kathy Shuh-Ries said,

> Two or three young couples ganged up and decided they were going to take over . . . They wrote on the walls, they wrote on the sheets. We had to ask them to leave. . . . [Another time] we had two men in the basement trying to rip off the food room. We had a person slashing their wrists on the second floor . . . a sick child who needed to go to the hospital. Sometimes you get crises one on top of the other and they made us think, "Do we want this going on here? Is this a safe place?"[22]

Gregory wrote that she "never saw an uglier apartment" than the one assigned her. "The toilet was in a closet just big enough to turn around and sit down." The main room was the Loft, where everyone was fed and meetings occurred. "The floor was rough and dirty— swept but not clean. Two toilets . . . stood along one wall. You would sometimes find wine bottles tucked into the grimy pocket behind the toilet bowl or crammed into the tank," wrote Gregory: "Once the Loft opened in the morning, some ate breakfast, some started to make the great vat of soup for the line at lunch, others wandered in when they felt like it, to answer mail, to talk to visitors or to sit around and talk with each other. The anarchism or personalism so often mentioned in the paper is probably more descriptive of the daily life at the *Worker* than of any ideal state."

The House was organized de facto by its two main activities. "The soup line would form earlier in cold or wet weather. Men and women climbed the stairs and waited. Slowly they would all be fed," said Gregory. "Every morning we got day-old loaves of crusty Italian bread made around the corner. We all ate the same lunch, and it was a good one: a hearty soup.... Some people liked to say the rosary every day. Millie ... would ring a bell and several people would gather outside the office to pray. Bob [Steed] would mutter some violent epithet, irritated by this sign of piety, fling down whatever he was doing, and get out of earshot as fast as he could."[23]

"The monthly cycle revolved around publishing the paper," said Gregory. "Articles would be written by us in New York or by friends and by others. Dorothy would read these or delegate someone else to do so. Articles were rarely edited. ... A truck delivered the papers and some of the men hauled these up to the loft. Keith produced the packets of cut address [labels], arranged geographically, by city, state or foreign countries. Most of us did our stint, folding, labeling, wrapping, chatting, watching the life of the loft." And Hennacy liked all this.

Steed offers an invaluable view of Hennacy in his most provocative period. Steed grew up in Memphis, joined Gethsemani monastery in 1951, and lived in silence under Thomas Merton until 1953. Then he left and volunteered at a hospitality house, where Ammon Hennacy showed up to give a talk: "He made a great impression," said Steed. "You could tell that he was a great man and you were a pipsqueak."[24] Like Hennacy, he went first to the Peter Maurin Farm. But without Maurin there was a void, he said, and "two other important people had just left, Robert Ludlow and Tom Sullivan." Unlike Hennacy, Steed said he was "eaten alive" by the bedbugs in their rooms. But he found fasting relatively easy, and once outdid Hennacy by going forty-seven days. This won Ammon's respect and, although Steed was not a strict vegetarian, he was enough of one to score points with Hennacy. Steed pointed out that Hennacy ate eggs in New York, just as he had in Arizona. But he admired Hennacy's toughness, his sang froid. "People denounced him as a communist when he sold CWs outside St. Patrick's," he said, "and one guy said he'd wipe the streets with him . . . Ammon just smiled."

After Day installed Steed as managing editor, "Ammon could write about whatever he wanted. He had a two-finger style of typing . . . and first draft was final draft."[25] Steed loved classical music and opera, which he played in the evening until Hennacy could not take it: he particularly disliked the *Kreutzer* Sonata. But Dorothy backed Steed's classical taste and Hennacy quieted down. In fact, they took him to an opera, but he dozed off in the second act. He "wasn't a big reader, like Dorothy, who loved murder mysteries; he'd read political stuff though. No interest in art or music." He did like films, though, especially if they were political. "Dorothy saw *On the Waterfront*," he wrote to a friend. "She says it is extra good."[26]

For Ammon politics was the main performance. He had heard every insult, every question, and he had formulated responses, his own lines. "I am having lots of fun, soap-boxing on Wall Street," he wrote in October 1954: "Sold 2 books there the other day and 50 papers. Sold 149 papers and 2 books at 43rd and Lexington yesterday. Speaking to the Vegetarian Society at the Belmont Plaza on Oct. 5." He perfected his art at the corner of Forty-Third and Lexington, which was his favored stage. There was a steady flow of commuters from Grand Central Terminal, a block away. The UN was three blocks east, though he never paid it much attention. Three blocks west was the New York Public Library, and the Eastside IRT subway met the Times Square shuttle there. These were the portals of the thinking classes, and he had a "door opener" or a reply for everyone who stopped. It was the best-situated corner in the world for a Catholic anarchist, but it was also close to that parish whose priest detested Hennacy. The priest had friends on the police force, and on this corner Hennacy was first arrested in New York on October 9, 1954. He wrote to Platt Cline,

> I spent 2 hrs. in jail last Friday for selling CWs on the street at 43rd and Lexington where I have been selling each Friday 11 to 3. I go to court this Friday and am out on my own. The Civil Liberties [Roger Baldwin] is defending me free. The charge is peddling without a license, and it is silly. I have a right to sell papers, but if they want to harass me every time I go

out, they can do it. So Dorothy, Eileen Fantino, and some others are coming along this Friday, and if I am pinched again, one of them will start selling, and if they are pinched, then one more, etc., like the old-time Wobs.[27]

This action plan did not materialize quickly enough though; Dorothy
came late and Fantino, with her back to Hennacy in the tumult, did not
see the police arrest him. He went to jail a second time. Dorothy and the
ACLU decided to make a test case for freedom of speech. But Ammon
did not mind jail that much, since he could write about it:

We jostled in the prison wagon up to the Tombs, which is near the City
Hall. After a time I was lodged in Lower D12 with Dan, in for drunken-
ness, who had bought a bottle of liquor when he cashed his $55 Lacka-
wanna check and had been rolled. Now he was picking up butts. I offered
to buy him a package of cigarettes from the trusty, but he said they
charged 50 cents after lockup and it was better to buy Bull Durham when
the regular commissary wagon came around the next day. . . . One aged
Jew got ten days for selling pretzels without a license (and the city won't
give you a license). He had not yet learned to pay off the cops.

These were not cotton pickers or conscientious objectors, but the urban
poor offered an abject experience that was, for Ammon, the backstory
of the "bums" that he met on the street.

In the morning my name was called "for Rikers," which meant Riker's
Island. . . . About 150 of us sat on benches in the big receiving room at
Rikers and were counted and recounted and fingerprinted. We all stood
naked and all body openings were examined, supposedly for dope which
we might smuggle in. The wine sores on the old men, the stooped and
broken bodies of many, presented a sorry spectacle compared to the
beautiful shiny black bodies of the Negros among us, for there was no
segregation here. Most of us were short timers who went to Dorm 8 in
the workhouse division. . . .
  My number was 419327, and Emil had the number next to mine. He
had done 30 days for drinking and had only been out a few days and by
some miracle of police inefficiency only drew 5 days this time for being
caught in a doorway drinking from a bottle. Emil is a counterman and

swears that in the future he will stick to beer, for this he can take, but not whiskey. After he had done his thirty days, he went to a blood bank, but his blood was too thin to be taken.

The food, the regimentation, and the dehumanization took Ammon back to his time at Atlanta. There had been no progress in prison reform: "This was the first time I had been in jail for 35 years. Was this all that our boasted civilization meant?"[28]

Five days later he and Emil were released, after being "checked and rechecked" by a guard who swore at them continuously. Emil accompanied Ammon to the CW House, where Murray Kempton, the *New York Post* columnist, interviewed them, writing, "We have no more radical instrument in our society than the Catholic Worker group. Its members are pacifists, reconcilers, and anarchists, and they believe that the service of Christ involves secession from the state." Hennacy "seemed altogether the least lonely man on earth," wrote Kempton.[29] The ACLU appeal lost initially but won unanimously in the state's highest court. These actions and publicity made Hennacy invaluable to the CW as it recovered its stature after World War II.

Hennacy remained in the city until the spring of 1954, when Catholic Worker Books released *The Autobiography of a Catholic Anarchist*, which he finished collating in the office. He was a celebrity, as Thomas points out: "His first speaking trip following the publication goes very well."[30] From the road he wrote pieces for the *CW*, such as the article "Greetings to the Spanish Anarchists from the Catholic Worker, May Day 1954."

When we think of Spain, we are with you ashamed of that Inquisition of Torquemada and of the bloody reign of Franco today. However, we are heartened by the memory of Francisco Ferrer, that martyr to freedom of education, whose memory cannot be obscured by decorations to Franco. . . . With this negative action there is also the positive one of brotherhood which we should seek to achieve on the land, in our unions, and in the support of our papers and literature, and above all in that sense of comradeship which we feel as a minority united to seek our goal of freedom only by means worthy of that freedom.—In Christ the Rebel, Ammon Hennacy.[31]

By September 1954, when reviews of his book began to appear, he was back in New York. "Here is something different and very different," wrote Daniel Poling in the *Christian Herald*. "From the cover to the last page, the volume is combative and stimulating. It is published by Catholic Worker Books! You will go in with temerity and come out with fists clenched." Nat Hentoff of the *Village Voice* also liked the book. And it gave ballast to Hennacy's public persona: with his flashing blue eyes and head of grey hair, Hennacy was a striking figure, and now a seriously published book author.[32]

Ammon without Dorothy

But publication did not spell success on other fronts. As Ammon wrote to his mother, "I don't see Dorothy very much, as she is at the farm. . . . Meeting her tomorrow at the Ferry." References to Selma disappeared entirely from his letters, and there were fewer notes about his daughters, although he mentioned them proudly to people at the CW House. But Ammon was lonely, in a fashion few suspected. He had come to New York expecting to be Dorothy's partner, if not lover, to work with her in a communion of true believers. Although he knew that she spoke and traveled extensively, that she went on retreats to the Maryfarm, and that she traveled even to put out the *Catholic Worker*, he never knew what those absences meant, how frequent they were. And when she was present, she was a mother, caretaker of the elderly and the wounded in the House, and she adjudicated quarrels. She dealt with inspectors, contractors, food suppliers, and the post office. She fended off the church hierarchy and the mob. People died on the premises and had to be buried. Day never let daily chaos dominate her spiritual life, however, retreating regularly to the Catholic Worker farms for prayer and community. But it would never be the experience they had together in Arizona.

She was in Minneapolis the week after Ammon was released from Rikers. She told him to open all her letters and respond, which seemed like a gesture of intimacy. He reported this in a letter to his mother, to show that the relationship was working. But in other letters he begins to mention other women: "Pat Rush came. . . . She liked me, as she had never seen her father, and at times introduced me as her foster father.

She helped me sell papers on the streets."[33] Later Pat would show up at the Joe Hill House in Salt Lake City. In truth, when Dorothy was gone, he began to appreciate the other female energy in the House.

Early in 1955 he planned a twenty-one-day fast, which he threatened in letters to Day to extend to forty days.[34] Dorothy was not much for fasting—she found her first six-day hunger fast too much—and some people at the *CW* were concerned about the health of the sixty-two-year-old Hennacy.[35] "Dorothy was in Montana and got scared that I would die after I had fasted 12 days, and came home and talked me into quitting it," he wrote.[36] It is not clear that she returned just for him, but after two years their relations had become a bit testy, as his description of one meal reveals:

> She told me not to wait until she came downstairs for supper, but to go ahead and eat, so one evening I waited about five minutes and then I commenced to eat. Then she stood in the door and said, "I told you that we're going out for chop suey." I got up and told her that she never told me. Maybe she thought she had. She called me a glutton and then asked me to ride over to the farm with her. All the time we were on the bus she grouched at me for not waiting on her. When we got by the ferry, she led the way to a restaurant and sat at a table and asked me what I had had for supper. I told her an omelet, so she ordered one and then held my hand and said she was sorry we had misunderstood each other. I had to go to Boston to speak the next day so she gave me the money for the fare and told me to wake her up in the morning with a cup of black coffee and she would make breakfast for "you glutton."[37]

Dorothy had her "ladylike" habits, as Harrington testified, while Ammon was blunt and matter of fact, but she also nagged, especially about fasting: Ammon should quit his Lenten Fast (for which he ate one meal a day and an apple) and stop extending his Hiroshima fast. He was disappointed that year when he only lost one pound, but Dorothy did not sympathize.

There were other young women around the CW. Some showed up pregnant, some were heartbroken, some were glamorous and wanted association with radicals. They basically ran the inside of the house during the day. One bought Ammon expensive dinners when he ended his fasts. Vivian Cherry, who became a celebrated street photographer, was clearly Ammon's favorite: "After a Friday meeting I would go over and take Dorothy home. Then I would leave. 'Are you going to Vivian's?' she would ask. 'Yes,' I said." "Do you sleep with her?" Dorothy would ask. "No," he answered truthfully, but his street performativity was spreading into the rest of his life. He wanted to appear more the bon vivant than he was, and his Gandhian reserve was at the breaking point.[38]

But Ammon and Dorothy reunited when Mayor Vincent Impellitteri announced a new civilian defense plan in case of nuclear war. A year earlier people had barely paused in their work when hearing air raid sirens, but now he announced a *mandatory* evacuation to fallout shelters for June 15, 1955. Historians describe what was supposed to happen:

> At 10 a.m., alarms [would] sound . . . at which time all citizens were sup-posed to get off the streets, seek shelter, and prepare for the onslaught. Each citizen was supposed to know where the closest fallout shelter was located; these included the basements of government buildings and schools, underground subway tunnels, and private shelters. Even President Dwight D. Eisenhower took part in the show, heading to an under-ground bunker in Washington, D.C. The entire drill lasted only about 10 minutes, at which time an all-clear signal was broadcast and life returned to normal. Civil Defense officials estimated that New York City would suffer the most in such an attack, losing over 2 million people.[39]

Hennacy saw this as an attempt to normalize nuclear war.

> I told Dorothy "we must get ready to disobey this foolish law." I contacted Ralph DeGia of the War Resisters League and he got in touch with others, the FOR, AFSC, and W.I.L., and so accordingly when the time came, we had a whole group in City Hall Park ready to disobey when the whistles blew. The television men were there and asked Dorothy to explain why we were acting as we did, but she asked me to speak because my voice would be louder. So I told them that if a bomb dropped there would be no police left to arrest us and that the whole thing was a farce.[40]

The police ordered Hennacy and Day to go underground, but they refused and with a dozen others were arrested. Not arraigned until

11:00 p.m., they offended Judge Louis Kaplan with impertinent answers, so he set bail at fifteen hundred dollars and sent Judith Beck (an actress then playing Phaedra at the Living Theater) to Bellevue's psychiatric ward for not saying "Your Honor" and for responding to his questions with her questions. Hennacy and the CW crew pled guilty and posted bail, thinking they would be free to agitate and, as in the past, still get the money back.[41]

Their protest was a media sensation. In addition to New York papers, the *Pittsburgh Post-Gazette* and *Chicago Tribune* covered (and praised) their stand, as did *Nation, Harper's*, and the *Progressive*. The Catholic press was divided, some journals feeling they should have obeyed the state. The *St. Louis Catholic Register* argued against them, but the *Boston Pilot*, the oldest diocesan paper in the United States, wrote that the nation had lost touch with its guilt over Nagasaki and Hiroshima. The *Catholic Worker* of course wrote copiously about the protest, thrusting Ammon and Dorothy to the forefront of the "Ban the Bomb" movement. Eichenberg, the resident artist, had been part of the event and made sketches that ran in the July and August issues. They expected to get prison time, but the case dragged on until December 22, when they were all found guilty, but their sentences were suspended (and their bail returned). When Ammon went to his desk on the morning of December 23, he found a card wreathed in black, from coworker Tom Caine: "'So Sorry! NO JAIL!'"[42] Ammon took this as irony rather than satire, but it reminded him of the missed opportunity, since he had come to New York for the dramatic stage. It is also indicative of office suspicion about his penchant for performance.

There were other, smaller disappointments. His Arizona world had been personal: Rik and Ginny, Lin Orme, Platt Cline, and Frank Brophy. He even knew the IRS officials by name. In New York City, aside from Dorothy, who was gone often, and some colleagues like Steed, he felt as though he was working every day against the impersonality of the big city. If his commitment did not register here, what was the point? Was he selling out his deepest beliefs on the streetcorners every day? He was thinking, he wrote to his mother, of returning to a smaller scale, maybe going "to Salt Lake City and working like I did in Phoenix a season or a year, and maybe some other places in the west." His life at hard labor looked attractive in the rear-view mirror.[43]

The small annoyances of Chrystie Street could pile up, like the inability to wash his clothes because "the indigent guests were always using the machine."[44] In Arizona, he had hung his clothes out to dry in the sun, picked his own vegetables, and made his own bread. Living in New York reminded him of the disputes and grievances of the 1920s, and the popular press still failed to distinguish between Socialists, Communists, and anarchists. True, the violent anarchist groups of the 1930s were as distant as the bohemian anarchists of the 1920s, but Whitaker Chambers and Joe McCarthy now blurred the public debate with their lies. "This capitalist system that breeds wars," wrote Ammon, seems "to exist on lies, deceit, and the dropping of atom bombs."[45]

As Christmas approached, he worried over gifts for Dorothy, for his daughters, and for his mother. After his morning chores in the kitchen, he worked on the newspaper. Its tasks were well divided, now that Steed was managing editor, and this left his afternoons free for picketing, lecturing, visiting, and selling papers. He argued, discussed, and debated: people came up after lectures or he debated them on streetcorners, always smiling, funny, sometimes with scathing comments. There was no question or comment that he had not heard before: it was like a play, but the audience moved on. Younger women asked him to manage their affairs, to take them to medical appointments, to babysit their children. There was even one who threw her laundry down the stairs for him to wash.

Through the spring of 1956, Ammon performed yeoman duties for Dorothy, accompanying her to St. Patrick's Cathedral for the reintroduction of the ancient ritual of footwashing, taking her statement to the *Daily Worker* and having it read from the podium in April, and picketing the New York offices of the IRS, where he was not much noticed. Most of his personal news he put in weekly letters to his mother: Sharon had married an I AM member who worked in a photography plant in southern California. Carmen was back in Santa Fe teaching music.

The air raid drills came again the next spring. An article in the *Chicago Tribune* suggested that they might not be mandatory, but Dorothy spoke to Quaker meetings against them, and Ammon was again galvanized: "We will likely get jail, as we are out under suspended sentences."[46] This time they chose for their protest Washington Square, already a gathering

Figure 7.2. Ammon Hennacy at Hiroshima Day Protest, August 6, 1957. Photograph by David McReynolds, permission of mcreynoldsphotos.org.

point for the Beat generation: "There were more reporters and television men than there were of us, and also the police," Ammon wrote, but "we gave our message to all of New York City." Once arrested, Ammon rode in the police van with a Purdue physics instructor, David Caplan, who became a cause célèbre in court, where he told the judge that it was foolish to tell civilians to stand in doorways since his studies showed they needed to be five hundred feet underground to be safe. "The figures [he gave] were that 4,372,939 would have died in the city in our mythical warfare," said Ammon," so Caplan was fined $25 and set free. Reporters present offered to pay his fine."[47]

Twenty had been arrested, the men spending five days on Hart's Island and the women in the tougher House of Detention, where protesters outside demonstrated for their release. Hennacy had taken books to read, but they were confiscated. "We each had a separate cell with a mattress, but the radio blasted until 9:30 p.m. . . . Dan and I went to Dorm 16. There were about 80 prisoners in a dorm, two-thirds of them Negros and very few grey-headed men. The light went out at 9:30 and we were up at 5:30 a.m. For the very first time in two years I had a good rest."[48] They were surprised at sentencing, however, when Judge Comerford "gave us a $25 fine or 5 days in jail."[49] Most of the CWs chose the sentence, and for Ammon it was time to reflect on his next endeavor—picketing the IRS in his annual August tax protest—but he was also reading about the Mormons "who went with push carts in the winter over the bad roads to Utah."

In the heart of the Cold War, life shifted a bit. "I was picketing again at the Custom House, and this was the first time since 1949 that I did not have the police or mobs bothering me," he wrote in August 1956: "A new Irish tax man had come to the CW office to collect my taxes, asking about my 'hidden assets.'" Although he sent news of his protest to the AP, UPI, *Times*, *Post*, and *Herald Tribune* and other papers, only the *Daily Worker* covered him that year.[50] This was disappointing, as if his fast and protest were losing publicity value, at the same time that he had increasing logistical problems. "Two T-men came from Washington and questioned Dorothy, Carol, and me several times at the CW and at 90 Church Street, saying that they would report their findings to Washington."[51] But Ammon retained his sense of humor when picketing:

While resting for five minutes in the park each hour, I noticed great shoots of Johnson grass disfiguring the scenery as they appeared between the neat evergreen border. Ordinarily I would exercise my anarchist prerogative and uproot them, but I was too tired to lift a hand. On the last day as I was again resting, along comes the park attendant and asked the occupants of each bench to move in order that he might sweep a few dead leaves from behind the benches. Then he proceeded to sweep this refuse under the hedge, pushing it along with his broom indifferently so that some remained along the hedge to blow around again. It was not his job to beautify the park by getting rid of the unsightly Johnson grass. It was nobody's job it seemed, so my last act in the park was to pull it up.[52]

The Old Pioneer would have approved. On this 1959 fast, Ammon lost more weight than usual, seventeen pounds in the first five days, and over a weekend break he gained back only one and a half. By the end of the second week he had lost eighteen pounds, a substantial amount considering that it was not as hot or dry as Arizona. Afterwards he rested at Dave and Tamar Hennessey's farm, where he and Dorothy babysat the five grandchildren while their parents took a vacation, with Ammon showing talent as a foster grandpa. At the end of November, the air raid protesters would have to appear in court again for sentencing; meanwhile, Dorothy set him to work on Best of "The Catholic Worker," which was time-consuming, he said, because Dorothy had written a column on every topic. Then the air raid sentencing was suspended, another anticlimax.

Ammon had lived for years with missing teeth and only one front tooth. "Seems that most of my teeth were chalky and broke off after all these years," he said, but the roots of the broken teeth remained, and he was experiencing increasing pain. In February 1957, he traveled to Waterville, Maine, where a sympathetic dentist extracted nineteen of his roots in four sessions and made him an upper plate. He took no anesthesia but confessed that it hurt and that he cried, "but I found I could now say 'Mississippi' without lisping." Lecturing his way back down the Atlantic seaboard, he arrived in New York City a more tolerable-looking man.[53] He went on a speaking tour immediately, to Canada this time, where he talked not only to labor and leftist groups but also at

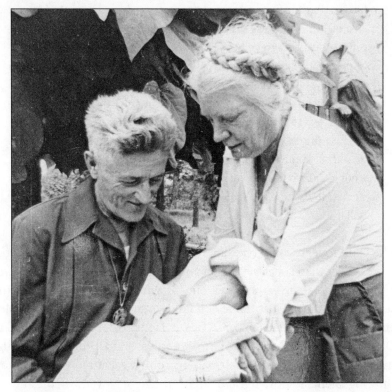

Figure 7.3. Ammon and Dorothy Day with one of her grandchildren. Permission of Josephine Thomas and Marquette University.

conservative seminaries and churches in Montreal and Quebec, then crossed Ontario, reentering the United States at Detroit. He lectured his way across Ohio and east through Pennsylvania, arriving back in New York City for Easter, 1957.

He had heard there was to be a "Prayer Pilgrimage for Freedom" on May 17, the third anniversary of the Supreme Court's *Brown v. Board of Education* decision. Organized by A. Philip Randolph, Ammon's friend Bayard Rustin, and Ella Baker, this march to the Lincoln Memorial was called a "prayer" action so as not to embarrass the Eisenhower administration. The final speaker would be Martin Luther King Jr., whom Ammon had only seen from afar. There would be thousands there, and he was excited, recalling his earlier visit with the Hopis. He was looking forward to working with the civil rights movement, but on the way there his bus broke down, three times, and he had to sleep in Philadelphia with friends.[54]

Picketing Las Vegas

Then he glimpsed another big project: picketing a major nuclear test site. He had his eye on Mercury, Nevada, a closed city run by the Atomic Energy Commission (AEC).[55] The Committee for Non-Violent Action (CNVA) had originated this protest, timed to the twelfth anniversary of the bombings of Hiroshima and Nagasaki, but they could not get into Mercury and had retreated.[56] Ammon had been thinking that nuclear tests might be connected to weather in a bigger way, writing to Nicholas Ross, a scientist at Woods Hole Oceanographic Institute, with questions about the effects of nuclear testing on the atmosphere. Ross said that there could be a link, and as it would turn out, weather would indeed make the tests deadly for ranchers and their flocks in Utah.[57] Hennacy also thought it would be better to picket the main AEC office in Las Vegas, which had scheduled smaller atomic tests for so many years that they had become tourist events. Norman Mailer had recently described in *The Deer Park* (1955) how Hollywood celebrities would drive up and, cocktails in hand, watch the blinding flashes and small mushroom clouds. Around one hundred tests were conducted above ground, paused only if the wind shifted so dramatically that it might blow fallout over St. George, Utah, which happened anyway.

Ammon's choice was astute: reporters had no interest in venturing out to remote Mercury, but Las Vegas was easy. Pope Pius XII had called for a halt to atomic tests, so that gave them a news hook. Ammon knew the AEC's PR chief, Grace Urros, and when he told her his plan, she sent word to Lt. Col. Hunter in Las Vegas that Ammon "was okay." She had "a guard named Don bring out a chair each morning that [Ammon] might rest in the shade at times." He ignited a controversy in the western states' media, which was happy to photograph and interview a famous pacifist. When the *Las Vegas Review Journal* asked the local bishop if he agreed with Hennacy, he equivocated, saying that Hennacy's protest was "directed to the whole world, and not limited to the Nevada proving grounds" but that while the *Catholic Worker* represented the church in organized labor, "this man does not have Episcopal approval." This was great PR, perhaps his most successful picketing, and the coverage could hardly have worked out better.[58]

But Ammon ended up needing that AEC chair. It was pure desert heat, over one hundred degrees every day, and each night it was all he could do "to crawl up the stairs to his Las Vegas hotel room and take cold shower after cold shower."[59] He later told Joan Thomas that was the one time he "thought he wasn't going to make it" through a protest. There were also logistical problems. Having taken the bus to Las Vegas, he had to assemble his posters from scratch on site. He bought poles and poster board at the hardware store, making two placards that both read "STOP ATOMIC TESTS" in large type.[60]

Tired as he was, after his evening shower Hennacy pounded out letters on a rented typewriter. To his mother he explained with amazement that his fifteen-dollar-a-week room included air conditioning. For the *Catholic Worker* he wrote that UPI and Hearst reporters had interviewed him, as well as a Japanese photographer, and that he would appear on local television. The problem was that due to the heat, "hardly anyone walks on this street, but cars are going by all the time." Col. Hunter had "asked me . . . to drink some of their cold bottled spring water, which I did." The office staff was cordial, even worried about his weight loss, which was dramatic, as much as three pounds a day. He wrote a long letter to Bayard Rustin, hoping to lure him out to the "big test," which "comes the day before I quit picketing."[61] He even sent Rustin maps.

Ammon focused on that "big test." Large numbers of troops were arriving, unconcerned that they were about to be exposed to a massive dose of radiation to test its effects on them. They hooted and whistled at him as they drove by, but the event was anticlimactic—the bomb failed to detonate. At the end of his last day, Hennacy drank sauerkraut juice to break his fast, then took the bus to Pasadena, where Sharon fed him avocado salad. He had lost nineteen pounds, which he regained. His son-in-law showed him a Pasadena paper with the headline "Atomic Test Foe Scores Victory." That California headline, for his solitary action, told him all he really needed to know.[62]

On his way back to New York City, Hennacy stopped in Phoenix for four days, reclaiming possessions left at Orme's farm and depositing them at Rik and Ginny Anderson's. He had made the Phoenix papers, so the mayor introduced him on a radio show. He wanted to go to Santa Fe to visit Carmen, and a young novelist, Edward Abbey, who had just published *The Brave Cowboy* (1956), drove him up there and back.[63] Then it was back on the bus, to the annual New York air raid drill protest. He arrived a day early, but this event was a cakewalk after Las Vegas. All the protesters were from the CW and the protest was in a park across from the CW House, so it was a kind of homecoming. About ten were arrested, including Dorothy, but "the judge this time was a tough old Catholic by the name of Walter Bayer," wrote Hennacy. "He told us to read the Bible and said that we were a 'heartless bunch of individuals who breathed contempt for the law.' . . . He gave us 30 days."

At the jail intake Ammon was given a yellow card that said "Unfit," which he thought was ironic after his Nevada protest. Then he remembered that exactly forty years earlier he had entered the Atlanta Penitentiary, so he decided to play the senior part, writing wryly that "I was put with the old men in Dorm 12. I helped as a houseman a little, spent the rest of my time pulling weeds from my favorite vegetables (eggplant and peppers) in a small garden nearby."[64] To his mother, on prison letterhead, he wrote, "I am having a good rest." Dorothy Day and the three other women arrested were not as lucky, going to the Tombs, a tougher jail.

On release all of them headed back to the CW House, where there was more than usual on the table. Eisenhower had initially been against dropping the atomic bomb, but in 1953 he quietly signed a document titled "NSC 162/2," which normalized the use of nuclear weapons. Secretary of State John Foster Dulles said that "local defenses must be reinforced by the further deterrent of *massive retaliatory power* . . . that permits of a selection of military means instead of a multiplication of means. As a result, it is now possible to get, and share, more basic security at less cost" (emphasis added).[65] As the *Catholic Worker* pointed out, this "economy" option meant the certain destruction of humanity.

Ammon began to speak about this threat up and down the East Coast, at colleges from Yale to Rutgers. At the former, where his announced topic was the Hopis, he turned the tribe's pacifism into a shaming of the US nuclear expansion. At the latter, he made his point via Thoreau, anthropology, and science. Appearing at an Amish event in Lancaster, he quoted John Woolman, William Lloyd Garrison, and their founder,

Jakob Ammann. On October 23, 1957, Ammon appeared on the *Night-beat* TV program, a forerunner of *60 Minutes*: "Radicals and Catholics phoned in saying it was very good," he reported. "I did not know what questions would be asked until they came, quite fast. I told of the Quakers and the Hopi."[66]

* * *

Ammon and Dorothy still went to Maryfarm in Easton if they had time, but Dorothy was busy developing a magazine titled *Liberation* and was irritated by Ammon's fasting, which to his annoyance she called his "specialty." "For each year that passes since Hiroshima, Ammon extends his fast by one day," she wrote: "He [also] undergoes a complete routine fast every Friday as a matter of health and discipline." He felt she was pigeonholing him, ignoring the Gandhian roots of his Friday ritual and the impact he was making.[67] But she added that the CW men "look up to Ammon for his readiness to go all out for his beliefs . . . for the many days he has spent in jail, for his refusal to pay income tax."[68] At other times she was less kind, mocking his rural accent and writing, "We call Ammon our American peasant. . . . Oh, he is right, irritatingly right, although it must be admitted that he is often hard to take."[69]

With his teeth fixed, Ammon appeared in more photographs, often giving advice to young people. Dorothy grew to resent it, since in wooing her he had said that age did not matter, that sex was not important. "He liked women," she wrote later, "especially young and pretty women and greeted them all with a swift embrace when he met them." He had privately accused her of being "afraid of sex," writes one biographer, going so far as to speculate that she "hated it."[70] She was equally brutal to him in her memoir: "Many people consider him egotistical and self-centered, and so he is, in a way—enough that he will appreciate my writing about him, rather than not. Ammon would prefer having people speak about him, rather than their not mentioning him at all. Hatred or love he can accept, but indifference, no."[71] She despaired of his ever understanding church history, the lives of the saints, or Mariology. Ammon felt those were unimportant; he felt unappreciated and, since Dorothy added whoever asked to the masthead of the *Catholic Worker*, he asked that his name be removed.[72]

Despite the deteriorating relationship, he did not leave because he felt that "Dorothy has no one here who is at all radical to speak of, and nearly all are too lazy or bashful to get out on the street and sell CWs. I meet hundreds who saw me on television and stop and talk."[73] After the deserted sidewalks of Las Vegas, he was happy to be back with the New York characters, even if the protests seemed more theatrical. One day on Wall Street he met John Moody, founder of Moody's Investment Services. On Saturday nights he returned to Union Square, selling CWs with Pat Rusk and Francisco and visiting their friends. "We would stop in afterwards to see a woman who taught English at Columbia and [her companion] who was some sort of an IWW." Another night he met a Jewish woman who married a "balmy kid from the south [who] came to CW meetings" and whose brother "brought a big, fat drunk Irishman to the warm rooms of the CW and said, 'This is Christ. Take care of him.' I told him to take care of him, for he had brought him in."[74] He also met Judith Malina, cofounder of the Living Theater, who later wrote that she "saw folks distributing copies of *The Catholic Worker*. . . . Ammon Hennacy gave me some to hand out and despite my religious difference I did so gladly. Ammon had seen 'The Idiot King' and treats me like a friend. I like his ornery plainness."[75]

This was the point at which Elmer Bendiner interviewed him for a classic study, *The Bowery Man*. "Ammon Hennacy is a remarkably pleasant man to be with," wrote Bendiner. "He appears to be in his fifties, but he is actually close to seventy. He is short, well-built, with iron-grey hair, mild blue eyes and ruddy cheeks, but these particulars can scarcely account for the uncommon sense of relaxation that he exudes. It is hard to pinpoint the manner in which this supreme effect is achieved. He wears clothes which seem not so much to have been chosen but rather to have happened to him."[76]

"Men who know their way around the Bowery know Hennacy and the Catholic Worker because it serves probably the best free grub on the street without a cover charge in the way of an ear-banging sermon or any compulsion to 'nose-dive'—which is the way Bowery Men speak of the energetic type of praying seen at missions."[77] Bendiner watched as con men hit up Ammon for money—he never gave and sometimes he told them to their faces that they drank "to keep on dying." One man who received free clothes, free meals, and a free bed turned to Ammon and said, "What the hell's the matter with you? Don't you know I'm a god-damned fraud?" Answered Ammon, "That's one problem you can't bring to us, Mac. If you're a fraud, that's between you and God."[78] Another man, annoyed that the *CW* did not have the "imprimatur" of Rome, stood behind Ammon yelling, "Don't buy from this jerk! Don't buy!" He followed Ammon down the street whispering, "I am your persecutor, I'm your persecutor." Hennacy just smiled and walked on, wrote Bendiner. Every day people told him to get a job, and every time he replied that he had one at the *Catholic Worker.*[79]

He liked that corner of Forty-Third and Lexington, which was fifty yards from the Church of St. Agnes, a venue used by Bishop Fulton J. Sheen for his radio broadcasts, and by Cardinal Spellman. Once a heckler asked him if he had been converted by the charismatic Sheen. He replied "that Sheen converted the big convertibles and I came in the Left door." Another heckler asked what he would do if the pope ordered him to pay taxes, and he replied, "The Pope can order me to walk on my hands. So what?" Said Robert Steed, "Remember that he liked Joan of Arc—he was fearless."

When Dorothy set off on a long trip to New Mexico, it made him homesick and he wrote to Platt Cline that he missed the desert. In fact, he was already dropping hints around the *CW* offices that he might move back to the West. Dorothy visited Carmen in Santa Fe, which pleased Ammon, but less than it should have. He went to St. Benedict's Farm at Upton, Massachusetts, with Lee Pagano, to see how stained-glass windows were made. Back in New York in January 1958, he planned not only his usual spring tax protest but also an antinuclear protest with a loosely affiliated group called the "Peace-makers" at Cape Canaveral on April 12, 1958.[80]

Among those protesters were to be Quakers and Christian Scientists, as well as Catholic Workers. Each chose a church of his denomination to picket the Sunday before the main action at the Cape, with Hennacy, unfortunately, picking the tough St. Mary's parish in Rockledge, where the conservative Father LeMay was close to the local police. Ammon had alerted LeMay to his coming, which usually defused the worst resentment, but on the front steps minutes before Mass, LeMay asked Ammon to remove the word "Catholic" from his signs. When he refused, four ushers grabbed his signs and destroyed them. Hennacy and the Quakers hung around three more days, speaking at churches and on the radio, and picketing on the highway to the base, but their protest was anticlimactic. "The Orlando and Miami papers gave us good coverage when we marched in the rain," he wrote.

But this was not enough for Ammon, since Dave Dellinger and others were picketing the AEC in Washington and fasting and getting good PR. In a grumpy mood, he disapproved of their "negative fasting" because it involved a sit-in and refusal to move. "Not good manners," he said, because penance should be pure. He preferred the protest model he had perfected in New York City, to which he returned. "We had been picketing the Atomic Energy Commission at 70 Columbus Ave for several years and there was a week of picketing going on when we heard that the air raid drill would be on May 6th," he said, but only ten people participated, all given suspended sentences by Judge Kenneth Phillips, who did not understand that they wanted to go to jail.[81]

Using his Las Vegas protest as a model, Hennacy next did a forty-day fast in Washington in late spring of 1958. Knowing from experience to pace himself, he roomed near the National Cathedral, where he went to Mass each morning, then picketed from 9:00 to 10:00, rested on the grass, and thereafter picketed twenty minutes and rested forty. When he saw that the pedestrian traffic peaked as the AEC shuttle bus arrived from Germantown, he modified his routine, having become a student of human traffic patterns.

Hennacy was almost sixty-five, and although some worried about his long fasts, he was rather dismissive of those who thought "loss of a pound or a meal is a disaster." He began to research long fasts—noting that many had occurred during the Irish Troubles. But the Washington forty-day fast (May 28 to July 6, 1958) caused him to lose twenty-five pounds in the first eighteen days, and thirty-one overall. Having overcome hunger through long practice, he no doubt felt a certain control, the lightness and clarity experienced by fasters. "I feel better than when I was eating," he wrote to Steed. "It is hard to believe. Didn't lose a pound the last week. The FAST beats down the old Adam."[82] The way that Hennacy fasted so easily was almost an affront to other protesters, especially the undertone of moral superiority, but he appeared increasingly tired.

Ammon tried to explain, in his Washington leaflet, that he was "fasting to awaken the consciences of those who are part of the war machine, those who are half-hearted pacifists and those Christians who see no contradiction in following both Christ and Caesar."[83] As usual, he wrote letters every night, but now they were briefer: "Pretty hot here for the past 8 days, but I went slow, and while a little weak, I felt very good generally." To his mother, who was growing frail, he said that he was dreaming of buttermilk and strawberries. Dorothy Day noted that during long fasts, "as the days went by, his voice got weaker; when he came home he lay down on one of the long, low tables in the office to rest until he could regain enough strength to climb the four flights to his bed."[84]

Sandstone 1959

Hennacy may have been weakening physically, but he was still burning spiritually. As he escalated the scale of his protests, the nuclear missile race was a perfect target. He had mastered the logistics, the publicity, the physical costs—all that he needed were bigger opportunities. He decided that he would fast forty days for Lent in the spring of 1959, beginning Ash Wednesday. There was probably a little cheating around the edges; he was known not to count Coca-Cola as food. On March 26 he wrote to his mother and Julia, "I feel fine; only 2 more days to do. Didn't lose any pounds the past 12 days. I'll think of all of you, especially on Easter morning when I break my fast with V8 juice heated up as soup."

Easter prompted him to think about jail, the sentence that he and the others might get for the previous year's air-raid-drill protest, their trial dates trailing behind them like a dust cloud. "No one can tell if we will get off with a scolding or get the limit of a year and $500 fine. . . . Bob Steed will write you if we get much time," he told his relatives. The CW was now starting to expand again, with new houses in Chicago, in Rochester, and on the West Coast. Dorothy had gone into retreat at the farm, and the newspaper missed publication in April and May. Gaining back only eight of the nineteen pounds he had lost, Ammon spoke to students at regional colleges and debated Communists, capitalists, and professors.[85] Steed was increasingly central, so perhaps Ammon thought he could be absent. In the summer of 1959 he planned, he wrote to the Clines, to go to Omaha and "get 6 months for 'going over the fence' at the missile base. Will stop in the spring and see you when I get out of jail."[86]

"Omaha," he wrote to several correspondents, "is the brains of the Missiles." He contacted Karl Meyer, a Catholic antinuclear protester in Nebraska, who had picketed the Offutt Air Base at the town of Mead (near Omaha). "I felt that I should offer him my sympathy," wrote Ammon, "so the day after my tax picketing was over I left for Omaha."[87] Given the economic recession of 1959, Nebraskans were enthusiastic about the missiles: they "meant more than jobs for the towns of Mead and Wahoo": "They came to mean patriotism, protecting one's country, and the opportunities of a new age. The county fair that summer had numerous parade floats featuring homemade rockets. Local support for the project was so great that when out-of-town peace protesters arrived in 1959, local residents rallied against them. The pacifists called themselves 'Omaha Action,' and set up a camp outside Mead's missile base. . . . The local people saw the group's very presence as an attack on their livelihood and patriotic spirit, and responded harshly with newspaper articles and counter-protests."[88] Ammon stopped in Chicago, picking up Dorothy, fresh from her retreat, and they spoke at a Quaker meeting. They picked up more protesters in Peoria; then Francis Gorgen drove them to Omaha. But base officials had new rules for protesters and were installing cyclone fencing around the perimeter, so even though Ammon had written ahead to the probable judge, "giving my reasons for wanting to be the last one 'over the fence,'" his arrest was almost slapstick.

As they drove up, the guard said to him, "'You're the pacifist? the picketing place is two miles down the road.'" In retrospect it appears they were duped. They drove down a dirt road to its end, where they parked and crossed a ditch, which they thought marked the base boundary, although they could not see a gate or missiles. So they doubled back and "finally a clerical worker took us ceremoniously to the brass at the front gate. They were waiting for us and we had somehow got in the back way." The officials opened the front gate so that Hennacy could go out, but then he pivoted and went back in, stepping over a small fence, and was officially arrested by Marshal Raab.[89]

"He was in ecstasy, going back to prison and for something longer than a mere 10 or 30 days," wrote Joan Thomas. The judge sent him to the reopened Sandstone Prison, between Minneapolis and Duluth. Hennacy and a Black prisoner were handcuffed, chained together, and transported in a car, to which they also were handcuffed. Perhaps Hennacy thought that he could reconnect with his epiphany in Atlanta, since Sandstone had been used for conscientious objectors during World War II (Bill Ryan had served there), but it was a new prison, in a new time. Ammon noted that some prisoners were in for having fed their pigs government-subsidized corn, a violation of the crop subsidy laws. Others had driven stolen cars across state lines. A few were dope dealers, but more were guilty of mail fraud, a catch-all category, although there was a Native American who had stolen a horse.

He objected to the required vaccines at first, volunteering to stay in solitary; he did not believe in shots, but he did recognize that they were designed to protect the general population, and he finally relented. He refused to have anything to do with meat, of course, and said he would teach "radical history" if assigned to the education department. This posturing backfired, and he was assigned to the library, where his subversive activity was limited to ordering books by Jack London, Erich Fromm, and Aldous Huxley.[90]

Eventually he came to enjoy the routine. The lights came on at 6:30 a.m. Breakfast was 7:00 to 7:30. He ate cereal, coffee, pancakes, sometimes scrambled eggs, always trying to sit with the Native American. He reported to the library at 8:00 a.m. and worked until 11:30 when lunch began. He took great delight in the variety of food: potatoes, several kinds of vegetables, white and whole wheat bread, Jell-O, cake, pie, and tea—it was a feast after the CW House. The food was "well cooked and really more than I can eat. So as an added penance and so I won't get fat, I'll fast the 42 hours from Thurs after supper to Sat. noon." His closest companion was Arthur Harvey, another vegetarian and his boss in the library.[91]

Instead of the grinding work details and solitary confinement cells of Atlanta, there was a skating rink, with inmate hockey teams. "In good weather baseball, volleyball, football and tossing horseshoes. . . . At this latter Arthur and I played and ran about even, but the Indian could make a ringer every time. We played 107 games of Scrabble and I only won 10, so there is no doubt that Arthur is smarter than I. You can buy a certain amount of candy, cigarettes, etc. at commissary and afterwards there is a scramble to pay gambling debts. Some of the most religious were the worst gamblers."

Hennacy began to have second thoughts about Catholicism because of what he saw in prison. "I attended Protestant services with a Lutheran friend," he wrote, but the whole idea of religion in prison offended him: "For a minister to be a chaplain in the armed forces or prison and accept the pay . . . in my mind as bad as to have a Prohibitionist wear the bartender's apron behind the bar." He was thrown back on his 1920s thoughts about prison reform, though many of the changes he championed had come to pass. Under the Huber Plan, first implemented in Wisconsin in 1957, some prisoners worked outside but slept at the prison, turning over all their salaries to support their families or to pay off fines.[92] Guards were recruited from the local farms, unlike the sadists at Atlanta, and "most of them seem to be afraid of their jobs, of us, and of themselves." Ammon still believed that "rehabilitation" was a joke, estimating that 85 percent of Sandstone inmates were repeat offenders. "There are bad boys and bad people who knowingly choose to do evil," he wrote, and one had to turn the other cheek to them. It was every Christian's duty to witness and to act. "My time in prison was not wasted," he said, for it reminded him of Eugene Debs saying that "while there is a lower class, I am in it, while there is a soul in prison, I am not free."[93]

Many people wrote to Ammon, but he was permitted to write only to family and five others. He could not write to Vivian Cherry or others he had befriended in New York, but he asked others to write for him. He had his mother pass on information to Dorothy; those letters were a full accounting of his actions and routines.[94] When he got around to writing to Father Casey, his Catholic patron, he signed himself simply as "Ammon Hennacy #3467": "You are the first person other than my relatives that I am allowed to write to. Not sure if I can write to Dorothy yet, for I am technically a married man."[95] As Joan Thomas noted, his time in prison helped Ammon to rest up from his New York activities and provided a respite from his long fasts.

It was also a respite from the personalist vs. distributist and other ideological battles, during which he had insisted on the importance of individual action. That had been wearing, but now he had a chance to assess his anarchism vis-à-vis the social activism and anarchism axis of Bayard Rustin and A. J. Muste and Paul Goodman. Muste was threatening to fire Rustin after he was arrested for having sex with two men in the back seat of a car; Dellinger and McDonald and others were struggling to manage FOR and *Liberation* and to get a foot in the emerging libertarian movement. These concerns seemed so beside the point to Ammon that he did not mind being out of it. "Sleep better than I have in years, as it is not noisy like New York City," he wrote to Carmen.[96] And being out of it hardly hurt his stature back in New York: "This prison vacation will add to the increased fame he's been enjoying since trekking to NYC," Thomas noted. If his ardor for Dorothy Day had cooled—in his letters she seems a business associate—his queries about other female friends had not.[97]

During the day, working in the library, he sampled the classics and read the *New York Times* (two days late) and many magazines. He watched television, seeing Khrushchev live for the first time, and pursued subscriptions to *Commonweal* and the *CW* for the library. The worst part of the job, he said, was checking out and reshelving the Zane Grey novels favored by inmates. After a while he was allowed to write to Dorothy, but she was often traveling and, he thought, did not receive his letters. He watched the deer grazing in the fields outside when the fall hunting season opened, fearing for their safety. A Halloween party was held, but Ammon and Arthur were so deep in Scrabble that they missed most of it.

When he was released on January 21, 1960, Father Casey came with Dorothy to meet him. With time off for good behavior, he had served four months.[98] But prison made him restless, as it had after Atlanta. By late January 1960 he was on speaking tour again, now flying the longer legs of trips, as Dorothy had for years. From Madison, Wisconsin, he traveled to Lafayette, Alabama, where he visited with Fairhope Colony members, then on to Nashville and New Orleans. By March 10 he was in Los Angeles, visiting Carmen for five days. On April 23, he visited Dorothy's niece in Seattle, then took the bus to Spokane to meet with Doukhobors, and finally, on May 1, he flew back to New York City.[99]

He was greeted by Murray Kempton of the *New York Post*, who wrote, "I hadn't realized how much touch I've lost with the consequential lately until I found out that Ammon Hennacy had been in and out of jail for five [*sic*] months with me not the wiser. . . . I cannot believe that Sandstone will ever be the same. It is obviously a sound policy for our society to keep Ammon Hennacy moving along." According to Elmer Bendiner, Ammon now exhibited "the relaxed self-confidence of a man who knows he is right." However, back at the *Catholic Worker*, the acclaim was more muted. "Just Ammon being Ammon," said Steed. "No big deal. He said Sandstone was much nicer than Riker's Island."[100] But for some younger women at the *CW*, Hennacy was a celebrity. There was Diana, divorced, Catholic, and mother of two boys: "I could have fallen in love with her, if she had not been so crabby with her boys," he wrote. There were Vivian Cherry and Janet Burwash, with whom he went to events. There were Carol Gorgen and her roommate (the granddaughter of Teddy Roosevelt, Ammon believed). Steed was sometimes the conduit between Hennacy and his young admirers, but Ammon was flattered by this attention, and years of emotional remove had made him a little needy. Some at the CW thought he was capitalizing on his prominence too aggressively, and after a visiting foreign student misunderstood his name, they too began calling him "Mr. Heresy."[101]

By 1960 American morals seemed more corrupt than ever to Ammon, who cited the case of a Milwaukee "postmaster who 'mishandled' $17,000 and was fined $1,000 and placed on 5 years' probation."[102] The height of hypocrisy, however, was the arming of submarines with nuclear missiles so that they could prowl undetected off the coasts of friends and enemies alike. The *Polaris* missile project, begun in secret by Eisenhower in 1956, was a delayed response to the Japanese surprise attack on Pearl Harbor, but in 1960 the US military also felt threatened when the Soviet Union put the Sputnik satellite in orbit. About fifty one-megaton warheads were to be mounted on nuclear-powered submarines that could patrol off Cuba, the Soviet Union, and China in order to deter war. Two young Christian Scientists, Brad Lyttle and Adrian Mass, began protests against this early in 1960 that were intended to culminate in a June march on the New London, Connecticut, submarine base. Protesters planned to converge from all directions, marching from Boston and from Providence, some coming by boat from New Jersey and Long Island.

Ammon joined the group marching from Columbia University, a 124-mile distance that was supposed to be covered in twenty-mile daily bites. Each night they would shelter with pacifist friends. This was no farther than Ammon usually walked while tax protesting, so even though he was fasting, he knocked off the march in three days, lifted spiritually by the "young atheistic anarchists" and their solidarity against the heckling crowd en route. He had not had any of this in a while. When they arrived at the base, Ammon and fourteen-year-old Timothy Hutchinson were in the lead and were attacked by a bartender who ripped away their signs. Punches were thrown here and there, for this town, like Omaha, was excited about its military jobs. "Where in the world was there another old man like this?" asked William Miller, the Day biographer: "Marching to New London, Connecticut to picket the launching of the atomic submarine *Polaris*, where he twitted the communists for opening their meeting by singing the *Star-Spangled Banner*?"[103] From June 6 to 19, Hennacy participated in the protests, which spread to nearby parks and even to the Harvard-Yale regatta.

Other protests also called out to Ammon; he went back to New York to help Steed, Gorgen, and others to picket the Park Avenue showrooms of the Kohler Company, whose unions were striking in Milwaukee. He and Steed were also picketing Woolworth's, and against the execution of Carl Chessman, and at SingSing against the execution of a young Bowery man. There were new young women at the CW: a willowy poet named Joan Thomas, visiting from Minneapolis, and Mary Lathrop, who began to accompany him on protests in December 1960.[104]

Mary Lathrop

Mary Lathrop was a twenty-six-year-old painter and Catholic convert who had met Dorothy Day through the novelist Caroline Gordon. She was looking to put her beliefs into action, so Dorothy invited her to move to the CW house. "Bob Steed came up to where I was staying, packed my drawings and whatever," she recounted, "and I came down to the Worker."[105] "I immediately latched on to Ammon, and we were picketing and fasting together. Picketing up at the Civil Defense Office against air raid drills. And we did the City Hall Park protest, where I cried because they wouldn't arrest me," Lathrop recalled. "Ammon had brilliant flashing light-blue eyes—and a great flashing smile. He had a very noble and expressive face." She was young, blonde, talented, and his favorite. "He had his stations," she said, like Fordham Gate, where "he tried to give a paper to a nun and she just charged ahead. He was a great conversationalist, he was good at repartee, but people said the worst things to him. He would find out who and what they were, concerned that they should understand."

The CW attracted many young spiritual seekers. Joan Thomas was another, but unlike Mary, she at first found Hennacy "unbearable" and called his *Autobiography* "boring." After returning to her husband in Minneapolis, however, she began to write to him. He confided that, since the air-raid-shelter laws had been dropped, his work in New York was done and he had plans for a CW "House of Hospitality" in Utah. He said that Mary Lathrop was going with him. Thomas vaguely recalled meeting Lathrop: "Was Mary mentally ill in that she was going to marry him?" At that point "Dorothy, as usual, was mad and not speaking to him. He seemed to be always quarreling with Dorothy." Joan put Hennacy out of her mind.[106] Lathrop, however, fell under Hennacy's influence, became a vegetarian, and took up fasting. "He was in great physical shape for his age," she said, although when he was fasting "he might be irritable at the beginning, but his energy was up. He would charge along as if not fasting. He had a very high energy level, not like kids today."[107] One day as they were picketing at Forty-Third and Lexington, they met Linus Pauling, who had just discovered vitamin C. This kind of event thrilled her: "He *knew* Pauling from some meeting. It was inspiring to be in his presence."

Hennacy took her to the Metropolitan Museum, where they sat in front of Jules Bastien-Lepage's *Joan of Arc*, a romantic 1879 painting of the teenage martyr. They drank in its call to action. "That was his favorite painting," said Steed. Ammon also took Mary to the nearby Frick Collection, but they did not go inside: Ammon liked to sit outside and think about Berkman attempting to assassinate Frick. He told Mary how Berkman had befriended him in Atlanta. "I like to be with Ammon," Mary told Dorothy, "because I love to show off and so does he." Dorothy detected a certain egotism, even bitterness, which she thought came from a broken home.[108] Hennacy began to take Mary on his speaking engagements at local colleges. "He would enter the room already talking while walking down the aisle. At one seminary, he strode down the aisle saying 'I have been sent here by God to wake you fellows up. You can go on the way you are, or you can wake up.' This had a huge impact on young men thinking about the 'vocation.' He was an actor. He had polished all his lines. He had a saying about 'love, courage, and wisdom' that I heard over and over." Indeed, he had been using that maxim since Milwaukee.[109]

Everyone living at the Catholic Worker House was single. "If they paired up and married, then they would move out," said Steed. Having dedicated herself to religious chastity, Mary felt a bit overwhelmed. "It was a 'singles' kind of place," she said, but then Ammon began to suggest that the two of them should get married. One day in the Bronx, walking behind her, she says that she heard him say, *sotto voce*, "If you could only give me a son." He may have been kidding but she was shocked. "I mean, we had not slept together, but it was pretty nearly that." She decided she had to tell Dorothy, but then she equivocated: "I thought . . . well, I've gone so far. And Ammon kept pestering me. . . . I know that his loneliness was extreme, but I didn't think he was in love with me. Finally, I said, 'all right.' I just got tired of saying 'no.' But I told him that if I had to choose between him and Dorothy, I would choose Dorothy."

Dorothy had a grim view of Ammon by now. Seeing Mary cling to Ammon's arm, she asked Steed, "Who would ever hang on to an old branch like that?" Nor was the relationship a fait accompli, since Hennacy was still married, as well as forty years older. As Miller writes, "Dorothy was troubled that, while a conformation to the standards of the Church was important to Mary, it seemed unimportant to Hennacy."[110] Lathrop said that Hennacy "told me he had a *verbal* contract with [Selma] that they would stay together as long as they were in love. . . . He didn't have a grudge against her. And he was very proud of his daughters."

The crux came, said Lathrop, "one day when Dorothy and Ammon and I were having coffee in some little coffee shop down near the *Worker*. And I was just getting ready to open my mouth and say 'Dorothy, there's something I have to tell you,' when Ammon jumped in and said 'Dorothy, Mary and I are going to be married.'" Day sensed a crisis and to free Mary from Ammon's pressure, she took her on a trip, with Ammon corresponding at each stop, keeping Mary on the hook. By the time they reached their Arkansas farm destination, "I was driving poor Dorothy crazy, with 'should I marry Ammon, or shouldn't I marry Ammon, or what should I do?' Right next to the farm was a large Stations of the Cross. On a hill. I went all around that hill and made all those stations. I said to myself, 'this has got to be decided once and for all.'" Returning to her room she opened a Bible, letting her fingers be guided by God to the "living word." Under her thumb appeared "Woe unto you that you should play the harlot and be his." She returned to New York City immediately, not to the Catholic Worker but to the Joan of Arc Rectory in the Bronx uptown, aiming to join the convent. When Dorothy returned to New York a few days later, she found that opinions about the affair were more divided but less intense than she expected. "'What convent will harbor that wild creature?' everyone around the office asked. 'She frightens young men; convents are too conventional.' . . . So all agreed 'she might as well marry Ammon.' It was as casual as that."[111]

As for Ammon, the New York period ended with a sense that he had learned much, but that he could use it better elsewhere. He loved the *Catholic Worker* and would always respect Dorothy Day, but the CW House did not have the elbow room or the order that he liked, and New York itself encouraged a kind of theatricality that he must have suspected in himself. Building on what he had learned there, he wanted to return to the West, to open a "house of hospitality" there, and Utah had the strongest grip on his imagination. "There are fewer Catholics there than in any other state," he said: "I like the Mormons because they accept no aid from the government but have their own mutual aid." He wrote to his mother, "Likely I'll go to Salt Lake City next spring to work in orchards and later start a small house there."

Perhaps "he had begun to miss the desert and the sky," Dorothy wrote, "the good hard labor and clean sweat. Perhaps he was taunting himself for giving up in practice his 'Life at Hard Labor.'" She was on target. But his new dream was almost derailed by the cardinal of New York, who forced another CW member to remove "Catholic Worker" from the name of a house he started in Chicago. "I would not obey [that], and would leave the CW, but not the church," Ammon wrote: "But I don't think he will do anything." Then he added, in his implied-metaphor style, "Too much rain in this country."[112] "He said he was going," Mary Lathrop said. "He kept after me. We had lunch together and so on. Finally I said, 'Well, if you're perfectly aware that there's nothing going on between us whatsoever, nothing at all. There will be fasting and picketing, and I'll help you with the house and do what I can. There will be no shenanigans.' He said okay."[113]

Through the fall of 1960 Hennacy remained in New York, "very much part of the 'we-ness' of the CW," wrote Joan Thomas. He picketed and protested. The names of Kennedy and Castro appear in his letters, and he wrote to Castro, Tito, Nehru, and Khrushchev. He wrote to his mother that the entertainer Steve Allen had praised him in his autobiography. But he wrote to Father Rombouts on September 23 that "I will be going to Salt Lake City to work in the Mormon orchards and farms in March [1961], but I will still write for the CW." He had made a huge impact on the Catholic Worker, raising it from its World War II doldrums, and he left as a legend. But it was his usual slow departure. For one thing, he was still negotiating with Mary Lathrop. He left New York on January 2, 1961, and wandered on the way, as he usually did, but by May, Ammon Hennacy was in Salt Lake City, eager to see where his Celestial Bulldozer led.[114]

8

In the Land of the Mormons

Hennacy's move to Utah was neither caprice nor desperation. He had an internal compass that guided him, as we have seen, to new venues apt for the exercise of the abilities and insights gleaned from the previous one. Intuition or Celestial Bulldozer, this instinct kept him from repeating or returning to old ways or places. Utah reminded him of New Mexico with its high, dry climate, but the main valleys were green with orchards, like Ohio, and the Mormon pioneers had built irrigation canals to deliver water to farms and back yards, an echo of his days as an *acequiero* in Arizona. But there were no water barons here, and no agribusiness yet. From the wide roads to the farming co-ops to the church-sponsored welfare system, Utah's development had been religiously inspired, but with many aspects that coincided with his own beliefs and practices. It was utopianism with rational planning, a bit like Fairhope. Deseret Industries, a Mormon project that reused clothes and furniture, was modeled on the Salvation Army. The Mormons were not vegetarians, but they led a healthy lifestyle, abstaining from tobacco, alcohol, and caffeine. If their origin story seemed *outré*, it was not as extreme as that of the I AM, and in practice they were almost as welcoming as the Catholic Worker had been. Above all, the Mormons had turned their backs on the federal government, rejecting its interference in their affairs— that was paramount to Hennacy. They were not anarchists, but there were strains of socialism and libertarianism in their practices, and they allowed dissenting factions to move out to the margins (in this case, the desert), as the Hopis and the Doukhobors did. They supported wars, but he had found that to be the case in every theocracy. "It is with a friendly feeling towards Mormons that I came here," he wrote.[1]

He had heard of Mormons while growing up. They were part of the abolitionist-era religious tumult in Ohio. Joseph Smith and his followers lived at Kirtland, north of Negley, though long before Ammon was born. When the Quakers had dwindled, they were replaced by Baptists, and then by Christian Scientists, Jehovah's Witnesses, and Mormons. These groups shared the common denominators of health consciousness and antinomianism (reading scripture according to one's own lights), but they had different and conflicting opinions about slavery. During Ammon's childhood, the number of Mormons living in Ohio was as high as twenty-five thousand.[2] "My great-great-grandparents," he said, "lived not far from the uproar of the Kirtland, Ohio, community. . . . If I had been a young man back then it's possible I would have followed Smith."[3]

He had many Mormon friends, such as the Clines and Udalls in Arizona, and he had met Mormon missionaries on the Hopi reservation. In his "life at hard labor" he had noted the Mormons' thrift: they "make juice from the grapefruit and orange culls, and trade all this for apples," he wrote, adding that "Mormons and Mexicans are the best irrigators." There were even Mormons who were IWW members, he claimed, but that was also part of a conspiracy theory that he found seductive: that the Mormon hierarchy had railroaded IWW leader Joe Hill to execution in Utah in 1915.[4] Thus the "Joe Hill House" that Ammon planned to start in Utah would be a flag uniting his labor, religious, and protest interests.[5] He would wave it for the next decade, imprinting himself on Utah's imagination.

On April 17, 1961, he spoke at the University of Utah. But this was only a reconnaissance, during which he stayed downtown at the Raymond Hotel, then "hurried home to NYC to take part in the air raid refusal." In letters he still called New York home, and he was traveling on CW funds.[6] But the CW had won the air raid protests, and as Coy has written, peace activism "was at a rather low ebb" there.[7] The event was canceled the next year. Back in New York, he pestered Mary Lathrop. "He said he was going," she recalled. "I hadn't definitely made up my mind. He said, 'When you make your decision, call me up and if you come, you come, and if you don't, you don't.' So two weeks later, I decided maybe there was something I could do out there better than working in a rectory."[8]

First there was a stop to see his family in Cleveland, where Mary joined him. They slept in different rooms, but she met all the relatives, and they traveled as a couple on the rest of the trip. Hennacy used "we" in his letters thereafter. Legally he was still married to Selma, but he acted as if that were "just common-law." They went to Notre Dame,

Figure 8.1. Hennacy and Mary Lathrop on their way to Utah. Permission of Josephine Thomas, University of Utah.

where he spoke, and to Nauvoo, Illinois, to see the grave of Joseph Smith and to absorb more Mormon history. Their trip stretched to Santa Fe, to visit to his daughter, then to Tucson and Phoenix, and finally to Flagstaff, where they hiked to the bottom of the Grand Canyon with Platt and Barbara Cline. Along the way Ammon, now sixty-seven, repeated that he wanted to work in orchards and to save money to open the Joe Hill House: "I will be glad to live poor and work daily as a migrant."[9]

Salt Lake City was then small enough that Ammon and Mary could commute from their hotel near the train station to orchards in the northern suburb of Bountiful, where they picked cherries for three cents a pound: "Mary is very brown and a good tree climber," he wrote to his mother, but "we make less than $6 a day for both of us." They could not cover their basics, he said, and would not visit her that year. Mary also worked as a hotel and house maid, living "at a hotel next door, and Ammon stayed at another hotel up the street."[10]

Despite the hard work, there were daily compensations. "This is a beautiful place, and we noticed at night that the whole sky is like a deep blue cup that cuts down over this valley," Ammon wrote, "I never noticed it that way any other place. . . . We are so tired at night that we go to bed at eight, get up at 5 and wait to . . . get picked up and back maybe by 8 p.m. We meet plenty of Mexicans, some Indians, and some drunk Okies." Sometimes Mary added a postscript to his letters—"Ammon is looking very healthy, as usual." To his delight, they found a Japanese-owned restaurant where a dinner of an omelet, hash browns, salad, and milk cost sixty-five cents.

If they had energy after work, they walked around skid row, looking for a site for the Joe Hill House. A Catholic student who had heard Hennacy speak in April said he had raised $240, and a friend back east (Yone Stafford) wired $100. She would fund Hennacy several times. They soon found a storefront at 72 Post Office Place, where the landlord said that if they paid three months down, he would give them two months of free rent. That would hold the store until November 1, when they planned to open. His parsimony being a reflex, Ammon moved in immediately, sleeping on the floor "to save the $28 a month from my room."[11]

The full name was to be the "Joe Hill House of Hospitality and St. Joseph Refuge." Dorothy had approved of that (she contributed money to the project), but there was no doubt which name was most important to Ammon, who got Mary to plan a mural of Joe Hill's execution. Then they set about furnishing the place. Ren Mabey, the first volunteer, cleaned and mopped the floors. They bought a rocking chair and a roll-top desk, to be used as the "office." Priests on the West Side gave them statues of saints, and a *CW* reader in Laramie sent fifteen dollars to turn on the electricity. A "sort of Rosicrucian brought us six cots and mattresses, but when he saw those statues," wrote Ammon, "he didn't come back."

Those priests also gave Ammon two stoves, but it took weeks to get city authorization to connect the gas for a "commercial kitchen." Francis Gorgen was visiting and, seeing the gas impasse, decided to buy a gas refrigerator and connect everything at once, for there was also a "donated" hot water heater. The water heater was stolen, however, and its owners came to reclaim it. Ammon got another one from a devout Baptist, who would not take money for it, then got two laundry tubs that needed welding. Gorgen stayed on three weeks, welding the tubs and connecting everything. The magic giving continued: there were buckets of grey paint, cases of toilet paper, boxes of crackers, cans of coffee, even cocoa tins from a Hersey's salesman. The Mormon community seemed to get behind them. Ammon and Mary "carried 120 lbs. of wheat on our backs for nearly a mile and ground it on the old coffee grinder from Milwaukee." Setting up led them to a circuit of donors: bakeries, a pie company, and even the Spudnuts franchise helped out. "Ammon was very, very energetic," said Mary. "A great enthusiast, with a wonderful sense of humor. He was in great physical shape for his age." As Day commented, this "Gandhi-and-Mira situation was not generally understood."[12]

Landing with a Splash

They took time off to protest, picketing for six days on the sixteenth anniversary of the bombing of Hiroshima. They also picketed at the state prison against an upcoming execution, until the state attorney general prohibited picketing there. But there was a rally protesting the execution in Liberty Park, so they spoke there, getting excellent publicity. The *Deseret News*, the afternoon Mormon paper, led with the headline "Anarchists Picket in City against Taxes, Killing." In the morning *Salt Lake Tribune*, columnist Ernie Linford, under the headline "Hennacy's Coming," wrote, "You may have lived such a sheltered life that you do not know this one-man revolution, but you likely will soon know him by reputation if not personally."[13]

So Ammon and Mary landed with a splash. The fact that almost everyone adhered to some Christian denomination made streetcorner proselytizing easier; they knew the Sermon on the Mount and his other biblical examples. His relations with the Mormons were better initially than his relations with the local Catholics, who felt themselves a beleaguered minority, with only eight churches in the state to the Mormons' two hundred–odd. Bishop Joseph Federal even interceded when a young priest asked Hennacy to speak at Lourdes High School, stipulating that nothing "controversial" was to be discussed. The Catholic hierarchy wanted the church to be middle-class and respectable, which became a factor in Ammon's disenchantment with it.[14]

"When he first arrived in Salt Lake City, Hennacy had written to Federal to explain his plans to open the Joe Hill House," journalist Jeremy Harmon has written. The bishop responded clearly: "I wish you to understand that your activities here do not have our approval and the name of the Diocese is not to be used in any way in connection with your actions." Hennacy wrote that "in this conservative community it is likely that folks have never heard of such radical Catholics." He still considered himself a Catholic, though left fringe. As Harmon explains, "While running his shelters, Hennacy continued to protest against capital punishment. He led annual protests on the anniversary of the bombing of Hiroshima. As the war in Vietnam intensified, he led anti-war marches that often ended at the Cathedral of the Madeleine, because Bishop Joseph Federal supported the war."[15] It was a challenge to the bishop to embody his beliefs.

Mary began to work on the mural. "Ammon wanted the death of Joe Hill and I didn't. He wanted a very large, twelve by fifteen-foot, mural of Joe Hill being executed. . . . He was strapped into a chair with a target pasted over his heart, a white target with a black or a red center. And I showed the firing squad there. And the mountains around Salt Lake City in the background."[16] Jesus rose out of the clouds above the mountain. The message was clear: Joe Hill, an IWW miner and inspiring labor songwriter, had been *crucified* for his part in the 1913 mining strike in nearby Park City.[17]

Ammon said, "As you see, Christ is in it, as another One who was framed."[18] Ammon believed that "the whole thing was a frame-up," a vendetta by a jilted lover of Virginia Snow, the daughter of the Mormon Church president. He wanted Utahns to reexamine their past. Photos of Mary's mural were rare for a long time: "The IWW won't print this picture because Christ is in it," wrote Ammon later, "and the Catholic papers won't print it because Joe Hill is in it." Mary also painted murals of the Holy Family, Russian pilgrims, a Russian icon, and St. Joan and the Wicked Bishop, the latter growing out of their New York interests. Ammon completed the interior with his favorite quotations from Debs and Dewey.[19] Once they were situated, Ammon felt he and Mary should wed. This presumption oozed male privilege, but he conceded to a "companionate" union (Mary was afraid of getting pregnant) and to a church wedding. However, he was not divorced, because that "common-law marriage" he kept shrugging off was legal, and he needed an annulment from Bishop Federal.

When they were ready to open, "Mary and I went around to the merchants saying 'We are pacifists, anarchists, subversives, and Catholics too radical for our Bishop, but we need sugar, etc.' We got it. Readers of the

Figure 8.2. Mary Lathrop's mural of Joe Hill as Jesus in the first Joe Hill House. Permission of Josephine Thomas.

CW over the country who know me send in bits of money at times, so I make it alright. $100 a month is enough."[20] There was generally good-will and support, but Hennacy got his first taste of resistance when a merchant suggested that he get the imprimatur of the Chamber of Commerce. "I went there and explained our ideas and was asked what my 'racket' was." He was deeply insulted. While preparing the House, they were still picking cherries, so "I told them that Mary and I would not be sitting on the cold curb in the morning waiting for some *padrone* to pick us up if we had any 'racket.'"

As soon as the House opened, "the health department came around and said that it was unsanitary to sleep men on the floor." With New York bravado, Ammon asked them "where *they* were going to sleep the men. They said I should have double bunks with mattresses. My reply was that the men would fall out of bunks. . . . I told them that there must have been some regulation from folks like them that Christ shouldn't have been born in a stable." His repartee did not win over the health department. Next were the police, who "wanted to know the name of some man. I told them I didn't ask any questions." The police said that he should, that he should be registering the men who slept there. Ammon replied that he was exempt, since he did not charge rent. Eventually these police would deliver drunks to his door, keeping them off the streets.

Then it was the FBI, four times the first year: they were also pursuing a name, but Ammon refused to help, saying he "didn't like that stinker, J. Edgar Hoover." The fire department followed, saying that drunks with matches posed a hazard. But Ammon said that he slept on the floor by the door "so that if there was any fire, I would know it, and that we took matches away from any drunks we kept in the cooler." Well, replied the inspector, "I guess 60 men in 60 doorways are more of a fire hazard than 60 men all in one room here."[21] It was a battle to get the bureaucratic breaks that Dorothy had in place in New York, and his "humor" did not work as well as Day's appeals to conscience.

But soon the Joe Hill House was sleeping twenty-five men a night and feeding three meals a day to fifty. They were "mostly guys dropping off freights," Ammon wrote to the Clines. "Three priests help us, but the Bishop still has thumbs down. . . . I can beg nearly all the food we need. Mary has moved to a rooming house nearby where the rent is only $18 a month." He included a snapshot of her mural of Joe Hill's execution, noting that her earnings paid the utilities.[22] "He took everybody in," said Bruce Phillips, a Korean War vet who had ridden the rails: "The police record shows night after night, at night court, 'Sent to Joe Hill House.' Instead of sending them to the drunk tank. Cause it saved the county some money."[23]

Mary was still thinking about a cloistered life. In Ammon's version, her departure was due to Dorothy's meddling: "She phoned and talked to Mary and offered her money to desert me and come back to N.Y.C." But Mary said that Dorothy "told me, 'You will get tired of that old flesh and start chasing younger men.'"[24] In Day's official version, which Hennacy, in an amazing act of self-effacement, used in his autobiography, Dorothy claimed that she had nothing to do with it: "A parish priest called [Mary's] attention to the fact that she was out of place with the crowd of men who began to come around. . . . He offered her bus fare to San Francisco any time she wished to go. . . . She, who was a most devout convert, had fought daily with Ammon over his anti-clericalism, so it should not have come as a surprise. But for Ammon it was a shock, and he was deeply hurt. He blamed me, because Mary regarded me as her mother, and he blamed the priest as well."[25] There is no evidence Ammon and Mary fought about clericalism, but much that Day used back channels to influence Lathrop.

The ugliness began when Ammon and Mary went to a Carmelite convent to which Mary wanted to donate art for a charity sale. Sister Mary Katharine took Ammon aside. She said that he was not welcome, then told Mary to stop picketing, to abandon the House, and to dissociate herself from Hennacy; otherwise she would be blackballed at all convents. "I got the impression that she thought that Ammon and I were living together," said Mary: "And I said, 'This is not a romance.' She said, 'Well, it certainly looks like it.'"[26] Shaken, Mary went to confession with Father McDougall, who advised her to follow the advice of Bishop Federal. A young Dominican priest visited the House: "I had a talk with him, and he said he didn't quite see what I was doing there. That kind of helped to give me the little extra push that I needed."[27]

Mary got on a bus without telling Ammon, thinking "I'm this far West . . . I might as well go to San Francisco." By the end of 1961 she was working there in the Palace Hotel as a maid. "But then I felt like I was breaking the ideals [of the CW] because I was getting paid a salary . . . and they were taking the taxes out."[28] Hennacy found her by sending mail to General Delivery, then he called and coaxed an address out of her. In the slack of winter he went for a visit. "He insisted on staying at my apartment. He stayed in one room and I stayed in the other, but I was furious that he insisted on staying, and I couldn't get out of it." It hardly needs saying that he left without her. Later she started a house of hospitality on skid row in San Francisco, painting a new set of murals, but the house only lasted for six months. They stayed in touch; in fact, she visited and later met Joan Thomas. After his death, Mary decided that Hennacy was probably a saint.[29]

Who Stayed at the Joe Hill House?

"About a third are 'Jack Mormons,'" Hennacy wrote, "a third Irish Catholics, and a third Okies or Arkies from the South, with a sprinkling of

Negroes, Mexicans, and Indians. About 25 town bums come and go. Many of them get kickbacks from their landlords for rent that the relief pays them; and also they sell their meal tickets for half price back to the restaurants and have money for booze." Hennacy had seen these scams on the Bowery, but he thought Utah made things worse. "Only beer is sold in taverns, and no taverns are on the main street in downtown Salt Lake City. You have to have a dollar permit to buy from the state liquor store."[30]

He was under no illusions about alcoholics, to whom he recommended Alcoholics Anonymous. "When a person wants to sober up, the AA is a great help, but the people I see here do not want to sober up: what they want is one more jug." Salt Lake City, he noted, was surrounded by five hundred miles of wilderness. When the men dropped off the freights, miles away, many were desperate for a drink before they hit skid row, and the state's restrictive laws pushed them to the edge. Hennacy allowed no alcohol in the House, but the men hid it under coats, under beds, in odd bottles and wineskins. He poured it out. He allowed drunks, but they were segregated in the "cooler." Aside from snoring, sleep-talking, and thrashing about, the drunks urinated everywhere. When not soiling themselves, they all urinated in one corner. Every morning the "cooler" where he put the drunks smelled poisonous. They claimed innocence, even when soaked in urine.[31]

The drunks were also thieves. Ammon started out with eight bath towels, but all were stolen in the first month. Then he installed a roller towel machine, but they cut the towels off the rollers. When he tried paper towels, they threw those in the toilet and clogged it. They stole the alarm clock and his gloves, they stole food, they stole from garbage cans. The cook, on whom Hennacy depended, was a thief. "The cooks who come here and help me say that all cooks are drunks, and in fact I have not found a sober one," Ammon wrote. "On our first Thanksgiving Day, in my innocence I thought that the cook was preparing the meal—a turkey given us by a woman who worked at the Post Office, with trimmings. But he was in the back room, passed out." To this particular rescue came Bill Ryan's wife, Alba, who stayed several days, running the kitchen. Another cook went to Mass with Mary, told her he was going to convert, and tried to bum drinking money from her. "In the beginning," Ammon wrote, "I used to buy them packaged cigarettes, but I found out they always had enough money for booze, so they could buy their own cigarettes too." In New York he never gave money to vagrants, though he did buy them cigarettes, but in Salt Lake he cut even that.[32] Yet it was the New York chapter of his life that prepared him for this, and without it he would not have been successful.

His daily routine started at 5:00 a.m. "I get up, turn the lights on, roll up my blankets, put jelly between two slices of bread, while the cook makes cocoa, and two others get the chairs and tables ready. Often someone offers to sweep the sidewalk, but if not, I do it. Then I read the morning paper or write letters until time to go to 6:30 mass. Back at 7:30 and have breakfast if I am not fasting. The first mail comes at 8:00 and by 8:45, I am on my way with the rubber-tired cart from the super-market for fruit and vegetables which they have saved for us, at two stores about a mile away. Often one of the men goes with me and we are back by 10:00 with potatoes, carrots, apples, onions, lettuce, and even avocados and strawberries and melons at times. One place gives us dented cans or cans with the labels off."

"On Mondays and Thursdays," he wrote, "I go to another store, coming through the Temple grounds where the guards greet me kindly.

Figure 8.3. Ammon in the "office" of the first Joe Hill House. Photo by Jerry Currier. Permission of Josephine Thomas.

Wednesday I go for candy to a wholesale house; and for salt, sugar, spices to other places when needed. At 3:30 three times a week I walk 18 blocks (long Mormon blocks like between the avenues in New York City) for bread, and twice a week I walk 35 blocks for Spudnuts and pies. I ride home on the bus."

Bruce Phillips worked as one of the cooks and described his routine.

I was making soup at the Hill House. Ammon would push a grocery cart sixty blocks a day. He was strong. Inhumanly strong. And he'd bring back unlabeled cans that they couldn't sell because the labels had fallen off and they didn't know what was in 'em. Well, I didn't know either. It could be cranberry sauce or Brussels sprouts. Whatever it was, it went into the pot. So the stew changed—evolved—over the winter. And the old hands, like sheep herders coming down from the mountains to winter in, they knew that the best part was at the bottom, caked up at the bottom. So they'd use a long-handled fork to dig that stuff out.[33]

Hennacy's work never paused:

If I have time in the afternoon, I try to sleep or rest for a few hours, but often drunks are making too much noise. During the day and before 9:00 p.m. visitors or students often come in to ask questions. On Friday night I always speak on some radical subject, with a notice being generally printed in the Mormon *Deseret News*. Students come to the meetings often. Afterwards we serve cocoa and cookies. This is a 24 hour a day job. Once I went away to Colorado speaking and the drunks had nearly taken over by the time I got back.[34]

Hennacy, in his Gandhi guise, counseled the residents constantly about drinking and other bad habits. "Ammon was spared," said Phillips. "No vices." When Phillips confessed to a capacity for rage because of what he had seen and done in Korea, Hennacy said, "Let's treat it like booze. Pacifism isn't a catalogue of beliefs. . . . It's an attitude, just like AA. Pacifist is something you're always *becoming*, but you're never really completely there. You've got to give up violent thought too, not just fists, guns, knives, clubs—overt violence. Nonviolence is going forth into the world completely disarmed. Disarmed of the weapons of privilege, the weapons of sexual privilege, the weapons of racial privilege, the weapons of economic privilege." Phillips said that Hennacy made him see "all that, as a white man in mid-twentieth century America, I had grown up with."[35]

Women showed up occasionally at the House, but Ammon sent them to a nearby hotel, where he paid for basic rooms. Native Americans appeared and, although he was partial to them, they had to leave alcohol outside. This made some angry: one Navajo threw a chair through the front window. "I was picking glass splinters out of my hair for a week," said Ammon. Despite all the work at the House, he did not stop protesting or picketing. Mary Lathrop recalled "a twelve-day fast on just water" while she was there. "We did fasting and picketing against the bomb and so on. Picketed the post office."[36] In January 1962, Hennacy had stationery printed up and began to write to the Board of Pardons on behalf of three young men facing execution for heinous crimes, named Garcia, Rivenburg, and Poulsen.[37] Executions were old-style in Utah, carried out by a firing squad of volunteers.

"I and others will picket the State Capital for an hour, weekdays, with our message for Mercy," he wrote, including Bishop Federal on the list of people to whom he sent this letter. He could not resist calling out the bishop personally: "If you have read in your student days of humane ideas or heard from others along the same line, it does not seem to have done any good, for you say nothing against this legalized murder."[38] The Catholic Church, he continued, "may convert a few Jack Mormons who want to be free to smoke and drink and play bingo, but what social message do you bring to them? Just the Old Testament message of an eye for an eye." Ammon was "in perfect ecstasy after writing the most shocking diatribe of a letter to the bishop in Salt Lake City," Joan Thomas said, "yet darn if he ever managed to make an enemy of that Bishop."

In his few spare moments, he read more deeply in Mormon history and theology, not only writings about Joseph Smith, Brigham Young, and other early Mormons but also writing by outside observers such as Mrs. Brodie and Richard Burton.[39] He appreciated the high level of Christian literacy in the general population; here were people who thought about the Bible during their daily lives. A number of local sympathizers appeared, beginning in 1961 with pacifists Ethel Hale and her husband, Paul Wharton. Hale had been among Utah's first female bus and taxi drivers and was a pioneer organic farmer. She picketed with Hennacy and substituted for him when he could not protest; during the war in Vietnam, she and her husband sued the FCC to prevent the renewal of Mormon station KSL's license because it reported the war unfairly.[40] Bruce Phillips began to appear at Hennacy's Friday-night lectures, singing the songs of Joe Hill, the Wobblies, and Woody Guthrie. He brought along a French visitor, Jean Chanonat, who described Ammon as having "a strong Irish ethnical radical power."[41] Phillips may have also introduced folk singer Rosalie Sorrels, who later included Hennacy in her song "Goodbye Joe Hill." He met local activist Robert "Archie" Archuleta, and Bob and Barbara Hood became friends, later lodging Ammon when the health department closed the House. From these people Ammon would hear about Dugway Proving Grounds, a weapons testing site to the west that he would soon picket.

Joan Thomas

Joan Thomas met Ammon in 1960 when, like Mary Lathrop, she came to New York City to meet Dorothy and look at the CW operation. She fasted in her own religious and aesthetic practice, so she found Hennacy's long fasts remarkable. In New York he had talked to her with disarming candor, but she felt that, though he was very funny, he was too self-involved. When she returned to Minnesota, however, he wrote letters to her, even describing his relationship with Mary. "These letters," Thomas wrote, referring to herself in the third person, "puzzled her . . . She could understand Dorothy's anger with him. The way he talked against the Church would anger anyone. . . . If she had been Mary, she wouldn't have let that old man touch her either."

Time passed, her husband left her, and she wrote to Hennacy in August 1962. To process the changes, she wanted to do a long fast: "Mightn't he, in return for her help with his charity house, help her in turn with her fast?" He told her to come; he would be glad to see her.[42]

When her bus arrived at 2:00 p.m., she would find him picketing at the state capitol against the trio of executions. She walked up the capitol hill, spotted him, and registered this impression: "Tanned and strong, his long white hair flaming out from his head, his magic blue stone winking on his chest, and carrying a large picket sign, 'Life for Poulsen,

Garcia and Rivenburg.' . . . He strode towards her, 'Hello, my dear, good to see you.' Before she could back up, he had kissed her on the cheek. This was just the second time in her life that she had met this man." He was on the nineteenth day of a fast and "kept telling her, as he bounced along down the hill into downtown, how fine he felt, light as a feather, fasting was easy as pie. When he wasn't telling her that, he was greeting every passerby and handing out leaflets against the execution. . . . She was almost embarrassed. Here she was, a reasonably pretty, innocent, young woman, only 27 years old, fooling around with an old codger."[43]

By the time they reached the Joe Hill House, her idea of him had changed. "What impressed her about the large, long room which they entered was the cleanliness. She hadn't received that impression about the charity house in New York, but wherever she went in New York City she felt the city's grime and grit."[44] This house was crammed with books, magazines, and newspapers and, in one screened-off corner, a paper-heaped desk: "My office," said Hennacy, "and went on to explain that the major part of the room was bare, being where his bums slept at night." It struck her that he had no illusions about them; he always called them bums. Sleeping bags and blankets were heaped against a wall. "On the other side was—under some stairs—a small cubbyhole known as the cooler, where the bums who came in drunk could sleep off the booze." The walls were covered with murals—the execution of Joe Hill, Joan of Arc, the flight of the Holy Family. As his "bums" wandered in, Hennacy introduced her: "She's from Minneapolis, she's come to fast with me." Then he sat down in the kitchen, pouring himself a cup of coffee. "You drink coffee when you fast?" she asked. "Once in a while," he said, opening the refrigerator door and pouring a generous dollop of canned milk into his cup. "But you're breaking your fast," she protested. "A little coffee isn't breaking a fast," he said calmly. "Every day at the Post Office after I get done there, I go inside and get a bottle of soda. It cleans out the gook in my mouth." These lapses had been reported by others in New York but not regarded as serious.[45]

"Maybe we should go find my room," she said. "Good idea," he said and, turning to the men traipsing in, "She's going to stay in that hotel where Mary stayed." This was the West Side Hotel.[46] "Not the best," said Hennacy. "But it'll do. When Mary stayed here, she had a rope hanging out of her window, and every morning I'd pull on it and she'd know to get up. Or we'd tie messages on it to each other." The next day Joan recalls that Ammon took her to 6:30 Mass, saying, "On Sundays it's the only one where you don't have to listen to a sermon by one of those five-fingered priests. When I'm not fasting, I go afterwards for pancakes to Walgreen's. When we come back, you can look at my scrapbooks." In church, she looked over from her missal to his, discovering the long list of people for whom he prayed. He started out saying "Great God of Truth and Light, bring courage, wisdom, peace, protection and love to . . ." and then repeated the names. There were hundreds, none of them saints, except perhaps Dorothy Day.

The next day he took her on his food-collection and picketing rounds. They visited three supermarkets with a grocery cart, stopping on the way back to give bananas to a favorite barber and day-old bread to the gypsy fortune tellers around the corner. At 10:00 a.m., with Hennacy still talking, they crossed the street to the post office to get the mail and picket against Hiroshima. Nearly everybody took a leaflet: "Sometimes a passerby would stop to talk to him—occasionally to argue: was he a communist that he wouldn't pay taxes? But in general, people were kind," she wrote, and no one cursed him, as they had in New York. When he ran out of leaflets, he left her to picket with his signs while he went to the House for more.

Finally, on the way home he insisted on stopping at a produce scale to weigh himself; he said he did that every day and he had not lost a pound in the three weeks of this fast.[47] "I was sure he was a fake," Thomas wrote. She was fond of the church, put off by Hennacy's anticlericalism, and horrified by her hotel room. Personally, she took fasting seriously, never cheating, and she was hungry every day, dreaming of food at night. After a few days, she excused herself from morning Mass and bought a ticket to Minneapolis.[48]

That fall (1963) Dorothy Day published *Of Loaves and Fishes*, with the section on Ammon that was withering, but he did not mind—she was right—because he was recognized. It went into detail about Mary Lathrop, but he did not mind that either. Joan Thomas may have left, but he had been writing, book reviews for the *Catholic Worker* now that Dorothy seemed to have forgiven him, even correspondence in his "Yours in Christ the Rebel" persona. He wrote appeals on behalf of Garcia et al. and continued his running battle with the Catholic hierarchy. Perhaps inspired by Dorothy, he was digesting his experiences since 1954 for a new autobiography, to be called *The Book of Ammon*. It would bring his life up to date, including his battle with the clerics, and eventually include Mary and Joan. It would cost nineteen thousand dollars—an almost impossible sum for him—but he had located a Mormon-owned union printer who agreed to start with a down payment, followed by installment payments from sales.

Unfortunately, the new edition was not edited by Dorothy Day. He added about a hundred pages to the end, resulting in a patched-up quality, with an unwieldly paratext of dedication, introduction (by Steve Allen), foreword (to the first edition, by Dorothy Day), a final word (from the author), three epigrams, two pages of very small photos, and a table of contents ten pages later. At the end were seventeen pages of index that Ammon labored over on file cards. But it was composed and printed by members of Local 66 of the Amalgamated Lithographers of America, which made him happy. By late fall he had pre-sold 330 copies, many of them at speaking events.

From these engagements and local friends, he drew volunteers for the picketing at Dugway over the winter of 1963–1964.[49] He had first picketed Dugway in April 1962. He had, in a sense, previewed it in his Las Vegas picketing. It was a military base with a generic front gate, eighty-five miles west of Salt Lake City, which lay in its wind shadow. This army testing ground for biological and chemical weapons covered 1,252 square miles of the Great Salt Lake Desert, an area the size of Rhode Island.[50] It was the largest of all federal "special use" areas and as remote as Mercury, Nevada, giving the military the sense that dangerous projects could be tried there. By the mid-1960s there were rumors (later confirmed) that the chemicals tested at Dugway caused livestock deaths.

In March 1968, 6,249 sheep died in Skull Valley, an area nearly thirty miles from Dugway's testing sites. When examined, the sheep were found to have been poisoned by an organophosphate chemical. The sickening of the sheep, known as the Dugway sheep incident, coincided with several open-air tests of the nerve agent VX at Dugway. Local attention focused on the Army, which initially denied that VX had caused the deaths, instead blaming the local use of organophosphate pesticides on crops. Necropsies conducted on the dead sheep later definitively identified the presence of VX. The Army never admitted liability, but did pay the ranchers for their losses.[51]

Hennacy recruited protesters to picket the site and they returned repeatedly during the 1960s. The Salt Lake City press covered them regularly, because Mormon ranchers suffering a sheep kill was a potent headline.

1963 and Joan Thomas

In August 1963, Hennacy received the first Health Department citation, as well as an order limiting to ten the number of people sleeping on the floor. He decided to comply with these, but he said that he would tear down any posted notices or padlocks on his doors. He had learned to use the media: "I told them go ahead, for when the newspapers hear my story, the people will wake up and make them look silly. That they had better not start anything they couldn't finish, for I would not obey any order of the court." His bravado would soon be tested, for this was not New York City, where Dorothy could draw on the sympathy of friends in high places. Here they played strictly by the rules.[52]

Then Joan Thomas returned, explaining that since her "divorce wasn't final," she had thought her husband "might change his mind and return." But he had not, whereupon she launched a twenty-one-day fast. Some confidence, she wrote, put her "in a sufficiently decent frame of mind to go visit Ammon again" in August 1963.[53] This time she walked to the YWCA on arrival and went to Sunday mass by herself. He walked by her without noticing, so she moved up to his pew, kneeling beside him. Afterwards they talked, and she checked out of the Y and into a hotel, deciding to end her fasting and picketing. She would "explore the city on her own hook—as she liked to do. The surrounding mountains fascinated her. When could she commence to climb them?" Walking around town with him, looking for an apartment for herself, she decided that she really liked those mountains. She said she was going back to Minneapolis to get her car, typewriter, and other things; then she could help him with shopping and speeches.[54]

In Minneapolis their forty-year age difference worried her parents. But she went back anyway in September 1963. Hennacy said that he was much happier in Utah than he had been in New York, but that he was lonelier than ever. When the trio of convicts got reprieves, he took a trip to San Francisco while Francis Gorgen watched the Joe Hill House. The landlord paid for the front window that the Navajo broke.[55] Joan had driven her 1960 Rambler from Minnesota through Colorado, car camping and visiting mountains that she liked, and when Hennacy returned from San Francisco, he helped her to find an apartment behind the capitol with a wonderful view over the valley. They had several heart-to-heart talks: she tested his pacifism, asking what he would do if she or his daughters were attacked in his sight. If he really would not fight back, she said, then she wanted him to stick to that position. She was not a pacifist, she said, but she did not believe in paying taxes for war. When he told her that he had lived a loveless life since Selma, and a sexless one since New Mexico, she saw the length and breadth of his solitary quest, and she said she would not try to make him "chicken out" if prison were his fate again. "He had been deeply hurt in his life," she wrote.[56]

By November 1963, she had decided that "we suited one another." It was the feast day of Christ the King, which Hennacy disliked because most Catholic churches played the "Star-Spangled Banner." They sat through it instead of standing, part of an evolving modus vivendi, a finding of common beliefs. Hennacy was constantly on speaking trips, but she had a car, so she became his driver, ferrying him all over the West. As the older, famous half of the couple, he assumed a lot of privilege, but she loved to drive, and she loved the West. Their first night on the road they "spent huddled in sleeping bags" near Bryce Canyon. He later called it one of the happiest moments of his life. The next night it was Death Valley. Then Los Angeles, where he introduced her to his daughters, and they all seemed to get along. At first his constant chatter annoyed her, but she learned to tune it out, and when he went off to speak, she found and climbed a peak.[57]

In the late 1960s Utah was a more liberal state than it is today. Its standard bearer in Congress was Democratic senator Frank Moss, first elected in 1959. An original sponsor of Medicare, Moss was an environment advocate, adding land in Utah's national parks and writing *The Water Crisis*. He was against the Vietnam War, unlike his counterpart Wallace Bennett, the Republican senator, who nonetheless gave Ammon a twenty-five-dollar contribution. Ammon was so shocked by

Figure 8.4. Joan Thomas. Permission of Josephine
Thomas.

the donation that he wrote to his mother, "$25 might not be much to
him, but now I have my bills paid until Sept. 1." Democratic governor
Cal Rampton responded to Hennacy's letters, sharing his concern about
Dugway, another sign Utah had accepted him.[58]

Merchants were now donating liberally, one giving him forty pounds
of herring. The postal workers across the street and the guards at the
Mormon Temple contributed to the House. From San Francisco Mary
Lathrop, now working in the fields with migrants, wrote a long adula-
tory poem for his birthday. Even the dispute with the Catholic hierarchy
eased, as Thomas Merton wrote Ammon a long letter confessing that he
himself was not "radical enough."[59] Ammon had discovered that some
Mormons fasted, and he attended meetings "where everyone gets up and
testifies, like Quakers. It may be good, and it may be tiresome, but I go
there every Sunday." These meetings, called Fast Sunday, were held the

first Sunday of the month, and those willing gave up two meals, donating the cost to a fund for the indigent.[60]

Appreciations of the Latter-Day Saints (LDS) dominated the last pages of his new biography, *The Book of Ammon*, which was published in ten thousand copies and could hardly be ignored locally. Ammon's idea was to sell books at three dollars each, netting eleven thousand dollars for the Joe Hill House, but the overall economics of the project were vague. The Mormon printer was allowing Hennacy to pay by installments, but it is not clear whether he recouped his costs. Steve Allen, creator of *The Tonight Show* and star of *The Steve Allen Show*, ordered five advance copies, which excited Ammon. He wrote to Wallace Stegner at Stanford, who returned a long, polite letter. Robert Steed had come out and was helping at the Joe Hill House, so Ammon could make appearances and talks. Momentum seemed to be gathering.[61]

But Hennacy's picketing lost some of its immediacy when Garcia got a commutation to life, Rivenburgh committed suicide in his cell, and Poulsen's appeals became legally complex. Ammon began to focus on Dugway and the war in Vietnam, which was escalating daily. College students were stopping in to visit, some with small stipends to support them while they worked at the House. Ammon had speaking dates from California to Colorado, from Washington to New Mexico, sometimes two in one day, so he traveled a lot, often with Joan driving, and he became well known in the West again. California was a favorite destination because he could also see his daughters.

Back in Salt Lake, journalists from TASS and Radio Moscow showed up to interview him, although he was out of town when the latter flew in (a Mormon bishop met the Russian and drove him around, indicating the entente between Ammon and the LDS). He also met various Mormon separatists, such as those in the Order of Aaron, who lived at Eskdale, and the Short Creek polygamists from Hildale, Utah, and Colorado City, Arizona. He was complimentary about the former, who ran a renowned music program and were, he said, "primitive pacifists and anarchists, for they had seceded from the state." He said nothing about the polygamists.[62]

Hennacy's political stances were as uncompromising as ever. John F. Kennedy was basically "a liberal opportunist senator." The assassination changed his view only a little: "Kennedy had the same charm as Franklin

D. Roosevelt, without so much of his guile. When he made his mistake at the Bay of Pigs, he admitted it. It is not likely that he would have gotten us deeper into the Viet Nam war, and if he had, he would have been honest about trying to get us out, instead of devious like Nixon."[63]

Despite Ammon's bluster, the Health and Building Departments did not relent, citing the Joe Hill House in the fall of 1963 and establishing a December 19 deadline for compliance. He got sympathetic coverage from the *Deseret News*, which helped him to get a hearing before the mayor and city council in early December. He won a reprieve from the council, but he did not foresee the Health Department pressuring his landlord, whom it told to expect more of the same. Hennacy, who was picketing at Dugway at the time, did not believe they would close the Joe Hill House. But in late January 1964, his landlord confirmed the worst, and on February 9, Hennacy served his last meal at the first Joe Hill House. The officials spent several days driving him around to look for a new location, to show there were no hard feelings, or to improve their PR.

Joan Thomas was still uncertain about a long-term relationship, retreating periodically to Minneapolis, where her mother finally surprised her by suggesting that maybe she should marry Ammon. On her third return, Hennacy told her that he could not take the emotional seesaw. He promised to get a legal divorce from Selma and marry her, though Joan had not said she would consent: in his patriarchal manner, Ammon just assumed. But she stayed, and they planned some travel, without any lecturing, to see new places.[64] These trips were happy ones. She made him take days off and nicknamed him "the Leprechaun," or "Leppy." He called her "Joey" or "Willow." They drove south through Utah to the Grand Canyon and then west, stopping when they saw an International House of Pancakes (Ammon's new favorite), stopping to run through a lettuce field, and stopping another time to raid an orchard. They stayed in cheap motels, they talked, and they decided to stay together.

Hennacy wrote to his daughters to say that he was filing for divorce, assuming that they would notify Selma (he did not have her address), but they did not tell her immediately. His presumptive ways with women continued. When she found out, Selma wrote a nasty letter, with no return address. Clearly she was hurt. But they had not lived together in thirty years, and she had never made any effort to contact him. On

November 9, 1964, the divorce came through, but it would not be final until ninety days later, due to the legal publication and waiting period required in Utah. He again sent the papers to his daughters to forward to Selma, who did not respond.

So there was a pause; the closing of the first Joe Hill House was muted. Before opening another house, Ammon decided to take a long bus trip, inviting Joan along. She accepted, but soon regretted being cooped up with his constant chatter, so after he appeared on the *Steve Allen Show*, she went to Minneapolis again. They met up there, and she drove them back to Utah. They stayed in a small motel south of Salt Lake, where the rent was one hundred dollars a month, while Ammon looked for a new Joe Hill House location. What he found was "a small house in a lower middle-class neighborhood," Thomas wrote, and she got an apartment nearby where "she got on with her life—Mass, hikes, writing, artwork."[65] The money for these ventures, which had come from the *Catholic Worker*, from Dorothy, from supporters like Yone and the Clines, was now slowing down. But Hennacy did not own a car, did not pay taxes, and could stretch a dollar.

Joan and Ammon were not particularly worried. He said that he had been broke before, and God had always provided something. But it was Dorothy Day who provided this time, sending a check for one thousand dollars. Half was for the new house, half for copies of his book. In fact, Day would send him rent money for the rest of his life, despite their conflicts. "Ammon never had anything. *Anything!*" she explained later.[66] He worked through the winter on his next book, for which he had already paid forty-one hundred dollars to the printer, though where he found that sum is a mystery.[67]

On February 8, 1965, Joan drove Ammon to Las Vegas to attend Mass and take communion at Joan of Arc Church, making of it a special but private occasion. Then they were legally married in Elko, Nevada, on April 12, 1965. "She is a vegetarian, natural born anarchist and pacifist," Ammon wrote to a friend, "and not too much of a Catholic to be nice to me when she wants to."[68] He was seventy-two and she was thirty, neither a vegetarian nor a pacifist, in fact, but strongly antiwar. She had decided that God intended for them to be together, and she began to enjoy what she considered a deepening friendship. She did not think of him as a "husband," she said, but as her own Mark Twain, confident and funny.

They went to Mass together every Sunday, and she helped mail out copies of the book: a hundred more had gone out by March 1. She did not feel overly involved in the Joe Hill House and suspected that long fasts were bad for him. "Married men shouldn't fast," she told him.[69]

The second Joe Hill House ran into problems early. Located south of the city, it was farther from merchant donors, though now they had Joan's car. More problematic were the residents, who traipsed twenty-some blocks from the railroad yards, panhandling at houses along the way. "Once there they would sleep out in the yard and urinate freely," Thomas wrote: "Neighbors all around were complaining." Ammon was "no great shakes at disciplining the men," and once went on a lecture trip, leaving three of them "in charge." On August 8, barely five months after it opened, the second Joe Hill House was shut down by the Salt Lake Health Department.[70]

Ammon and Joan made the most of their free time, driving back to Cleveland, where Ammon's ninety-three-year-old mother, still cogent, shared her collection of "Dear Heloise" columns with Joan. They drove to Negley, where Ammon showed her Peter Brown's house, but the new owner would not let them on the property. They turned northwest and headed for her parents in Minneapolis, where Hennacy spoke at the university, and Joan's father found her a newer car. Then Ammon got on the bus to return to Salt Lake, to search for a third Joe Hill House location.

By July he had located a house at 3121 South Second West, but news of his mission preceded him, and the neighbors were offended. This was a working-class area, with a homeowner across the street threatening to break every window if the house were opened. Hennacy thought he had a rent-to-own arrangement worked out, but in September, the landlord, who had been charging fifty dollars a month, told Ammon that he was selling the place.[71] By accident Hennacy and Thomas found another house for rent just a few blocks away, without neighbors. Surrounded by weedy fields and junked cars, it was owned by the proprietor of a nearby wrecking yard, who rented them the house for forty dollars a month. He owned a second two-bedroom house that they rented to live in for seventy dollars, so in April 1965 Hennacy was able to return to picketing in commemoration of the Hiroshima bombing.[72]

In 1965 the anti–Vietnam War protests were just beginning: at first Hennacy read about them in the *Catholic Worker* more than he participated, but that changed quickly. A *CW* follower named Roger LaPorte immolated himself in front of the UN, the third such suicide of the year. Then Father Daniel Berrigan, a prominent antiwar activist at Yale who had burned Selective Service records with the Catonsville Nine, was seemingly "exiled" to South America by Cardinal Spellman.[73] News of the grassroots struggle for control of the church reached Hennacy through his *CW* network, Dave Dellinger came to speak against the war, and Joan Baez sang at the Mormon Tabernacle. The antiwar protest reached Utah.

But Hennacy's energy was flagging. In July he had mentioned feeling tired while picketing for the first time, noting that "Joan [drove] me down and back for my picketing." Fortunately, Bruce Phillips was helping out at the House and had become a regular feature of Ammon's Friday evening meetings. These were held closer to campus and attracted more students—potential conscientious objectors—now that the military was pouring men and money into the war. Phillips obtained a copy of a CBC film on Joe Hill, which he and Ammon began to show around Salt Lake, using it as an antidraft, antiwar rallying point. There had been an influx of students from both coasts to the university, bringing antiwar politics with them, founding chapters of the SDS and other organizations.[74]

Hennacy and Thomas were getting by on donations from supporters, but Joan was writing a novel for publication, and she urged Hennacy to write about his favorite American radicals. In one sense he had been preparing for this his whole life, but now he read more history and biographies, for a book to be titled *The One-Man Revolution in America*. It would be a distillation of his ideas about a native tradition of American anarchism, but the subjects changed and the book was delayed while they waited for permissions (Ammon himself did not believe in copyrights and never sought any), reducing its income-producing possibility. They still picketed for Poulsen, they acquired a puppy they called Hopi, and cats surrounded the new House. Ammon found a piano for Joan, just as he had for his daughters at Bisanakee, so that she sometimes suspected him of trying to recreate that life. She did not protest: she had time to write and paint and plenty of open roads on which to ride her bike.

By January of 1966, Hennacy was speaking at antiwar rallies locally and planning a road trip to Denver, Omaha, Chicago, and Minneapolis.

The University of Utah had some free-thinking professors, antiwar Unitarians and Quakers running its campus ministries, and a student radio station that could get out the news, so it became the focus of some of his activities. Hennacy was invited to write on pacifism by the Mormon journal *Dialogue* and was soon speaking more of Dave Dellinger than of Dorothy Day.[75] This being the presidency of Lyndon Johnson, Hennacy went on attack, characterizing Johnson as "the wheeler-dealer of them all, the super-politician who could lie and blackmail and nearly get away with it." Johnson had said, "We are not about to send American boys nine or ten thousand miles away from home to do what Asian boys ought to do for themselves," but Ammon noted that "while he was uttering these reassurances, administration plans were under way to escalate the war by bombing North Vietnam. Steps had already been taken to dispatch large numbers of troops to southeast Asia."[76]

Though the latest Joe Hill House lacked indoor plumbing and heat, on return from the long speaking trip, Joan and Ammon slept on its floor in sleeping bags. Then Bruce Phillips secured a kerosene lantern, and some Unitarians produced a gas heater. This new house was supposed to be rent-free until September 1 if they fixed it up, so Hennacy started work on the plumbing, while Joan moved into their rental. Outside the new house he erected a sign that read,

SHAME!
HIROSHIMA
NAGASAKI
VIETNAM

This third Joe Hill House was a one-story frame bungalow, with a small ground-level front porch where Ammon and the residents could sit. Joan drove Ammon on his collection route now and also most other places.[77] She said that "Ammon was remarkably easy to live with now, was never or rarely hungry, thirsty, tired, or if he was, he never complained. . . . When we weren't working, Ammon was always ready and eager for a walk, a car drive, a mountain hike. He was always exuberant about visiting friends."[78] Sometimes they even went to a movie—his favorites were *Brigadoon*, *South Pacific*, *The Sound of Music*, and Pasolini's *Gospel according to St. Matthew*.

But the Joe Hill House did not run smoothly in the winter of 1968. It was only a block from a rail yard and the men jumped off around midnight, creating a disruptive schedule for the neighborhood and for Hennacy, who no longer slept at the House. They lived close by, but there were other distractions. Hennacy cut back his Hiroshima fasting a bit and some of his picketing against the Poulsen execution. On April 7, 1968, after the Martin Luther King Jr. assassination, he sent the *Salt Lake Tribune* the poem "Mourn Not the Dead" by Ralph Chapin in tribute. He was writing about King for his new book as well.

Then some misfits moved into the House, including a schizophrenic named Dale, while other key helpers left. "Red, the very able cook and housekeeper, hitched a freight to Denver with one of his lovers, and later one of the men said that he was working as a cook in a whorehouse there," wrote Joan, and "Dale, whose drinking was growing worse, acquired a knife and a revolver, and during his drunken sprees, threatened the other men, so that many were afraid to stay there. The number of men dwindled at times to maybe Dale and one or two friends." Considering that Dale's disability check was three hundred dollars a month, they wondered if it was worth keeping the House going for him and his buddies.

"Though the men kept this house immaculately clean," Joan noted, "one time they let the toilet run for some days before Ammon noticed a thirty-dollar water bill for that month." Someone else bought an electric heater and turned it on high at night, resulting in a huge electric bill. Then Dale returned from the VA hospital saying he had leukemia; Ammon and Joan suspected a lie and were patient, but finally they concluded that the House was "too far out from the downtown section where the men prefer to hang out." In May 1968, they closed the third Joe Hill House and headed for Phoenix, where they had stored many possessions, before starting another cross-country trip to the East.[79]

They lingered in Minnesota a while, because it was not clear what they could do back in Salt Lake. Joan pushed Ammon to finish up *The One-Man Revolution*. He wanted to return to Utah by August 6 to start his annual Hiroshima picketing, but he was mildly irked that, since the Joe Hill House had moved in Salt Lake, he did not have the notoriety that he once enjoyed. Picketing was the important thing, he decided, so they returned for that briefly, but in September they moved to Phoenix, where few seemed to remember Ammon Hennacy anymore.

With no income, he fell back on his oldest skill, door-to-door selling for Fuller Brush.[80] But something was wrong. "He looked very bad, exhausted, returning from long days on his route," Joan said. Looking for a respite, she got him to write "Forgotten Aspects of My Youth," which she appended to her book *The Years of Grief and Laughter*. Then in November he came down with a serious bout of flu, coughing continually until Joan made him see a doctor.[81] As he wrote to the Clines,

> I had to quit selling the brushes when I got the flu twice, for there is no use in dying for Consolidated Foods, which bought out Fuller and increased prices. I had a positive reaction to a skin test for TB, so I'll have to rest and be careful. Guess that sleeping on those floors all those years was not good for me. The chest x-ray was not so bad. I'll concentrate on my new book. Finishing up on Thoreau now. Going west in May speaking and will be in Salt Lake in July and August picketing. Have to depend on alms from CW readers for a while now.

A few days later the Clines sent him a check, for which he wrote a letter of thanks, adding that he considered it to be "spiritual social security coming from my years of feeding tramps."[82]

They kept a quiet life in Phoenix. "We enjoy visits with Rik and Ginny, and with Joe and Ida Stocker," he wrote. "We found a quiet place to live where vines grow all around a locked gate in the front. We told only Joe Craigmyle where we lived, so no one bothered us, and Joan has felt better and got her artwork and writing done after I quit my brushes."[83] He kept a journal in which he recounted their conversations about God and morals: "If the man I shake hands with, doesn't want to shake hands and kills me, maybe he will reform and become better than I am. If I killed him or tried to, it wouldn't solve anything, except that I went against my ideals—against God." His pacifism was still absolute.

In April 1969, they headed north to Utah, in part because the heat of Arizona bothered him. He could not believe that he once dug ditches in these temperatures, but he also thought Phoenix had gotten too big: "It used to be a chicken shit town, like Salt Lake." He was no longer on a first-name basis with Phoenix radio and TV announcers or the chief

Figure 8.5. Ammon and Carol Gorgen picketing in Salt Lake. Permission of Josephine Thomas.

of police. Having sent their goods ahead by truck, they swung over to Albuquerque and Santa Fe.[84] In Taos they visited Frank Waters, author of *The Book of the Hopi*, and attended "the best mass ever" in a Hispanic church. They loved this "gypsy life," as they called it, but wondered how long it could go on. In June, back in Minnesota at Joan's folks' house, Ammon finished *The One-Man Revolution*.[85]

When they returned to Salt Lake in August 1969, Ammon was seventy-six and Joan was thirty-five. "They were staying at the house of friends while looking for a new place, which shortly they found. It was the back half of a duplex, the front half of which was occupied by a woman named Millie, who was slightly younger than Ammon." But "Ammon had developed a cough," Joan wrote, "or rather never seemed to have gotten over the cough acquired from his sickness in Phoenix the past winter."

While he was picketing the post office on August 6, she went again to climb Mt. Timpanogos, where she had an intuition that their days together were numbered. In November Ammon got the flu twice more. When that round of picketing was over, she took him to a doctor friend who had examined him in the past. "The results were that Ammon was in excellent shape for a man of his age." They went to Timpanogos Cave, and then on November 11 to Mt. Timpanogos.[86] It was the anniversary of the Haymarket martyrs, which he had observed since Atlanta, but there was a somber tone in his voice. "We can always remember that we visited the mountain for the last time on November 11," he said. The foreshadowing continued. While she was doing a tarot reading, he asked if they had a happy marriage: the deck produced the Sun, denoting a happy *and* fortuitous marriage. On other days he would complain that she was overfeeding him, though she had cut back the size of his meals.[87]

Ammon started picketing on Monday, January 5, 1970. "A bus line ran directly in front of our house," wrote Joan, "so he was taking the bus downtown, getting his picket signs and leaflets kept at the house of a friend [Ethel Hale] a couple of blocks from the downtown section, then parading through the downtown area (the best part of picketing) up to the capitol, where he walked back and forth from twelve to one in front of the building."[88]

Joan had been making him wear a stocking cap and gloves when he went out in winter, even though he protested that Salt Lake never got that cold. "I remember putting his cap on him that morning of January 8th, his fourth day of picketing." Then she settled down to write.[89] "At a quarter to one I heard him at the living room door," she wrote. He explained that, on walking up the hill to the capitol, he had fallen, and upon rising, he had vomited. "His face was ashen, he put a hand to his chest. 'I'm sick,'" he said. He took off his gloves, cap, and overcoat. "I'll lie down for a while, I'll be all right." On his bed, he told her how a passerby had driven him to Ethel's, how Paul had driven him home. About ten minutes later she decided to call Dr. Edison.[90] "Maybe you better . . . I don't seem to be getting any better." Frightened by his acquiescence as much as by his appearance, she went to Millie's apartment to phone the doctor. "He says he has indigestion, but could it be a heart attack?" The doctor told her to go to the drugstore, get some medicine and if it did not work, to call him back.

Instead, with Ammon lying across the back seat under a blanket, she drove him to St. Mary's Hospital. He was taken in a wheelchair immediately to emergency, where the admitting doctor told her that Ammon's chest pains all winter could have been warning signs from a waning heart. Minutes later another a doctor came back: yes, he had had a heart attack. When she went up to visit him, he looked better—color had returned to his face and he said that he was no longer in pain.[91]

Joan went in his place on January 9 to the capitol, where she picketed with Al, one of the Joe Hill House regulars, and Ethel Hale. But neither Joan nor Ethel could stand the hecklers, nor did they feel much sympathy for the murderers whose execution they were protesting (Lance and Kelbach, serial killers who killed and raped six people in five days, then escaped from prison). Returning to the hospital, she amused Ammon with their failings. He said that Dr. Edison had okayed his spring speaking tour.[92] The next day was a Saturday, so there was no picketing because the state offices were closed. Instead, Joan brought Ammon newspapers, and he was moved out of intensive care. On Monday and Tuesday she picketed again with Al, recounting their adventures to Ammon that afternoon. Cards and flowers began to arrive. "You know," he said, "this heart attack might turn out to be the best thing that ever happened to us. It got you out picketing and brought us closer together." But he did not look so good.

She had given the hospital Millie's number, in case they needed her. Millie would pound on the door if they called. On Wednesday when Millie pounded, Joan was in the kitchen and felt immediately that he had died. It was January 14, 1970. There was a nun with the body when she arrived, and Ammon had received last rites and was later cremated. Joan had stayed in contact with Carmen, who spoke with her sister, and the daughters paid the hospital bills. Dorothy Day learned of the death within days, and soon a circle of friends, including Selma, assembled in Salt Lake to commemorate Hennacy's life. It went more smoothly than anyone could have foreseen.

As he wished, Hennacy's ashes were scattered over the graves of the Haymarket anarchists in Waldheim Cemetery in Chicago on March 27, 1970. Joan drove through a snowstorm to begin the ceremony and returned on August 27, 1972, to finish the job. A few ashes she saved and placed on Mount Timpanogos and in its glacial lake. In 2019 the last of his ashes were scattered by Jeremy Harmon in Sugarhouse Park, at the spot where Joe Hill was executed.

Conclusion

Fearless Speech

At the time of his death, Hennacy had just been named "Pacifist of the Year" by the War Resisters League. The *Salt Lake Tribune* announced his passing in an all-block-caps headline: "AN AMERICAN LEGEND." Dorothy Day reminded people that he had "given up everything in life for his beliefs—he never had any money, possessions, home, or stable family life."[1] There were already people who considered Ammon a "saint," a notion he would have dismissed, and others, including academics, who wrote that he had been a "prophet."

The irony was that, after a formal embrace of some fifteen years, Hennacy had left the Catholic Church, though he continued to attend Mass. That does not phase followers who argue that he embodied pacifism, the Sermon on the Mount, and Christian anarchism with a preternatural clarity. Dan Wakefield's account in *New York in the Fifties* is representative:

> He stood on street corners from Union Square to Broadway selling copies of *The Catholic Worker*, spoke to Quaker meetings and student groups at colleges. . . . What impressed me most of all was that Hennacy, as a teenage Ohio farm boy, had joined the IWW. . . . He was a real Wobbly, like those I'd read about in Dos Passos . . . and heard praised by C. Wright Mills, as the only truly homegrown American radicals. . . . The most surprising part of all this was that Hennacy conveyed it with a sense of delight and humor. There was nothing heavy or dour about him, but rather a feeling of joy and discovery.[2]

But if he had been only this "home-grown" streetcorner idealist, Hennacy would have been forgotten by now. Why does he endure? Wakefield's comment about joy and discovery is a clue.

Like Dorothy Day, he was a powerful writer. His books and articles trail behind him and allow us to trace the evolution of that "teenage Ohio farm boy" into one of twentieth-century America's most important pacifist/anarchist voices. Indeed, scholar William O. Reichert writes that "in many respects, Ammon Hennacy's autobiography, *The Book of Ammon*, is one of the finest sources of anarchist philosophy and theory available."[3] But unlike Day, he never stood down and, not facing her daily realities, his uncompromising stands therefore still seem pure and relevant. His moral framework was personal responsibility: if you do not trespass against your neighbor, your neighbor will not trespass against you. He presses us to add this uncompromising quality to our daily appreciation of the joy and discovery of God, or the good, as he liked to quip.

Hennacy's regard for the neighbor, that each be treated as a God-created individual, was the heart of his particular personalism. But the embodiment of this philosophy was difficult and something that Ammon worked on every day. He was not always successful, as his patriarchal and sometimes intolerant attitudes attest. But he tried, like a Zen *roshi*, to embody his philosophy in his smallest actions. How far did his attitude carry him? Did he combine Christianity and anarchism? After fifty years, what had he learned?

The One-Man Revolution

One turns to his final work, *The One-Man Revolution*, for answers, to learn whether, after a lifetime of practice, he actually united the strands of anarchism, pacifism, and personalism. His purpose in writing this book seems to have been to trace the development of an indigenous American anarchist tradition. While profiling his heroes and heroines, he also argues that the tools for a better way of living are lying in plain sight in America. But he also wanders tellingly into other topics. Just as we had to learn to read Ammon's "implied metaphors," we have to discern a subtheme about "directness" in this book. The volume stretches from John Woolman and Thomas Jefferson to Dorothy Day and Malcolm X, a particular selection of rhetorical performers who relate to Hennacy's own verbal brashness. There are no shrinking violets in this bouquet, but several curious selections. The subtheme can be recovered by laying aside our suspicions about his feuds, disputes, and patriarchal attitudes, while recovering the deeper meaning of his humor and "fearless speech" as a daily practice.

The place to begin *One-Man Revolution* is at the end, in the section on "Introspection," where Hennacy writes of his motivation:

> While writing this book one morning, I happened to look into the mirror on the wall. While in solitary there was no mirror, yet in my loneliness and silence, I at times, seemed to "come out of myself," and look at myself from a distance. That morning, as I was dissecting one of the people of whom I was writing, in this same "come out" attitude I looked at myself, and I commenced a sort of Devil's Advocate process; "Am I a pacifist because I never liked shooting and hunting? Am I an anarchist because I did not want to come out second best in political strife? Am I a vegetarian because I am squeamish about blood, and not, out of love for animals? Do I refuse to pay taxes because I want to be 'different'"?[4]

The "coming out" of one's self was self-examination in the manner of Socrates and Thoreau, but also self-encouragement toward "fearless speech," a form that dates to ancient Greece and its practitioners, called rhetors, whom Hennacy had studied in high school. "Come out from behind your social mask and daily social practice," Ammon says, and show me how you have lived your beliefs. The figures that he treats had done so.

Hennacy begins this book with the Quaker John Woolman, whose embrace of the fundamental freedom provided by the so-called antinomian heresy (1525) is key.[5] The "heresy" was the freedom to interpret the Bible personally and apart from tradition, and it took place in a community. In Ammon's view, after the Puritans established themselves in America, they lost that interpretive independence and became corporatist.[6] The Quakers' community was constituted so as to preserve freedom of interpretation: Ammon understood the Quakers not only as his personal heritage but as a force against restrictions on Bible interpretation. As *Catholic Worker* historian William Miller points out, Hennacy's interpretations of society were binary: the Quakers, with their unfettered religious idealism and opposition to political obedience, were always good.[7]

Quakerism had started with John Fox, but Hennacy lays his foundation with the uncompromising American outsider John Woolman.
Respect for the outsider was a second absolute for Ammon. Woolman
applied the Sermon on the Mount absolutely, as Ammon did, and he
was against all taxes that supported war or official churches, like those
in Maryland and Virginia. So he met Ammon's religious standard. In
terms of anarchist theory, these outsiders should be in voluntary cooperation with others. Hennacy tells of Woolman, camping at a settlement
of friendly Indians, threatened by an armed member of another tribe.
He "extended his open hand with grave dignity and walked up to the
Indian" and all was resolved, an echo of Hennacy's Hand or Knife parable. There is an association, by analogy, with General Bouquet, who
made the peace with Indians near Ammon's birthplace of Negley. Thus
the first figure in Hennacy's anarchist history is a Quaker, with Ohio
connotations, and an outsider. Hennacy also finds in Woolman an early
advocate of race emancipation, not unusual for a Quaker, but he was
also a vegetarian and health advocate "who blazed the way for himself
and us in the deep forest of compromise and greed."[8]

Ammon's next building block is Thomas Jefferson, a small-
government, nonchurch Christian but not an anarchist. The "Jefferson
Bible"—a folio into which he cut and pasted the sections he believed—
included the Sermon on the Mount, and Congress had published an
edition in 1904, so this inspiring document was available to Hennacy.
But Jefferson was "not a pacifist," as Hennacy admits, even if "he never
ceased to attack privilege." It is the agrarian Jefferson that appealed to
Ammon. "The earth belongs to each of these generations in its course,"
wrote Jefferson. "The second generation receives it clear of the debts and
encumbrances of the first." This invokes the anti-agribusiness lessons of
Ammon's time in New Mexico and Arizona. In Ammon's apologetics,
Jefferson was a reluctant slaveholder, who might have recognized his
white privilege later on. Jefferson's relation to Sally Hemings was not yet
known, but Hennacy's soft-selling of Jefferson on race is regrettable.[9]

What redeems Jefferson for Hennacy is his rhetorical boldness, his
absolute advocacy for "states' rights against the Union, for county rights
against the state, for township rights or village rights against the county,
and for private rights against all." If this is a concession to some government, uncomfortable for Ammon, it is also a recognition of the urban

life that he met in New York and Salt Lake. Jefferson says, in effect, "only this much government, no more." It is that absolutism that Hennacy admired. He omits most of Jefferson's time in Europe, focusing on his youth—"'that government is best which governs least, as with the Indians'"—and later life, when he belatedly advocated freeing the slaves and developed varietal grapes, cinnamon, and herbs at Monticello.[10] At least the case for Jefferson's ecological consciousness is strong, as Peter Ling has detailed. He was against monoculture farming (tobacco) and embraced crop rotation.[11] In Jefferson's personal habits, Hennacy sees the "embodiment" that he prized: "There were never twelve consecutive hours, except when sleeping, when he was not working on some project. In this he was the very opposite of Thoreau, who 'rested through life.' He was always horseback riding and rode horses hard until three weeks before his death. He was the original jogger, for from his college days he was to be seen walking or running in the evening along woody paths." Looking into that mirror, one can imagine Hennacy repeating Jefferson: "Action will delineate and define you."[12]

Of all the colonial figures, it was to Thomas Paine and his experience in Europe that Hennacy paid the closest attention. Why not Paine in America? Paine in Europe provides an assay of political ideas that Ammon never imbibed at the source. Paine lived through the French Revolution, which Hennacy thought was underexamined on the Left: with government swept away, what had happened? "Anarchists generally believe these details will be adequately taken care of by popular ingenuity," Patrick Coy notes: "It is presumed that the freed spirit will require little or no guidance and that natural patterns of decentralized organization will evolve."[13]

Hennacy was not that naïve. After the Terror, he writes, Paine faced execution more than once: he "would not have been a Communist, nor was he an anarchist [but] he knew what the anarchist knows and what the Communist does not know, that government is evil. . . . We have had too many Socialist and Communist theorists who can tell for centuries what should happen according to Marx, and this very slavery to theory has kept them from advancing the revolution they have wanted."[14] If Woolman and Jefferson were the raw synthesis of religion plus libertarianism, then Paine was that synthesis schooled by the chaos of the crowd and a suspicion of theory. It was unnecessary for Hennacy to add that

Paine was among the first to recognize what we now call "the banality of evil": Ammon agreed and believed in calling out even small increments of evil, of compromise, of bad faith or habit, which sometimes gave others the impression of fanaticism. As Joan Thomas has written, "He knew in his heart there could never be an anarchistic society other than as it is embodied in an individual person."[15] It appears that Jefferson and Paine went to Europe for Hennacy, and then later Berkman, Debs, Mother Bloor, and the Nearings brought back a follow-up report. All these people that he trusted had sieved Europe's political thought and found it wanting in practice.

With great relish Hennacy passes on to Henry David Thoreau, who was obviously a literary model. Quoting mostly from *Walden*'s "Economy" and "Civil Disobedience" chapters, Hennacy edits Thoreau liberally, deleting many rhetorical, humorous, and self-referential flourishes. What remains is the present-oriented focus on nature that Ammon reproduced in his own "Life at Hard Labor": "To anticipate, not the sunrise and the dawn merely, but, if possible, Nature herself! How many mornings, summer and winter, before yet any neighbor was stirring about his business, have I been about mine! No doubt, many of my townsmen have met me returning from this enterprise, farmers starting for Boston in the twilight, or woodchoppers going to their work. It is true, I never assisted the sun materially in his rising, but, doubt not, it was of the last importance only to be present at it."[16] In that last sentence we see some of Hennacy's inspiration to humor and metaphor. Some of his edits, however, seem curious. In order to arrive quickly at "the mass of men lead lives of quiet desperation," he cut "as if you could kill time without injuring eternity." Why? Probably because the line is purely metaphoric speculation. He also cut Thoreau's politics of soft resistance: "If the injustice is part of the necessary friction of the machine of government, let it go, let it go; perchance it will wear smooth—certainly the machine will wear out." These are more signs of Hennacy's subtheme of rhetorical boldness. He does not speculate, nor does he "let it go."

By the time we get to the chapter on Berkman, we understand Ammon's structure and method: plunge into the best prose of the subject for up to half the chapter, letting us hear each figure speak fearlessly. After that, Ammon will enter the chapter, sometimes with context on the subject's life, sometimes with a critical overview, always pointing to the value he sees. But now comes Berkman, whose writing style was bombastic and Victorian. Describing the run-up to his assassination attempt on Frick, Berkman wrote that "Perfidious Carnegie shrank from the task" and "the world stood aghast. The time for speech was past."[17] The modern reader may look for a villain to "enter, stage right." But when Ammon intervenes this time, he imagines Berkman's stream of consciousness as he shoots Frick. He does not endorse Berkman's violence per se, but he does exalt Berkman's fearlessness. Berkman and Hennacy now seem to move on the same stage: "They presented themselves for a hearing December 5. On that date I was released from Delaware, Ohio, prison, having gone there from Atlanta. I was in New York City on December 12, but of course could not see them."[18] Ammon continues to appear in Berkman's life for several pages. This seems like egotism, but it is an identification of the self with a greater spiritual force, like that he saw in Gandhi's identification of his body with greater India. At this point in the book Ammon steps, immodestly for some readers, onstage with his models, including Emma Goldman, the Haymarket figures, Debs, and Vanzetti. *The One-Man Revolution* becomes a meditation on the power of *parrhesia*, or fearless speech.[19]

Once this subtheme is discerned, subsequent chapters may be read as elaborations on the power of pacifism or anarchist practices, and sometimes on both. Other chapters, such as those on Sacco and Vanzetti and Malcom X, have little to do with pacifism and everything to do with the power of rhetoric. Bartolomeo Vanzetti (chapter 13) represents the pair of anarchists executed in April 1927. As we saw in chapter 3, this event affected Hennacy powerfully if belatedly. He was in prison when they were arrested initially, and he was living semi-rurally in Waukesha when they were executed. But the objective facts of the case hardly matter; Ammon was called back to his credo and became a devotee of a cause célèbre that prefigured his later interest in Joe Hill. What matters is that Vanzetti, the more articulate, said things such as "I neither boast nor exalt, nor pity myself. I followed my call. I have my conscience serene . . . hoping for the little knowledge of the enormous mystery surrounding us and from which we sprang. . . . All what is help to me without hurting others is good."[20]

The following chapter on Malcolm X begs the question, Why not Martin Luther King Jr.? Hennacy had lived in the segregated South and worked with Black Americans, but never met King or Malcolm X. He writes that in April 1969—a time of race riots and tensions across the United States—he read *The Autobiography of Malcolm X* (written by Alex Haley) and "was impressed by the real spirit of suffering and learning, rather than the more bourgeois life of King."[21] This is so antithetic to Hennacy's general philosophy as to require an alternate explanation. It probably lies in Malcolm's rivalry, recounted by Haley, with the more famous and effective speakers Elijah Muhammad and Martin Luther King Jr. Hennacy takes the side of outsider in this competition, feeling that Malcom X, like himself, had lost a pacifist competition with Muhammad and King when he in fact had firmer principles. The last two pages of this chapter, parsed in the context of sixties radicalism, especially support such a reading. Ammon surveys the Black radicals of 1969—King and Malcolm dead now—and finds the latter preferable to Eldridge Cleaver, whose "message is somewhat like Malcolm had arrived at when he came back from Mecca." But "Malcolm was learning that which Cleaver has not understood or believed: 'That he that taketh the sword shall perish by the sword.'" But no one knew this or exemplified it better than King, although Ammon seems to have missed his point.

"Yukeoma, the Hopi" (chapter 12) is an endorsement of Native American decentralization and self-government by secession from the state. Native Americans always seemed to Ammon to embody a nobility of speech, in a stateless society governed by avoidance of violence and by voluntary poverty: the choice of "God's Coward," but on native ground. Chapter 13, on John Taylor, an early leader of the Mormon Church, should have something critical to say about the violence and polygamy of the early church—these are stunning omissions. But Taylor, the third president of the Mormon Church, is redeemed as the leader who did not accompany Brigham Young on the great migration, who retraced Paine's footsteps and, finding the same lack of solutions in Europe, presents the case for a different and distant relation to federal government: the experiment called Utah. If the reader has followed the Jefferson argument, this makes sense.

Hennacy closes his book with chapters on Dorothy Day and Helen Demoskoff, a measure of the putative importance of strong women in his life, such as his mother and grandmother. But his treatment of Day is severely wanting, even misogynistic.[22] Bruce Phillips saw the manuscript while living in the Joe Hill House in 1968, and he said, "Ammon! Dorothy's not in the book!" To which Ammon replied, "Well, she's still alive. She could chicken out at any time. If you've got to have heroes, make sure they're dead so they can't blow it."[23] The wounds were clearly not healed, but the quotation underlines Ammon's ingratitude, and recalls his battles with Selma and questionable relation to Mary Lathrop. Hennacy goes on to characterize Day as "a journalist and basic radical," gives a jumbled account of her life, then breaks from his editorial model "to tell her story rather than to give quotes of her statements," as though he can ventriloquize her life. His subtheme of bold speech does not excuse him here. He breaks into Day's story for parenthetical comments on what he was doing at the time. Within twelve pages, he joins the *Catholic Worker* and makes himself the central figure of the first part of her chapter. Perhaps this was his belated response to *The Long Loneliness*: "There are many events in Dorothy's life that I do not feel like speaking about," he admits.[24] But to call Peter Maurin a "peasant" who shows up at her apartment is vindictive, and to term his program of agrarian self-sufficiency, long a belief of Hennacy's, "a sad story of hope and despair," is contradictory.[25] Only at the end of the chapter does he acknowledge the stress and complexity of Day's life. "She has been understanding with me when I later left the Church," he concedes. Indeed, she paid his rent, paid a subvention for *The One-Man Revolution*, and promoted the Joe Hill House.

Hennacy's final chapter, about Helen Demoskoff, looks back to Tolstoy, one of his original influences. In an overview of Hennacy's life, the Doukhobors may seem like a sidelight, a lost tribe recently arrived in North America, not yet in command of English, and certainly not in the Woolman-Jefferson-Day tradition. But Demoskoff had served eleven years in prison and given up all her possessions, litmus tests for Hennacy, so she serves as a medium though whom Hennacy can think again about Tolstoy.

He imagines her, at age sixty-one, with "the patience and the wisdom to deal with the young folks who may seek her guidance," a note of futurity that many readers of the book will desire. "She has proven herself in not becoming disillusioned," he writes: "Alone among the people of whom I write in this book, she has fought a fight all her of life and found that the enemy has won, yet she is not embittered, and she feels that this battle must continue, but by different methods."[26] Demoskoff allows Hennacy a summing up: a general assessment in which he sees "the family" withering, the state stepping into many of its functions, and the church becoming "of diminishing importance." More important than ever will be people true to Tolstoy's vision, who "chose the power of love," not "the love of power."[27]

The Power of Rhetoric

The One-Man Revolution in America is clearly not only about Christian anarchism but also about the power of speaking fearlessly. We know that Hennacy struggled from high school onward with self-expression, struggled to articulate and embody a syncretic religious practice. That he was able to digest what he learned in each phase of his life and use it as a building block in the next is certainly one sign of a successful life. Without his Arizona life, there would have been no New York phase. In the *Catholic Worker* community, he finally flowered as the all-occasions rhetor, preaching on streetcorners from Wall Street to the Bronx, giving each passerby his full attention, his full presence. "He walked into college classrooms already talking," said Mary Lathrop, "and they listened."[28] Ammon Hennacy was about speech.

Berkman, Debs, and Hennacy: each one used "his freedom and chosen frankness instead of persuasion, truth instead of falsehood or silence." Those are Michel Foucault's words, but they could be Hennacy's, practicing his "obligation to speak the truth for the common good, even at personal risk."[29] Foucault defined this *parrhesia* as a speaker's avoidance of "any kind of rhetorical form which would veil what he thinks."[30] That is Hennacy par excellence, uniting his health and ecological interests with the politics of a truth-speaking loner. Strip away all veils! Remember that his high school classmates tagged him "Philodemus," the ancient philosopher who disdained those too lazy to practice the Epicurean truths—they already recognized this quality in him.

This idea of truth speaking is ancient. As opposed to techniques of manipulation, Plato associates *parrhesia* with "free speech." The degree to which one could practice it was the basic test of democracy. In assembly or court, Athenians were free to say almost anything; in the theater, Greek playwrights such as Aristophanes ridiculed whomever they chose. A related use of *parrhesia* spilled over into the Greek New Testament, where "bold speech" meant that believers could hold their own in argument with the authorities: "Now when they saw the boldness of Peter and John and realized that they were uneducated and ordinary men, they were amazed and recognized them as companions of Jesus" (Acts 4:13).

Ammon embraced that kind of *parrhesia*, not only because of high school but because after emerging from prison and reading widely, he found buttressing practices in Tolstoy, Thoreau, Whitman, and Gandhi. In diluted form, this "embodiment" was even present in the pedagogy of developing the "whole child" at the Ferrer School (recall Selma's interest in Isadora Duncan and John Dewey). Hennacy was already practicing straight speech and embodiment at Fairhope, in his "Life at Hard Labor," and ultimately at the Joe Hill House.

The question is how such a practice can unite anarchism, Christian pacifism, and personalism. We get a hint from Patrick Coy, who writes that "Hennacy's Christian anarchism seeks to establish the Golden Rule by working from within the consciousness of the individual while all other systems of society, working from without, depend upon human-made laws and the violence of the state to compel people to act justly."[31] In Hennacy's case, the Golden Rule was implanted so strongly that it became his "Celestial Bulldozer," a metaphor with connotations of force and predetermination. There is only one answer: no hesitation. "Turn the other cheek" must become a reflex, but so should speaking the reasons for doing so. Speak fearlessly of pacifism while practicing it. He practiced this self-consciously.

Does *One-Man Revolution* show us Hennacy's final version of anarchism/pacifism? The answer would have to be a qualified "yes." He does not give blueprints, but he indicates the direction that he and others, chiefly Helen Demoskoff, had figured out. Just as important as a plan is a focus on the purity of the protest and the practice of "fearless speech." Does *parrhesia* change things? Sometimes—look at Gandhi and Martin Luther King Jr.—but not always (Berkman). The important thing is that it exists, and that one embraces it. It is a radical affirmation of "the Good, or God," as Ammon liked to say.

If the topics and figures in *The One-Man Revolution* are more secular and less religious than one would expect, that is perhaps one reason why it still draws an audience. Ammon makes the lessons interesting. The book is about individuals who did not work well in groups, a durable attraction. After visits to Fourierist towns and time in Fairhope, Hennacy never tried the planned community again; the unplanned community in New York City was more to his liking, in part because in New Mexico and Arizona, even while writing his best prose, he had fallen in love with the immediacy of streetcorners, of engaging in person—lower-case "personalism." At the *Catholic Worker*, he cast himself as the provocateur, the all-occasions rhetor. He "came out" of himself daily, enacting a call on the Other to do likewise, even as he exposed himself to verbal and physical harm on the street.

The evidence that he made the right decision was his increasing stature in the 1960s. "Ammon had a tremendous influence," Karl Meyer writes. "If you're going to talk about the Vietnam war generation in the Catholic Worker movement . . . you're going to talk of people who were deeply influenced by Ammon because Ammon threw up that radical challenge."[32] Having entered completely into his belief that others could do as he did, he became more personalist than anarchist. Anarchists need governments to protest against. Having discovered "Christ in you," Hennacy never needed governments, but rather an audience to activate.

"The profound effect Hennacy had on resistance in the 1960s," writes Coy, "is exemplified by the memorial article Jim Forest published in the Milwaukee Catholic Worker paper, the *Catholic Radical*. Forest, who wrote from the Waupan state prison where he was incarcerated for his participation in the Milwaukee Fourteen draft board raid of 1968, titled his article 'Men Acted Differently according to Whether They Had Met Him or Not'": "For myself, however, it is no pious funeral effort to suggest that he was a saint. And is. By which I mean he was not only one who rarely if ever failed to be responsive to the voice of conscience within himself—but that he was one of those raised up to show others how much is possible. He was the saint as prophet: the one who, with his life, widens the frontiers of imagination for others."[33]

After Hennacy's death, the number of military-tax resisters grew. Archbishop Raymond Hunthausen publicly withheld 50 percent of his federal income taxes in 1981. In 1982 Franciscans for Peace began an annual forty-day Lenten witness at the Nevada test sites so familiar to Ammon. In 1987 several Catholic bishops were arrested, for the first time in US history, for committing civil disobedience at the same test site. Also in 1987 the Catholic Worker movement hosted a three-day international celebration of Dorothy Day's ninetieth birthday at that site, attended by over four hundred Catholic Workers and supporters. Over two hundred were arrested for civil disobedience. There are 150–200 Catholic Worker houses now, most funded entirely by private donations, and several inspired by Hennacy's go-it-alone venture in Salt Lake. On the eightieth anniversary of the Catholic Worker movement (2013), one of the oldest houses, in Los Angeles, was renamed the "Hennacy House of Hospitality."[34] There is widespread interest in Hennacy, especially in Salt Lake City, where the plight of the homeless is again an issue.

"All that I'm trying to do is to go a bit farther like Christ did—that those without sin should first cast the stone," said Ammon from his bed in the intensive care unit on January 11, 1970: "I have been picketing and saying this for the last nine years in Salt Lake City and will continue to do so as long as I live." Those last words were to be read at Lance and Kelbeck's pardons hearing on January 14, the day he died.[35]

ACKNOWLEDGMENTS

This book would not have been possible without the help of Joan Thomas, Ammon's widow. She generously provided me with her own biographical materials and read the chapters for accuracy. In many letters and conversations, she helped to sculpt and balance the narrative. Also invaluable was Jeremy Harmon, who put me in contact with Joan and later with Mary Lathrop, gave freely of his own archive, and led me to materials. Prof. Raili Marling and my editor, Jennifer Hammer, read these chapters, asked insightful questions, and surveyed the narrative from high ground. Thanks to each of you.

Hennacy began to send his papers to the Labadie Collection at the University of Michigan when invited by Agnes Inglis. I benefited from a grant to visit the Labadie, where Julie Herrada was an invaluable help. Marquette University has a wonderful collection of Catholic Worker and Dorothy Day materials, and Phillip Runkel was a great mentor there, helping me track down missing manuscripts. Liz Rodgers and the librarians at the University of Utah put up with my many visits. I spent time at the Tamiment Library's Robert Wagner Labor Archives at New York University, finding material on Ammon's early days in New York, and at Northern Arizona State University, where Cindy Summers went out of her way to provide me with audio files of Hennacy. Mary Lathrop and Robert Steed consented to interviews at the Catholic Worker House, key to portraying Ammon's life in New York City. I am grateful to these people and institutions.

NOTES

ARCHIVES

Labadie   Ammon Hennacy Papers, Labadie Archive. University of
                   Michigan, Special Collections Research Center.
Marquette   Ammon Hennacy Papers, Dorothy Day–Catholic Worker
                   Collection. Marquette University Archives.
Northern Arizona   Cline Library, Special Collections. Northern Arizona University.
NYU   Tamiment Library & Robert F. Wagner Labor Archives. New York
                   University Special Collections Center.
Utah   Ammon Hennacy Papers, 1823–2001. Archives West, Special
                   Collections, J. Willard Marriott Library, University of Utah

CHAPER 1. EARLY LIFE

1 This account of his prison time is based on Hennacy's *Book of Ammon*, abbreviated *Book* hereafter. I have used the first edition (1964), since it was closest to the events narrated. After spending months at all major archives, I found nothing that contradicted this account of his life, though some documents amplified it or suggested modest exaggerations, which I have indicated. I also rely on Joan Thomas's *Years of Grief and Laughter* and her meticulous "Unpublished Biography" from 2000. The "Unpublished Biography" at Marquette is divided into four sections, noted herein as I, II, III, and IV. Again, the archival record supports the book, and Thomas's biography includes an extraordinary summation of documents, letters, and observations by Hennacy not available anywhere else. There are thousands of documents in archives, but I found nothing that contradicted Thomas's work. That much said, it should be noted that Hennacy saved mostly documents by or about him, not as much correspondence from others. Thus the archive is intrinsically one-sided. There are few letters from his daughters, his wife, Selma, his siblings, or his mother, to whom he wrote almost weekly. He did save letters from important people, photographs (of himself usually), and news stories and editorials. Early on he conceived of himself as an ideological and rhetorical subject, so he sought out repositories as early as the 1930s. Readers in search of his "interiority" should understand that it increasingly turned on the criterion of embodying a lived ideology. Dimiter Popoff was twenty-six, from Toledo, and convicted of counterfeiting and a murder in Atlanta. "Atlanta Penitentiary Case Files," National Archives at Atlanta, https://www.archives.gov/atlanta/, accessed April 3, 2021.

2 Hennacy, *Book*, 25.

3 County history from Mack, *History of Columbiana County*; W. Ensign & Co., "History of Columbiana County, Ohio," Internet Archive, accessed May 24, 2021, https://archive.org/; "Columbiana County, Ohio, Free Public Records Directory," Online Searches, accessed October 2, 2018, https://www.publicrecords.online searches.com/.

4 Mack, *History of Columbiana County*, 22, 31. Baltazar Young had come to the colonies as a child from Wurttemberg, Germany, in 1760, fought in the Revolution, and married Anna Elizabeth Dentler in 1788.

5 Mack, *History of Columbiana County*, 95.

6 Mack, *History of Columbiana County*, 195. Levy, *Quakers and the American Family*, 42. Levy notes that because of the clay-ridden soil of Cheshire, the old-country Quakers preferred to keep their land in grass and raise cattle, avoiding disastrous crop losses. Thus they specialized in cheese making, blacksmithing, tanning, shoe making, and tailoring, professions that "required little capital to enter or pursue."

7 The wedding certificate of Deborah Vale and George Ashford was a document that Ammon treasured his whole life.

8 Hennacy spells the name "Vail" in *Book*, 1. Also Box 4, folder 1, "Biographical materials 1823–1970," Utah. The certificate reads "married November 13, 1823, at the hand of Squire Jackson."

9 Hennacy, *Book*, 23, 1, 2. Ammon was only a few months old when Coxey's Army, a mass of unemployed men, marched following the National Road, fifty miles to the south of Negley, although sometimes local groups met up with the main body. The family name was possibly "Henessey" and "misspelled in transit." There were several other Hennacys in the area, possibly relatives that he came to visit.

10 Hennacy, *Book*, 1. Death certificate, Utah.

11 Hennacy, *Book*, 19–20.

12 Hennacy, *Book*, 20–22. In many records the Irish progenitor is named Benjamin Franklin Hennacy too. Benjamin Franklin Hennacy was born October 23, 1872, in Newton Falls, Ohio, about fifty miles north of Columbiana County. Hennacy, *Book*, 1. Hennacy suspected a common-law relation with the maid. Thomas, "Unpublished Biography," I: 43.

13 Hennacy, *Book*, 3. The farm was strip-mined in the early 2000s, as were the riverside meadows and the hills around the Achor Baptist Church. Although Ammon recalls his father buying a house in Negley for three hundred dollars and selling it for double that, land maps from the period do not show that B. F. Hennacy ever owned land. The town to the west is Rogers, Ohio. Indeed, his obituary listed him as mayor of Rogers. Hennacy to his mother, in Thomas, "Unpublished Biography," I:73–74. See also Hennacy, "Forgotten Aspects of My Life," 275.

14 Columbiana County Map and Atlas Company, "Middleton Township, Rogers, Negley, Clarkson," Historic Map Works, accessed May 24, 2021, http://www.historicmapworks.com/.

15 Hennacy, *Book*, 2–4.

16 Hennacy in Thomas, "Unpublished Biography," I: 2, 3. Hennacy, *Book*, 4.

17 Hennacy, *Book*, 4.

18 Hennacy, *Book*, 2–3.

19 Hennacy, *Book*, 2–4, 33. He would also have learned *McGuffey's Reader* by heart, and used William D. Henckel's math and spelling books. The arrowheads he found were on land owned by W. H. Pancake, along the current Pancake Hill Road. Brush Creek and Beaver Creek come together here, one mile south of the Valley Farm. K. F. and R. F. Randolph owned land here in 1870.

20 Hennacy, *Book*, 3; in Thomas, "Unpublished Biography," I: 272.

21 Hennacy, *Book*, 3.

22 Hennacy, *Book*, 4–5; Bryan in Sicius, *The Progressive Era*, 182.

23 Hennacy, in Thomas, *The Years of Grief and Laughter*, 274; Hennacy, *Book*, 4–5.

24 Hennacy, *Book*, 4–5. "My father was in the real estate and insurance business on West Chester St." *Ohio Lisbon Buckeye State*, Thursday, January 31, 1907. Ammon wrote that "my father ran for Auditor and was always beaten, but he nearly made it." Thomas, "Unpublished Biography," I: 122, 278. This is incorrect; he sometimes won. In the early years of the last century, rheumatic fever was a big killer even in developed countries. In the United States in the 1920s, it was the leading cause of death in individuals between five and twenty years of age and was second only to tuberculosis in those between twenty and thirty years. The only treatment was salicylates and bed rest. The majority remained at home for weeks, more often for months, with a smoldering illness; in the United States and Europe, the sicker children were managed in foster homes or special institutions for the chronically ill.

25 Grades handwritten by Elsie A. Roberts, principal of Lisbon High School for Ammon's admission to Hiram College, Hiram College Registrar's records, Hiram, OH. Accessed April 20, 2017.

26 Hennacy, *Book*, 5.

27 Frankenberg, *Billy Sunday*, 215–16. A "sum considerably in excess of any to that time contributed," according to local businessman E. L. McKelvey.

28 Betts, *Billy Sunday*, 36; Hennacy in Thomas, "Unpublished Biography," I: 122.

29 Hennacy, *Book*, 5.

30 Hennacy in Thomas, "Unpublished Biography," I: 279.

31 Hennacy, *Book*, 7.

32 Hennacy's East Palestine High School report card shows that he was in the Latin (precollege) track; it is signed by May Templer, principal. Accessed at the Hiram College Registrar's Office, April 20, 2017; the (Lisbon High School) *Olympian*, 1913, 68.

33 It is doubtful that Hennacy understood the national and international potential and dimensions of the IWW until later, but he sensed early that its egalitarian spirit was compatible with his religious outlook. During his high school and college years, the IWW made more headlines in the West, with its mining actions,

than in the East. The execution of Joe Hill, later Hennacy's favorite, passed without his notice. The IWW staged actions in Pennsylvania in 1916, and Frank Little,
the IWW's most outspoken opponent of World War I, was lynched in Butte, Montana, in 1917, four months after the war started. But Hennacy appears to have been
more focused on promoting a Marxist socialism in Ohio at this point. For general
background see *The Wobblies: The Story of the IWW* by Patrick Renshaw.

34 *Lisbon (OH) Buckeye State*, December 14, 1911, n.p.; Hennacy, *Book*, 5.

35 Hennacy, *Book*, 5–6. His full report card: English: 90, Plane Geometry: 86; S. Geometry: 72; German: 75; Political Economy: 93; Physics: 72. East Palestine report
card accessed at the Hiram College Registrar's Office, April 20, 2017.

36 Hennacy, *Book*, 6; Thomas, *The Years of Grief and Laughter*, 280. The "old"
McKinley house was that of the president's grandparents in Lisbon, so Hennacy
appears to conflate the two locations.

37 Hennacy, *Book*, 6.

38 This phrase refers to a door-to-door salesperson who blocks the door with one
foot so s/he can complete the sales pitch.

39 Hennacy, in Thomas, *The Years of Grief and Laughter*, 282.

40 Hennacy, *Book*, 6. Another Manchester reverend, William Metcalfe, who was
a homeopathic physician, in 1817 led a group of these Christian vegetarians to
Philadelphia, where he became "the first public advocate of vegetarianism in
America." The group met on North Third Street and gradually recruited members.
Carson, *Cornflake Crusade*, 16.

41 Carson, *Cornflake Crusade*, 22.

42 Hennacy in Thomas, "Unpublished Biography," I: 282–84.

43 Cornell, *Unruly Equality*, 23.

44 The *Olympian*, published by Lisbon High School, 1913. Columbiana County Historical Society, n.p.

45 Hennacy senior report card, signed by Elsie Roberts, 1912–13, from the Hiram
College Registrar's office, accessed April 20, 2017. Hennacy in Thomas, *The Years
of Grief and Laughter*, 284.

46 Treudley, *Prelude to the Future*, 197.

47 From the Hiram College Registrar's office: Public Speaking: 82; Economics: C;
Philosophy: 89; Biology: 84; English: 70. Quotes, Hennacy in Thomas, "Unpublished Biography," I: 281–84.

48 *The Advance of Hiram College*, October 4, 1913, 4–5; October 14, 6; October 22, 5;
October 28, 1.

49 Intercollegiate Socialist Society Records, TAM 048, Microfilm R-7124, NYU.

50 Hennacy in Thomas, "Unpublished Biography," I: 281.

51 Lewis quoted, *The Advance of Hiram College*, October 4, 1913, 5. *The Spider Web*
yearbook for 1913–14 says that Lewis "bested" Phelps on November 14. The Lewis/
Hennacy exchange is on 147. *The Spider Web*, vol. 24 (Alliance, OH: Albert E.
Bradshaw, 1915).

52 Treudley, *Prelude to the Future*, 197.

53 *The Advance of Hiram College*, November 25, 1913, 6. Kautsky was available in English translation by Daniel DeLeon: Kautsky, *The Class Struggle*.

54 *The Advance of Hiram College*, November 25, 1913, 6.

55 Hennacy in Thomas, "Unpublished Biography," I: 280–82. Strickland lecture in *The Advance of Hiram College*, March 3, 1914, 2. Hennacy to Day, May 19, 1950, Marquette.

56 Treudley, *Prelude to the Future*, 198.

57 Hennacy, in Thomas, "Unpublished Biography," I: 280–81;*The Spider Web* 24: 129.

58 *The Advance of Hiram College*, January 20, 1914, 1. Striker Stamps on p. 2. Strickland lecture in the *Advance*, March 3, 1914, 2.

59 *Lisbon (OH) Buckeye State*, Thursday, April 2, 1914, 8.

60 Hennacy, *Book*, 7; Thomas, "Unpublished Biography," I: 283–84.

61 Ammon claimed that "Arthur M Schlesinger Sr. was my very good friend at the university," but this seems chronologically doubtful. Hennacy, *Book*, 8; in Thomas, "Unpublished Biography," I: 285. Schlesinger graduated in 1910; Hennacy arrived in 1915 when Schlesinger would already have been matriculated at Harvard. Hennacy, in Thomas, "Unpublished Biography," I: 286.

62 Hennacy, *Book*, 6–7.

63 Hennacy, *Book*, 7; Hennacy in Thomas, "Unpublished Biography," I: 285. Poems in the Agnes Inglis Archive, Labadie Collection, University of Michigan, Box 1, "Correspondence Outgoing," and Catholic Worker Archive, Marquette.

64 He spent the first part of the summer in Wisconsin selling Wearever aluminum cookware door to door.

65 Hennacy in Thomas, "Unpublished Biography," I: 285–86. Poem, Agnes Inglis Archive, University of Michigan.

66 Hennacy remembers Nearing as teaching at Ohio State University, but according to his *New York Times* obituary, Nearing was dean of arts and sciences at the University of Toledo, near where Hennacy's parents lived, after being fired from the Wharton School at the University of Pennsylvania. Glen Fowler, "Scott Nearing, Environmentalist, Pacifist, and Radical, Dies at 100," *New York Times*, September 2, 1983, D-21. https://www.nytimes.com.

67 Hennacy in Thomas, *The Years of Grief and Laughter*, 287.

68 Cornell, *Unruly Equality*, 55–60.

69 Hennacy, *Book*, 8. In Thomas, *The Years of Grief and Laughter*, 287.

70 Allan L. Benson, "What's Wrong with the Socialist Party," *New Appeal*, June 15, 1918, 1, http://www.kyforward.

71 Hennacy in *Ohio State Lantern*, January 17, 1916; "Discussion on Capitalism," *Ohio State Lantern*, December 6, 1915.

72 Hennacy, *Book*, 10. This may have been the summer they first visited the Rand School in New York City, where they would have scholarships after his release from prison in 1920.

73 "Alumnus Teaches," *Ohio State Lantern*, September 28, 1916. Despite the title, Ohio State University has no record of Hennacy graduating.

74 "Sticker" and poster from Hennacy, *Book*, 10. The sticker was put on storefronts, Hennacy writes, indicating that perhaps it was glued, while the "poster" seems to have been a placard. There are no copies extant and no evidence of how or by whom they were printed outside of these in FBI Archives, Atlanta.

75 Hennacy, *Book*, 10–11.

76 Hennacy, *Book*, 11.

77 Hennacy, *Book*, 11.

CHAPTER 2. PRISON

1 I have not been able to find any such headline in a 1917 Ohio newspaper. The paper shown to Hennacy was probably the *Morrow County Republican*, with the headline "Three Charged with Treason." Columbus newspapers of the period are not indexed or available online. Other sources include Richard A. Folk, "Socialist Party of Ohio: War and Free Speech," *Ohio History* 78, no. 2 (Spring 1969): 104–14. As for Wilson's claim about registering, Ammon later learned that he told them the same lie.

2 Hennacy was still indexed in the Columbiana County Archives and Research Center, 129 South Market Street, Lisbon, Ohio, under "draft dodger" in 2017 when I researched there. The center is currently creating a master index but was staffed by gracious volunteers who performed the research when I went there. "Mission Statement," Columbiana County Archives, accessed May 25, 2021, http://www .columbianacountyarchives.org.

3 "Hennacy Trial to Be Resumed Early This Week," *Buckeye State*, July 2, 1917, 200, in bound volume of *CCARC Newsletter* reprint of June 15, 2017, 6.

4 Hennacy, *Book*, 12.

5 *Alliance (OH) Review and Leader*, June 28, 1917, 2. The subpoenaed were Hosea Ward, Jesse Danner, Chester Green, R. G. Putnam, J. A. Johnson, Robert Boda, Paul Spence, and J. A. Johnson. Hennacy et al. Document #941, Chicago Archives, in possession of the author. Chicago Archives, Dept. of Justice, Corrections Division, Chicago Federal Records Center, 7358 South Pulaski Road, Chicago, IL.

6 These pamphlets are in Box USCD #941, exhibit #22, "Young Men Refuse to Register," Chicago Archives, Dept. of Justice, Corrections Division, Chicago Federal Records Center, 7358 South Pulaski Road, Chicago, IL.

7 Hennacy, *Book*, 13.

8 *Buckeye State*, July 5, 1917, 201, Columbiana County Archives and Research Center, http://www.columbianacountyarchives.org.

9 Cantina, Rainer, and Meters, *Prison Etiquette*. Cantina, a draft resister in World War II, was later a friend of Hennacy. There never was a "Peter Brockman" in the Atlanta Penitentiary, according to records at U.S. Government, "Atlanta Penitentiary Case Files," National Archives at Atlanta, accessed May 25, 2021, https://www.archives.gov/atlanta/. This is certainly a pseudonym. The mostly white prisoners had been convicted of a variety of crimes, ranging from

bootlegging to bigamy to mail theft. Relatively few were in prison for murder or violent crime. Most were in for "white collar crime," including failure to pay income tax.

10 Hennacy, *Book*, 14.

11 Hennacy, *Book*, 15.

12 Hennacy, *Book*, 15.

13 Hennacy, *Book*, 16. Johnny Spanish was a genuine criminal, the likes of whom Hennacy had never seen. His business was extorting garment workers. This was no doubt an education for Ammon. "'Johnny Spanish' Slain in East Side: Shot Down at the Entrance to a Restaurant Where He Was to Have Met His Wife," *New York Times*, July 30, 1919, 4.

14 The Atlanta records at U.S. Government, "Atlanta Penitentiary Case Files," National Archives at Atlanta, accessed May 25, 2021, https://www.archives.gov /atlanta/, show John T. Dunn with number 7970 (not 7979 as Ammon recalled), which is proximate to Hennacy's. But it lists his crime as "desertion," meaning that he had been inducted. He was twenty-nine and from Fort Adams, Rhode Island. Hennacy says the warden was defying orders from Washington on this matter.

15 Hennacy, *Book*, 17.

16 This play is summarized by Thomas, "Unpublished Biography," I: 50–70. Hennacy wrote the play in 1934, sixteen years after the incident. Thomas wrote that the Black man's actual name was Kid Smith, and that his death was described by Alexander Berkman in a special article for the *Atlanta Constitution*. However, in Berkman and Goldman's *Prison Experiences*, Kid Smith is shot dead for not walking fast enough while being taken to the hole. See "A Fragment of the Prison Experiences of Emma Goldman and Alexander Berkman," Internet Archive, accessed May 25, 2021, https://archive.org. Neither of them, however, witnessed the event.

17 Although they sometimes worked together, as on the construction site where Hennacy protested, Black and white prisoners were typically housed in separate wings in 1918 in the United States.

18 Hennacy, *Book*, 19.

19 Hennacy, *Book*, 19.

20 Hennacy, *Book*, 36. In a letter quoted below he dates his entry to June 7, 1918. Hennacy, *Book*, 19.

21 Hennacy, *Book*, 19.

22 Hennacy, *Book*, 23.

23 Hennacy, *Book*, 26. Girardeau's name is not mentioned in Hennacy's published manuscript, but it is in his notes to his unpublished play, summarized by Thomas, "Unpublished Biography," I: 162.

24 Hennacy, *Book*, 21–24. Hennacy's letters, in Thomas, "Unpublished Biography," I: 37–39. Also in the Platt Cline Archives, Northern Arizona.

25 Hennacy, *Book*, 21–24.

26 U.S. Government, "World War I Draft Registration Cards," National Archives, accessed May 25, 2021, https://www.archives.gov; *Book*, 23. Ammon Hennacy's letters, in Thomas, 2000, I: 37–39. Also Northern Arizona University, Platt Cline Archives. Warden Zerbst was famous for repealing inmates' "good time" while they were in solitary, and he was the defendant in several high-profile court cases because of this: See "Lupo v. Zerbst, Warden, et. al," Justia, accessed May 25, 2021, https://www.justia.com. He also debated his techniques in the *Atlanta Constitution* with Berkman, October 1–4, 1919. While at Atlanta he bent the rules to ensure the survival of Eugene Debs. He was later warden at Leavenworth..

27 Details in Thomas, "Unpublished Biography," I: 38.

28 Hennacy, *Book*, 23–24. Popoff would end up in St. Elizabeth's Hospital for the Criminally Insane. "Missouri, U.S., Death Certificate for Dimiter Popoff," Ancestry, accessed May 25, 2021, https://www.ancestry.com.

29 Hennacy, *Book*, 24.

30 Hennacy, *Book*, 24–25.

31 About 675,000 would die in the United States, about fifty million worldwide. U.S. Government, "1918 Pandemic (H1N1 virus)," Centers for Disease Control and Prevention, accessed May 25, 2021, https://www.cdc.gov.

32 Hennacy, *Book*, 25.

33 Hennacy, *Book*, 25. Second Hennacy letter in Thomas, "Unpublished Biography," I: 38–39.

34 Hennacy, *Book*, 26.

35 Hennacy, *Book*, 27.

36 Hennacy, in Thomas, "Unpublished Biography," I:139.

37 Hennacy, *Book*, 29

38 Heanncy, *Book*, 30.

39 Zinn, *People's History*, 364; Coffman, *The War to End All Wars*, 25–28.

40 Hennacy, *Book*, 30.

41 Tolstoy, *The Religious Writings*, 211, 215.

42 Webb was nineteen and flamboyant. After his sentence was commuted to life on the chain gang, he escaped, and when captured posed with a cigar in his mouth. *Atlanta Constitution*, January 3, 1920, 5. Details on his conviction in the *Southeastern Reporter* 1, no. 99 (1919).

43 Samuel Castleton letters, Series I: Correspondence, 1899–1955, Eugene V. Debs Collection, TAM 020, New York University. See also Lucy Fox Robins Lang, *War Shadows: A Documental Story of the Struggle for Amnesty* (1992); Joseph W. Sharts, "Death for Me or Release for All," *Missouri Valley Socialist* (Dayton, Ohio), September 26, 1919, 1, 3. Debs would arrive in the Moundsville Penitentiary in 1919.

44 Hennacy, *Book*, 31.

45 "Bobby Bolshevik" in Thomas, "Unpublished Biography," II: 30.

46 Selma Melms, ms. dated October 9, 1919, titled "Workers Awake!" transcribed by Thomas, "Unpublished Biography," II: 31.

47 "Unpublished Biography," II: 33.

48 "Unpublished Biography," II: 33.

49 "Unpublished Biography," II: 41.

50 Several of the cities important in Ammon's wanderings—Toledo, Atlanta, San Francisco, Los Angeles—were major Fuller distribution centers, and there were 175 regional offices, in every state in the United States. "Fuller Brushes Factory Promotional Film: Door-to-Door Salesman 47384," YouTube, accessed April 1, 2021, https://www.youtube.com/watch?v=ooSXzMPalEI.

51 Thomas, "Unpublished Biography," II: 41–42.

52 Thomas, "Unpublished Biography," II: 44–45.

53 Thomas, "Unpublished Biography," II: 46.

54 David Kuebrich, "Religion," in J. R. LeMaster and Donald D. Kummings, eds., *Walt Whitman: An Encyclopedia* (New York: Garland, 1998), available at https://whitmanarchive.org/.

55 Hodder, "Thoreau's Religious Vision," 92.

56 Pfeifer, *The Making of American Catholic Worlds*, 5–15.

CHAPTER 3. NEW YORK CITY AND THE BIG HIKE

1 Hennacy, *Book*, 33; Thomas, *The Years of Grief and Laughter*, 288.

2 Thomas, "Unpublished Biography," I: 209.

3 Thomas, "Unpublished Biography," I: 212.

4 Thomas, "Unpublished Biography," I: 211.

5 Thomas, "Unpublished Biography," I: 211–12. Ammon wrote that "Selma did not know that she should reach a climax until a few weeks after we were married; then we read *Married Love* by Mary Stopess which taught us quite a bit. It was always hard for me not to have a premature ejaculation. Several of our scrapes . . . were due to the fact that she was out of sorts because she did not reach the climax. When this was improved, we had less trouble." Hennacy, *Book*, 33; Thomas, "Unpublished Biography," I: 155.

6 Thomas, "Unpublished Biography," I: 210–14.

7 Thomas, "Unpublished Biography," I: 191–92.

8 U.S. census document, Supervisor's District 7693, Enumeration District 861, sheet 16, 12th Ward, John Jay enumerator. FamilySearch Document ED861, accessed December 5, 2020, https://www.familysearch.org/. "Yiddish-speaking" was a convenience term used by census takers, apparently when nationality was murky.

9 Hennacy, *Book*, 33.

10 Cornell, *Unruly Equality*, 46–47.

11 Thomas, "Unpublished Biography," I: 213. They had to abstain from sex for six weeks. However, after the abortion, "Selma got a silver wishbone pessary which has proved okay."

12 Loughery and Randolph, *Dorothy Day*, 96.

13 Thomas, "Unpublished Biography," II: 193, 195.

14 Hennacy, *Book*, 34–35.

15 Lindsay, *Tramping across America*, 23.

16 Thomas, "Unpublished Biography," II: 214.

17 For more information on this unusual congregation, see Ivens, "New York's Croatians," and Dunlap, *From Abyssinian to Zion*.

18 Thomas, "Unpublished Biography," I: 203–13.

19 Thomas, "Unpublished Biography," II: 200, 201.

20 Thomas, "Unpublished Biography," II: 213. One of the purely mystical experiences that Hennacy would write about was a vision of a blue flame in the Southwest.

21 Thomas, "Unpublished Biography," II: 214.

22 Hennacy letters in Thomas, "Unpublished Biography," II: 203.

23 Hennacy, *Book*, 35; Thomas, "Unpublished Biography," II: 205–7.

24 Eaton S. Lothrop, "The Brownie Camera," *History of Photography* 2, no. 1 (January 1978): 1–10. https://doi.org/10.1080/03087298.

25 Thomas, "Unpublished Biography," I: 222.

26 Thomas, "Unpublished Biography," I: 229.

27 Lindsay, *Tramping across America*, 8.

28 Thomas, "Unpublished Biography," I: 269. The trip dates and mileages are as Ammon computed them for *High Roads and Hot Roads*, the manuscript of these trips, which Joan Thomas, "Unpublished Biography," transcribed into the biography. For this trip he includes the time spent working in Atlanta.

29 The dates given in Thomas, "Unpublished Biography," I: 308 (June 21, 1924, to July 30, 1924) must be a typo, because the couple lived in Berkeley for several months. In Hennacy, *Book*, 41, Hennacy gives the date of return to Milwaukee as "my birthday," which was July 24, 1925.

30 In Thomas, "Unpublished Biography," I: 335. In Mrs. Hurray's house "Ammon notices a Catholic magazine on the table and reads an article, the substance of which was that the simple Catholic peasant who appeared to the modernist to believe many foolish superstitions was at heart more kindly in his ignorance to those in need than the more educated and liberal Protestant who gave cold charity, if anything at all."

31 Thomas, "Unpublished Biography," I: 260.

32 Thomas, "Unpublished Biography," I: 261.

33 Thomas, "Unpublished Biography," I: 286–87.

34 Thomas, "Unpublished Biography," I: 318.

35 Thomas, "Unpublished Biography," I: 267.

36 Thomas, "Unpublished Biography," I: 350.

37 Fuller, *A Foot in the Door*, 85.

38 Thomas, "Unpublished Biography," I: 105–6.

39 Thomas, "Unpublished Biography," I: 92.

40 "The Ups and Downs of the Fuller Brush Co. (Fortune, 1938)," *Fortune*, February 26, 2012, https://fortune.com/.

41 Thomas, "Unpublished Biography," I: 204–5.

42 Thomas, "Unpublished Biography," I: 268.

43 Thomas, "Unpublished Biography," I: 268–69. Savings on 280.

44 Thomas, "Unpublished Biography," I: 305.

45 Thomas, "Unpublished Biography," I: 267.

46 Thomas, "Unpublished Biography," I: 281.

47 Thomas, "Unpublished Biography," I: 288.

48 Alyea and Alyea, *Fairhope*, 121, 89.

49 Hennacy, *Book*, 38.

50 Hennacy, *Book*, 39.

51 Hennacy, *Book*, 39.

52 Thomas, "Unpublished Biography," I: 369.

53 Thomas, "Unpublished Biography," I: 308.

54 Thomas, "Unpublished Biography," I: 371.

55 Thomas, "Unpublished Biography," I: 327.

56 Thomas, "Unpublished Biography," I: 371–72, 377.

57 Thomas, "Unpublished Biography," I: 329.

58 Thomas, "Unpublished Biography," I: 373.

59 The Wikimedia Foundation, "Ella Reeve Bloor," Wikipedia, accessed September 16, 2020, https://en.wikipedia.org/. Hitchhiking was legal and safe, even for women, in the United States in the 1920s.

60 Thomas, "Unpublished Biography," I: 330.

61 Thomas, "Unpublished Biography," I: 330.

62 Thomas, "Unpublished Biography," I: 331.

63 Thomas, "Unpublished Biography," I: 333.

64 Thomas, "Unpublished Biography," I: 338, 367.

65 Thomas, "Unpublished Biography," I: 339.

66 Thomas, "Unpublished Biography," I: 351.

67 Thomas, "Unpublished Biography," I: 352.

68 Walt Whitman, "A Prophecy," *Christian Science Sentinel*, January 12, 1899, 1.

69 Thomas, "Unpublished Biography," I: 332.

CHAPTER 4. BISANAKEE AND MILWAUKEE

1 Ammon went from 134 to 151, Selma to 160. Thomas, "Unpublished Biography," I: 386.

2 Thomas, "Unpublished Biography," II: 4, spells it "Zidker," but it is "Zicher" on maps and land plats. Waukesha Historic Society. Plat "Town 6 North" on Rt. 59 near Rt. 20 East. Marling personal correspondence with John Schoenkneckt, Waukesha Historical Society, email December 5, 2017.

3 Hennacy, "Forgotten Aspects of My Life," 293.

4 Thomas, "Unpublished Biography," II: 1, 3.

5 *Waukesha Daily Freeman*, December 7, 1925, 3, 5. Thomas, "Unpublished Biography," II: 1–3.

6 Hennacy to his mother, February 1926, Thomas, "Unpublished Biography," II: 3.

7 Hennacy, *Book*, 42; Thomas, "Unpublished Biography," II: 2, 373.

8 Thomas, "Unpublished Biography," II: 4.

9   Hennacy, *Book*, 41; Thomas, "Unpublished Biography," II: 6; Hennacy, "Forgotten Aspects of My Life," 293.

10 Thomas, "Unpublished Biography," II: 8; Hennacy, letter to Lida, February 2, 1927, in Thomas, "Unpublished Biography," II: 5.

11 Hennacy, "Forgotten Aspects of My Life," 293; Thomas, "Unpublished Biography," II: 5.

12 Thomas, "Unpublished Biography," II: 8, 12, 19, 23, 25–27. Hennacy, "Forgotten Aspects of My Life," 294–95.

13 Hennacy, *Book*, 43.

14 Thomas, "Unpublished Biography," II: 41; Hennacy, *Book*, 42. Ammon later claimed that he paid fifteen hundred dollars, in Thomas, "Unpublished Biography," II: 31.

15 Hennacy, "Forgotten Aspects of My Life," 297.

16 A Wisconsin state law of 1906 set up poor houses, insane asylums, orphanages, and tuberculosis houses, as well as "departments of outdoor relief," akin to a social work service. As a state service, it was not bound by federal laws that might have prevented Hennacy's employment. U.S. Government, "The Laws of Wisconsin, Chapter 619," Wisconsin State Legislature, accessed May 25, 2021, https://legis.wisconsin.gov/.

17 See Alter, *Gandhi's Body*.

18 Hennacy, *Book*, 45–48.

19 The incident happened May 10, 1933. See Thomas, "Unpublished Biography," II: 69. The couple are Marion and Helen Myszewski, of 2141 South Fifteenth Street. Thomas says that Hennacy immediately began to retell the story. Thomas, "Unpublished Biography," II: 68–72.

20 Hennacy, *Book*, 44.

21 Details from Hennacy's case notes in Thomas, "Unpublished Biography," II: 69–72.

22 Deming, *Revolution and Equilibrium*, 21.

23 Hennacy letter to his father, March 6, 1933, cited by Thomas, "Unpublished Biography," II: 64, 68.

24 Mrs. Millis letter of February 6, 1933, quoted by Thomas, "Unpublished Biography," II: 61. Mrs. Millis herself had switched to the Fellowship of the Universal Design of Life, a breakaway sect started by Annie Bill, an English woman who was convinced that she was Mary Baker Eddy's real heir. In his letters Ammon asked Mrs. Millis about the respective attitudes of Christian Science and Design of Life towards war, pacifism, and conscientious objectors. For him these were foundational issues. She responded that Annie Bill thought disarmament to be "folly." When Ammon described himself as a "Christian anarchist," Mrs. Millis replied that, religiously speaking, she didn't see how there could be such a thing.

25 Thomas, "Unpublished Biography," II: 297.

26 Thomas, "Unpublished Biography," II: 68.

27 Hennacy, letter to his mother, quoted in Thomas, "Unpublished Biography," II: 69. He also corresponded with a progressive educator in Mt. Kisco, New York, named

William H. Bridge, who was trying to open a Fellowship of Faiths school. But Bridge eventually let on that he was most interested in investors. The girls' education would be the wedge that eventually split the couple, but there were other factors.

28 Putnam and Campbell, *American Grace*, 296 ff.

29 Pfeifer, *The Making of American Catholic Worlds*, 125–50.

30 Day, *Loaves and Fishes*, 8.

31 Hennacy in Thomas, *Years of Grief and Laughter*, 298. In 1920s slang, "Yipsels" referred to young Socialist Party members

32 Thomas, "Unpublished Biography," II: 172.

33 Hennacy, *Book*, 54; and Ammon Hennacy Papers, Folder 2 (G-R), Labadie.

34 The Labadie materials show an extraordinary range of correspondence in a period when Hennacy might logically be expected to be depressed. His sense of humor is evident in a letter to Ab Heisler, a close friend from his Hiram College period, to whom he wrote, "I still have hopes for you, Duke, that you will end up as an ultra-conservative. Bill Young called on me yesterday. . . . has been with the Goodyear Tire and Rubber Company, in the 'Zeppelin' Dept." Folder 2 (G-R), August 29, 1935, Labadie. The catholicity of Hennacy's contacts in this period is attested to by a letter of thanks from the American Legion, which invited him to its annual dinner on May 21, 1936, "in appreciation of the effort you expended in our behalf." He had apparently represented the antiwar position in a debate the Legion staged., Labadie.

35 Hennacy, March 18, 1936, letter from Madison WS church to 2613 N. Downer St., Milwaukee, paying him three dollars for a talk. Labadie Archive.

36 Thomas, "Unpublished Biography," II: 150–52.

37 Whitman's term had been "American personalism" in his essay "Personalism," published in the *Galaxy* in May 1868. *CW* circulation in Loughery and Randolph, *Dorothy Day*, 167. Details on Peter Maurin's life, Loughery and Randolph, *Dorothy Day*, 132–64.

38 Loughery and Randolph, *Dorothy Day*, 134–36, give an idea of how murky Maurin's life was.

39 Maurin, in Miller, *Dorothy Day*, 256–57; and Mark Zwick and Louise Zwick, "Why Not Canonize Peter Maurin, Co-Founder with Dorothy Day of the Catholic Worker Movement?" *Houston Catholic Worker*, July 1, 2010. cjd.org, retrieved June 16, 2013.

40 Klejment, *American Catholic Pacifism*, 39.

41 Dorothy Day, in Klejment, *American Catholic Pacificism*, 40.

42 Carmen Hennacy letter, Thomas, "Unpublished Biography," II: 156.

43 Selma Hennacy, in Thomas, "Unpublished Biography," II: 161. She touted the location ("right above the furnace"), convenience ("one block from the Oakland Ave car line"), and privacy ("a separate side entrance which can be used, if you like").

44 Thomas, "Unpublished Biography," II:10.

45 Nunn, in Thomas, "Unpublished Biography," II: 174.

46 Hennacy, in Thomas, "Unpublished Biography," II: 180.

47 Hennacy, in Thomas,"Unpublished Biography," II: 180. When they arrived in New York on July 28, they stayed at a tourist camp in Orchard Beach in the Bronx, then found an apartment at 60 West Eighty-Third and finally a cheaper one at 41 West Eighty-Seventh.

48 Thomas, "Unpublished Biography," II: 182, 188–89, 189, 10, 191. The Stratton Arms was more upscale: "They are 2nd floor front with two rooms, maid service, etc., $12 a week," Hennacy wrote. Thomas, "Unpublished Biography," II: 192.

49 Thomas,"Unpublished Biography," II: 2, 172, 199.

50 Kaufman in Thomas, "Unpublished Biography," II: 201–2; Hennacy in Thomas, "Unpublished Biography," II: 204–5, 206.

51 The Wikimedia Foundation, "Guy Ballard," Wikipedia, accessed May 25, 2021, https://en.wikipedia.org: "A new Dispensation was given so that the *Ascension* could be gained (in the finer body) without taking the physical body, as Jesus had done."

52 The Wikimedia Foundation, "Guy Ballard," Wikipedia, accessed May 25, 2021, https://en.wikipedia.org. See also Godfrey Ray King, *Unveiled Mysteries* (Schaumberg, IL: St. Germaine Press, 1989).

53 Thomas, "Unpublished Biography," II: 218, 220, 225, 231, 254, 235–36, 236.

54 Dorsa Beach folder, May 4, 1940, Labadie.

55 Thomas, "Unpublished Biography," II: 243.

56 U.S. Government, Mitchell International Airport, Milwaukee County, Wisconsin, accessed May 25, 2021, https://county.milwaukee.gov/.

57 Elkinton, *The Doukhobors*, 10–15.

58 Hennacy, *Autobiography of a Catholic Anarchist*, 51.

59 Thomas, "Unpublished Biography," II: 251–52, 255, letter to Roger Baldwin October 28, 1940, quoted 256.

60 Thomas, "Unpublished Biography," II: 255; "Objector Relief Aide Not to Be Prosecuted," *Milwaukee Journal*, October 20, 1940, 1.

61 Hennacy, *Autobiography of a Catholic Anarchist*, 54.

62 Hennacy, Labadie. On November 16, 1940, he wrote his first letter to "Brother Dallas" and seven fellow COs in Danbury. He had been reading Ibsen's *Enemy of the People* and quoted from it, a recurring motif in his letters. Thomas, "Unpublished Biography, II: 261, 265.

63 Hennacy to Mrs. Ackerman, February 15, 1941, and also to Abe, February 22, 1941, in Thomas, "Unpublished Biography," II: 271–72.

> I was listed as a "C" and the C's were to be laid off. I had an A plus rating for seven years, a C rating for two years and now a B plus rating, but they take only the last two years and not your whole record. The rating is a joke and no one takes it seriously. If you work for a straw boss who rates liberally, you get a good rating, and if you work for one who is stingy, you get a poor one. Also, if you play poker, bowl, and go to drinking parties, you rate better. I do not do this. I know my head boss Glassberg well, but would not go to him

and ask for a better rating as I do not consider their opinion worth anything. I know when I am doing good work.

64 Sharon Hennacy, in Thomas, "Unpublished Biography," II: 275, 277, 278, 293, 298.

65 Hennacy, "Forgotten Aspects of My Life," 302.

66 Thomas, "Unpublished Biography," II: 313, 308–10, 299, 304.

67 Thomas, "Unpublished Biography," II: 304. Two large boxes went out on December 6, 1941, the day before the United States officially entered World War II. Thomas, "Unpublished Biography," II: 306.

68 Now he lived farther out at 1534 North Sixtieth Street in Wauwatosa with his brother-in-law.

69 Thomas, "Unpublished Biography," II: 334–35.

70 Hennacy, letter March 22, 1942, Box DD-CW, Series D-1, Box 9, Marquette.

71 Hennacy, letter March 22, 1942, Box DD-CW, Series D-1, Box 9, Marquette.

72 Cornell, *Unruly Equality*, 207.

73 Hennacy letter, April 12, 1942, Box DD-CW, Series D-1, Box 9, Marquette.

74 Hennacy to Dorothy Day, April 2, 1942, Box DD-CW, Series D-1, Box 9, Marquette.

75 *Milwaukee Journal*, May 16–17, 1942, 1.

76 Thomas,"Unpublished Biography," II: 318. He found a temporary job at a cornflakes mill, but it was harder than he expected. The corn came in one-hundred-pound sacks, which he offloaded from railcars and carried to a cold, dusty warehouse that was in dangerous disrepair: it had caught fire the previous year. The cornflakes left the plant in large, loose bags that also weighed one hundred pounds and were hard to carry because of their formlessness. He worked several weeks there.

77 Cornell, *Unruly Equality*, 167.

78 Hennacy later dated his departure to the Fourth of July 1942, but at Marquette there are letters from him in Denver dated in June 1942.

CHAPTER 5. LIFE AT HARD LABOR

1 Ellis, "The Legacy of Peter Maurin," 298; Williams and Bengtsson, "Personalism," 2.

2 Hennacy, "Forgotten Aspects of My Life," 303.

3 City Park Dairy was on Lettsdale Road, south of downtown, and used some horse-drawn delivery trucks until 1946. Dairy Max, "Western Dairy Association Timeline," Western Dairy Association, accessed May 25, 2021, https://www.dairymax.org.

4 "Glendale History," Glendale Colorado, accessed May 25, 2021, https://www.glendale.co.us/.

5 Hennacy, "Forgotten Aspects of My Life," 305; Thomas, "Unpublished Biography," II: 2.

6 Hennacy, "Forgotten Aspects of My Life," 304.

7 Hennacy in Thomas, "Unpublished Biography," III: 4.

8　Hennacy in Thomas, "Unpublished Biography," III: 5.

9　Hennacy, *Book*, 59–61.

10　Thomas, "Unpublished Biography," III: 16–20.

11　Thomas, "Unpublished Biography," III: 21.

12　Thomas, "Unpublished Biography," III: 18, 22, 28–35. The addresses could be reversed, as the Delgado Street house, twelve hundred square feet, appears more likely to have had two fireplaces than the 820-square-foot Canyon Road address, which is in a compound. Their first house seems to have been at 225 Delgado Street.

13　Thomas, "Unpublished Biography," III: 23. Hennacy, "Forgotten Aspects of My Life," 304.

14　Hennacy, "Forgotten Aspects of My Life," 304–5.

15　Miller, *Ruth Hanna McCormick*, 21.

16　Miller, *Ruth Hanna McCormick*, 124.

17　Phillips, Hall, and Black, *Reining in the Rio Grande*, 119.

18　Thomas, "Unpublished Biography," III: 26–27.

19　Hennacy, "Forgotten Aspects of My Life," 306.

20　Hennacy, *Autobiography of a Catholic Anarchist*, 61.

21　The manuscript is now in the Labadie Collection, University of Michigan.

22　Hennacy, "Forgotten Aspects of My Life," 306–7.

23　Thomas, "Unpublished Biography," III: 28.

24　Hennacy, *Book*, 63.

25　Hennacy, "Forgotten Aspects of My Life," 308.

26　Hennacy, doc. 02798, Labadie. By September 8, 1943, Hennacy had a phone.

27　Thomas, "Unpublished Biography," III: 97.

28　Hennacy, letter, June 16, 1943, Labadie.

29　Hennacy, *Book*, 63. This is the revised version of his tax statement.

30　Shirk's orchards most likely became part of the historic Manzano Orchard, although some of Hennacy's letters from the period are on letterhead from Upland Orchards. His move to Shirk is confirmed in his October 7, 1944, letter to Dorothy Day, Box DD-CW Series D-1 Box 9, Marquette.

31　Hennacy letter, October 7, 1944, Box DD-CW, Series D-1, Box 9, Marquette. Though a vegetarian, Hennacy consumed milk and eggs. Hennacy in Thomas, "Unpublished Biography," III: 51.

32　Hennacy, letter to Francis, June 16, 1942, Labadie.

33　Hennacy in Thomas, "Unpublished Biography," III: 70–80.

34　Hennacy, April 18, 1945, Box DD-CW, Series D-1, Box 9, Marquette.

35　Hennacy in Thomas, "Unpublished Biography," III: 71–74, 77.

36　Hennacy Papers, Utah, March 30, 1945, November 15, 1945, and August 1948.

37　Selma Melms Hennacy to Ammon Hennacy, in Thomas, "Unpublished Biography," III: 282–85. Ammon sent Selma's originals and carbon copies of his responses to his mother, who preserved them.

38　Hennacy, in Thomas, "Unpublished Biography," III: 285–86.

39 Hennacy worked for Shirk, who sold the orchard to Gibson, who mismanaged it and lost it back to Shirk, who left Hennacy working in it, but told him he would be moved to Shirk Dairy in January 1945. Hennacy to Dorothy Day, October 7, 1944, Marquette. See also November 30, 1945, to Erich and Genevieve, and Hennacy to his mother, Thomas, "Unpublished Biography," III: 77.

40 Hennacy, February 25, 1945, Marquette; Hennacy to Day, n.d., Marquette, DSC03004.

41 Hennacy, July 6, 1945, DSC03006, Marquette.

42 Hennacy to Day, June 24, 1945, Marquette.

43 Hennacy to Day, Box DD-CW, Series D-1, Box 9, Marquette. Thomas, "Unpublished Biography," III: 71.

44 Thomas, "Unpublished Biography," III: 66–67.

45 Thomas, "Unpublished Biography," III: 98.

46 Hennacy, *Book*, 74.

47 Hennacy in Thomas, "Unpublished Biography," III: 95.

48 Hennacy, *Book*, 77–79.

49 Hennacy in Thomas, "Unpublished Biography," II: 92.

50 Thomas, "Unpublished Biography," II: 92.

51 Thomas, "Unpublished Biography," II: 94.

52 Mark Van Steenwyk, "Anarchist Reflections on Christianity," Jesus Radicals, accessed May 25, 2021, https://www.jesusradicals.com/: "Some, such as Ammon Hennacy, have claimed that a 'shift' away from Jesus' practices and teachings of nonviolence, simple living and freedom occurred in the theology of Paul of Tarsus" (7).

53 Hennacy, *Book*, 81.

54 Hennacy to Dorothy Day, June 2, 1946, Box DD-CW, Series D-1, Box 9, Marquette.

55 Hennacy in Thomas, "Unpublished Biography," III: 96.

56 Hennacy to Day, June 11 and 20, 1946, Box DD-CW, Series D-1, Box 9, Marquette.

57 Hennacy to Day, September 14, 1946, Box DD-CW, Series D-1, Box 9, Marquette; and Cooper, *Claude McKay*, 364–65.

58 Rudnick and Wilson-Powell, *Mabel Dodge Luhan and Company*, 124. Luhan was soon married to Mabel Dodge, the patron of the arts.

59 Haley, "Ammon Hennacy and the Hopi Traditionalist Movement," 140.

60 Thompson in Haley, "Ammon Hennacy and the Hopi Traditionalist Movement," 135–88.

61 "Pueblo of Isleta," Wikipedia, accessed April 2, 2021.

62 Hennacy, *Book*, 84–85.

63 Hennacy to Selma, February 14, 1947, in Thomas, "Unpublished Biography," III: 99–100.

64 Thomas, "Unpublished Biography," III: 102–3.

65 This was before overgrazing was recognized as a problem by the tribes.

CHAPTER 6. BECOMING "AMMON HENNACY"

1 Molokans are a sect of non-Orthodox Russian pacifists.
2 Hennacy, *Book*, 87.
3 Hennacy to Day, July 7, 1952, Marquette. His fifty-fourth birthday was July 25, 1947.
4 Hennacy, *Book*, 87–88.
5 Hennacy, *Book*, 89.
6 Hennacy, *Book*, 88.
7 Heanncy, *Book*, 90.
8 Citizen Printing & Publishing Company, "*Arizona Weekly Citizen*, June 30, 1888," image 4, Library of Congress, accessed May 25, 2021, https://chroniclingamerica.loc.gov.
9 Information on both Ormes, Citizen Printing & Publishing Company, "*Arizona Weekly Citizen*, December 25, 1880," Library of Congress, accessed November 16, 2020, https://chroniclingamerica.loc.gov.
10 Hennacy to his mother, July 4, 1948, in Thomas, "Unpublished Biography," III: 277.
11 Thomas, "Unpublished Biography," III: 268.
12 Hennacy, *Book*, 92.
13 Hennacy, *Book*, 92–93.
14 Hennacy in Thomas, "Unpublished Biography," III: 268.
15 Thomas, "Unpublished Biography," III: 270. Hennacy wrote that "after twelve years of separation, I felt that morally my wife and I were divorced, although legally we were married by the common law of the state of New York." See also Thomas, "Unpublished Biography," II: 302.
16 Hennacy to his mother, in Thomas, "Unpublished Biography," III: 270.
17 Haley, "Ammon Hennacy and the Hopi Traditionalist Movement," 155, points out that Hennacy ignores those aspects of Hopi culture that contradict his beliefs. They had, for example, a war chief who was extremely influential. They depended on government subventions for schools, roads, and especially wells for their livestock. In the 1970s they sold mining and water rights to Peabody Coal for the Black Mesa mine.
18 Haley, "Ammon Hennacy and the Hopi Traditionalist Movement," 155.
19 Hennacy to Gerald Williamson, September 2, 1949, Box 4, Folder 5, Utah.
20 Hennacy to his mother, in Thomas, "Unfinished Biography," III: 327.
21 Hennacy contrasted the "true Hopis"—such as Thomas and Fermina Banyacya, Dan Kuchongva, Andrew Hermequaftewa, David Monongye, and the former draft resisters—with their enemies, the federal and state governments, the tribal council, and its supportive "stooge Republican Christians." Haley, "Ammon Hennacy and the Hopi Traditionalist Movement," 149.
22 Haley, "Ammon Hennacy and the Hopi Traditionalist Movement," 150, 169.
23 Haley, "Ammon Hennacy and the Hopi Traditionalist Movement," 152.
24 In January 1956, Hennacy published "Hopi Indians vs. the Government or, Democracy vs. Dictatorship" in the *Catholic Worker* about the federal government's

Hopi hearings that were held on the reservation. Returning to KPFA in 1958, he repeated his notion of the Hopi traditionalists: "These people are anarchists and pacifists—they don't know what the words mean even, but they went to jail during the wartime. They're good people. But they are getting messed up by the government and the government missionaries—you know that." When the Hopi hearings resumed in Washington in 1958, Hennacy attended for a day. In May 1959, after Kuchongva, Monongye, Tawangyawma, Banyacya, Paul Sewemaenewa, and George Nasewesewma were denied entrance to the United Nations, having hoped to deliver their apocalyptic prophecy, they visited Hennacy before going to a meeting with the Onondaga "traditionalists" in New York State. Hennacy publicized the Hopi traditionalists' opposition to bills before Congress in June 1957 and was asked to speak to a sociology class at Yale in November as a Hopi expert. His last work on the Hopi traditionalists was "Yukeoma, the Hopi" in *The One-Man Revolution*. Although Hennacy's advocacy diminished after August 1953, those he had lured to the Hopi cause carried on. George Yamada continued to collaborate with the Andersons in Phoenix from his new home in Mexico in an effort to persuade an attorney to challenge the legitimacy of the tribal council. Haley, "Ammon Hennacy and the Hopi Traditionalist Movement," 172–73.

25 Haley, "Ammon Hennacy and the Hopi Traditionalist Movement," 169–70.
26 Haley, "Ammon Hennacy and the Hopi Traditionalist Movement," 170.
27 Haley, "Ammon Hennacy and the Hopi Traditionalist Movement," 138. It is important to note that Hennacy, having started with a blanket endorsement of Native Americans, had to progressively reduce his enthusiasm to "true Hopis," as he learned about war-prone tribes and nomadic and carnivorous lifestyles.
28 Hennacy, draft of *One-Man Revolution*, 2, Utah.
29 Hennacy, draft of *One-Man Revolution*, 2, Utah.
30 Hennacy, draft of *One-Man Revolution*, 5, Utah.
31 Shelton self-published his first book, *Fundamentals of Nature Cure* (1922). Seeing importance in the hygienic movement (launched in 1832 by Dr. Isaac Jennings and Sylvester Graham), he changed the title to *An Introduction to Natural Hygiene*. A later book, *The Science and Fine Art of Fasting*, exerted an influence on Mahatma Gandhi, who consulted the book before undertaking public fasts. Shelton is credited with reviving the natural hygiene movement.
32 Hennacy to Day, January 1, 1950, Marquette.
33 Hennacy to Day, September 22, 1950, Marquette.
34 Sheldon funeral condolences, March 1970, Utah.
35 Trepanowskiand Bloomer, "The Impact of Religious Fasting on Human Health."
36 Studies by Patterson and Speers, "Metabolic Effects of Intermittent Fasting"; Antoni, Johnston, Collins, and Robertson, "Effects of Intermittent Fasting on Glucose and Lipid Metabolism"; Sundfør, Svendsen, and Tonstad, "Effect of Intermittent Continuous Energy Restriction."

37 Hennacy to Day, August 24, 1950, Marquette:

> Was a working fool this last week. Worked 100 hours, mostly irrigating at night. Slept all last night and to 11 a.m. today then hoed big weeds in the garden and will finish it tomorrow, then irrigate for 5 more nights. Have my round-trip fare saved: $100.89. I can zig zag around a lot on this kind of a ticket. . . . Can rest at Platt's in Flagstaff some hours. Will drink orange juice and eat fruit on my way. Stomach shrinks and your eye bigger than your stomach. Can't eat much at once. Have to nibble along the way. I am strong and as Dr. Shelton says have no poisons of meat, medicine in my body so can stand a lot of strain.

38 Hennacy to Day, August 24, 1950, Marquette.

39 Hennacy to Day, August 17, 1950, BOX DD-CW, Series D-1, Box 9, Folder 7, Marquette.

40 Hennacy, *Book*, 258.

41 Fernald, Baker, and Guldan, "Hydrological, Riparian, and Agro-Ecosystem Functions."

42 Hennacy to Day, January 31, 1951, Marquette.

43 Hennacy, February 8, 1953, Marquette.

44 Hennacy, March 27, 1947, Marquette.

45 Hennacy, June 7, 1950, Marquette.

46 Hennacy to Day, April 26, 1951, Marquette.

47 Hennacy, February 8, 1953, Marquette.

48 Hennacy, *Book*, 172–73.

49 Hennacy, June 10, 1950, Marquette.

50 Hennacy, January 29, 1953, Marquette.

51 Hennacy to Bob Ludlow, in Thomas, "Unpublished Biography," II: 370.

52 Hennacy to Day, March 26, 1953, Marquette.

53 Robert Ellsberg, "Dorothy in Love," *America: The Jesuit Review*, November 15, 2010, accessed May 25, 2021. https://www.americamagazine.org/.

54 Hennacy, *Book*, 51.

55 Hennacy to Day, February 22, 1940, Marquette.

56 Ammon Hennacy, "God's Coward," *Catholic Worker* 9, no. 1 (1941). Cited in McKana, *"The Catholic Worker" after Dorothy*, 69. Also Hennacy in Thomas, "Unpublished Biography," II: 182.

57 Hennacy to Day, June 4, 1941, December 12, 1941, Marquette.

58 Hennacy to Day, January 14, 1942, January 17, 1942, Marquette. Hennacy proudly informed Day that he "sent 170 pounds of clothes to the Doukhobors."

59 Miller, *Dorothy Day*, 425. Miller is sarcastic about Hennacy throughout his biography, which generally moves from one archival source to another. He dismisses Hennacy's role in Day's life, and he is often factually wrong. On a single page (410), he makes four mistakes: Hennacy did not go to Cleveland to sell cornflakes in 1913, Selma was neither "willowy" nor the daughter of a "state senator," and Ammon did not "give up college" because of "straitened circumstances." His

account of Selma omits any mention of the I AM movement and its influence. Miller even attempts to cast doubt on Hennacy's leadership in the fish boycott at the Atlanta Penitentiary, while admitting that he alone went to solitary for it. "He never 'grew up,'" in Miller's assessment (409).

60 Loughery and Randolph, *Dorothy Day*, 217–18.
61 Hennacy to Day, November 1, 1944, Labadie.
62 Hennacy to Day, April 1945, Marquette.
63 Hennacy, August 10, 1945, Labadie.
64 Dorothy Day, "We Go on Record: The CW Response to Hiroshima," *Catholic Worker*, September 1945, accessed May 25, 2021, http://www.catholicworker.org.
65 Hennacy, *Book*, 107. As mentioned in chapter 2, the origin of this experience could have been the 1920s Broadway play starring Theda Bara.
66 Hennacy to Day, May 23, 1951, Marquette.
67 Patrick Coy, in Thomas, "Unpublished Biography," II: 5–6.
68 Miller, *Dorothy Day*, 411–12; Hennacy to Day, May 19, 1950, folder W–16, Marquette. Loughery and Randolph are vague about the time and events of Day's Arizona trip, seemingly placing it in January 1950 and only saying that Hennacy "reminded her of Mike Gold, tireless and passionate and cocksure of himself. He was the most dedicated anarchist she, or anyone, had ever met" (246).
69 Hennacy to Day, May 19, 1950, Marquette.
70 Hennacy to his mother, January 4, 1950, in Thomas, "Unpublished Biography," III: 304.
71 Hennacy to Day, July 1, 1951, Marquette. Also February 19, 1951.
72 Hennacy, doc. 1229, Labadie.
73 Loughery and Randolph, *Dorothy Day*, 253. Miller, *Dorothy Day*.
74 Miller, *Dorothy Day*, 424–25.
75 Dorothy Day, doc. 02770, Labadie.
76 Dorothy Day, doc. 02770, Labadie.
77 Hennacy in Thomas, "Unpublished Biography," II: 391.
78 Thomas, "Unpublished Biography," III: 301.
79 Thomas, "Unpublished Biography," II: 2–9.
80 Hennacy to Day, March 18, 1953, Folder W, Marquette.
81 Thomas, "Unpublished Biography," III: 300.
82 Thomas, "Unpublished Biography," 302.
83 Thomas, "Unpublished Biography," 304.
84 Coy, *A Revolution of the Heart*, 141.
85 Day, *The Long Loneliness*, 296–98. Hennacy to his mother, January 18, 1952, in Thomas, "Unpublished Biography," III: 330.
86 Hennacy, August 13, 1952, Marquette.
87 Hennacy to Platt Cline, May 19, 1952, in Thomas, "Unpublished Biography," III: 341.
88 Hennacy to Day, August 13, 1952, Marquette. Around this point in his conversion to Catholicism, Hennacy began to date his letters according to the saints' birthdays: "St. Teresa Day" was October 15, 1952. In this letter he writes, "Remember in

1950 when I first realized that you loved me, and you said it was to make us both love everybody."

89 Hennacy to Helen Ford, May 20, 1952, in Thomas, "Unpublished Biography," III: 342.

90 Thomas, "Unpublished Biography," III: 348.

91 Thomas, "Unpublished Biography," III: 350.

92 Hennacy, *Book*, 223.

93 Hennacy, *Book*, 274–75.

94 Hennacy to Platt Cline, January 19, 1953, in Thomas, "Unpublished Biography," III: 363; meets Orme, 372.

95 Hennacy to Day from Tucson, January 8, 1953, Marquette.

96 Hennacy, January 9, 1953, Marquette, on Arizona-themed stationery.

97 Hennacy to Day, April 23, 1953, Marquette.

98 Hennacy to Mr. Killoran, in Thomas, "Unpublished Biography," III: 376.

99 Hennacy in Thomas, "Unpublished Biography," III: 379.

100 Hennacy letter, September 5, 1952, Marquette.

101 Hennacy to Day, December 18, 1952, Marquette.

CHAPTER 7. THE NEW YORK YEARS

1 Cornell in Troester, *Voices from "The Catholic Worker,"* 78.

2 Hennacy, *Book*, 247. Letters that Hennacy wrote to Helen Ford and Platt Cline before leaving Arizona indicate that one motive for going to New York was to learn what he needed to run his own "house of hospitality" eventually, possibly to be called the Vanzetti House. "Unless I was a Catholic, I wouldn't run a CW house myself, but I could work and earn money to pay the rent, gas, light, etc." Hennacy to Ford, May 20, 1952, in Thomas, "Unpublished Biography," II: 342–24.

3 The Sermon on the Plain, in Luke, with its level setting and reduced set of blessings and greater enumeration of woes, may have been a bit more to Hennacy's taste. In place of Matthew's "Blessed are those who are persecuted because of righteousness, for theirs is the Kingdom of Heaven," Luke has, "Blessed are you when people hate you, when they exclude you and insult you, and reject your name as evil, because of the Son of Man." The greater sense of opposition might have appealed to Hennacy.

4 For an overview of distributism, see Mary C. Segars, "Equality and Christian Anarchism: The Political and Social Ideas of the Catholic Worker Movement," *Review of Politics* 40, no. 2 (April 1978): 196–230. Segars writes that scholars trace distributism to Pope Leo XIII.

5 See Ludlow's general statement of CW philosophy at http://old.catholicworker.org/. It echoes Marxism in some places: "From each according to his ability, to each according to his needs"; and "the laborer is systematically robbed of that wealth which he produces over and above what is needed for his bare maintenance."

6 Robert Steed, interview with Marling, New York City, January 4, 2019.

7 Hennacy to Helen Ford, May 20, 1952, in Thomas, "Unpublished Biography," II: 342–44.

8 Steed, in Troester, *Voices from "The Catholic Worker,"* 149.
9 Harrington, in Troester, *Voices from "The Catholic Worker,"* 74.
10 Harrington in Loughery and Randolph, *Dorothy Day*, 253.
11 Judith Gregory, "Some Memories of *The Catholic Worker*," National Catholic Reporter, June 20, 1997, accessed May 25, 2021, https://www.ncronline.org/.
12 Gregory, "Some Memories of *The Catholic Worker*."
13 Hennacy, *Book*, 247.
14 Gregory, "Some Memories of *The Catholic Worker*."
15 Thomas, "Unpublished Biography," IV: 23.
16 Thomas, "Unpublished Biography," IV: 20.
17 Thomas, "Unpublished Biography," IV: 41.
18 Hennacy, *Book*, 359–61.
19 Gregory, "Some Memories of *The Catholic Worker*."
20 Hennacy to Dickerson, October 30, 1954, in Thomas, "Unpublished Biography," IV: 40.
21 Thomas, "Unpublished Biography," IV: 40.
22 Kathy Shuh-Ries, in Troester, *Voices from "The Catholic Worker,"* 172.
23 Gregory, "Some Memories of *The Catholic Worker*."
24 Robert Steed, interview with Marling, January 4, 2019, New York City. See also Thomas Merton, "Merton's Correspondence with Robert Steed," Thomas Merton Center at Bellarmine University, accessed March 12, 2019, http://merton.org/.
25 Robert Steed, interview with Marling, January 4, 2019, New York City.
26 Hennacy to Yone Stafford, in Thomas, "Unpublished Biography," IV: 38. "Gandhi's birthday" in Hennacy's dateline, which is October 2.
27 Hennacy to Platt Cline, October 13, 1954: "I spent two hours in jail last Friday for selling CWs on the Street at 43rd and Lexington." In Thomas, "Unpublished Biography," IV: 39.
28 Hennacy, *Book*, 284–85.
29 Hennacy, *Book*, 286.
30 Thomas, "Unpublished Biography," IV: 32.
31 Hennacy quoted by Thomas, "Unpublished Biography," IV: 32–34. Little documentation survives from this trip.
32 Thomas, "Unpublished Biography," IV: 37.
33 Hennacy in Thomas, *The Years of Grief and Laughter*, 313. Thomas, "Unpublished Biography," IV: 50.
34 Hennacy to Douglas MacArthur, in Thomas, "Unpublished Biography," IV: 48.
35 Day, *The Long Loneliness*, 88.
36 Hennacy in Thomas, *The Years of Grief and Laughter*, 313.
37 Herrnnacy in Thomas, *The Years of Grief and Laughter*, 313.
38 Thomas, *The Years of Grief and Laughter*, 318.
39 A&E Networks, "This Day in History: First Nationwide Civil Defense Drill Held," History, accessed June 1, 2021, https://www.history.com/.
40 Hennacy, *Book*, 286.

41 Opinion on the left was not uniform. Bayard Rustin advised against the risk of a five-hundred-dollar fine and a year in jail. Some protesters passed out the leaflet, signed by Ammon and Dorothy, then ducked for cover.

42 Hennacy, *Book*, 289.

43 Hennacy to his mother, in Thomas, "Unpublished Biography," IV: 61.

44 Hennacy to Warren Largay, in Thomas, "Unpublished Biography," IV: 65.

45 Hennacy to his mother, in Thomas, "Unpublished Biography," IV: 42–43.

46 *Chicago Tribune* article in Thomas, "Unpublished Biography," IV: 70.

47 Hennacy, *Book*, 289.

48 Hennacy, *Book*, 290.

49 Hennacy, *Book*, 290.

50 Hennacy, *Book*, 298. Hennacy to Platt Cline, in Thomas, "Unpublished Biography," IV: 72.

51 Hennacy, *Book*, 298.

52 Hennacy, *Book*, 298.

53 Hennacy, *Book*, 339.

54 Hennacy to his mother, May 19, 1957, in Thomas, "Unpublished Biography," IV: 98.

55 The Wikimedia Foundation, "Mercury, Nevada," Wikipedia, last edited March 6, 2021, accessed June 1, 2021, https://en.wikipedia.org.

56 This protest was launched by the Committee on Non-Violent Action. CNVA's action was a vigil outside the atomic weapons test grounds in Las Vegas, Nevada, in 1957. The following year their ship *Golden Rule* set sail for the South Pacific test area, but its crew was stopped and arrested in Honolulu. Earle and Barbara Reynolds continued the effort aboard the *Phoenix* and successfully entered the test waters. CNVA sponsored an Omaha Action in 1959 to protest construction of intercontinental ballistic missiles, and, in 1960, Polaris Action began, aimed against the missile-carrying Polaris submarine being constructed in New London. Hennacy thus would participate in three of their actions. "Committee for Nonviolent Action Records, 1958–1968," Swarthmore College Peace Collection, accessed June 1, 2021, https://www.swarthmore.edu/.

57 Hennacy, September 27, 1958, Marquette.

58 Hennacy, *Book*, 300. Thomas, "Unpublished Biography," IV: 78. Another group, led by Larry Scott, had gone as close as possible to the proving ground to picket, but received little publicity.

59 Thomas, "Unpublished Biography," IV: 78.

60 Thomas, "Unpublished Biography," IV: 79.

61 Thomas, "Unpublished Biography," IV: 81. *Catholic Worker*, June 18, 1957.

62 After Hennacy left, another group got onto the actual test grounds at Mercury and were arrested, but they were offered a suspended sentence if they went home. When they took it, Ammon scoffed: "To chicken out is a poor way of advancing a cause." Hennacy, *Book*, 302.

63 Hennacy in Thomas, "Unpublished Biography," IV: 81–83. Hennacy, *Book*, 342.

64 Hennacy, *Book*, 290–91. To his mother on August 2, 1957.

65 Dulles, to Council on Foreign Relations 1954, from Brodie, *Strategy in the Missile Age*, 248; and McGeorge Bundy, *Danger and Survival*, 256.

66 Hennacy in Thomas, "Unpublished Biography," IV: 86.

67 Day's appreciation of Gandhi was minimal. See "We Mourn Death of Gandhi Non Violent Revolutionary," *Catholic Worker*, February 1948, 1.

68 Day, *Loaves and Fishes*, 103.

69 Day, *Loaves and Fishes*, 105, 104.

70 Miller, *Dorothy Day*, 467.

71 Day, *Loaves and Fishes*, 112.

72 Miller, *Dorothy Day*, 466–67. Day, *Loaves and Fishes*, 133.

73 Hennacy to Platt Cline, December 18, 1957, in Thomas, "Unpublished Biography," IV: 87.

74 Hennacy in Thomas, *The Years of Grief and Laughter*, 320.

75 Malina, *The Diaries of Judith Malina*, 45.

76 Bendiner, *The Bowery Man*, 119.

77 Bendiner, *The Bowery Man*, 119.

78 Bendiner, *The Bowery Man*, 118.

79 Hennacy, *Book*, 360.

80 Hennacy, *Book*, 272. Robert Steed, interview with Marling, January 4, 2019, New York City; Mary Lathrop, interview with Marling, January 3, 2019, New York City; Hennacy, *Book*, 363. Pagano was apparently among the CW's tax-resisting members, a protest that had grown, according to an article in the April 15, 1957, *Intelligencer* of Doylestown, Pennsylvania, which mentions six residents of Bucks County and fifty-one nationwide, among them Pagano.

81 Hennacy, *Book*, 302, 304, 291–92.

82 Hennacy to Steed, in Thomas, "Unpublished Biography," IV: 92.

83 Hennacy in Thomas, "Unpublished Biography," IV: 92.

84 Day, *Loaves and Fishes*, 110.

85 Hennacy to his mother, in Thomas, "Unpublished Biography," IV: 102.

86 Hennacy to Cline, in Thomas, "Unpublished Biography," IV: 104.

87 Hennacy, *Book*, 306.

88 U.S. Government, "Small Town, Big Missile," History of Nebraska, accessed April 6, 2021, https://history.nebraska.gov.

89 Hennacy, *Book*, 306.

90 Thomas, "Unpublished Biography," IV: 104; Hennacy, *Book*, 308.

91 Hennacy to Father Casey, in Thomas, "Unpublished Biography," IV: 108; Hennacy, *Book*, 309.

92 Hennacy, *Book*, 310–11. For an account of the Huber Plan, see Sheridine Rucker, "A Study of the North Carolina Work Release Program," Robert W. Woodruff Library, Atlanta University Center.

93 Hennacy, *Book*, 311.

94 Hennacy to his mother, September 18, 1959, in Thomas, "Unpublished Biography," IV: 108.

95 Hennacy to Father Casey in Thomas, "Unpublished Biography," IV: 106–7.

96 Cornell, *Unruly Equality*, 218–22. Hennacy to Carmen, in Thomas, "Unpublished Biography," IV: 111.

97 Thomas, "Unpublished Biography," IV: 108.

98 Hennacy to Sharon, September 25, 1959, in Thomas, "Unpublished Biography," IV: 111. He gives the January 21, 1960, date in Thomas, *The Years of Grief and Laughter*, 320.

99 Dates and places in Hennacy letter to his mother, January 13, 1960, in Thomas, "Unpublished Biography," IV: 119–20.

100 Bendiner in Hennacy, *Book*, 331–32. Kempton in Hennacy, *Book*, 330. Robert Steed, interview with Marling, January 4, 2019, New York City.

101 Hennacy in Thomas, "Unpublished Biography," IV: 320.

102 Hennacy, *Book*, 311.

103 Miller, *Dorothy Day*, 467.

104 Henancy, *Book*, 312–13.

105 Mary Lathrop, interview with Marling, January 3, 2019, New York City; and interview conducted by "RO" of Catholic Worker Archives, January 18, 1988, Marquette.

106 Thomas, *The Years of Grief and Laughter*, 14.

107 Mary Lathrop, interview with Marling, January 3, 2019, New York City.

108 Day in Hennacy, *Book*, 418.

109 Mary Lathrop, interview with Marling, January 3, 2019.

110 Miller, *Dorothy Day*, 466.

111 Lathrop, interview conducted by "RO" of Catholic Worker Archives, January 18, 1988, Marquette, 6. Lathrop quoted by Day and Day quoted by Hennacy in *Book*, 419.

112 Day, *Loaves and Fishes*, 115. Hennacy to his mother in Thomas, "Unpublished Biography," IV: 120–21; Day, *Loaves and Fishes*, 115; Hennacy to his mother, in Thomas, "Unpublished Biography," IV: 121.

113 Lathrop, interview conducted by "RO" of Catholic Worker Archives, January 18, 1988, Marquette, 9.

114 Thomas, "Unpublished Biography," IV: 133, 124, 128.

CHAPTER 8. IN THE LAND OF THE MORMONS

1 Hennacy, *Book*, 429.

2 The Ohio History Connection. "Mormon Church," Ohio History Central, accessed June 1, 2021, https://ohiohistorycentral.org/.

3 Hennacy, *Book*, 430.

4 Hennacy, *Book*, 67, 95, 116, 118.

5 Hennacy to Bill Ryan, January 22, 1951, Marquette.

6 Thomas, "Unpublished Biography," IV: 138; Hennacy, *Book*, 403.

7 Coy, *A Revolution of the Heart*, 163.

8 Mary Lathrop, interview conducted by "RO" of Catholic Worker Archives, January 18, 1988, Marquette, 9.

9   Thomas, "Unpublished Biography," IV: 134; Hennacy to "Friend Strojie," November 29, 1961, Thomas, "Unpublished Biography," IV: 137; Hennacy, *Book*, 403.

10 Lathrop, interview conducted by "RO" of Catholic Worker Archives, January 18, 1988, Marquette, 9. Hennacy to mother, in Thomas, "Unpublished Biography," IV: 167.

11 Hennacy to mother, in Thomas, "Unpublished Biography," IV: 167–68.

12 Lathrop in Troester, *Voices from "The Catholic Worker,"* 109. Day in Hennacy, *Book*, 419.

13 Hennacy, *Book*, 404–8.

14 Number of churches is Hennacy's estimate. Other data, Hennacy, *Book*, 404.

15 Jeremy Harmon, "Fifty Years Ago, a Catholic Anarchist Tried to Help Solve Homelessness in Salt Lake City: Here's What Happened," *Salt Lake Tribune*, September 24, 2017, accessed September 27, 2017, www.sltrib.com.

16 Lathrop, interview conducted by "RO" of Catholic Worker Archives, January 18, 1988, Marquette, 9.

17 More information on Joe Hill in Adler, *The Man Who Never Died*, which introduces new evidence about the trial; and Smith, *Joe Hill: The Man and the Myth*.

18 The 1914 trial of Joe Hill was somewhat like the trial of Sacco and Vanzetti that Ammon held dear: it depended on circumstantial evidence, eye-witness accounts later recanted, and sketchy ballistics. President Wilson asked twice for a commutation of Hill's sentence, but Utah's governor refused.

19 Hennacy, *Book*, 407.

20 Hennacy, *Book*, 408.

21 Hennacy, *Book*, 409.

22 Hennacy to Clines, November 11, 1961, in Thomas, "Unpublished Biography," IV: 173.

23 Phillips in Troester, *Voices from "The Catholic Worker,"* 112.

24 Lathrop in Troester, *Voices from "The Catholic Worker,"* 110.

25 Hennacy to Stafford, in Thomas, "Unpublished Biography," IV: 170; Day, *Loaves and Fishes*, 116.

26 Hennacy in Lathrop, interview conducted by "RO" of Catholic Worker Archives, January 18, 1988, Marquette, 10.

27 Hennacy in Lathrop, interview conducted by "RO" of Catholic Worker Archives, January 18, 1988, Marquette, 11.

28 Hennacy in Lathrop, interview conducted by "RO" of Catholic Worker Archives, January 18, 1988, Marquette, 11.

29 Hennacy in Lathrop, interview conducted by "RO" of Catholic Worker Archives, January 18, 1988, Marquette, 12. Repeated in interview with Marling, January 3, 2019, New York City.

30 Hennacy, *Book*, 412.

31 Hennacy, *Book*, 414.

32 Hennacy, *Book*, 412–13.

33 Phillips in Troester, *Voices from "The Catholic Worker,"* 112.

34 Hennacy, *Book*, 414–15.

35 Phillips in Troester, *Voices from "The Catholic Worker,"* 112.

36 Lathrop, interview conducted by "RO" of Catholic Worker Archives, January 18, 1988, Marquette, 9–10.

37 Poulsen raped and killed an eleven-year-old girl. Rivenburgh and Garcia cut the head off a fellow prisoner. Thomas, "Unpublished Biography," IV: 177.

38 Hennacy in Thomas, "Unpublished Biography," IV: 177–78.

39 Hennacy, *Book*, 435.

40 Ethel Hale, in Hennacy, *Book*, 200–201; and "Ethel C. Hale: 1922–2016," Legacy, April 10, 2016, accessed June 1, 2021, https://www.legacy.com. There is also an interview at Kathryn French, "Interview with Ethel Hale," Utah Valley University Digital Collections, November 2, 2006, accessed June 1, 2021, https://contentdm .uvu.edu. An overview of her life: Colby Frazier, "Salt Lake City's 'Conscience' Remembered: Ethel Hale Passes Away at Age 94," *Salt Lake City Weekly*, April 20, 2016, accessed June 1, 2021, https://www.cityweekly.net/.

41 Jean C. Chanonat, PhD, letter to Marling, August 1, 2019. In author's possession.

42 Thomas, *The Years of Grief and Laughter*, 15, 17, 18.

43 Thomas, *The Years of Grief and Laughter*, 18, 20–21.

44 Thomas, *The Years of Grief and Laughter*, 24.

45 Thomas, *The Years of Grief and Laughter*, 25–26.

46 The West Side Hotel, owned by Utah natives Misao and Elsie Doi, and kept scrupulously clean in Marling's experience. See Legacy Incorporated, "Misao and Elsie Doi Obituary," Legacy, August 22, 2015, accessed June 1, 2021, https://www.legacy .com.

47 Thomas, *The Years of Grief and Laughter*, 30–31.

48 Thomas, *The Years of Grief and Laughter*, 22–23, 35.

49 Details in Hennacy letter to Yone, October 7, 1963, Thomas, "Unpublished Biography," IV: 212.

50 Thomas, "Unpublished Biography," IV: 189.

51 The Wikimedia Foundation, "Dugway Proving Ground," Wikipedia, accessed July 21, 2018, https://en.wikipedia.org/.

52 Hennacy in Thomas, "Unpublished Biography," IV: 209, 210.

53 Thomas, *The Years of Grief and Laughter*, 37, 41–42.

54 Thomas, *The Years of Grief and Laughter*, 44.

55 Thomas, "Unpublished Biography," IV: 189.

56 Thomas, *The Years of Grief and Laughter*, 52.

57 Hennacy in Thomas, *The Years of Grief and Laughter*, 336.

58 Thomas, "Unpublished Biography," IV: 192.

59 Thomas, "Unpublished Biography," IV: 193.

60 Thomas, "Unpublished Biography," IV: 201. The Wikimedia Foundation. "Fast Sunday," Wikipedia, accessed June 1, 2021, https://en.wikipedia.org/.

61 Thomas, "Unpublished Biography," IV: 204. Stegner letter on 205.

62 Hennacy letter in Thomas, "Unpublished Biography," IV: 208; Hennacy, *Book*, 382.

63 Hennacy, *The One-Man Revolution*, iv, vii.
64 Thomas, *The Years of Grief and Laughter*, 85.
65 Thomas, *The Years of Grief and Laughter*, 87, 89.
66 Day in Troester, *Voices from "The Catholic Worker,"* 113.
67 Hennacy letter to Yone, May 1964, and other info. in Thomas, "Unpublished Biography," IV: 4–8, 221, 393, 230.
68 Thomas, "Unpublished Biography," IV: 232.
69 Thomas, *The Years of Grief and Laughter*, 106.
70 Thomas, *The Years of Grief and Laughter*, 108–9.
71 Hennacy to "Dearest Gertrude," January 5, 1966, in Thomas, "Unpublished Biography," 259, says that "they sold it for the $7,640 that I still owed on it, so I got nothing out of it."
72 Thomas, *The Years of Grief and Laughter*, 148–49; Thomas, "Unpublished Biography," IV: 268. Locations given in back-to-back letters to Yone.
73 There is controversy about Spellman's action. Van Allen, "What Really Happened?"
74 Hennacy to Power in Thomas, "Unpublished Biography," IV: 252; letter to Yone Stafford, December 17, 1965, in Thomas, "Unpublished Biography," IV: 258. An overview of the anti–Vietnam War protests in Utah may be found in *Utah Historical Quarterly* 78, no. 2 (2010): 154 ff.
75 Hennacy to Yone, February 4, 1967, in Thomas, "Unpublished Biography," 4–10.
76 University of Houston, "Lyndon B. Johnson," Digital History, accessed June 1, 2021, http://www.digitalhistory.uh.edu; Hennacy, *The One-Man Revolution*, vii.
77 Thomas, *The Years of Grief and Laughter*, 151.
78 Thomas, *The Years of Grief and Laughter*, 161.
79 Thomas, *The Years of Grief and Laughter*, 165, 170; Thomas, "Unpublished Biography," IV: 273.
80 Thomas, *The Years of Grief and Laughter*, 161.
81 Thomas, *The Years of Grief and Laughter*, 171, 161.
82 Hennacy to Platt Cline, January 1, 1969, in Thomas, "Unpublished Biography," IV: 394, 4–14.
83 Thomas, "Unpublished Biography," IV: 300.
84 Thomas, "Unpublished Biography," IV: 400; Thomas, *The Years of Grief and Laughter*, 184–89.
85 Thomas, *The Years of Grief and Laughter*, 188.
86 Thomas, *The Years of Grief and Laughter*, 189, 191; Thomas, "Unpublished Biography," IV: 394.
87 Thomas, *The Years of Grief and Laughter*, 191–94, 195.
88 Thomas, *The Years of Grief and Laughter*, 197.
89 Thomas, *The Years of Grief and Laughter*, 197. It was January 8, 1970.
90 Thomas, *The Years of Grief and Laughter*, 198.
91 Thomas, *The Years of Grief and Laughter*, 199–200.
92 Thomas, *The Years of Grief and Laughter*, 202.

CONCLUSION

1 Loughery and Randolph, *Dorothy Day*, 254.

2 Wakefield, *New York in the 50s*, 72–75.

3 Reichert in Coy, *A Revolution of the Heart*, 141–42.

4 Hennacy, *The One-Man Revolution*, 333–34.

5 David Como, *Blown by the Spirit*, 36, provides an overview of antinomianism.

6 Levy, *Quakers and the American Family*, 78. Levy details how John Fox developed new conceptions of family and community that emphasized "holy conversation": speech and behavior that reflected piety, faith, and love. With the restructuring of the family and household came new roles for women; Fox and Margaret Fell viewed the Quaker mother as essential to developing "holy conversation" in her children and husband. Quaker women were also responsible for the spirituality of the larger community, coming together in "meetings" that regulated marriage and domestic behavior. David Yount, in *How the Quakers Invented America*, writes that Quakers first introduced many ideas that later became mainstream, such as democracy in the Pennsylvania legislature, the Bill of Rights (Rhode Island Quakers), trial by jury, equal rights for men and women, and public education.

7 Miller, *Dorothy Day*, 411, 467; also in Coy, *A Revolution of the Heart*, 146, note 33.

8 Hennacy, *The One-Man Revolution*, 12.

9 Hennacy, *The One-Man Revolution*, 18, 16. Jefferson's relation to Sally Hemings was unknown until Fawn Brodie's biography raised the issue seriously in 1974, well after Hennacy's death. In 2000, a consensus emerged, generated by the DNA study titled "Jefferson Fathered Slaves' Last Child," that Jefferson was the father of Hemings's children.

10 Hennacy, *The One-Man Revolution*, 17, 18.

11 Ling, "Thomas Jefferson and the Environment."

12 Hennacy, *The One-Man Revolution*, 25. The Jefferson quotation may be spurious, according to Thomas Jefferson Encyclopedia, "Do You Want to Know Who You Are? (Spurious Quotation)," Th. Jefferson Monticello, accessed June 1, 2021, https://www.monticello.org. But it was common currency in Hennacy's day.

13 Coy, *A Revolution of the Heart*, 144.

14 Hennacy, *The One-Man Revolution*, 34.

15 Thomas in Coy, *A Revolution of the Heart*, 145.

16 Thoreau in Hennacy, *The One-Man Revolution*, 40.

17 Berkman in Hennacy, *The One-Man Revolution*, 90.

18 Hennacy, *The One-Man Revolution*, 99.

19 Merriam-Webster defines "*parrhesia*" as "boldness or freedom of speech." See Marling and Marling, "Reparative Reading and Christian Anarchism."

20 Marling and Marling, "Reparative Reading and Christian Anarchism," 236.

21 Marling and Marling, "Reparative Reading and Christian Anarchism," 256.

22 Marling and Marling, "Reparative Reading and Christian Anarchism," 280.

23 Phillips in Troester, *Voices from "The Catholic Worker,"* 114.

24 Hennacy, *The One-Man Revolution*, 294–96.

25 Hennacy, *The One-Man Revolution*, 289.

26 Hennacy, *The One-Man Revolution*, 328.

27 Hennacy, *The One-Man Revolution*, 335.

28 Mary Lathrop, interview with William Marling, January 17, 2019, New York City.

29 This theme is fully developed in Marling and Marling, "Reparative Reading and Christian Anarchism." See also "The Meaning and Evolution of the Word 'Parrhesia,'" in Foucault, *Discourse and Truth*.

30 Foucault, *Religion and Culture*, xv. Also Foucault, *Discourse and Truth*.

31 Coy, *A Revolution of the Heart*, 142.

32 Meyer in Coy, *A Revolution of the Heart*, 78, 164.

33 Forrest in Coy, *A Revolution of the Heart*, 53, 155.

34 Statistics from Coy, *A Revolution of the Heart*, 166.

35 Coy, *A Revolution of the Heart*, 85, 168.

BIBLIOGRAPHY

Adler, William M. 2011. *The Man Who Never Died: The Life, Times, and Legacy of Joe Hill, American Labor Icon.* London: Bloomsbury.

Alter, Joseph S. 2000. *Gandhi's Body: Sex, Diet, and the Politics of Nationalism.* Philadelphia: University of Pennsylvania Press.

Alyea, Paul E., and Blanche R. Alyea. 1956. *Fairhope, 1894–1954: The Story of a Single-Tax Colony.* Tuscaloosa: University of Alabama Press.

Antoni, Rona, Kelly L. Johnston, Adam L. Collins, and M. Denise Robertson. 2017. "Effects of Intermittent Fasting on Glucose and Lipid Metabolism." *Proceedings of the Nutrition Society* 76: 361–68.

Avrich, Paul. 1995. *Anarchist Voices: An Oral History of Anarchism in America.* Princeton, NJ: Princeton University Press.

Bendiner, Elmer. 1961. *The Bowery Man.* New York: Nelson.

Bestor, Arthur Eugene, Jr. 1950. *Backwoods Utopias: The Sectarian and Owenite Phases of Communitarian Socialism in America, 1663–1829.* Philadelphia: University of Pennsylvania Press.

Betts, Frederick William. 1916. Reprint 2015. *Billy Sunday, the Man and Method.* Boston: Murray Press.

Brodie, Bernard. 1959. *Strategy in the Missile Age.* Princeton, NJ: Princeton University Press.

Bundy, McGeorge. 1988. *Danger and Survival.* New York: Random House.

Butalia, Tarunjit Singh, and Diane P. Small. 2004. *Religion in Ohio.* Athens: Ohio University Press.

Cantina, Holley, Duchene Rainer, and Phillips Meters, eds. 2001. *Prison Etiquette: The Convict's Compendium of Useful Information.* Carbondale: Southern Illinois University Press.

Carson, Gerald. 1976. *Cornflake Crusade.* New York: Arno Press.

Carter, April. 1971. *The Political Theory of Anarchism.* London: Routledge & Kegan Paul.

Christoyannopoulos, Alexandre. 2010. "Christian Anarchism: A Revolutionary Reading of the Bible." In *New Perspectives on Anarchism,* ed. Nathan June and Shane Wahl, pp. 149–67. Washington, DC: Lexington Books.

Coffman, Edward M. 1998. *The War to End All Wars: The American Military Experience in World War I.* Lexington: University Press of Kentucky.

Como, David R. 2004. *Blown by the Spirit: Puritanism and the Emergence of an Antinomian Underground in Pre–Civil War England.* Stanford, CA: Stanford University Press.

Cooper, Wayne F. 1996. *Claude McKay, Rebel Sojourner in the Harlem Renaissance: A Biography*. Baton Rouge: Louisiana State University Press.

Cornell, Andrew. 2016. *Unruly Equality: U.S. Anarchism in the 20th Century*. Oakland: University of California Press.

Coy, Patrick G., ed. 1988. *A Revolution of the Heart*. Philadelphia: Temple University Press.

Crammer, Gibson Lamb. 1891. *History of the Upper Ohio Valley*. Madison, WI: Brandt and Fuller.

Day, Dorothy. 1942. *The Catholic Worker*, January, 1, 4.

———. 1952. *The Long Loneliness*. New York: Curtis Books.

———. 1963. *Loaves and Fishes*. New York: Harper & Row.

———. 1967. "Interview." In *Protest: Pacifism and Politics*, ed. James Finn. New York: Random House.

———. 2015. *House of Hospitality*, ed. Lance Richey. Huntington, IN: Our Sunday Visitor.

DeLeon, David. 1978. *The American as Anarchist: Reflections on Indigenous Radicalism*. Baltimore, MD: Johns Hopkins University Press.

Dellinger, Dave. 1970. *Revolutionary Nonviolence: Essays by Dave Dellinger*. Indianapolis: Bobbs-Merrill.

Deming, Barbara. 1971. *Revolution and Equilibrium*. New York: Grossman.

Dittmore, John V., and E. Sutherland Bates. 1933. *Mary Baker Eddy: The Truth and the Tradition*. London: Routledge.

Dunlap, David W. 2004. *From Abyssinian to Zion: A Guide to Manhattan's Houses of Worship*. New York: Columbia University Press.

Elkinton, Joseph. 2016. *The Doukhobors: Their History in Russia, Their Migration to Canada*. Sacramento, CA: Creative Media Partners.

Ellis, Marc. 1984. "The Legacy of Peter Maurin." *Cross-Currents* 34, no. 3: 294–304.

Ellsberg, Robert. 2010. "Dorothy Day." *Love, America: The Jesuit Review*, November 15. https://www.americamagazine.org/faith.

Farrell, James J. 1997. *The Spirit of the Sixties: Making Postwar Radicalism*. London: Routledge.

Fellner, Gene. 1992. *Life of an Anarchist: The Alexander Berkman Reader*. New York: Four Walls, Eight Windows Press.

Felski, Rita. 2015. *The Limits of Critique*. Chicago: University of Chicago Press.

Fernald, A. G., T. T. Baker, and S. J. Guldan. 2007. "Hydrological, Riparian, and Agro-Ecosystem Functions of Traditional Acequia Irrigation Systems." *Journal of Sustainable Agriculture* 30, no. 2: 147–71.

Fisher, James Terrance. 1989. *The Catholic Counterculture in America, 1933–1962*. Chapel Hill: University of North Carolina Press.

———. 2000. *Communion of Immigrants: A History of Catholics in America*. New York: Oxford University Press.

Forest, Jim. 1970. "Men Acted Differently according to Whether They Had Met Him or Not," *Catholic Radical*, February: 2.

Foucault, Michel. 1983. *Discourse and Truth: The Problematization of Parrhesia (Six Lectures)*. University of California. Available at https://foucault.info/parrhesia/.

———. 1999. *Religion and Culture*, ed. Jeremy R. Carrette. London: Routledge.

Frankenberg, Theodore Thomas. 1917. *Billy Sunday, His Tabernacles and Sawdust Trails: A Biographical Sketch of the Famous Baseball Evangelist*. Whitefish, MT: Kessinger.

Fuller, Alfred C. 1960. *A Foot in the Door*. New York: McGraw Hill.

Gregory, Judith. 1996. "Some Memories of *The Catholic Worker*," September 2. Unpublished version provided to the author by Robert Steed. A different version was published in 1997 in *National Catholic Reporter*, http://www.natcath.org/.

Gross, David. 2019. "The One-Man Revolution (The Only One That's Coming)," *Moon Magazine*, http://moonmagazine.org/.

Haley, Brian D. 2016. "Ammon Hennacy and the Hopi Traditionalist Movement: Roots of the Counterculture's Favorite Indians." *Journal of the Southwest* 58, no. 1.

Harrington, Michael. 1970. "Ammon Hennacy: Combined Pacifism, Moral Passion, Irish Humor." *Catholic Worker*, February: 7.

———. 1993. "The Ideals of One's Youth," in Troester, ed., *Voices from "The Catholic Worker*," 120–35.

Hartshorne, Charles. 1984. *Omnipotence and Other Theological Mistakes*. Albany: State University of New York Press.

Hennacy, Ammon. 1941. "God's Coward." *Catholic Worker*, November.

———. 1954. *Autobiography of a Catholic Anarchist*. New York: Catholic Worker Books.

———. 1955. "Why I Am a Catholic Anarchist." *Individual Action*, January 25: 3, Marquette, W-11.1.

———. 1956. "In the Market Place." *Catholic Worker*, April: 2 and May: 2.55.

———. 1958. "In the Market Place." *Catholic Worker*, June: 382.

———. 1964. *The Book of Ammon*. Salt Lake City, UT: Self-published.

———. 1970. *The One-Man Revolution*. Salt Lake City, UT: Ammon Hennacy Publications.

———. 1974. "Forgotten Aspects of My Life." In Thomas, *Years of Grief and Laughter*, 272–336.

Hill, Christopher. 1984. *The World Turned Upside Down: Radical Ideas during the English Revolution*. New York: Penguin.

Hobbes, Thomas. 1651. Reprint 2005. *Leviathan*. Hamburg: Meiner Verlag.

Hodder, Allan D. 2003. "Thoreau's Religious Vision." *Ultimate Reality and Meaning* 26, no. 2 (June): 88–108. https://doi.10.3138/uram.26.2.88.

Hogan, William. 1965. "Hennacy, a Unique American Rebel." *San Francisco Chronicle*, February 26. Box 8, Folder 20, Utah; FBI, "Subject: Hennacy," file 100A—SU-9531— sec. 2, pp. 114–16. In author's possession.

Ivens, Molly. 1976. "New York's Croatians: Close-Knit and Fiery."*New York Times*, September 18.

Jennings, Chris. 2016. *Paradise Now: The Story of American Utopianism*. New York: Random House.

Jones, Malcolm V. 2005. *Dostoevsky and the Dynamics of Religious Experience.* New York: Anthem Press.

Jordan, Patrick, ed. 2002. *Dorothy Day: Writings from "Commonweal."* New York: Commonweal.

Jun, Nathan, and Shane Wahl, eds. 2009. *New Perspectives on Anarchism.* Washington, DC: Lexington Books.

Kautsky, Karl. 1899. *The Class Struggle.* Daniel DeLeon, trans. New York: New York Labor News Co.

Kempton, Murray. 1970. *The Village Voice.* Cited in Wakefield, *New York in the 50s,* 73–77, 82–83.

Klejment, Anne. 1996. *American Catholic Pacifism: The Influence of Dorothy Day and the Catholic Worker Movement.* Westport, CT: Praeger.

Kuebrich, David. 1998. "The Soul." In J. R. LeMaster and Donald D. Kummings, eds., *Walt Whitman: An Encyclopedia.* New York: Garland.

Levy, Barry. 1988. *Quakers and the American Family.* New York: Oxford University Press.

Lindsay, Vachel. 1914. Reprint 1999. *Tramping across America (Adventures While Preaching the Gospel of Beauty).* Springfield, IL: Rose Hill Press.

Ling, Peter. 2004. "Thomas Jefferson and the Environment." *History Today* 54, no. 1.

Loughery, John, and Blythe Randolph. 2020. *Dorothy Day: Dissenting Voice of the American Century.* New York: Simon & Schuster.

Love, Heather. 2010. "Truth or Consequences: On Paranoid Reading and Reparative Reading." *Criticism* 52, no. 2.

Lynd, Staughton. 1966. *Non-violence in America: A Documentary History.* Indianapolis, IN: Bobbs-Merrill.

———. 1968. *The Intellectual Origins of American Radicalism.* New York: Pantheon.

Mack, Horace. 1897. *History of Columbiana County, Ohio: 1879.* Philadelphia: D.W. Ensign. https://archive.org/.

Malina, Judith. 1984. *The Diaries of Judith Malina.* New York: Grove Press.

Marling, Raili, and William Marling. 2021. "Reparative Reading and Christian Anarchism," *LIT: Literature, Interpretation, Theory* 32, no. 2 (Fall).

McKana, Dan. 2008. *The Catholic Worker after Dorothy: Practicing the Works of Mercy in a New Generation.* Collegeville, MN: Liturgical Press.

McNeal, Patricia F. 1978. *The American Catholic Peace Movement, 1928–1972.* New York: Ayer Press.

Meyer, Karl. 1986. "Interview with Patrick Coy," Milwaukee, June 21. Cited in Coy, *A Revolution of the Heart.*

Miller, Kristie. 1992. *Ruth Hanna McCormick: A Life in Politics, 1880–1944.* Albuquerque: University of New Mexico Press.

Miller, William D. 1973. *A Harsh and Dreadful Love: Dorothy Day and the Catholic Worker Movement.* New York: Liveright.

———. 1982. *Dorothy Day, a Biography.* San Francisco: Harper & Row.

Nisbet, Robert. 1976. *The Social Philosophers: Community and Conflict in Western Thought*. New York: Crowell.

Nozick, Robert. 1974. *Anarchy, State, Utopia*. New York: Basic Books.

Patterson, Ruth E., and Dorothy D. Speers. 2017. "Metabolic Effects of Intermittent Fasting." *Annual Review of Nutrition* 37: 371–93.

Pfeifer, Michael J. 2021. *The Making of American Catholic Worlds: Region, Catholicism, and American Society*. New York: NYU Press.

Phillips, Fred M., G. Emlen Hall, and Mark E. Black. 2015. *Reining in the Rio Grande*. Albuquerque: University of New Mexico Press.

Piehl, Mel. 1982. *Breaking Bread: The Catholic Worker and the Origin of Catholic Radicalism in America*. Philadelphia: Temple University Press.

Putnam, Robert D., and David E. Campbell. 2010. *American Grace: How Religion Divides and Unites Us*. New York: Simon & Schuster.

Reece, Erik. 2016. *Utopia Drive: A Road Trip through America's Most Radical Idea*. New York: Farrar, Strauss, and Giroux.

Reichert, William O. 1976. *Partisans of Freedom: A Study in American Anarchism*. Bowling Green, OH: Bowling Green University Popular Press.

Renshaw, Patrick. 1999. *The Story of the IWW and Syndicalism in the United States*. Chicago: Ivan R. Dee.

Rudnick, Lois Palken. 1987. *Mabel Dodge Luhan: New Woman, New Worlds*. Albuquerque: University of New Mexico Press.

Rudnick, Lois Palken, and Malin Wilson-Powell, eds. 2016. *Mabel Dodge Luhan and Company: American Moderns and the West*. Albuquerque: Museum of New Mexico Press.

Saltmarsh, John A. 1991. *Scott Nearing: An Intellectual Biography*. Philadelphia: Temple University Press.

Sharts, Joseph W., ed. 1919. "'Death for Me or Release for All,' Says Debs: 'I Trust in My Comrades.'" *Missouri Valley Socialist*, Sept. 26.

Shelton, Herbert. 1922. *Fundamentals of Nature Cure*. San Antonio, TX: Self-published.

Sicius, Francis J. 2015. *The Progressive Era: A Reference Guide*. Denver: ABC-CLIO.

Sillito, John, and John S. McCormick, eds. 1995. *A World We Thought We Knew: Readings in Utah History*. Salt Lake City: University of Utah Press.

———. 2011. *A History of Utah Radicalism: Startling, Socialistic, and Decidedly Revolutionary*. Logan: Utah State University Press.

Sluiter, Ineke, and Ralph Mark Rosen, eds. 2004. *Free Speech in Classical Antiquity*. Leiden: Brill.

Smith, Gibbs. 1969. *Joe Hill: The Man and the Myth*. Salt Lake City, UT: Gibbs Smith.

Sundfor, T. M., M. Svendsen, and S. Tonstad. 2018. "Effect of Intermittent Continuous Energy Restriction on Weight Loss, Maintenance, and Cardiometabolic Risk: A Randomized 1-Year Trial." *Nutrition, Metabolism & Cardiovascular Diseases* 28: 698–706.

Symes, Lillian, and Travers Clement. 1934. Reprint 1972. *Rebel America: The Story of Social Revolt in the United States*. Boston: Beacon Press.

Thomas, Joan. 1974. *The Years of Grief and Laughter*. Phoenix, AZ: Hennacy Press.

———. 2000. "Unpublished Biography." Boxes 5–6, Marquette.

Thoreau, Henry David. 1854. Reprint 1906. *Walden*. Boston: Houghton Mifflin.

Tolstoy, Leo. 1960. *The Religious Writings of Leo Tolstoy: Lift Up Your Eyes*, ed. Stanley R. Hopper. New York: Julian Press.

Trepanowski, J. F., and R. J. Bloomer. 2010. "The Impact of Religious Fasting on Human Health." *Nutrition Journal* 9, no. 57. https://doi.org/10.1186/1475-2891-9-57.

Treudley, Mary Bosworth. 1950. *Prelude to the Future*. New York: Association Press.

Troester, Rosalie Riegle. 1993. *Voices from "The Catholic Worker."* Philadelphia: Temple University Press.

Van Allen, Roger. 2006. "What Really Happened? Revisiting the 1965 Exiling to Latin America of Daniel Berrigan, S.J." *American Catholic Studies* 117, no. 2 (Summer): 33–60.

Vishnewski, Stanley. 1980. *Wings of the Dawn*. New York: Catholic Worker Press.

Wakefield, Dan. 1992. *New York in the 50s*. New York: St. Martin's.

Ware, Norman. 1964. *The Labor Movement in the United States, 1860–1896*. New York: Vintage.

Williams, Thomas D., and Jan Olof Bengtsson. 2020. "Personalism." In *Stanford Encyclopedia of Philosophy*, ed. Edward N. Zalta. Stanford, CA: Metaphysics Research Lab, Center for the Study of Language and Information, Stanford University. https://plato.stanford.edu.

Woodcock, George. 1965. Review of *Book of Ammon* in *Freedom*. Box W-11.1, Marquette.

Zinn, Howard. 2003. *People's History of the United States*. New York: HarperCollins.

INDEX

Page numbers in italic indicate illustrations.

Haley, Bruce, 21–27, 155; cites Hennacy's importance in promoting Hopis, 158; on Hopis, 287nn17–18
Hammond, John Lewis (co-defendant, 1917), 40
Harlem, New York City, 68
Harmon, Jeremy, 225, 251
Harrington, Michael, 187; on Hennacy habits, 187–88, 195
Harvey, Arthur, 212
Haymarket protests of 1887, 53
Hemingway, Ernest, 69, 113
Hennacy, Ammon: Ashford ancestors, 9, 7–15; canning line at the Valley Farm, 12; family, 11–39; Quaker grandmother, 7, 8; family moves to Lisbon, 15–18; family name in Ohio, 270nn10–12; Third Great Awakening, influence of, 14–16; life in Negley, 8–10; Julia Hennacy, sister, 10; high school socialist, 18–23; high school grades, 32, 271n25; Hiram College, 23–28; influence of Bible begins early, 13, 17, 47, 48–49, 80, 170; at Ohio State University, 32–36; early Wisconsin travels, 29–30; anarchist thought, 9, 19–20, 24, 34, 41, 45, 55–56, 57, 60–61; anarchistic thought fading by 1920s, 93, 103; WWI anti-war activities, 35–38; tried for WWI draft resistance, 39–42, 41; conviction served in Atlanta Penitentiary, 1–2, 7–8, 39–54, 44; cousin Selma Melms, 39, 60, 65; Big Hike with Selma, 45, 59, 70, 72–88, 74, 100, 141; Bisanakee homestead, 89–97, 90, 94; Fox Dairy job, 96–97; Fuller Brush employment, 32, 59–61, 75–85, 96, 248; job actions, 96; in Milwaukee, 30–31, 60–75, 88–91, 90, 97–118; Milwaukee social work job, 96–97; move to New York City where relations grow strained, 64–72; passport photo of Ammon (1923), 70; Catholic Church

and struggles with thoughts of conversion, aided by Claude McKay, 87–99, 145, 171, 178–179; marital ties loosen in Winnetka, 102; WWII, organizes WWI objectors against WWII, 103; considers jail for WWII draft resistance, 111; satirical about churches, 117; on New Mexico, 119–148; praises Albuquerque climate, 127; relationship with Hopis, 131, 136–58, 174; 1945 cross-country trip, 141–45; picks cotton with Blacks and Navajos, 150; picketing in Phoenix, 159; as acequiero, 162; and Green Revolution, 161–63; mystical experience, 172; returns to New Mexico, 183–220; message to Dorothy Day from Albuquerque includes phone number, 171; mentioned in Day's autobiographical The Long Loneliness, 177; New York City speaking locations, 188; New York picketing shifted to Custom House, 200; picketing shows sense of humor, 201; in Las Vegas, pickets office of AEC, 203–5; at Catholic Worker offices, performs chores for Day, 198; edits Day's columns for Best of "The Catholic Worker," 201; major teeth extraction, 201; relations with Day grow testy, 195–96, 206; reads about Mormons and breakaway groups, 201, 241; pickets with Peacemakers at Cape Canaveral, 208; Omaha missile protest, 211; Joe Hill Houses, 144, 222–51; third House closes, 247; Hiroshima Day protests, 188, 195–97, 199, 203, 206, 225, 236, 244; plans long fast in 1955, 195; plans for Prayer Pilgrimage for Freedom, 202; opinion of Martin Luther King, after assassination, 202, 247, 259–63; Salt Lake City non-cooperation with, 228–38; Salt Lake Health Dept citation, 238; on Franklin Roosevelt, 241 opinion of John Kennedy, 241;

ABOUT THE AUTHOR

WILLIAM MARLING is Professor of American and World Literature at Case Western Reserve University. He has written seven books and over fifty articles on subjects ranging from anarchy to Edgar Allan Poe, Hawthorne, and Fitzgerald to Marcel Duchamp's influence on William Carlos Williams. His scholarship has been published in French, Spanish, Japanese, and Estonian.